THE BANDIT QUEEN
OF INDIA

THE BANDIT QUEEN OF INDIA

An Indian Woman's Amazing Journey
from Peasant to International Legend

Phoolan Devi
with
Marie-Thérèse Cuny
and Paul Rambali

THE LYONS PRESS
Guilford, Connecticut
An imprint of The Globe Pequot Press

Printed in the United States of America

1   3   5   7   9   10   8   6   4   2

ISBN 1-59228-038-2

The Library of Congress Cataloging-in-Publication Data is available on file.

Some Hindi Terms

Amma	Mother
Bahanji	Sister
Bajra	A type of grass
Baraat	A procession led by groom to bride's village
Beti	Daughter
Bigha	Approximately one square hectare
Bappu	Father-in-law
Buppa	Father
Chapati	Unleavened bread
Dal	Yellow lentils
Dhoti	Cotton cloth wound around the waist and between the legs
Gauna	Day of wife's departure to husband's village
Ghee	Clarified butter
Ghoonghat	Veil or shawl created by gathering the loose end of a sari
Haldi	Turmeric
Hora	A black lentil, salted and eaten dry
Jatav	A Shudra sub-caste of leatherworkers
Kanya-daan	Ceremony where parents offer bride's hand to groom
Khat	A wood-framed, thatched bedstead
Kurta	Long, loose shirt
Lathi	A long stick, sometimes ringed or tipped with iron
Mallah	A Shudra sub-caste of boatmen
Panchayat	A council of village elders
Panches	Village council members
Pandal	A decorated mat and canopy
Pradhan	Head of district village federation
Sadhu	Holy man
Sarpanch	Head of panchayat
Sipahi	Army or police officer, bully, henchman
Sorghum	Genus of grass including Indian millet, eaten as porridge or cake
Teeka	First wedding ceremony when groom is received at bride's house. The teeka, a vermillion dot, is made on his forehead.
Thakur	A sub-caste of ruling Kshastriyas

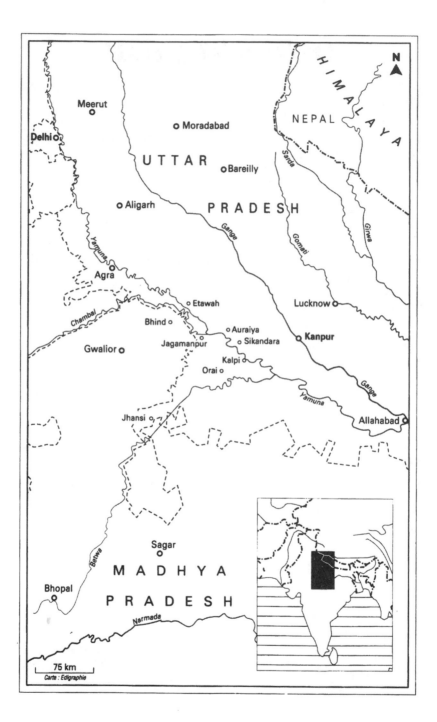

Introduction

*I*t was just before lunchtime when Phoolan Devi returned to her house in Delhi's Green Park, a leafy residential zone less than a mile from the Indian Parliament. She had been at the legislature all morning and she was dropped off by a fellow MP. As she walked to her front door, three masked gunmen jumped from a car that had been following her and opened fire. The former Bandit Queen crumpled to the ground, her saffron sari drenched in blood.

Two days later, Delhi newspapers received a call from someone who claimed to be her assassin, and who said that he was going to surrender. During a meeting at the Dehra Dun Press Club, Sher Singh Rana, a twenty-five-year-old, announced, "I killed Phoolan because she committed the Behmai carnage," and "since my childhood I have been against anyone who insulted Thakurs." Sher Singh Rana was too young to appreciate the shock felt throughout India when a gang of *dacoits*, or bandits, led by a low-caste girl had staged a dawn raid on a village of Thakurs, a caste of privileged landowners, and had left twenty-two Thakur men dead. Although he was not a Thakur himself, this was his professed reason for gunning down the bandit girl who had become a heroine to India's outcasts, the subject of films, books, and comics, and an elected Member of the Indian Parliament.

Despite what he told journalists, Rana may not have sought vengeance by murdering Phoolan. He reportedly told police later that he had killed her to get into politics. Perhaps he thought that the gun would be his ticket—as some said it had been for Phoolan. She wasn't the only ex-bandit in the Indian Parliament; thirteen MPs and nineteen ministers in Uttar Pradesh had criminal records at the time. More likely, Rana sought the favor of the Thakur community. Despite convening the press to surrender—an eerie, pathetic echo of his victim's life—he wasn't after fame since, though his plans quickly unravelled, he had prepared an alibi by arranging for an accomplice to impersonate him in jail.

Phoolan Devi had always feared that the Thakur community might seek revenge, but relatives of the Behmai Thakurs denied any link with her assassin, and police weren't able to find a connection. Her death on the doorstep of her government residence was, for many, a necessarily violent end to a violent life.

On that day, Durga, the Hindu goddess of *shakti*—power and strength—to whom Phoolan prayed for guidance, deserted her. In her home, she had pictures of Ghandi and Buddha, saintly figures for low-caste Indians, many of whom turn to Buddhism, as she had, to escape the perpetual damnation of the Hindu caste system. Even in death, the Bandit Queen remained political capital. She was cremated in Mirzapur, her constituency, against the wishes of her family who wanted her cremated in Delhi. Mulayam Singh Yadav, who is widely believed to harbor aspirations for the office of Prime Minister, coolly declared that his Samajwadi Party was her family. Flights were arranged to bring Phoolan's mother, sister, nephew, and nieces to the funeral, as well as her husband Umed Singh, whom she married after her release. After numerous tributes from her followers, Phoolan's ashes were scattered on the Ganges.

Phoolan Devi was born in the rural heartland of the state of

Uttar Pradesh, in a village on the banks of the Yamuna, one of the great rivers that flow down from the Himalayas and across northern India. Nearly a billion people live in such villages, with a few hundred thatched roofed huts, cows lying under the ample trees, and a well where girls like she once was come every day to fetch water. Phoolan was the daughter of a poor fisherman, born into one of the lowest castes—so low, it was even beneath the Brahminical order. She didn't exist, unless it was to perform harsh or unpleasant chores or to satisfy the lusts of men belonging to wealthier castes. Phoolan's first and perhaps greatest crime was to defy this ancient system.

She was made to suffer a series of terrifying ordeals as a result of a dispute between her father and her uncle over a meager scrap of land, a heritage that meant the difference between dignified survival and pitiful serfdom. With a child's keen sense of fairness, Phoolan cried to see her father wronged, but her tears invoked only contempt and this in turn fired her rage. Instead of meekly going to the well with the other girls, she pleaded before the village elders; she grew into a nuisance, a troublemaker said her uncle. To get her out of the way, he had her married off soon after her eleventh birthday, a common enough fate for pre-adolescent girls in rural India. But Phoolan was not meek like them; she fled her husband—a fat, middle-aged man who kept his child-bride in a dark hut—and returned to her village, only to be treated as a pariah, a loose woman. Her anger wouldn't abate, and her protests at the shame the village heaped upon her became increasingly irksome to the villagers. Finally, her uncle paid to have her abducted by a gang of local bandits to dispose of as they pleased. She was only saved from death when one members of the gang fell in love with her.

Vikram was low-caste, a Mallah like Phoolan, and he watched for several days as the gang's leader—who was from a higher caste—toyed with the slight young woman with a flat nose, full cheeks, and a fierce glint in her dark eyes. Even among the gangs of outlaw *dacoits* that roamed the Chambal region, hiding in the deep ravines and raiding and kidnapping for ransom, caste was all. Finally, Vikram could stand it no longer. He killed the leader and took over the gang, making Phoolan his second-in-command. He taught her how to use a gun, how to run all night along the soft banks of the Yamuna without leaving footprints, how to escape police—how to survive unbeholden to anyone. She commissioned a rubber stamp that said, *Phoolan Devi, dacoit beauty; beloved of Vikram Mallah, Emperor of Dacoits*. Phoolan took the lessons to heart. Her uncanny instincts for survival and her ability to stay one step ahead of the police inspired her men. She won the respect and protection of villagers by her vigilante actions, as she castrated rapists and punished Thakurs who abused poor, landless peasants. She was transformed into the Bandit Queen of Uttar Pradesh, the cruel *dacoit* beauty of legend, and her destiny was fixed the day she lead a dawn raid on Behmai— the same village where she had been brought bound and gagged in the night to be brutally and repeatedly raped.

There is a long history of *dacoity* in the hinterlands of Uttar Pradesh, a state nearly the size of Texas with a largely rural population of over 150 million, but Phoolan Devi was only the third recorded woman bandit leader. No photographs existed of her, and after what happened that morning at Behmai she turned into a potent legend—a female Robin Hood of the Chambal who defied the rich and defended the poor—and a potentially dangerous element in Indian national politics where, ever since Ghandi took up the cause of the Untouchables, there has been a fear among the nation's ruling castes. Politicians throughout the country called for the Bandit Queen to be caught and hung; the government worried that this would only make her even more dangerous, a martyr to the low-caste cause.

Finally, weary of being relentlessly hunted, she agreed to surrender in exchange for a promise from the Home Minister, or governor, of the Indian state of Uttar Pradesh that all charges against her and her gang would be dropped. She was barely twenty-one years old when, on a makeshift stage, under a portrait of Ghandi and with Hindi film music blaring—another scene in what, if it wasn't so harrowingly true, might seem a relentlessly melodramatic life—she gave herself up. For Phoolan Devi, it was the end of a long and desperate fight not just for survival, but for justice and respect, a fight she relates in this book.

For the next eleven years, the authorities did their best to forget her, leaving her to languish in prison, penniless and suffering from medical problems after years of living on a daily diet of fear and hunger, with charges still hanging over her. In the public imagination, however, her fame grew. The legendary Bandit Queen became a star of popular comics and Hindi films. In February, 1994, the new Home Minister of Uttar Pradesh, Malayam Singh Yadav, ordered that all charges against her be dropped and signed her release. Yadav, who also hailed from a low caste, appointed himself her political mentor, recruiting her to his Samajwadi Party and encouraging her to stand for Parliament. In a democracy in which 85 percent of the voters are low-caste and illiterate, the Bandit Queen had a powerful appeal. Eventually, the instincts that had served her so well in the ravines of the Chambal would enable her to survive in the undergrowths of Indian politics.

Meanwhile, Phoolan Devi's story had spread beyond the Indian subcontinent. Susanna Lea, a British-born editor working for French publisher Robert Laffont, boarded a plane for Delhi with a proposal for Phoolan to write her autobiography. The first substantial problem she faced was that Phoolan could neither read nor write. The only book she had ever known was the Ramayana, the Hindu mytho-logical epic that she remembered being read aloud under a tree in her village, when she was still an innocent girl who went every day to the well. Moreover, the vastly more shrewd and wary woman that Phoolan had become sus-pected she would just be exploited yet again. She was wary of media, of the journalists and film-makers whom she sensed were only interested in violence and sensation. For Phoolan, they seemed to forget as they grilled her about her humiliations that rape, beatings and death was the silent lot of millions of powerless girls in Indian villages. Yet she was ready to play their game, as well as that of the politicians who sought her support, because she believed that by relat-ing her experiences she could relieve the shame of these frightened girls, such as she once was, and that by becom-ing a Member of Parliament she would be able to speak for them. Susanna Lea persuaded Phoolan that an autobiogra-phy would mean the telling of her story in her own words—not somebody else's version of events and feelings they hadn't known—and Phoolan agreed.

Over the following summer, for days and nights, Phoolan related her extraordinary life via an interpreter to Susanna. Recorded and transcribed, the typescript ran to two thou-sand pages. Writer Marie-Thérèse Cuny and I shaped this into a first draft. Then, over several weeks in 1995, and with the aid of translator and journalist Vijay Kranti, Susanna and I read it back to Phoolan page by page. She would interrupt to correct errors, clear confusing contradictions, and add more recollections as they came to her. Phoolan signed her name at the bottom of each page, the only word she knew how to write. She listened carefully and seemed proud and even excited by what she heard; finally she was being allowed the hearing she had never received, not from the village elders, nor from the courts, nor in the press.

One part of the story made her uneasy, however: the massacre at Behmai. During the years she had been in prison, relatives of the victims had brought new charges. If they reached the courts, she might face prison or a capital sentence.

The following year, 1996, Phoolan would to be elected MP for Mirzapur, in Uttar Pradesh, and with the parliamentary seat would come immunity from prosecution. But at that point, as we worked, it was as though the powerful Thakurs could still drown out the lone voice of a mere girl crying for retribution. Phoolan's account of what happened that morning—what must stand, because of tragic subsequent events, as her last testimonial—can be found in these pages. There was no doubt in Phoolan's extremely sharp mind that the men who died at Behmai had been among the ones who had raped and humiliated her by parading her bedraggled body through the village, but whether or not she gave orders to kill that day, the ghosts of Behmai returned to slay the Bandit Queen.

Sher Singh Rana, a law school dropout who ran a liquor store in the town of Roorkee, was a familiar face around Phoolan's official residence at 44 Ashoka Road. According to Phoolan's younger sister Munni, who lived with her to the end, a constituency worker named Uma Kashyap had introduced Rana to Phoolan. On the morning of July 25, 2001, someone—either Rana or possibly Kashyap—drove

Phoolan to an annex of the parliament building in the green Maruti that would later be used as the getaway car. Rana and his alleged accomplices Shekar Singh and Dhan Prakash were following Phoolan in this car as she returned from the morning's parliamentary session. The assailants shot her at close range with country-made revolvers and wounded her bodyguard, who managed to fire back, damaging the windscreen of the Maruti. They soon abandoned the car, putting police on their trail.

Phoolan Devi, dacoit beauty, beloved of Vikram Mallah, Emperor of Decoits, died from her wounds before she reached Delhi's RML hospital. In the villages of India and in the pages of this book, her spirit remains.

—PAUL RAMBALI
AUGUST 2003

Prologue

My father-in-law had shut me in the dark. The only light in the cowshed was a thin shaft coming from under the door and all I could see were the rusty tools and cooking pots amid the rat droppings. I sat on my heels with my face in my hands. I was hot. My cheeks were stinging me . . .

I had been crying, calling for my mother, and my father-in-law must have been afraid I would run away after I told him my husband had threatened to beat me. That must have been why he locked me in the dark. He must have thought it was my fault.

When he asked me why his son was cross with me, I had been too frightened to tell him at first, but he insisted.

So I told him.

'He wanted to touch me! He unbuttoned my blouse.'

I had shouted for help. I knew that men weren't supposed to see my body. Since the spring, my mother had been telling me that I was ten years old now and I shouldn't go around with my blouse open.

'Did he hurt you?' my father-in-law had asked, becoming very serious. 'Stop crying and tell me what he did . . .'

'He said I was a little pigeon . . . he said he didn't know when I was going to grow . . . He touched me all over with his hands!'

I had pleaded with my father-in-law to take me back home to my mother. He just told me to calm myself, and said he would bring me some milk. But I couldn't stop crying. So he shut me in the cowshed. I begged him to open the door but it was no use. He must have gone away somewhere and left me there.

I had been alone with my husband and his father for three days. They had told my parents they needed me to do the housework because my husband was a widower, and we left for his village the day after my wedding. I had been doing everything they asked. I did all the housework, but I was forbidden to go to the well because they were afraid I might fall in and I wasn't allowed to cook because the old man was worried I might burn my fingers. The only good thing there was the food. I was allowed to eat four chapatis with every meal, and I only wished I could have saved some for my sisters and my brother. But when I wanted to go and play in the street with the other children, my husband made me stay inside.

'One day I'll take you home,' he said, 'and you'll have lots of nice things to eat, but if you cry or try to run away, I'm going to beat you, understand?'

Then he had unbuttoned my blouse and touched my chest. He had squeezed my ribs and giggled. The look in his eyes had scared me, but it wasn't my fault that he had stared at my chest and touched me. I had tried to get away from him, and if his father hadn't come back at that moment, I'm sure he would have beaten me.

After my big sister's wedding it had been a while before she went to her husband's village. He never threatened to beat her, he protected her, and she did the housework and cooked for him. My husband smelled of sweat and he made a funny noise with his mouth whenever he saw me. I wanted to go home and ask my mother what I was supposed to be doing there.

I cried so much my head hurt, and my skirt was damp

from my tears. After a while, I heard them arguing outside.

'She's just a child,' the old man was shouting. 'You shouldn't go near her!'

'What do you expect me to do? You're the one who chose a bloody infant for me!'

Then I couldn't hear them any more. They left me locked up alone in that dark empty cowshed.

I decided that when they came back, I would stay near the old man from then on. I would go with him to the well, so that his son wouldn't be able to touch me again. I would wear my skirt and my petticoat as well as my blouse and wrap my sari over that, and then tie it so tightly he wouldn't be able to undo it. I didn't even know him, he wasn't even one of my family, and he was trying to frighten me!

'Phoolan! Where are you hiding, my little pigeon?'

It was Putti Lal's voice.

'Now that we are married, I'll show you what married people do . . . Don't be scared. I'm going to teach you a new game . . .'

1

My mother squatted in front of a cow-pat. She took a handful of the cow dung and with a movement I had watched her make since I was a little girl, kneaded it into a cake that she set alongside the row of dung cakes in front of her.

At the far end of the field, cakes she made a few days ago were drying, ready for us to pile up. It was hard work. The dung stuck like honey to our hands. First I made one circle of cakes, then another, until I could no longer reach the top of the mound of cakes. Then my sister Rukmini, who was taller than me, took over, and I started the next pile. By the end of the day, the field was full of mounds of dried dung – no longer dark brown but ochre red, the colour of the dry, dusty soil that clogged our toes and stained our feet red too.

With a straw basket balanced on my head, I set out along the path from the field back to our house in the village. By my side, my little sister Choti also carried a basket on her head. The colour of my village was red, like the soil. The walls of the houses were shaped out of the earth by the hands of the villagers, just as we shaped the dung cakes that we burned to keep us warm in winter and to cook our food, the same dung that gave strength to the soil to make the hora grow.

In the little courtyard of our house, my father was waiting

for us to prepare his meal. Because she was the eldest, Rukmini had to make the chapatis. She began by cleaning the grindstone to mill the wheat to make dough, and then, squatting on her heels like my mother, she lit the fire with some twigs. With one hand on her knee, she leaned sideways and pulled her hair back to blow softly on the brazier. Her face glowed in the firelight. Rukmini was thirteen years old, she was beautiful and her skin was pale, not like mine. Father had told us she was soon to be married.

'Phoolan, where are you going with that stick?' my father asked.

I didn't answer. The setting sun was making long shadows in our little yard. All that day, I had been thinking about something very serious.

'Father,' I asked, 'where does God live?'

Deep furrows lined his brow above a large, flat nose, like my nose. His skin was dark like mine, too. It seemed to me he was always sad. Sometimes, he scratched his head for hours, as though he was trying to relieve it of thoughts that must have itched him like lice. But as he looked at me with my stick, the worried expression lifted from his face.

'Where do you think God lives, Phoolan?'

'In the jungle, Buppa. I'm going with Choti. I've got a stick to beat off the snakes.'

Choti and I intended to climb over the wall of our yard, run along by the ditch and then follow the river until we reached the jungle.

This time it was our mother who called to us.

'Phoolan! Go and fetch some water!'

Father smiled. His teeth were black, and so many of them were missing that I used to wonder how old he was. I was nearly nine years old then – I think. Nobody, not even my parents, knew exactly which year I was born. But I was born on the day of the flower festival so they named me Phoolan,

which means flower. My parents had already had one daughter, Rukmini, and after me another girl, Ramkali, was born.
We nicknamed her Choti because she was so small. Then
they had a boy, Shiv Narayan, who was still just a baby. And
in the belly of our mother, there was a secret . . .

'God is everywhere, Phoolan, not just in the jungle,' said
my father. 'Now go and fetch water, and don't speak to
anyone on the way.'

We ran along the street and up the path between the
houses to the well. It was so deep that Choti and I had to
hang on to the rope together to pull up the pail. We had to
pull hard with our toes hooked under the stone base to stop
ourselves being pulled in. The water at the bottom was black
and I was sure there were demons living down there.

I wanted to find God to ask him something. I had been
thinking about it for some time – while I was taking the
cows to graze, or fetching water from the well or going to the
toilet in the field – but first I needed to know where I could
find the God who decided I would be born in this village on
the plains, next to the river.

In our village everybody gossiped, and they often bick-
ered when they weren't too tired from working in the fields.
I thought it must have been hunger that made them quarrel
the way they did. Over the mud walls of the courtyards, you
could hear women arguing over a pot of milk or shouting at
their children – except in the hot season, when the air was so
heavy the flies seemed to float, and the cries of the birds
were stifled in the trees. A warm wind blew and only the
monkeys picking each other's fleas in the shade of the
banyans had any energy left, and the mosquitoes that sucked
lazily at our skin. There was almost no air left to breathe by
the time the rains came to wash the dust away.

The only place I could be alone, to have time to think,

was in the field on the outskirts of the village, squatting down among the long grasses to pee.

To reach the field, though, I had to go along the path and by the big house that belonged to Bihari. And he always tried to beat me. He was old, cruel and mean. With a smile like a rascal pretending to sell sugar-cane juice, he used to call out to me as I went by. 'Come, little girl, come Phoolan,' he would say, 'come and see your uncle Bihari . . .' I was meant to obey my elders, but I knew that if I put a foot inside his yard, he would try to catch me and beat me. He beat Choti too with his stick. And he beat my big sister Rukmini if she was foolish enough to pass by his house. He even beat my mother if he was very angry with us. He pretended we were spying on him or doing something we shouldn't. He was the one who was always spying – there by the doorway inside his courtyard stretched out on his bamboo khat with its soft straw matting. He didn't work like my father but spent the days lying in wait for us, watching his servants sweep away the dust.

If he got up from his khat, it was usually just to shout at my mother over the walls. 'Can't you keep your filthy daughters inside?' he would yell.

Bihari the bully lived at the end of the little row of houses along our path. His house was built of concrete. It had two floors and a balcony. Around the doorway, the wood was carved like the palace of a rajah. There was even a well in his yard, so his wives didn't have to wait their turn in the village.

The walls of our house were coated with mud and the roof was made of straw. Around our wooden door there were no carvings. Inside was a little courtyard with some rooms: two for us – one where we slept in winter and one with a clay hearth for the cooking – and another for the cows. There were no windows or doors, so it was always dark and cool in the rooms. For the evenings, we had an oil-lamp made from an old tin box with a hole in the lid for the wick. The only decoration was our little shrine, there was no furniture apart from three old khats in the bedroom and one in the yard by the doorway where father lay when he had no work. In the hot season, my father liked to sleep in the yard, but the cows always slept inside. We had two cows. Someone might have stolen them if we left them out and they were all we possessed. We were poor mallahs, with only what the river gave us to live.

If I crossed Bihari's field with our cows, he beat me. If I passed his house, even if I just ran past to pee in the field, he tried to beat me! I didn't know why he wanted to hurt us. My mother used to say that he just wanted to be rid of us. All I knew was that he was always complaining to her that we were causing mischief, that we were trespassing on his property, and that we were ugly and dirty.

To avoid him, I used to go the long way around to reach the fields, but when I was little there had been times when I wasn't able to wait, I needed to pee so urgently. I would run along the path close to the wall of his courtyard, twisting my feet to avoid stepping in the gutter, running as fast as I could because I was afraid of wetting myself. But he would be lurking there . . .

'Here, Phoolan! Where do you think you're going?' he would shout. 'You're on my property!' His vile old wife would cackle in the courtyard, squatting on her khat and flapping her sari.

If I went the long way around and peed in my dress, I would have to wash it in the river and then wait without any clothes until it dried. I had only one dress. And no shoes. Nobody in our family owned any shoes.

I couldn't understand why we had to endure insults and beatings from Bihari. I used to imagine that one day, Choti and I would creep up on Bihari as he lay on his khat snoring

through his big hooked nose and would hit him on the head /
with a heavy stone, to pay him back for what he did to us! It /
was as if I wasn't allowed to exist in my village, as if my family was worse than the fleas on a dog. Was it just because we
were mallahs, poor people? That was why I wanted to find
God, to ask him.

When I was little, I loved the smell of wet earth. I used to
gather up handfuls of mud from the riverbank and eat them.
My mother always scolded me. She even had to tie my hands
to stop me eating the rich red clay. It nourished the crops
that grew beside the river and covered the walls of the
houses. Its smell overwhelmed me. But you couldn't eat it.

That was another reason why I wanted to know where
God lived – to ask him why we never seemed to have
enough to eat. My little sister Choti wanted to come with
me. We had been talking a lot about this God who decided
that we would be poor, and we had made up our minds to go
to the jungle and ask for his help. God, we intended to say,
give us everything we need: a house like Bihari's with two
floors, a field to grow wheat, a mango tree, lots of cows, a
buffalo and a cart. Choti wanted piles of batasas, those
crumbly sweets made of milk and sugar, and we were going
to ask for plenty of rupees for our father.

At times it felt as though I was always hungry, and there
was never enough to eat. I liked to eat lentils and mangoes,
but often all we had was potatoes. If we had some wheat,
Rukmini ground it to make chapatis. And sometimes mother
smothered the chapatis with delicious ghee – the rich butter
oil we gave to the gods in the temple – and we scooped up
our vegetables with them. For some wheat or a little pot of
ghee, my father had to work all day making something in the
house of a rich family. When we were working in the fields
all we had for lunch was salted peas. The main meal was in

the evening and father was always served first. Once he had taken his food, the rest of us were served from what was left. The last one to eat was the one who did the cooking, and that was Rukmini. I often watched her preparing the food, and always eating last. It must be hard to always be last to eat, I thought, knowing that once she was married, it would be my turn to prepare the food.

When I finished my work in the house or out in the fields, I had to do chores for anyone in the village who asked. My father said it was my duty. Look after their cattle, gather their crops or pick the lice from their scalps, and you might get something to eat in return.

One day, the Pradhan had ordered me to come and massage his head, and there on the concrete courtyard floor in front of him was a big pile of mangoes that had just been picked from his tree.

Usually, I would never speak in his presence, and I would certainly never ask him for anything. He was an important man, the head of all the villages in the district, and I was too timid to utter a word. But the mangoes were so fresh and plump, and red as the evening sun. At home we never had mangoes like those. We could only afford the cheapest sort, green and sour, that you had to suck hard to get any juice. Those were the best mangoes I had ever seen. I dreamed of tasting the soft pulp in my mouth and feeling the sweet juice trickling down my throat. Finally, the smell of them was so strong, it overcame me.

'Please can I have a little piece of mango?' I asked.

The slap was so fierce I heard it resound in my head. I was stunned – I couldn't see clearly, everything was spinning around me, and I fell over.

The Pradhan was furious. 'How dare you ask me for a mango! Today you want a mango and tomorrow it'll be something else!'

I was in so much pain, and so afraid, that I wet myself.

I ran back to my house, hoping my mother wouldn't see me. But there she was.

'What is it now?' she asked. 'What have you done this time?'

I wanted to hide.

'I'm never going back to his house,' I cried. 'I don't ever want to do that work. I hope the fleas eat him!'

Even though I was sure she would beat me too, I told her what had happened. As I did, I saw my mother's dark eyes bulging with fury. She grabbed me by the arm, but she didn't try to beat me. Instead, she dragged me back to the Pradhan's house.

There, she started to shout at him from the street, her voice full of rage.

'You think we bring children into the world just to be your slaves? Instead of hitting her like that you should have just killed her! Go on, kill her! Then she won't ask you for any more mangoes. Kill her if you want!'

When he came home and heard what had happened, my father was ashamed. He said it was our duty to serve them. That was how the world was. If we did what they asked without complaining and bowed our heads and touched their feet to show them respect, they would give us food. He said the world was like that because God made it that way.

'Father, what does God look like?' I asked him.

'God has many faces, Phoolan!'

'Does he look like me?'

My father tried to hide his smile.

I knew I wasn't pretty like Rukmini. My skin was too dark, although not as dark as Choti's, and my nose was too big. I was too small, too thin and too weak to be beautiful. Rukmini had light skin; my mother and father loved her very much. He always saved some of the food he was given by people he worked for and brought it home for her: a pot of milk or a chapati that he had put aside specially. Rukmini was to be married, he explained, so she had to stay beautiful and healthy. But I could climb trees better than other girls and I could run faster too! I could swim in the river and I could do all kinds of work. I could cut grass with my sickle and thresh it for the animals, I could carry heavy baskets and jars of water on my head.

We didn't have very much to eat, so it must have been anger that gave me my strength.

I was born with my mother's anger. 'I vomited everything I ate when you were inside me,' she once told me.

'If I made you so ill,' I asked her, 'why didn't you just strangle me the day I was born?'

Every time she moaned at me because I was a girl, or because I had made her ill, or because I only brought her worries, I wanted to cry too. But I didn't. I kept quiet or I did mischievous things instead, so she beat me, and carried on wailing at the God who had given her just one boy.

Was it a boy or a girl growing in my mother's belly, we wondered? Choti and I could scarcely believe there was a baby in our mother's belly. It was very mysterious. We couldn't understand how it was that her belly had grown so large, while her body remained so thin. All day long she held her belly, supporting it from beneath with both hands. She looked as though she was in pain, and there were tears in her eyes. 'Please, God,' she kept moaning, 'let it be a boy!' It was the only thing I had ever heard her ask of God.

The last time, he had given her two girls at the same time, and they had both died. On that day, I heard a woman tell her, 'The first died in the morning, and the second in the evening.' I don't remember their faces, I don't even remember if I saw them. My mother came out of the room where she had hidden herself, where we weren't allowed to go, and said she was happy. 'God has taken them,' she announced. 'God will look after them in another life, but not here. So many girls! Why, why?'

When I asked her where God lived, my mother just laughed. She never prayed like my father. She preferred to wail about the misfortunes God had sent her. 'If he would even just give me enough food for all these girls . . .' Once, she took a little statue of one of the gods from our house and threw it down the village well. She even made fun of my father while he was praying to Durga, the goddess, which he did twice a day at the little shrine in our house decorated with butter-lamps and flowers. And if she caught me doing something naughty, she beat me on my behind shouting, 'Where is your God now, eh? Call him to come and help you! How many times do I have to tell you? You were trespassing in Bihari's field again!'

For a while I thought that God must live in the river, at the place where the ashes of the dead were thrown, so I held on to the tail of a buffalo as it waded out. I wanted to look under the water, to see if I could catch a glimpse of God in the river. But I could see nothing beneath the water but mud.

If God had taken the baby girls, I reasoned, then he must live elsewhere: far away in the jungle with the tigers, the hyenas and the snakes.

Father told us God was everywhere, and that he was watching us, though we couldn't see him.

How were we going to find him, I wondered, if he hid even from the eyes of men?

'If you want to reach him, you must have patience, you must persevere,' said my father. 'You must pray often and meditate like the priest in the temple.'

I had no idea what it meant to meditate, but I knew I didn't have patience. I couldn't wait. I wanted to find God right away.

'If you want to find God, Phoolan, don't go looking for him in the jungle, go to the temple.'

But that was no good. I had already looked in the temple. There were many statues in the temple, many gods. Father had told me once that if you prayed hard enough, the statues would come to life to show you the way of Brahma.

I had gone to the temple in the village with Choti to see the statues. I stood right in front of them and looked them straight in the eye, but nothing happened. They didn't come to life.

I began to give up the idea of finding God.

That night, the belly of my mother burst . . .

We all knew a baby was coming. Choti and I had talked about the mysterious thing that was happening, the way the belly of our mother had swollen and there was a baby inside. Our Amma went into a room in the house where we weren't allowed to go and came out later carrying a new baby!

The next day, we made up a new game. I went into the house wearing my mother's sari, pretending to have a swollen belly, and then I came out again saying a baby had been born. Choti beat on the metal dish to announce the news to the village.

But our mother was very angry and her eyes were even bigger and darker than usual in her thin face, because the baby was a girl, another girl. Her name was Bhuri, a fourth girl to feed.

My mother made a decision. She would not give her milk to Bhuri, only water. We other girls would have to look after the baby and feed her; our mother said she had too much work to do in the fields. We would have to find milk for her somewhere, even if it meant stealing it from other people's goats.

If a goat strayed near our house, first of all we made sure nobody was looking then we led it through our front door and into our yard where we milked it quickly, being careful not to take too much so the owner wouldn't notice. Then we would quietly let the goat loose. We mixed the milk with water and gave it to Bhuri. I knew it was wrong to steal, but surely God hadn't meant her to have no milk?

If I found God, I made up my mind to ask him.

In the meantime, I was glad this baby had survived. Ever since the other two baby girls had died and our mother had said it was good that God had taken them, I had been scared that we would be joining them and that we too would be going to live up in the dark night sky.

When we cried in the night, our mother used to point upwards and say, 'Look! Your sisters are up there . . . They've become stars in the sky!' There were so many stars up there, big and small, that I was afraid I would be lost. 'Amma,' I asked, 'when I die, will I become a bigger and brighter star than the others?' Because of her colouring, I would tease Choti by saying she would become a *kara*, a black star that gives only shadow, while I would become a *tara*, a star that gives a brilliant light.

I didn't know very much the year Bhuri was born.

The world that my father described, under the stars where God – though you couldn't see him – had taken my sisters, was my village, which was called Gurha Ka Purwa. At the centre of my world, past Bihari's house at the corner and up the steep, narrow paths lined with many other little houses like ours, was the well, deep and dark, where I went to fetch water with a pail attached to a rope. Beside our house was a river, the Nadi, where we washed, that flowed into the Yamuna, where we scattered the ashes of the dead.

The waters of the Yamuna were soft and clear in the spring, and blue in the hot season. Insects danced on the glistening surface and snakes slithered along the shores, shining in the sun. With the monsoon rains the river turned brown and muddy, a wide, raging torrent that carried all the dust and dirt away. The rains poured through the village, unearthing snakes and toads, and sometimes the houses nearest the steep bank were swept away. The Yamuna flowed from the mountains where the gods in the temple live. Upriver were the badlands, ravines where only thorny bushes grew and the jungles full of wild animals: tigers, leopards, jackals, owls and snakes. Beyond the jungle, where the sun went to sleep at night, the world came to an end.

It was better that a boy burst from the belly of a mother, because his family wouldn't have to pay a dowry when he married.

That's all I knew, all I had learnt, not from school books, but with my own eyes and ears.

One day, my father said to me, 'You must show respect to Bihari. He is your uncle!'

I didn't believe him. How could someone so rich be my uncle, someone with servants and a house with floors made of concrete? If he really was our uncle, surely he would try to help us, not beat us and insult us! Bihari despised us. When I was little, he used to sneer at me and my baby sister running around without any clothes on. 'Look at these children, they're naked!' he would shout at my mother. 'It's disgusting!' He told the whole village that we were the ones who caused all the trouble.

But it was because he stole my father's land that we couldn't afford any clothes, and my first dress had to be made from a piece of my mother's sari.

Bihari and my father were brothers. They had the same

father, but different mothers, and Bihari was rich because he had kept for himself the share of the land and cattle that should have gone to my father. He said my father had no right to it. 'When your mother arrived at our father's house,' I heard him shouting, so the whole village could hear, 'she was dragging you with her!'

After that, my father spent all the rupees he earned as a carpenter on going to court to fight my uncle. In the local court at Kalpi, my father won, and we all went together to the temple to lay garlands of flowers at the feet of the gods. But Bihari was cunning. He went to a bigger court, far away in Orai, and then it was as if nothing had changed. To reach the court in Orai, my father had to walk for a whole day, and he always returned more disappointed than ever, sighing and saying he would have to find more rupees to pay another lawyer.

Our father talked about it almost every day, and even when he didn't talk about it, you could tell he was thinking about it. And I began to loathe this uncle who had the look of the hawk that circled over the ravines. He behaved like a thakur, like somebody important and powerful, someone who owned land but wouldn't think of dirtying his hands in the fields. Because he was rich, Bihari thought he had the same power as a thakur, but really he was a mallah just like us.

One day, my father was summoned to the Panchayat, the village council. 'You know what you should do, Devidin?' the Sarpanch, the chief of the council, told him. 'You should give up your lawsuit against Bihari. Have you considered your daughters? You should be thinking about their marriages. You've got four girls now. How are you going to be able to afford their dowries if you go on with this lawsuit?'

My father pleaded with them. 'I beg you, just give me justice. Let the court decide.' But nobody listened. Even when he wept, they ignored him. The village elders were all rich, the friends of Bihari.

When he came home and told us what had happened, I became very angry. My poor father was timid and kind. There wasn't a flicker of hatred in him. He never beat us. He only used his stick to lean on as he walked home at night, for his thin back was already bent. He even pleaded with the other villagers, 'You are my brother mallahs. Help me! Go and tell the court whether Devidin is the true son of his father or not! Just tell the truth!' But the other villagers were afraid of Bihari. They knew what he had done, but they would never speak out for my father. They were poor like us and they did whatever the Sarpanch told them. And if a villager tried to help my father, Bihari would have had him beaten by the men who worked for him.

Then, as the day was nearing when my father would have to go to the court again, Bihari came to talk to my father. He said he would give him a field of sixty bighas if my father forgot about the lawsuit. My father agreed, but it turned out to be a trick. When my father went to him, Bihari just scoffed. 'Your case came up but you weren't there,' he said to him. 'And anyway, they can't make me give you any land, because I don't have any!'

He had sold a field of eighty bighas and spent the rupees building his big house with the well in the courtyard. He had given another field to his son, Mayadin, and he had put his own land in the name of his daughter.

That was why our Buppa always looked so sad.

Apart from a patch of land where my father had planted a neem tree, we had no fields of our own. To survive, we depended on our kachwari, the land on the far shore of the Yamuna that was left dry when the swollen river subsided after the monsoon. This land belonged to no one. For six months of the year, it was given to us by the Yamuna as she hurried on to join the waters of the Ganges.

The boatman charged five rupees for us to rent his boat for the day. We had to row it across ourselves after filling it with baskets of manure to mix with the sandy soil so that we could grow watermelons and cucumbers. We had to make several trips a day to take the manure over, and there were times when the current was so strong we had to row for hours just to make one crossing.

I had learned to steer the heavy boat across the river against the current when I was very young. Mallahs are small but agile like the dragonflies that skip across the surface of the water. I already knew how to swim when I was four or five. I knew how to collect the manure, carry the basket down to the river on my head, and haul in the boat. I knew how to help Rukmini and my mother plough the soil and sow the seeds. Once it had grown, the crop from our kachwari belonged to us. We could eat it ourselves or take it to market and sell it. It was the only thing God had given us and father told us we should be contented with it.

'When he's happy with people, God gives them many blessings,' he said.

Mother didn't agree. 'There's no point going in search of God, Phoolan. God only gives to the rich. He gave everything to Bihari and nothing to your father.'

In the village there were mothers who kissed and cuddled their children and gave them nice things to eat, but our mother couldn't have loved us the way they loved their children. 'Our Amma is a demon,' Choti said. 'She's always angry with us.' We had mouths and stomachs, so we were always hungry, and we were girls.

We were afraid of our mother when she wailed, 'What's to become of all these girls? Who is going to marry them?' Sometimes her face grew strange and terrifying. Her eyes became big and dark, bigger than the eyes of a buffalo, and she would groan, 'There isn't enough food. I don't know why we had to have so many girls . . .' As though *we* were the thieves! As though it was us who had stolen the food from our house.

Once she had yelled at my father, grabbing us by our arms as though she was going to tear them from our bodies, 'I'm going to throw myself down the well! I'm going to throw these girls in first and then I'm going to throw myself in!' I was scared, and Choti was trembling with fear. 'Don't throw me in, Amma,' she wept. 'Don't, please! If you throw me in the well, I'll die.'

It was the cold season, and she was angry because we had nothing to eat, while Uncle Bihari had everything. She was angry too because my father never wanted to quarrel or fight with him. My father just worked like a slave and prayed. My mother said he was a weak man. 'Uncle Bihari decides for him,' she said. Whenever Uncle Bihari beat me, my father said nothing. He just came afterwards to console me. He would put me on his knee and say, 'Your uncle is a demon, not a man.'

Well, if that was so, I said, I was going to become a demon too. Then I would be able to stand up to him and fight back.

It seemed to me that I had been beaten ever since I was born. My sister Choti and I were always showing each other our marks and bruises from the beatings we received. Were all children beaten, I wondered? Sometimes I had the feeling that every day of my life meant another hiding. When it wasn't Bihari, it was the Pradhan, or else it was my mother.

Father tried to explain to me that in the village there were two sorts of people: the rich who owned land, and the poor like us who had to wait for the waters to go down to grow crops on their kachwari, land that belonged only to the river.

'A rich man can give orders, he can beat you and punish you, because he is a landowner, he has the power of life or death over us. He owns the fields and gives us work. If he didn't, we would starve.'

The poor had nothing, neither land nor rupees nor power. They were born only to serve.

'That's the way it is, Phoolan,' said my father. 'You have to bow down and touch the feet of those who are superior to you, because they protect you.'

I looked at the timid face of my father, the lines on his brow, his old cotton shirt, his worn hands, his dusty skin the ochre colour of the earth, the colour of our lives. Then I thought of Uncle Bihari in his long flowing white kurta with a chapati in his hand, scooping up mouthfuls of lentils; I thought of him waving the menacing stick he always had with him. I didn't understand the difference between us, why he should be rich while we were poor.

It had always been so, according to my father. The poor must bow down and touch the feet of the rich. The poor eat a few grains of millet while the rich feast on mangoes. The pain of hunger in the belly of the poor produces fear and submission. I tried to submit, as my father said I should, but I was unable. I was like my mother. There was too much anger in me.

2

The Brahmin came to talk about school again.

Once, when I was little, my father had taken me to the school in the Pradhan's house. I must have been four or five years old, not yet tall enough to touch the nose of a buffalo. Father had sat down on his khat in our yard and called me over.

'It's time you learned to talk, Phoolan,' he had said. 'Why don't you ever say anything? You never laugh and you're shy of everyone. Are you frightened of me, Phoolan?'

I shook my head. Afraid of my father? No. I was afraid of my mother, yes, and intimidated by my sister Rukmini too, because she was bigger than me, but I was not afraid of my father. When he looked at me, it was always with tenderness. But it was true that, at that age, I hardly ever uttered a word.

'I'm going to take you to school,' he decided. 'The Brahmin. He will teach you to speak. You must listen carefully to him and do exactly as he tells you.'

Father took my hand and we walked along the path to the end of our row of houses, past the empty house that belonged to an old woman we never saw named Kamlesh; past the house of Makhan, the fisherman, who was one-eyed and very poor; past the house of Ram Sevak, who was also a fisherman; and past the pukka house that Uncle Bihari had built for his daughter, Bitoli. And then we hurried past the big house on the corner that belonged to Uncle Bihari himself.

There was one road that led to the school and another that wound up the hill, past the well and past the Panchayat (the house where the village council met) to the temples. Our village had two temples, one dedicated to Kali where my father went all the time to make offerings to the goddess and pray for help, and another, much more beautiful, dedicated to Shiva, where the rich went to give thanks for all they possessed. The Brahmin was the village priest. He looked after the temples.

My father led me down the other road a short way to the Pradhan's house. He stopped in front of a wooden door with letters painted on it. 'Look, Phoolan, it says "Primary School". This is where you're going to learn to read and to count.'

The Pradhan's house had a concrete courtyard where we children were made to sit down. We were each given a little book with drawings in it; we looked at the pages and the Brahmin pointed with his stick at letters on the blackboard. But the Brahmin was an impatient man who punished children. He tried to teach us the letters with blows from his stick. He insulted us when we didn't repeat what he had said correctly, and when he was very angry, he struck us on our heads, which had been shaven bald because of lice.

'Ek . . . Do . . . Tin . . . Char . . . Panch . . . REPEAT!'
'One . . . Two . . . Three . . . Four . . . Five . . .'

I didn't stay there very long, and I never went back. We were too poor, and I had to work. That's why I never learned to count or to read, though my father needn't have worried about me talking. Within a few years, I was talking all the time.

But the letters that made up the words we spoke remained a mystery to me. The only book I ever saw was the

Ramayana, the story of Rama, the incarnation of Vishnu. The Brahmin used to read it to the villagers gathered under a tree. Sometimes he would ask other Brahmins to come and read some of it with him because the book was very big and the story very long and very beautiful. I only ever saw the book from afar. Women were not allowed to touch it.

The readings lasted for hours. Even though I didn't like him, the Brahmin's voice enchanted me with the adventures of Rama, who married Princess Sita. The princess was kidnapped by a demon and Rama set out to rescue her. He had to struggle against many fierce demons and afterwards, in the night, I dreamed about Rama and the demons he fought.

At first, when I was little, I spoke only silently, I spoke only with myself. I watched the waters of the Yamuna flowing, changing colour with the seasons, and I saw the big white clouds come to drink the waters of the river, and I thought about the clouds taking the water up into the sky to pour it on the crops. There were two elements in the sky: water and fire. The sun was fire. Then the clouds came to drink the water and the sun fought with the clouds, provoking the thunder. And then rain fell on the crops in the fields, making them grow green and high.

I used to watch the big wooden boats moving slowly along the river between other villages like mine. My father had told us that in Orai, electric lights came on without anyone lighting them and they shone brighter than stars without making any flame. There was a train that ran on iron rails from Orai to Kanpur, a city where jatavs cut and sewed animal hides, where shops sold beautiful saris made with gold thread, where there was a temple as big as a mountain, painted white and garlanded with coloured stars. In our village, there were no electric stars in the trees, only monkeys, those little fruit thieves who chattered away in the branches of the trees, speaking a language of their own.

I wished I could understand what they were saying, just as I sometimes wondered if the big black bullocks chewing at the forage I gave them were thinking about their past lives. Ever since Bhuri was born, I had been having the same dreams. I dreamed that in my past life, I was buried alive with my baby. In the dream, I ran towards my father, crying and pleading for him to find my baby and give it back to me. Or I dreamed I was married to an old maharajah and, because I did something that was forbidden with a servant, the maharajah had me buried alive. I could even remember the place where I had been buried, under a date palm, near a stream.

Whenever I was beaten, I would go by myself to the river to cry. At those times, I wished God had let me be born an animal in this life. They were neither rich nor poor, they were fed and looked after, and they knew all they needed to know without having to learn it. Even the rat who stole our grain was cleverer than us.

Mother sent away the Brahmin who came to talk about school, saying we were too busy to learn to read and write.

I was told I would never have to go back to school, and nor would my sisters. My little brother Shiv Narayan would go, later, and learn to read and to count. My mother said we girls didn't need to learn anything except how to grind wheat, cook chapatis, weed the soil, thresh grass to feed the animals and fetch water from the well. She told me the main thing I had to learn was to stay out of danger. She was always warning me that I was going to get myself into real trouble one day, and I wondered what this trouble might be. It must have been something terrible as my mother's eyes were full of dread when she said it.

And like God, it was everywhere . . .

It lay at the bend in the river, I knew, because she wouldn't let us go to bathe there without permission. And we were absolutely forbidden to take the shortest route, through the Pradhan's field behind his house, at the point where the Nadi flows into the Yamuna. That danger seemed clear enough: he had ferocious dogs that he set on anyone who trespassed on his land. If we went that way we had to run very fast. But I knew how to run fast, jump over walls and dive into the river where the water was deep.

I had done no more chores for the Pradhan since he slapped me for asking for a mango. The Pradhan was the head of our village federation. His name was Kisna. He was rich and, like Uncle Bihari, he never seemed to do any work. He was always sitting on a khat in his courtyard, right where the women passed on their way to bathe in the river. He was short and fat with a thick neck and the eyes of a cock, alert and shining.

He was always there watching us pass and his sons were just as bad. Whenever a woman went by, they made remarks. 'Ah, what a beauty!' they would shout. 'Come over here! Come with us!'

The Pradhan used to try to lure women to the back of his house, or over to the far side of the Yamuna. That was why our mother would never let us go and bathe alone at the bend in the river or dash across his field. She was always worried that he would take her daughters, and that the danger would happen to them. Rukmini was soon to be married and would leave our house, so she must have known what the danger was, but when I asked her, all she said was: 'A girl mustn't speak to any man apart from her father or her husband, Phoolan. If a man takes her without marrying her, then she is everybody's, and no husband will want her after that.' It was hard to understand . . . If a girl went across the river with the Pradhan or one of his sons, did it mean she would be beaten by everybody, because she belonged to everybody?

Rukmini knew things that I didn't. She had been a woman for several seasons now. Father had been keeping a careful watch on her since she was fourteen or fifteen, because after that age men had to be prevented from coming too close. She stayed near our mother working in the home or in the fields, like the other girls of her age, and mother no longer beat her. Rukmini was always busy with the cooking and we hardly talked. I played instead with my little sister Choti and looked after baby Bhuri.

Nearly a year had passed and Bhuri was still alive. She had been born in the month of Kartik, the autumn month when we began to plough our kachwari, and we had to wait six months until the cold season had passed for the crop. For a while, there had been so little to eat my parents thought she would die. Mother didn't want to know about this hungry baby girl, one too many to feed. She couldn't take care of the baby because she was working in our kachwari all day. But Bhuri survived her first winter and spring had come. She didn't die, though she cried often. She ate porridge made of millet and soon she would be able to eat chapatis.

Four girls in a family was a great misfortune. In the village, they said it took four boys and one girl to make a happy family. Sons brought rupees when they married, the dowry from the bride's family. Girls were just more mouths to feed.

Dawn was the time of day I loved best, when Choti and I went to meet our friends to bathe. Far away across the plains, the sun would be edging up over the horizon, spreading a soft pink light over the steep sandy banks. The sky was pale blue and the air was still clear, not yet hazy with the ochre dust.

The river was wide and my mother always warned us to

stay near the shore and not to go in the water any deeper than our knees. You had to plunge your right hand in, scoop the water up and pour it over yourself to know the truth of the river – to be pure. And she repeated her warnings about the Pradhan. Above all, we were not to speak to him if he was lurking at the bend in the river to bother women. The path that lead to the river was too close to his door, and if you didn't hurry, you were caught between his house and the river. That was why we went to bathe very early, before he was up.

I liked to bathe and I would have been happy to spend all day playing with Choti and my friend Ram Dhakeli by the water. She was about the same age as me, with skin that was paler than mine. She had become my best friend since she started working in the fields with me after her father, the blacksmith, died. She had been eight or nine years old at the time.

One morning, as we were lying on the sand after bathing, waiting for the sun to warm us, Ram Dhakeli told us how it had happened.

'That bastard the Pradhan killed my father!' she said.

Ram Dhakeli's mother was very pretty, with the same light colouring. Men like women with pale skin, and the Pradhan's big, shining eyes had been on her for a while. The fat little rooster had been watching her and one day, as she was taking a bullock to the river, the horror happened. The animal bolted into the Pradhan's field. Before it could do any damage or eat anything, the blacksmith's wife managed to lead it out. But his servants were like their master, always spying on everybody. They called the Pradhan like frightened chickens. 'Kisna! Kisna! Look!'

He saw the blacksmith's wife with her bullock and realised right away that she was alone, which was unusual, as her husband was always keeping a close eye on her. The

Pradhan had never been able to find a way to lure her to his house, and he couldn't just force her to come with him. When she was with other women on the path to the river, she usually hurried past without replying to him, covering her head with her sari.

The Pradhan rushed out and barred her way, twiddling his moustache. He told her she was very beautiful, and that she would have to pay for letting her bullock stray on to his field.

Ram Dhakeli was at home that day. She said her father became very angry when her mother returned and told him what the Pradhan had said. The blacksmith was brave enough to go to his house and complain, and the Pradhan summoned his men. Ram Dhakeli and her mother had followed behind. They saw the Pradhan's men start to beat him with their bamboo lathis. The blacksmith was left lying on the ground, his face in the dust and his long white kurta covered in blood. Ram Dhakeli was terrified, and ran back to her house. Her father wasn't moving, she said. Later, his family came and put him on a khat to carry him back to his house. He died the next day.

If her father was still alive, Ram Dhakeli wouldn't have to work as a labourer in the fields. He was a blacksmith who earned plenty of rupees; he didn't have to work for others like a slave. 'Now my mother has to stay locked up in my uncle's house until she can find another husband. And I'm just a field hand,' she said.

We lay on the sand, watching the flat, calm surface of the water. God must have taken his ashes from the river by now, I thought. The pyre had been immense. I had watched it burn for a long time from the terrace of our house.

When I pictured the beating he had received, I felt my blood boil.

Once, I had seen the Pradhan beat a fisherman. The poor

man had spent the whole night tending his nets, but he had caught only one fish. He was going back to his house when the Pradhan came by him and saw the fish he was carrying. The fisherman tried to hide it but it was too late.

'If you caught anything, it's mine!' the Pradhan had said.

'Please, Kisna!' the fisherman had begged. 'I only caught one fish and I have to feed my family. Look, just one, and I have so many children.'

The Pradhan became furious and began to hit the fisherman. We all ran to hide in our houses. Whenever he started to beat someone, it was better to hide. No one ever protested or tried to interfere because if they did he would beat them too.

'If anyone beat my father to death I'd break all the bones in his body!' I shouted, not caring if the Pradhan heard me.

Ram Dhakeli was much more obedient than me. She never did anything silly or mischievous and her mother never beat her. I watched as she combed her hair and twisted the braids to wring the water out. She had pretty arms that shone like gold in the sunshine. Mine were thin and dark as a starless night. I told her not to worry, she would have a husband to protect her one day.

'If your father died, Phoolan, and the time came for you to have a husband, it would be hard for your family to pay the dowry,' she said sorrowfully. 'My uncles already have to find the rupees for a dowry for a new husband for my mother.'

I couldn't see our Uncle Bihari giving any rupees for the dowry of my sister Rukmini. I told Ram Dhakeli I wanted to leave our village, I said it was cursed for us.

'Where would you go, Phoolan?' she asked.

'There are other villages along the Yamuna. My father has worked in them. When he makes khats or stools he takes them to other villages. I know there are villages that are much bigger, with lights in the trees.'

'Not for us,' said Ram Dhakeli, shaking her head. 'My mother came from her father's village, and one day you'll go to your husband's village. And it'll be the same as here. You can't go alone to another village. A girl can't go anywhere alone.'

Choti had been listening to us, and asked, 'Will Rukmini be leaving soon for another village?'

'Amma says she will, but not right away. There'll be a party for her wedding. The groom will arrive on a horse with his family. There'll be dancing and presents and rupees for him, and then he will leave again for his village.'

She looked amazed.

I would soon be ten years old and Choti was still only seven or thereabouts, but we told her everything and she did the same naughty things as we did – like stealing rags from the ghoora to make dolls.

There was never enough cloth left over at home to make dolls, but in the village there was a tailor who threw out the pieces he couldn't use. Near his shop there was always a pile of scraps of cloth in different colours, called the ghoora. When no one was looking, we went to the ghoora to search for pieces to make dolls.

When we returned from bathing with Ram Dhakeli, I promised Choti that after we had done our chores we would go and rummage in the ghoora. Mother had told us to collect manure and bring it down to the river for our kachwari. She had already gone across the Yamuna with Rukmini.

It was tiring work. Choti and I had to gather the manure and carry it in baskets on our heads to the boat. We sang to ourselves as we worked:

> *Work hard, and the harvest will be good*
> *Work hard, and the harvest will be bountiful*

As we laboured, lodged in my head, like the fang of a snake, was the thought that if we worked hard enough, my father would be able to afford to go to Orai and win the case against his brother. Then we would have land – a whole field to grow big yellow lentils, enough to eat for the rest of our lives.

Father had marked the site of our kachwari with vines. He had needed to be there as soon as the water fell to mark out our plot from our neighbour's. Once our cucumbers and watermelons were ripe, we would harvest and sell them to buy grain to store for when we couldn't grow anything. Rukmini and I would walk all the way to the main road behind our parents carrying baskets of fruit on our heads. Choti would have to stay behind to watch over the rest of the crop and make sure cattle didn't trample or eat it. During the harvest, we even slept at the kachwari to guard our melons and cucumbers in case somebody stole them. That wouldn't be until the month of Jeth, in the hot season. We had planted the crops in Magh, the cold season, and now it was spring and we had to add manure to help them grow.

In the cold season, our bare feet went blue as we planted the seeds. We didn't have any extra clothes for the winter; we never earned enough rupees from what we grew to be able to buy clothes. And in the hot season, our feet turned red on the blazing sand. The hot season was coming, and the rags from the ghoora would serve to make sandals as well as dolls, but even with our feet wrapped in rags we would have to hop on the sand to avoid getting burned.

The ghoora was full of bright colours and we loved going there. To make a doll you had to find the thickest pieces, then you needed the most colourful bits to dress it.

When we weren't working in the kachwari, Choti and I minded animals. We looked after animals for other people as well as looking after our own. When I was little, we had only two cows, but now we had five cows and some goats, but no buffaloes. They were much more expensive than cows. And a male calf had just been born. When he was two or three years old, we would be able to sell him for more than a thousand rupees, if Bihari didn't steal him, like the last one, the year Bhuri was born. We spent the whole night looking for it, asking everyone in the village if they'd seen a large calf with little horns. It was no use, because everyone knew who the thief was, and they were all afraid of him. He waited until the calf passed his house, then he tied it up and led it into his house for a few days. He knew we wouldn't dare to come and ask for it back.

We kept some milk from our cows but our mother sold the creamiest milk at market, to buy wheat that Rukmini ground into flour for chapatis. I knew that my father would have liked to have buffaloes, to be able to have enough milk for the whole family.

We worked all day in our kachwari, and the sun was almost setting by the time we got back to the house. Father went to the temple to pray for a good harvest while Rukmini cooked chapatis. I told mother that Choti and I needed to pee, but it was just an excuse. I knew that if I asked her permission to rummage in the ghoora, she would have threatened to beat us.

Squatting with our shorts down, pretending to relieve ourselves, we searched through the pile of cloth. Once we had made sure no one was looking, Choti plunged her head into the pile until she had almost disappeared, then stuck out her arm with a piece of bright yellow cotton!

Suddenly Choti turned, looking startled.

Bihari's servants had spotted us! From the terrace of his big house you could see everything that happened in the village.

Clutching our shorts in one hand and the rags in the other, we ran faster than goats back towards the river.

Bihari had come out behind us, waving his lathi. I cried out to our mother, 'Amma, help!'

If he caught us he would beat us. It was as if even the ghoora belonged to him. Everything belonged to him.

The only thing to do was run down to the river, plunge in the water and hide among the buffaloes, swimming right under their noses. After a while we slipped behind a little hill so we couldn't be seen from the village and, keeping low in the ditches, we reached the wall of our neighbour's house. Every time we jumped over it and ran across his yard Dhakeli the fisherman told us off, but he was a nice man who didn't beat us.

Unfortunately, Bihari was at our house already, screaming abuse at our mother. 'Your rag-picking daughters are giving my family a bad name!' He struck my mother with his lathi. 'The little bitches are ruining my reputation by doing these things. Moola Devidin, you should lock them inside!'

He hit her again, and my mother cowered, trying to dodge his long bamboo stick. I knew that as soon as he had finished beating her, she would beat us, and after that, she would cry over her misfortune again.

It was always the same. I couldn't even count how many times the thieving dog had chased after us because we were rummaging in the ghoora. But we were mad about dolls. One more hiding for a doll was worth it.

It had been a long day. We had filled the baskets with manure until our backs were aching. Once the sun had ceased to burn our heads, it became the turn of the mosquitoes to pester us. Our feet were swollen and I could still smell the manure in my hair. We had been beaten again because of Bihari, but at least we had our rags from the ghoora. We sewed the arms and legs and stuffed the rags with straw. Our doll had an orange sari, a shawl to cover her head and a red mark on her forehead. Choti cradled her the way we cradled Bhuri, who was still too small to play dolls. But we never beat our dolls, we played at marriages with them.

In winter we slept inside. Rukmini had a blanket to herself, but I shared a khat with Choti and we spread straw under us to make warm bedding. Choti was always turning over and kicking me in her sleep when she wasn't taking up all the space. Sometimes I fell out and ended up on the floor. Once when that happened, a scorpion stung me. Mother didn't believe me at first but I screamed so loudly a Brahmin had to be called to pronounce a mantra to rid me of the evil poison.

But that night the air was warm and we were going to sleep under the stars in our yard for the first time that year. Before I fell asleep, I liked to stare up at the stars. I imagined all the gods and goddesses up there, and the things that had happened during the day piled up in my mind like the rags of the ghoora. And as I lay there, I heard the calves begging for milk and the soft slap of my father's footsteps as he returned from praying in the temple. Perhaps mother was right, I thought. Praying to the gods wasn't enough. But I loved my father and I couldn't bear to see him cry.

My father only really beat me once. It was soon after Bhuri was born. I had to prepare feed for the cattle, mixing the grass with some millet. I began to put the mixture in some pots, but father wanted me to fill a basket first and then fill the pots with the rest. I didn't want to have to start all over again. I put the basket down and looked him right in the eye.

'You do it!' I said.

Never before had I been cheeky to my father, nor looked him straight in the eye like that. It was something you should never do. But I was angry. 'I can't carry that much. What do you think I am, a bullock?'

He slapped me.

It was a hefty slap and I cried so hard that mother came running. 'Why did you hit my daughter?' she demanded. 'Who are you to hit my daughter?'

'I'm her father,' he said, 'and you, her mother, you beat her every day, for nothing! Today is the first time I've ever hit her, and I'm sorry, I didn't want to do it.'

They began to argue while I cried even more loudly. For three days, whenever I saw my father coming, I hid from him, afraid he would slap me again. But he never did. He was even more affectionate towards me, and when he brought food back to the house after working somewhere, he called me over to share it.

'Come, Phoolan, don't be afraid. Come and eat.'

He gave me pots of milk that tasted creamy and delicious, and thick chapatis made from the best wheatflour. I ate them hurriedly, without lifting my head, and he laughed and said, 'Don't be afraid, don't eat too fast.'

After that, whenever I had to carry feed for the cattle I filled the baskets to the top, so he wouldn't be angry with me, and so that he would always speak to me tenderly.

But just as I was about to fall asleep, I saw the faces of evil men like Uncle Bihari and the Pradhan. I spat at their feet. It made me so angry that our family had nothing. We had to avoid the bend in the river because of the Pradhan saying things to the women there. We had to take the long way around Bihari's house to relieve ourselves in the fields because Bihari was friends with the Pradhan. We had to feed and tend to their animals and only after that could we look after our own, hoping that they wouldn't steal them from us. It was as though even the ground that we walked on in the village was forbidden to our feet. We were almost as wretched as untouchables, who were less than animals.

And being a girl meant being even lower. A girl didn't exist without her father, her brother, her uncle or her husband —
or any man at all belonging to her family or her caste. She couldn't even walk without fear between the village and the river.

I had heard that there were Brahmins who were gentle, the priests of Brahma, the God I had given up hope of finding. But in my village the Brahmin beat the children to teach them. In my village, there were only those who lay around all day wielding sticks and eating the bounty of their lands — and those who cowered from the sticks and worked the lands, eating what they could.

Uncle Bihari, his ugly wife, and his son Mayadin thought they were more important than us. They had stolen our land and they were trying to poison our lives like snakes. But I wasn't afraid of the snakes that slithered through our village with the monsoon rains. I prayed like my father to Durga, the fierce goddess who rode on a tiger through the endless night. She was the only one I wanted help from now. I asked her to show me how to slay demons as she had done, and to give me a stick too, so I could fight back.

3

I never asked my father where he was going when he left
the house. It would bring bad luck.

Our father worked all day long. Sometimes he rented the
fields of the rich; he prepared the soil and bought seed and
when he harvested the crops he was given a share. But it was
never as much as he expected and, if the harvest was poor, it
was even less. As well as working as a farmer, he was a
mason and a carpenter. When he left carrying on his head a
wooden stool he had made, I knew he was taking it to someone who had ordered one. He knew how to make all kinds of
nice things out of wood; he could make khats, doors and
even boats. His work was always well done, but sometimes
he was paid with only one bowl of flour.

When he left that day, a strong wind was blowing the
grass flat and the dust was everywhere. In a few days or
weeks, the monsoon would come. Though he had said nothing to us, we knew our father was going across the Yamuna
to Teonga, the village where Rukmini's future in-laws lived,
to discuss her dowry.

I was going to have a Jeeja, a brother-in-law! I had already
seen weddings in the village and I knew he was going to
arrive on a mare loaded with presents and flowers – if his
family accepted the dowry our father was going to offer. I
had heard talk of five thousand rupees, plus a cow, a buffalo
and a set of cooking pots.

It would be a long time before Rukmini saw her husband. She didn't know if he was dark with a big nose, ugly as an ape, or strong and handsome as an eagle; if he had a limp or whether he was already a widower.

I couldn't wait to go and bathe in the river to talk about it with Choti, but our mother caught us as we were trying to sneak out.

'Phoolan, where are you going?' she asked. 'You haven't collected enough cow-dung! Who's going to do it? Rukmini has to grind the wheat. Take your basket and go.'

I collected so much dung there was enough to burn for the entire winter.

'I've finished all my chores! Please, Amma! Can we?'

I wanted very much to go and bathe that day for another reason too, but I couldn't tell her. Choti and I had found some treasure, a piece of soap. A crow flying over the village had dropped it from its beak. I had snatched it up, quick as I could, and hid it under my shirt.

'We're going to the temple later and Choti is covered in mud. Look at her hair! Please, Amma! Please!'

I always had to beg my mother at least ten times before she let me do anything. I had to do everything she asked and make as many promises to her as there were stars in the sky: don't speak to strangers, don't go near the Pradhan, don't do this, don't do that! It was always the same story with Amma. 'If you meet a man and he tries to touch you or if he tries to force you to go with him, don't let him! If a man offers you money, you mustn't speak to him. Run and tell me as fast as you can. Even if he says very ugly things, you must tell me. If you don't obey me I'll cut you into little pieces and throw you into the river!'

I promised.

I knew by then that the danger of being caught by a man meant a great humiliation. A girl in the village had been caught by a gang of men; as many as twenty, she said. She was engaged to be married but hadn't yet seen her future husband. And then the whole village could see that her belly had started to swell. The Panchayat had met and everybody wanted to know who was the father of the child that was coming. They had said she was a bad girl, that it was her fault; someone even said she should be tied up and thrown in the Yamuna! But her father defended her. He even dared to say to one of the Panches, 'It was your son who committed this crime!'

In the end the girl was made to go to her husband's house and her mother-in-law forced her to get rid of the baby before it was born. After that we never saw her again. She wasn't allowed to come back home to see her parents. Her father was very unhappy. He was a sweet, kind man who once, when I was very small and didn't know how to swim properly, had saved me from drowning in the river. He spoke a lot with my father about his daughter's humiliation, and about how much he longed to see her again.

I promised my mother I wouldn't let myself get caught like that, and that I wouldn't let Choti out of my sight either.

The water bubbled around our bare feet as they sank in the mud, stirring up a cloud of golden sand. We laughed so loudly that the birds fluttered from the bushes along the banks. Our father always told us we were not to laugh in public and draw attention to ourselves, but he was far away on the other side of the Yamuna on the road to Teonga, and we were free in the water, freer than we were in the village and more free even than in a field of tall grass. The water quenched our thirsts, cleaned our bodies, and purified our spirits.

The bar of soap was hard as a stone. I had never held a bar of soap before, and I rubbed with all my strength, until my skin turned red. Then I threw it to Choti and she did the same before throwing it back to me. We rubbed as hard as we could, but there was no milk. I had seen women using soap. It made a milk as light and white as the froth on a pot of boiling millet, but all that happened was my skin became sticky. Sand stuck to it from the riverbed and I couldn't even rinse myself. Choti looked at the bar of soap in despair, her hair stuck together in great clumps. Was it just that we didn't know how to use it properly? I tried it on my clothes, scrubbing them fiercely. Perhaps the soap was too old?

Two women had seen what we were doing and came over.

'What are you up to, Phoolan?' asked one of them.

'Can't you see?' I said. 'I'm washing my clothes with this soap.'

'What sort of soap? Show me . . .'

I held out the hard, sticky tablet. The woman took it and began to laugh. 'You wash yourself with a sweet?' she said with disbelief.

She handed me back the thing I had taken for a piece of soap. I bit off a piece and spat it in the river. It tasted vaguely of fruit. The woman was right to laugh at us with our skin rubbed raw and sticky and our shirts and petticoats stuck together. We couldn't help laughing too. There was nothing else for us to do but rub ourselves with sand until we got it all off.

We could have stayed there laughing and floundering in the mud for the rest of the afternoon, but as usual we had chores to do; we had to go back to the fields to cut grass for the animals.

While I did this, Choti had to watch the calf, a nasty little animal who kept running away. He was difficult to hold on to, and Choti was soon out of breath. She shouted at him and sat down on the ground.

'I've had enough,' she said. 'I'll cut the grass and you can chase after the calf!'

'No. Amma said you must look after him, not me.'

'I'm too little, and that calf is a little devil who wants to make me go round and round like a fly. Catch him yourself!'

'No!'

Choti took a stick and started trying to beat me with it. We fought and she ran home crying. 'Amma! Phoolan hit me! She doesn't want to look after the calf.'

She cried so much that in the end I was the one who got told off. My mother grabbed me by the hair before I could get away and beat me so hard on my behind with a stick the pain almost paralysed me.

It still hurt the next day. There were two big weals on my left buttock, and another came up the following day, as swollen as a mango.

'Amma,' I told my mother, 'you hit me too hard, I can't even sit down. It hurts too much.'

The abscess grew bigger each day and it burned as though it was eating my flesh. Soon I couldn't even walk. I had to lay on the khat and I couldn't even go to the field to relieve myself.

When he came back from his trip, my father was horrified.

'Phoolan, my poor girl!' he wailed. 'Oh mother Durga be gentle with my poor little girl! Help her to get well.'

Even Amma began to pray. 'God help my little Phoolan,' she sobbed.

I supposed that only God knew if the abscess was the result of the beating she had given me, but I had never felt so much pain. Even when the Pradhan's dogs chased us and Choti was bitten on the ankle, she wasn't in as much pain as I was then.

Amma put warm mud on the abscess and that made the pain go away for a moment. But once the mud had cooled the pain returned. I cried the whole day long. Mother made a poultice from the leaves of our neem tree. It grew on the little patch of land that belonged to my father. He had planted it himself, long ago, and we used the bitter-tasting twigs to clean our teeth in the mornings. Our neem was like a Brahmin for us: it kept the bad spirits away, healing our wounds and sicknesses.

Choti mocked my sufferings, making fun of me. She didn't realise it was all her fault. 'Your behind is one big bump. You'd be better off dead because you're not going to be able to walk for the rest of your life!'

The days turned into weeks, until one day, as I was trying to sleep on my right side so as not to touch the enormous violet ball that pounded with blood under my skin, I felt a sudden need.

'I have to pee,' I whispered to my mother.

She told Rukmini to help me over to the pot in the corner of the yard. My sister left me there. I felt helpless, no longer able even to go outside to relieve myself any more. Suddenly I saw an animal approach, a ferocious dog. I shouted at him, and he bared his teeth as he came towards me, drawn by the smell of the wound.

I screamed to my father for help. 'A giant dog! He wants to eat me!'

My father rushed in with a large stick, shouting at the dog, who ran into the stable. In a few seconds, he had killed two baby goats and torn their bodies to pieces, before scurrying out of the shed.

I had been terrified by the yellow eyes and gleaming teeth, but the sight of the dead baby goats made me even more afraid. I knew they would live again, perhaps as dogs since it was a dog that had killed them, but I hated to see an animal die. I began to sob, and my father tried to comfort me.

'It wasn't a dog, Phoolan, it was a hyena! Now I know my

little girl isn't going to die. If the hyena couldn't eat her, then the abscess isn't going to kill her.'

The only good thing about those weeks of suffering was the little pot of milk I was given every evening. It was the only moment when I was able to forget the pain and discomfort. The rest of the time I had to squirm and crawl on the ground, and I had to beg Rukmini, who already had plenty to do, to help me if I wanted something.

On the day of Diwali, the festival of light, I was left alone in the house. That evening, oil-lamps were lit in the temples and all the houses in the village in honour of Lakshmi, the wife of Vishnu, goddess of beauty and fortune. Lakshmi can't abide sorrow or poverty. The festival of light celebrates her triumph over the dark forces. I silently begged mother Lakshmi to take pity on me. As I prayed, I felt the evil pour out and run over the floor. I had the impression that I hadn't been able to contain myself, and that I had urinated all the liquid from my body.

The house had been cleaned for the festival. On the walls, father had spread a fresh coat of mud and dung. Amma had dusted the ground and I feared that she would be angry when she came back, but it hurt so much I was unable to move my body to see what had happened.

It was my mother who returned first. She saw a stream of blood flowing from the room where I was sleeping and gave a terrible shriek, thinking another hyena had come to attack me. She found me lying on the bed, unconscious. The lower half of my body was covered in blood. A rancid smell filled her nostrils. Turning me over, she discovered that the abscess had burst and the pus had come out. She wiped the vile black blood from me and there was a hole in my buttock big enough to put her fist in. My leg still hurt and I wasn't able to work for many more days. I was still a burden to the family.

My friend Kusumi, who lived two houses away from us, said she was very glad I didn't die. Kusumi and I often played together. She was thin and tall – much taller than me, though she was the same age as me and dark-skinned like me. She said she was happy I would be back to play with her and the other girls. When the others tried to climb a tree, sometimes they couldn't find a way, but I always could. They used to make me the leader because my games usually worked best. But not always . . .

It was Kusumi's turn to play dead, a game she loved to play. She had to lie down on the sand by the river and not move while we pretended to give her a funeral. A girl named Maya brought a sheet to cover her, a white sari with gold embroidery that had been a wedding present to her mother. Her mother was very fond of that sari and Maya had taken it without her knowledge. I used my sickle to cut some dry sticks to make the pyre. It was a game we often played. Usually, we piled the grass under Kusumi, and then we pretended to burn her corpse while we sang the mantra of the dead: 'Ram nam Satya Hai . . .'

After we had sung it long enough for her to find a way to another life, we carried her to the river. Just as we were about to throw her in, she would wake up and frighten us by saying, 'I'm a ghost and I'm going to eat you!' We had to run away, pretending to be scared, shouting, 'Kusumi is a ghost! Kusumi is a ghost!' Then she had to catch us and if she did, she would pinch us with her sharp nails. Then we would take her prisoner and pull her hair. But Kusumi had grown so tall that we couldn't even reach her hair any more, so we jumped around her, pretending.

Usually, that would be the end of the game. Pulling her hair would hurt the ghost so much that she disappeared and Kusumi would be herself again. And then we would go back to our chores in the fields.

That afternoon, we found a way of improving our game. We laid Kusumi out as usual, but on a nice bed of dried leaves and branches, a real pyre, like the ones we saw when a corpse was brought to the river for burning. One of the girls said, 'I've got some matches. Shall we have a real fire, to see what happens?' We had often seen the men setting fire to the funeral pyres. There was a point on the Yamuna where people came from all the nearby villages to cremate their dead. They lit the pyre from a burning torch.

I carried the torch, approaching the pyre slowly to light it. We watched the flames rise towards the motionless body of Kusumi, retreating slowly as we had seen mourners do. You had to pray silently for the soul that was leaving one of its lives. But our ritual quickly ended.

In no time, the beautiful embroidered sari that covered our corpse had caught fire. Kusumi jumped up like a billy goat and ran to the river. But instead of throwing off the burning cloth, she ran with it, screaming. There were flames all over her by the time she reached the water. She plunged in and we heard a terrible hiss.

There was no sign of her.

After a moment, her body floated up to the surface. She stood slowly and came towards us, covered in mud and ashes. She had become a real phantom!

We ran back towards the village in terror, with the spirit of Kusumi running after us brandishing the sickle I had used to cut the branches.

'Kusumi is a ghost! Kusumi is a ghost!' we cried.

This time we were convinced. The other girls hid in their houses and I did the same.

My mother saw me rushing in out of breath and without my sickle. She frowned at me, accusing me with her black eyes.

'Where is the grass for the animals?'

I had forgotten the grass as usual. I had left it in the field. I was going to be beaten again.

'I cut all the grass, Amma, and I tied it in bundles, but Kusumi turned into a real ghost! All the girls ran back home when she chased us and I did too! It's true!'

My mother stared at me thoughtfully. She was squatting at the grindstone, and she put down the tray of grain and shook her head.

'Phoolan, why are you always causing problems! I told you to cut grass from three fields and bring it back to the house.'

I didn't get the chance to answer. Kusumi's four brothers were at the door of our house. They had already rounded up the other girls and they had come for me. Since I was the one who had lit the pyre, I was the one who had the most to answer for. Kusumi's brothers were big and strong. The eldest one spoke to my mother.

'Your daughter Phoolan burned our sister. You have to punish her.'

Soon, the whole village was in an uproar. My father was summoned and a punishment was decided upon.

My parents were extremely angry. My mother gave me a hefty slap with her bare hands, and then she went to cut a long blade of bajra to whip me. I couldn't make her understand that I didn't really mean to burn Kusumi, I was only playing. But she didn't care about our games. She was mainly vexed because I had left the grass in the fields. I had abandoned my chores.

My behind was still sore from the abscess and now it was stinging again from the whipping my mother gave me. It was late in the afternoon by then, but my mother sent me back to finish my work. And I had to get my sickle back from Kusumi.

When I reached her door, her mother shouted at me. I

had to ask her as politely as I could to let me have my tool back.

'Look at what you've done,' said Kusumi's mother. 'Look at my daughter.'

I lifted my head to face my friend.

Her eyelashes had turned red. Her hands had been burnt and her hair had frittered away. I thanked the goddess she had been able to jump in the river before she really caught fire.

'Are you angry with me, Kusumi? Will you ever play at funerals again?'

'The next time I become a ghost, I'm going to eat you up! And I'm going to throw your bones in the river afterwards!'

She gave me back my sickle.

I ran as fast as I could back to the fields, rubbing my sore bottom, with Choti running after me laughing.

'Phoolan is afraid of the ghost! Phoolan is afraid of the ghost!'

That night, I had nightmares. Spirits dragged me by my feet to the depths of the earth, and I had to struggle to get back to the surface to find my sickle.

4

U ncle Bihari had been unwell for several moons now. Deep croaking noises came from his throat whenever he tried to shout at us, which happened less and less often. We rarely saw him lying on his khat by the door of his courtyard waiting to catch us. There was something wrong with his breathing, a sickness that the juice from the heart of the neem tree couldn't cure. But perhaps it was the gods who didn't want him to get better.

Rukmini had seen her husband for the first time. He arrived with the *baraat* procession riding on a mare, handsomely dressed in a pink turban with a gold headband. He had a vermilion mark on his forehead and carried a sword at his side and his family and friends followed behind dancing to the musicians' drums. They went to the temples to make offerings before they came to our door. Rukmini was waiting with her head covered by a beautiful sari. She was wearing lots of jewellery and bangles. Our mother welcomed the groom with gifts and a blessing. She had a large tray with grains of rice, flower petals and some vermilion powder. She turned the platter around his head and dipped her finger in the powder to make a mark with it on his forehead. Then she showered him with rice and flower petals.

After the meal, in the evening, the bride and groom sat on a mat made of four of the wide green leaves of a banana palm, under a canopy decorated with garlands of flowers, mango leaves and coloured cloth. The Brahmin lit the homa, the sacred fire, and Rukmini and her groom had to turn seven times around it while the priest said the mantras. At each turn, her future husband had to vow to cherish and respect his wife, and in between, the relatives one by one gave presents to Rukmini. It seemed to go on for hours, and it was so beautiful, I wanted to cry. Rukmini was still wearing her sari with the heavy veil. All you could see were the palms of her hands. Then my parents made the *kanya-daan*: they rubbed turmeric on my sister's palms, and on her husband's, and then they put my sister's hand into his. Finally, the barber's wife, who had been guiding Rukmini because she couldn't see a thing behind her veil, lifted it for the first time and the groom made the *sindoor* – he applied vermilion powder to the centre-parting of her hair.

The ceremony was over, and the celebration began, a lavish feast that never seemed to end. Fireworks exploded and there was music and dancing and lots of sweets to eat. There were so many guests, more than a hundred. And it kept on raining.

Once, when I was fighting with Rukmini, I had been so angry I screamed at her, 'I hope it rains on your wedding day! I hope it rains so hard you'll have to get married under an umbrella!' It did rain that day, heavy monsoon rain, all through the ceremonies. The whole house was water-logged. Rukmini was annoyed with me about this but I was sorry that it rained because I was happy to have a Jeeja, a brother-in-law. My Jeeja had been given a dowry of five thousand rupees, lots of presents, a cow, and a buffalo. He was two years older than Rukmini and he was very nice. I followed him around everywhere, pulling the tail of his dhoti. His name was Ramphal, and Rukmini said he loved her very much.

Eventually, she told us, she would go to live in the village of her in-laws, but for the time being she would stay with us.

Rukmini was so happy that day. Uncle Bihari had already managed to put a stop to three marriages that had been arranged for her. The previous time, he had called the police on the day the *baraat* procession was supposed to arrive. The groom was on his horse at the head of the procession. He and his family had come all the way from Kanpur, but they never reached our house. Uncle Bihari stopped them on the main road at Kalpi, before they turned off the road for our village. 'The girl is a minor,' he told them. 'She's only fourteen years old and her father wants to sell her! It's against the law.' He conspired with the Pradhan and they brought the police with them. The groom was from a good family, and they had been so embarrassed they turned around and went back without a word to my father. My sister was ashamed; she sobbed and said she was going to commit suicide by throwing herself on a fire. Before that, Bihari had prevented people in the village from lending money to my father for her dowry by telling them my father would never be able to pay them back. The first time, he had told the groom's family that Rukmini was adopted. It wasn't true. Our mother had lost three babies before Rukmini was born. Rukmini was her fourth, but the first to survive.

Mother said Bihari was worried Rukmini would marry into an influential family because then he would lose his power over us. But Rukmini had her husband now, and my mother and father were contented because her new in-laws might even be able to help us get the land we should have inherited, the nice field of hora. His family wasn't afraid of Bihari. They had warned that they would cause problems for our uncle if he tried to prevent the marriage. My mother argued a lot about this with my father. I wasn't supposed to listen and when they argued they chased me out of the house, but I heard them anyway.

*

The wedding party had been going on for three days. It was late and Choti and I both needed to go to the field to relieve ourselves. My little sister was desperate. 'Let's run past Uncle's house,' she whispered, 'I can't wait!'

But we weren't fast enough. We heard the hoarse voice of Bihari as we passed.

'Phoolan, come here.'

I held my breath. He had heard us whispering. I thought he was going to beat us again and my first instinct was to flee, but there was something about his voice that made me hesitate. I realised all the rainfall must have been making him ill.

'There's something funny about his voice,' I said to Choti.

'I'm not going in there, Phoolan. He's probably hiding behind the door waiting for us.'

'He sounds as if he's sick. Come on.'

Choti didn't want to go inside.

'He won't do anything to us now,' I told her. 'We've got Rukmini's in-laws here to protect us. Listen! He's calling again.'

'No! Ask him from here what he wants.'

'I'm going in on my own then. Wait for me here. If he tries to beat me, you run back home and tell them.'

Bihari groaned again. 'Phoolan, my little niece, I'm thirsty.'

I entered warily, but there was no one in the courtyard. Then I saw Bihari curled up on a khat inside the doorway of his room, his eyes burning with fever. I approached him warily. He called me his little niece again, and with his hands clasped together thanked me for coming, so I touched his feet dutifully, but quickly, in case he tried to grab me.

'What's wrong uncle? Are you sick?'

I was careful of what I said. He seemed very ill indeed. His voice came from his throat like the rumble of distant thunder, and for some reason his bushy black eyebrows didn't frighten me as they had done before.

'It's my asthma, Phoolan, you know,' he croaked. 'This monsoon is going to kill me. Get me a drink of water.'

I lifted the jug of water I was carrying to wash myself. 'I was going to the toilet. This water is for washing. Why don't you go back in your house and ask for a drink? Is there no one home?'

'Go and fetch your father, please.'

It was the first time he had spoken to me politely, and he was asking me to get my father, something he had never done before. I ran back to our house.

'Come, father! He's very sick.'

Mother interrupted us. 'Your father isn't going.'

She always decided things for him. But this time, my father spoke up. 'Bihari has been sick for a long time. Who knows? Perhaps he wants to give me some land.'

She muttered something under her breath, the usual curses about Bihari the thief, the rascal, the liar.

'He's sick. Perhaps he wants to settle his affairs, talk about the inheritance.'

Father decided to go. I followed him with Choti, excited by the prospect of this death that might mean land for us – land that should have been ours in the first place.

'Father, you should ask him for more than just a few bighas, you should ask for a hundred!'

'God will decide for us, Phoolan. Don't be greedy! We must accept whatever God wills.'

Bihari was lying on the concrete floor of his house when we arrived. His eyes were closed. Father kneeled down near him and started to cry.

'What are you crying about, Father?' I asked.

'My brother is dead!'

Dead? I didn't believe it. A few minutes earlier he had

been asking for water and now here he was – dead. If it was true, it meant he would no longer beat us!

Choti looked at him with disgust. 'We're safe now,' she said.

'Are you sure?' I asked her. 'What if he gets up again in a few days?' I asked her.

'Don't worry, they're going to burn him tomorrow. There'll be no chance of him coming back.'

Just then, Mayadin, our uncle's eldest son, rushed into the room in tears. He knelt in front of his father with his head in his hands. 'What did he say? Who was here? Who was with him at the end?'

'Me,' I said. 'He spoke his last words to me.'

'What did he say, little cousin?'

It surprised me to hear that I was his 'little cousin' now.

'He wanted water.'

Mayadin began to sob loudly. 'I wasn't even here to give him water at the end,' he moaned. Some villagers had gathered in the courtyard and I heard someone say you should never refuse water to a dying person. I should have given him the dirty water I was carrying. I would have liked to pour it over his head!

The next morning, his body was taken for burning. There was a long procession and the whole village was there, but my mother didn't want my father to go. She said they could go later to pay their last respects, and afterwards they would bathe in the river, as is the custom. But there was no question of going to the funeral. Bihari wanted to be like the rich, like a thakur. Father always told us that if God had decided we should be born mallahs, it was wrong to want to belong to another caste; we had to respect God's will. Bihari had wanted to be a thakur, but he was dead now and everything was going to be different.

As Bihari's corpse burned on the pyre, the sky turned

dark and menacing with monsoon clouds, but I felt as light as a butterfly. Afterwards, his teeth and some of his bones were put in urns. Mayadin would take these to be thrown in the Ganges at Kanpur. His son would have to bring back some water from the sacred river and on the thirteenth day, we would all drink some of it.

When the funeral rites were completed, Mayadin came to our house. He had a face like a lizard: a flat nose with big wide nostrils and lying eyes. He addressed our father respectfully as his Chacha – his uncle!

'Now you are the eldest member of the family, Chacha,' he said. 'It doesn't matter how my father behaved, I don't intend to go on like that. From now on, we belong to the same family.'

My parents were pleased to hear this. My mother smiled, and when she smiled, her face lit up suddenly. She looked relieved; perhaps she was thinking she would no longer have to beat us because of Bihari. She seemed to feel that Mayadin was a good man who was going to give us our share. I listened joyfully to the conversation between my father and Mayadin, both sitting there together on the same khat. I had never imagined I would see such a thing.

Father told his nephew he had it in mind to cut down the neem, the tree that grew on the one little patch of land we possessed, a plot of just three bighas. Our handsome tree had been planted there by our father and the trunk was so large that Choti, Rukmini and I had to hold hands to reach around it. Father said he was sure to get enough rupees for the lumber (perhaps more than a thousand rupees) to pay for my wedding.

'You can sell the tree, Chacha and what's more, instead of working your kachwari or renting land from other people, you can come and work for me,' said Mayadin. 'While we're waiting for the crop I'll pay you every month in grain. I'll keep proper accounts and we'll settle up at the next monsoon.'

Father sighed deeply with relief. We were going to have enough food to eat for a year.

'I'm very grateful,' he said humbly. 'My wife's family has had a marriage proposal for our daughter Phoolan. The man is a widower who lives in Maheshpur. It's a good family for Phoolan to marry into.'

His nephew seemed to be ready to agree to whatever my father asked.

'I'll help you with the arrangements, Chacha. I'll organise the *kanya-daan*. Your daughter Phoolan will have a very nice wedding!'

So I was to be married!

I imagined that there would be a party that went on for days, like Rukmini's. I would wear a lovely sari and bangles, and there would be plenty of nice food. And then my husband would return to his village, as Rukmini's husband had done, and Choti and I would be able to play at weddings with our dolls.

My mother had once told me that when uncle Bihari got married, he hired sixteen elephants for the *baraat* procession. He had wanted to let everybody know how rich he was. Of course he was rich, I thought, he had stolen my father's inheritance! But now his son wanted to make amends. Father would be able to sell the wood from the neem tree and he was going to work the family land for a share of the harvest. I wanted to go to the temple to give thanks for all the things Mayadin was going to do for us. I decided, after studying him, that he didn't have his father's jackal face. His nose was large, like the beak of an eagle, and when he smiled he had a nice wide mouth. He had put his palms together in devotion when he greeted my father, saying he was now the eldest of the family. And he was speaking to him now with the respect due to an elder.

'If the man is a widower, the dowry will be smaller, Chacha. That is a good arrangement,' he said.

My father nodded. 'His name is Putti Lal. His first wife was from the family of my wife Moola. She is going to see her brothers there to organise the *baraat*. The astrologer is deciding on the date of *teeka*.'

That would be the day my father would go to my husband's village to give him the first part of the dowry and put a vermilion mark on his forehead.

I ran outside in the heavenly rain. Drops of water fell like beads from the end of my big nose, and I thought of the beads of juice that formed on the bark of the neem, our handsome tree with the pale green leaves that bloomed with pretty yellow flowers. There were other neems in the village, but this one was mine. Our neem was going to pay for my wedding. I ran to the end of the street, past my cousin Mayadin's house, and down a path across the fields to the tree. I spread my arms to embrace the rugged trunk. I was going to miss the fruits it made, yellow as the sun, that smelled of onion. The squirrels were going to have to find somewhere else to live. So many rupees from one tree! But he was the king of trees, and he was far older than me.

It was dawn and the stars were beginning to vanish from the sky. My eyes suddenly opened as I lay on the khat in our yard with Choti. A noise had woken me, and I heard it again. It was the noise of an axe splitting wood. The blows were regular and repeated, but where was the noise coming from? I closed my eyes to listen, and as I did my heart began to pound with anguish. I shook my sister awake.

'Choti, wake up. Someone's cutting down a tree.'

'So?'

'The neem. It's *our* tree they're cutting!'

'Why would they do that? Maybe father asked the wood-cutter to do it.'

'Come on!'

'*No-oo!* Are you mad? If we go out all alone at this hour something terrible could happen to us!'

We had been left on our own. Our mother was still at her brothers' village. She had gone with Rukmini to organise my wedding, I supposed. Father was working in a village upriver. He had said he would be gone for six days. He was making bricks to line the well in a rich person's courtyard, but I had lost count of the days and I didn't know when he would be back. It couldn't be our tree they were cutting, I decided. I tried to go back to sleep. It was still too early to go to the well or to bathe. But I couldn't sleep, thinking of the tall, handsome tree and hearing the blows from the axe.

When I saw the first ray of sunlight on our roof, I could no longer wait. I pulled on my green shirt over my petticoat.

'Come on, Choti, let's go and see!'

We ran through the village, brushing against the walls and jumping over the gutters to reach the little patch of earth where our father grew some millet under the neem. But the tree was no longer there! The field was full of labour-ers loading logs onto a wagon pulled by a tractor. Next to it was a cart pulled by two healthy white bullocks. The cart was elaborately painted and the bullocks had silver orna-ments dangling from their harnesses. I knew that cart, it belonged to Mayadin!

Where was my tree? Where was the king of trees?

He was in Mayadin's cart, dead, and cut into pieces! They had murdered him! That was the noise I had heard in the night, the noise of axes dismembering my handsome tree. I saw the pinkish-yellow heart of the tree bleeding its rich juice. The thick branches were being cut with a saw and piled up too, waiting to be taken away and sold. My heart pounded in anger. I felt as though I was suffocating with rage. Mayadin had lied! The swindling son of his father didn't want to help us at all. He had taken advantage of my father's absence to steal our tree. He had done it in the night like a robber. When he had said to my father, with his hands together in supplication, 'Take the tree, Chacha, and sell it,' his smile had really been the treacherous smile of a jackal after all.

The little patch of earth was all the land we possessed and the tree that grew on it was ours, and ours alone. I was speechless as I watched the tractor moving off but when I saw Mayadin climb up on his rich man's cart in his clean white dhoti hanging loose between his knees and his silk kurta buttoned up to the neck, I flew into a rage. He hadn't even dirtied his hands, but they were covered in the blood of my tree. I leapt at the cart and grabbed the rope harness that ran through the nose of one of the bullocks.

'You swindler!' I screamed. 'Give us back our tree.'

From the seat, Mayadin whipped me with his crop, but I wouldn't let go of the rope. The bullock's nose was his most sensitive spot and the animal's eyes rolled wide with terror in front of mine as I hung on and kicked at his legs. It must have hurt the poor beast, but I was blind with fury.

'You aren't taking this wood! I won't let you steal it from us like this!'

Mayadin kept on viciously whipping me, harder and harder. He must have feared that I would tear the nose right off his bullock and that the animal would bolt. I wouldn't let go. I felt his crop sting me on my arms and my back, and then on my head and my ears. I could hardly see, blood ran in my eyes, but I held on tight.

'I'm not going to let you take it!'

Choti had run off when I jumped onto the nose of the bullock. I could hear her shouting in the village, 'Save my sister. Come and help her! Everybody!'

They all came, but they just stood there, laughing as though it was a show. I heard one villager say, 'That crazy girl has managed to stop Mayadin's cart!'

Once he realised I wasn't going to let go no matter how hard he struck me, and he could not advance, Mayadin called his bullies. Four men came up, punching me and trying to grab me to pull me off. The animal roared in pain and I let go. I was being held by a huge man who swung me by the feet and hands to the ground like a bundle of straw.

Before Mayadin could ride off, I picked myself up, ran back and climbed up on the enormous cartwheel, I shouted at Mayadin that if he wanted to ride off he could only do it by crushing me under the wheel. He hesitated. There must have been hundreds of people there watching, nearly half the village.

'It's our tree!' I screamed. 'You are a thief!'

I had just enough time to tear his silk kurta and see his eyes redden with anger. Powerful hands grabbed me by my clothes and pulled me from the wheel, not letting go of me this time. I was choking, but my tears sprang from helpless rage as much as from the pain of being strangled by the arms that were still holding me back. I watched helplessly, unable to struggle free, as the men cut the rest of the fallen branches, piled them up and put them on the cart.

'Leave them . . . Leave them,' I begged. 'They belong to my father!'

The man who was holding me had a hard time gagging me. 'God knows what this girl is made of,' he exclaimed. I bit his hand hard and spat the blood in the dust. He dropped me with a yelp.

But it was over.

I could only stare as Mayadin left on his cart with all my father's wood, the wood that had been going to pay my dowry. The cart disappeared down the road with the slow shuffle of the bullocks. There was nothing left, not a twig; in the middle of our patch of land was just a stump. Even the millet that had been growing under it was ruined, trampled by the woodcutters. My handsome tree would no longer give us shade, and all it would bring my father now was a fresh humiliation.

The wood was valuable, it would have fetched us more than a thousand rupees. I had been happy for a while, but this new pain, a crushing pain, the pain of being a slave, of being less than a dog, turned my stomach. I wanted to vomit. We were poor, and because of it we were powerless. Exhausted, I sat on the ground, amid the dust and the grains of millet at the feet of Mayadin's men, sobbing. The four men picked me up and pushed me ahead of them back along the path to our house. They threw me in the yard and barricaded the door from the outside. It made no difference. I had no strength left by then. Lying face down on the hard earth, I couldn't even cry. I felt my heart beating so hard I feared it was going to explode under me. I had done all I could, but I was alone.

The villagers had been laughing. When I was struggling, not one of them had tried to help me. And when it was over they had slipped away to hide in their homes. There were several men from the village among Mayadin's gang of labourers, including one I knew. 'Why are you doing this? You know it's my father's tree!' I had shouted to him.

'He's paying me, Phoolan,' the man had answered. 'Mayadin told me he would pay me a sack of millet.'

Mayadin was learning how to use the power he had inherited from his thieving father. And all the cowering dogs in the village had obeyed him. But he had been red with fury, he was sweating in his fresh clothes and I had seen his eyes blink with disbelief that I had dared to attack him in the absence of my father. I began to calm down as I thought about his embarrassment. It must have infuriated him. He must have thought that I took myself for the head of our household! If I had a knife with me, I would have stabbed him as he sat on his cart with its rich silver decorations, but my knife was made of wood and it was only good for peeling vegetables.

Choti managed to get in over our neighbour's wall and came and sat down next to me. 'I wet myself. I was afraid they were going to kill you, Phoolan. Look, you're still bleeding!'

Her voice was weak, worn out from shouting for help. But nobody ever came to the aid of Devidin's daughters – nobody.

'Choti . . . Come, sister.'

The blood on my body was drying in scabs, all my muscles ached and there were bruises all over me. We got out over the wall and took the path down to the river. There we could soothe our wounds, we could wash away the blood, the urine and the tears in the holy waters.

The sun had set by the time our mother returned carrying little Bhuri. Above the village, the moon had risen, round and pale as a pearl, and I stared at it as I told her what had happened. She felt my arms first and then my legs to see if any bones were broken and then she sat on the khat, her head in her hands, and began to cry.

'Phoolan, all you do is cause trouble for us.'

It was a sermon I had heard before, but this time her voice was low and pained. She wasn't shouting, and she didn't try to beat me. She was too weary that night to beat me. My dowry had disappeared on that robber's cart and I was the one causing trouble? By fighting with Mayadin I had caused trouble? It was my fault, always my fault! I was a dirty brat who showed no respect, insulted everybody and caused only mischief. And then I was beaten for it.

I called on Durga, the goddess, to give me force, but my prayer was interrupted.

'God? You're asking God?' My mother was still crying. Her voice was dry and bitter. 'How are we going to marry you now? Ask him that?'

After Rukmini's marriage, we had had nothing but potatoes to eat for months. I had already decided that when I grew up I would be a mason or a carpenter like my father, then I could work hard and earn lots of rupees and bring plenty of wheat home, enough to feed us all. I was sure I could do the work of a man, and no one would be able to cheat me the way they cheated my father. Someone from the village had gone to tell him what had happened. It was past midnight and the moon was high when he returned, exhausted from the long walk home.

Mother's tears had dried and she was angry by this time. 'Tomorrow morning I'm going to the police to make a complaint!' she declared.

'The tree has gone, Moola! What can we do?'

'You never fight back, Devidin! Phoolan fights harder than you!'

The next day, she forced my father to go with her to the police station at Kalpi. They touched the feet of the officers to beg them to come and inspect the field. But there was no trace of the tree, not one branch, not even a single leaf. The stump had been burned, and the hole filled with earth.

'How dare you accuse Mayadin? He is already a rich man,' the policeman said, 'what would he want with your tree?'

He threatened to bring charges against my parents if they persisted with their accusations. Only the broken stalks of millet bore witness to the tragedy, but it could have been cattle that trampled them. Could we bring a charge against the cows?

The trunk of our tree was so big it took three of us to reach around it holding hands. Father was very fond of the tree. He had planted it and watched it grow, but he was happy to cut it down to pay the dowry to the husband my mother had found for me.

We didn't eat for many days. We felt grief for our murdered tree; it was like a member of the family who was no longer with us, and we were in mourning. One evening, not long afterwards, the whole family went and sat where our neem used to tower in the sky. My father told us, 'Concentrate, children . . . Close your eyes, look, see . . . Our tree is still with us. It's there above our heads. Smell it, touch it.' We sat there – Choti, little Bhuri (who was just starting to walk), our brother Shiv Narayan, father and myself – in a circle under the white moon, remembering the smell of the leaves. Against my cheeks I thought I could feel the rough bark.

Mother went back to her village again, this time to ask for help from her brothers to pay the dowry to my future husband. Father made bricks and built houses and walls, whatever people asked, putting the rupees away carefully in a fold of his dhoti. And I had nightmares. I dreamed that I was whipping Mayadin until he bled; I dreamed I was cutting off his arms with an axe, as he had cut off the branches of our tree.

Lying next to me, father woke.

'Phoolan! What is it?'

In my sleep, I had been hitting my father.

'Are you ill? Do you have a fever?'

It wasn't fever but anger that burned in me.

Mayadin's mother resembled a little old monkey. She was tiny, hardly as tall as the wall of her courtyard, with little round eyes that had lines around them like stars. She spied on everything that went on in the village and she kept a special watch on me. I knew that she was the one behind most of the beatings I used to receive from her husband Bihari. She was worse than their servants. First it was, 'Bihari! Devidin's daughter ran through our yard!' Then, after he died, it became, 'Mayadin, thrash this little brat!'

After Mayadin cut down our tree, I began to threaten her. I used to tell her that if she shouted to her son for help, I would strangle her. I was growing fierce. I admit I liked to tease her – it made her agitated, and she looked just like a monkey. Just for her I made a little drum like the ones used by monkey tamers, using the neck of a broken clay pot left over from Diwali. I stretched a piece of cloth over the rim, then I drummed on it with sticks as I passed their house, singing, 'Dance, monkey, dance!'

It infuriated the old woman. She would stamp her feet and call for her son, but her voice was too weak for him to hear, and the harder she stamped her feet, the louder I beat the drum to make her dance!

One day, after I had made certain her son was out of the way, I went into their courtyard with Choti. We dragged her khat from her usual vantage point by the door over to the well. I had a big stick and threatened to beat her if she moved. Bihari had dug the well because he didn't like the thought of his women being stared at in the village, and he wanted to show that he was rich, too, by digging it. He had threatened many times to throw me in the well, so I decided to do the same thing to his widow. I dangled her by the feet over the dark abyss.

She bawled and screamed, and when she had no voice left I told her, 'Your husband was a thief and your son is a thief. You're the widow and the mother of thieves! If you tell on me, I'll let you drop to the bottom of the well next time.' From that day on, she was terrified of me.

Sometimes I would bring back a live snake from the river just for her. I had to catch a toad first, which I attached to a hook at the end of a piece of string. When the snake came out of the water to try to eat the toad, I grabbed it. Sometimes I was able to free the toad by squeezing it out of the throat of the snake before he had time to swallow it. Then I hid the snake in the gutter by the house, attached with a washing peg to a piece of string tied to a tree. My friends would tell me when Mayadin had left the house and, with the snake behind my back, I would creep up on her khat and wake the old woman by waving the snake in her face.

When she jumped with fright, I shouted, 'When are you going to give back the land you stole, you mean old hag?' I liked to put the head of the snake right in front of her beady eyes, and then I let the snake's body slide over her scrawny bare arms. 'Take the snake away!' she always pleaded. 'Mayadin will give you back your land! He will! I promise!' Every time I did this, she trembled in terror. I knew that the snake from the river wasn't dangerous, but she didn't know where I had got him.

I began to feel that snakes were my allies. Whenever I thought about snakes, I knew it meant there would be one near me somewhere and, if I searched a little, I could usually find it. It was often the same sort of snake: very long, with a large head and brightly coloured scales.

Another monsoon passed, and another winter, and then one day, I heard from my friend Ram Dhakeli that the old monkey woman had been on her deathbed for almost a week. We decided to go to her house and find out why she was taking so long. When Mayadin asked me what we wanted, I said I had come to pay my last respects.

He let me in.

She was curled up on her khat in the courtyard with the

dhurry all the way up to her chin. Her monkey face was even more shrivelled and it had turned as grey as her hair.

Her breathing was faint. 'She's delirious,' said Mayadin. I leaned close and spoke softly.

'My dear great-aunt, your little Phoolan is here.'

She opened her eyes wide when she saw me and her tongue popped out.

She died that instant.

I shuddered . . . It was as if she had been waiting to see my face before she died. I feared the old woman had become a spirit, and that now she was going to haunt me! Mayadin leant over and closed her beady eyes. The pupils had turned white.

'She didn't want to die before she had seen you,' he said, suspecting nothing. 'I should have called you earlier.'

I knew the truth. She had died of fright when she saw me!

The last memory she took with her from this life was me. I had hung her over her well, I had waved snakes under her nose, and her son thought she wanted to bless me! It was more likely that she wanted to curse me with her dying breath.

Goodbye vile little monkey, I thought. May you never be reborn, may your spirit be imprisoned forever at the bottom of your well!

5

Choti wanted to play weddings with our dolls. 'You can be the husband and I'll be the bride,' she said.

I didn't have much time left for playing after Rukmini finally went to live with her new family.

Mother said I was eleven years old, but she wasn't sure. I was still small, so small it seemed that Choti might soon outgrow me, though she was born after me. My mother could only say that I was born in the month of Bhadrapad, during the wet season, on the day of the flower festival. She couldn't remember how old Rukmini, Choti or little Bhuri were very clearly either. But she knew the age of Shiv Narayan, our brother, because she knew one day she would have to register him for school. All I knew was that one day I would be big, and I would have more strength to work. With Rukmini gone I was the eldest and I had her chores to do. I had to grind the wheat for the chapatis and the stone gave me blisters on my hands. I had to gather manure and row it across to the kachwari, feed the animals, get mud to repair the wall when the rain washed it away, fetch water, light the fire, clean the stable, and wait until everybody else had eaten.

After her wedding, it had seemed that Rukmini would never leave to live in her husband's village, and we were always asking her when it would be. But now that she had gone, I missed Rukmini. She used to teach me things. When she performed the *gauna* ceremony and went to live in her new village, we went with her along the road and cried until long after she was out of sight. Since then, I had often wanted to cry, or vent my anger somehow, to hit someone, and hurt them. There was no one to defend me from our mother now, the way Rukmini did at times. I was the eldest and I had to do as she said. If I daydreamed at the threshing machine, Amma scolded me and told me I was good for nothing. It seemed as though I didn't have the wisdom and calm of Rukmini. Even my little sister was starting to get on my nerves.

Choti never stopped asking about marriage. With her nose red from the cold, chewing on the hard millet cakes that were all we had to eat that winter, she would ply me with questions. When are you getting married? Will it be my turn after? Will you be going away like Rukmini? Will your husband be nice? How old will you be when you get married? And me?

I, too, would have liked to know the answers. I was to be married, but it was only a ceremony to me, and I was looking forward to getting presents like Rukmini. I was told that my husband would come from a village called Maheshpur, one day's walk away, that he had already been married and he owned land and would help our family. I was told I would leave our house to live in his village in three or four years time, when I was an adult. I couldn't imagine what it meant to wait four years. How many nights and days, how many moons, how many harvests was that? I wondered.

'It's a long time,' explained father, 'nearly half your age again. Don't worry about it.'

So I stopped worrying about it.

It was dawn, still dark, and I didn't want to go out in the cold to fetch water.

There was a knock at the door. 'Phoolan!' It was the voice

of my friend Sukhdei. 'I'm going to cut some grass from our field. Ask your mother if you can come too. We'll cut some for your cows.'

Sukhdei was tall and graceful. She dressed like a woman in her yellow sari with her long hair plaited and tied with a ribbon. She was already married, though she hadn't yet gone to live in her husband's house, and she treated me like her little sister. I had no sari to wear yet, only my cotton shorts and my blue shirt, and my hair usually hung in tangles down my back.

'If you want to come you'll have to hurry up,' said Sukhdei.

Mother called out to us to be careful. It was spring and the rivers had gone down but they were still treacherous. Amma thought I was careless, but I wasn't afraid of the waters.

When we got down to the banks of the Nadi, we could barely see the opposite shore in the pale light. It was cold, and a blue mist hung over the grey waters as we stripped off our clothes. Sukhdei kept her petticoat on even though nobody could see us as we waded across, holding our clothes and our sickles above our heads. I walked behind Sukhdei, shivering as I trod through the cold, muddy water that came all the way up to my chin and made my teeth chatter. We dressed quickly as soon as we reached the other side. I noticed that Sukhdei was already a woman, with rounded hips. My body was as formless as the bodies of my dolls.

To reach Sukhdei's field, we had to go past a field of hora. The plants were set in neat rows that came up to my waist. They were ripe, with little green pods. I felt a sudden pang of hunger. I had eaten nothing for breakfast so I knelt down, cracked open one of the pods, and the little black peas rolled into my hand. As I ate, I had an irresistible urge to take more.

Sukhdei looked at me with fright. 'What if Mayadin sees? This is his field.'

'It's too early. The lazy dog is still in bed.'

'You'll get a beating.'

'I don't care . . .'

Bent double in the rippling green field we reaped the plants with our bare hands. In no time I had a nice bundle, almost as big as me. I tried to imagine the look on Mayadin's face if by some magic power I could have reaped it all and carried it off! At harvest time he would only let us have the stalks left after he had taken all the leaves and the peas, yet we were the ones who sowed the seeds and spread manure in his field. We fed the stalks to our cows. Our cows were hungry, and so were we. I knew that he ground a sack of hora every day just for his animals, while we had only millet to eat.

As I turned around to put another sheaf of hora in the sack that was slung over my shoulders, I noticed a figure moving in the clear dawn light. It was a well-dressed man. It could only be Mayadin! He wanted to look like one of the important people in the village, but I couldn't have mistaken his nose. It wasn't the nose of an eagle, I had decided, it was the nose of a vulture. And he had been watching us . . .

Fearfully, Sukhdei drew close to me. 'When we passed behind your house I saw one of his wives,' she whispered. 'She must have told him we were going to the river. He'll be furious!'

There was nowhere to hide in the open field and soon he was upon us. He grabbed us both by the hair, Sukhdei with one hand and me with the other, and he dragged us along like reluctant goats. Sukhdei was crying but I was silent. I stumbled and fell at his feet, expecting him to try to beat us, but he contented himself with insults.

'Thieves! Dirty little robbers! I'm going to have you sent to prison!'

Sukhdei struggled desperately, probably fearing that Mayadin would drag her to the bend in the river and do to her what my mother was always warning me about. She clutched her sari around her tightly and looked at me reproachfully. But I knew Mayadin by then; he was like his father. There was only one thing he wanted, and that was to beat and punish me.

I heard his stick whistle by my head and felt it land with a sting on my back, but then he seemed to change his mind. He ordered us to gather up the hora we had stolen and he made us walk in front of him back to the river, slapping the backs of our heads and cursing us. When we reached the river he pushed us in fully dressed at the deepest point. To keep the bundle of hora dry I had to lift my arm as high as I could. My mouth was full of water and I had to swim, almost choking, to stay afloat. I could hardly even hear the insults he showered us with as he crossed on the back of a buffalo to avoid getting his nice clothes wet.

Then I thought of our parents. I realised Mayadin was going to make them pay a fine to the Panchayat. Bihari had done it once. My father had to pay five hundred rupees when I took a little bit of hora from his field. It had been a bad season, we only had cakes of millet to eat, and Bhuri was so thin she cried all the time. To punish me, mother had deprived me of what meagre food we had for several days.

Mayadin was forcing us to walk towards the house where the Panchayat, our village council, met. As we passed, people came out to stare at us. My shirt clung to me and my shorts were covered in mud. Sukhdei was still shivering and her sari was twisted around her.

'Look at Devidin's daughter!' Mayadin told them. 'Look at the little robber! She stole hora from my field!'

When we arrived, he made us sit on the ground while the village elders assembled. Kisna, the fat little Pradhan with the rooster eyes, was one of them, of course. Kisna was in league with Mayadin – they were both jackals in my mind. The village guard was sent out to beat his drum to announce that there was to be a meeting and one of the villagers was instructed by the Sarpanch, the village chief, to light a fire in the yard. Sukhdei and I had to wait to one side, sitting on the ground by the door to his courtyard.

We were trembling with cold in our wet clothes, but nobody let us sit near the flames to warm ourselves. Wives and servants coming to fetch water from the well whispered to each other and nodded in our direction. I could hear my name being uttered with contempt. *Phoolan Devi is a thief! Phoolan Devi has dishonoured her parents! One of these days, she'll go to prison!* But I heard other voices too . . . *That Mayadin ought to be ashamed of himself! What's wrong with a child taking a bit of hora? It's not as if it's going to make him any poorer . . .*

My mother came running in panic when she heard the guard's announcement. My father was walking behind her slowly, with his head bowed in disgrace. Mother seized me by the neck and hauled me up on my feet. 'When you get home I'm going to give you a lesson you won't forget!' she hissed. My father said nothing. He sat down silently without looking at us under the large banyan tree where the village council met in the hot season, with his hands over his face, as though he was praying. But I knew he was crying.

It was nearly midday before all the panches arrived. They were all rich men who owned land. They shut themselves in the Sarpanch's house and we could hear Mayadin shouting, 'Why did these girl steal hora from my land? Because their parents put them up to it! Devidin should be fined!' I stared at the bundles of hora that Mayadin had placed on the concrete platform under the big tree in the centre of the courtyard: one was large, and the other, which Sukhdei had gathered, small. Sukhdei had a father, a husband, brothers, people to defend her. Even though she was poor like us, nobody bullied her. She wasn't Mayadin's hated cousin like me; she wouldn't be punished like I would be. I was the dirty thief, the daughter of Devidin who was praying under the banyan for forgiveness. I loved my father, but he didn't know how to defend me. He was a peaceful, kind man whose back was bent from working in the fields whatever the weather. He never complained about the pittance he earned.

By the time the Panchayat reached its decision it was mid-afternoon, and it seemed as though half the village had gathered there. The Sarpanch came out and stood on the platform under the tree. He was tall, with thick hair, and his name was Brij Bihari. Usually he said little to us but I knew he was in league with Kisna and Mayadin. He announced first of all that Sukhdei's family would have to pay a fine of a hundred rupees. A hundred rupees! For a bundle of hora that you could hold in one hand! But for me it was different. Wide-eyed with surprise, I listened as the village chief declared in front of all the villagers that my father had rights to Mayadin's land; and that, until then, Mayadin had denied him his rights; and that since Devidin's family had no other land to grow food themselves, their daughter could not have legitimately gone to take hora anywhere other than in Mayadin's field!

I had won! The Panchayat had decided I wasn't the thief; it was my cousin and his family, who had refused my father his rights. They had turned my family into hungry dogs.

I jumped up from where I sat and ran to my father. He was still staring at the ground, weeping.

I was so delighted I pushed his shoulders. I was almost

hysterical. I couldn't stop myself from giggling with disbelief. 'Father! You see! I won! I'm not a thief – we have rights to Mayadin's land! They said so. Why are you still crying, father? The field is ours now!'

He wiped his tears. 'Why did you do it, Phoolan, why?' He shook his head.

I didn't know what to say. I had nothing to fear any more – not Mayadin, not being beaten by my mother, nothing! I had won, but he was still crying.

Mayadin approached and my father stood up, his head still bowed, his eyes bright with embarrassment. He said nothing. It made my heart ache to see how ragged his clothes were compared to those of Mayadin. And I felt an even deeper unease at my father's bent, compliant posture, the posture of a slave, in front of his arrogant nephew with the fat, lazy hands.

Mayadin was so angry his nostrils flared like an angry bull. His voice was choked with frustration. 'Devidin! This is an outrage! You put her up to it! You sent her to my field to steal hora from me! You should have been made to pay a fine. The panches haven't given me justice. You listen now to what I have to say, Devidin. I'm going to make your life a misery! You hear me? A misery!'

I wanted to jump with joy. I laughed at Mayadin and ran to get the bundles of hora from the platform. As I did, a woman from the village spat at me saying it was going to encourage stealing in the fields.

The bundles were heavy but even struggling with the weight I had the strength to run back to the house and straight to the animals. It was the happiest moment of my life! I fed the hora to the animals stalk by stalk, one for each cow, one for the goats, one for the chickens. I held out the precious branches one by one and let them chomp on the crisp pods full of peas.

'Eat! You *can* eat them. They come from *our* field!'

Waddling in her cotton shorts, little Bhuri came up and held on to me full of curiosity.

'Look Bhuri, it's food, good food! We're going to be rich now!'

I danced with joy among the animals as I shared out our bounty. They hadn't punished me. I was the princess of the stable, of the house, of the whole village!

The only one who still wanted to scold me was my mother.

'Why did you giggle in front of the panches?'

'You heard what they said. Father has rights! We can go to Mayadin's field whenever we like and take whatever we like to feed our cattle!'

And she began to laugh too.

Over the following days, Choti and I went to forage happily in the family field. Choti was caught once by Mayadin's wives and they chased her with a stick, but Mayadin did nothing to me. He didn't dare to lift his hand against Phoolan Devi. I just laughed at my little sister's annoyance as she showed me the marks on her arms and legs.

Three months after my victory over the field of hora, there was a sudden commotion in the house: lots of activity and many people from our village and other villages coming and going. I was too busy working in the fields with Choti to pay much attention. Late one afternoon, while I was gathering manure, my mother came to get me. She told me to forget the manure. Turning me around, she led me down to the river, where she washed me, combed my hair, and rubbed my body with oil mixed with haldi, a yellow powder ground from sweet-smelling turmeric. I glowed like the statue of a goddess, and it would be three days before I was allowed to go to the river to wash it off.

I continued with my work. There were other girls painted yellow like me, and they kept on working too.

On the third day, a small procession came along the road to our village, led by a cart pulled by two large white bullocks. From a distance I could see that in the procession there were only men. When I realised they were making their way to our house, I ran and hid in the bedroom at the back.

The men who were riding the cart came through the door and sat on khats in the courtyard.

'Show yourself, Phoolan!' my mother called. She had to come to find me.

I was still yellow from the oils she had rubbed on me but I was wearing my cotton shorts and blue shirt and I was layered with dust from the fields. The women of the village were crowding outside our front door, trying to see what was going on. I felt like a goat that was being sold at market. The man sitting in front of me was big and fat, with light skin. With him there was an even older man. The fat man seemed too old to be my husband. He was at least as old as Mayadin and I assumed he must have been the father of my husband.

My mother spoke to him.

'She's too young, she's not a woman yet. A man aged thirty ought to have a bride of at least fifteen.'

My father shook his head anxiously.

'She's too young,' he said. 'You won't be able to take her for some time.'

The man sat there looking at me, saying nothing. His eyes were very dark under brows that creased as though he was weighing up some sort of bargain, but what sort? What was he calculating? I thought. I was feeling more and more uneasy. I didn't know the meaning of his look. My mother made me stand next to her for him to compare and I barely reached to her waist. But the older man announced, 'She is suitable.'

And they were gone. The old man gave me a pat on the head and a smile.

They left the village the same evening and by the next day, I had forgotten them.

Then Choti asked, 'Are you going with this Putti Lal?'

The question surprised me. 'No,' I replied.

'But Rukmini went to live in Ramphal's village!'

'Rukmini waited until *gauna* before she left for her husband's village. She was sixteen.'

'What is marriage for, Phoolan?'

'I don't know, Choti.'

As far as I could tell, it was an elaborate feast parents made for their daughters. I told her that many girls in the village were married, and after the wedding they stayed with their parents and played with their sisters and came back to work in the fields with us.

Choti thought about this. 'So let's play with our dolls,' she said brightly. 'You can be the groom and I'll be the bride!'

She set about parading our rag dolls yet again in the yard, sitting them down and introducing them to one another, the way we saw our parents doing at Rukmini's wedding. I put a garland around the neck of my doll and a red mark on her forehead, but like Choti I had no real idea what any of it meant. For me a husband was a man in the same way that a brother or a father was a man. He was someone who would protect you, not a man like all the others that you had to be wary of. One far off day, the day of *gauna*, I would leave like Rukmini to live in my husband's village, and my mother and father would have one less mouth to feed. That, I supposed, was why they struggled to pay my dowry. Since our neem tree had been carried off on Mayadin's cart, I guessed that my mother had borrowed the rupees from her brothers to pay my dowry.

I didn't know anything about this Putti Lal. I didn't know

who he was or what he looked like. I didn't know he was a demon, and that despite the promises he made to my parents, he wanted to carry me off the day after the ceremony.

Until then, life had been hard. It comprised beatings, hunger, and tears, but also laughter and hope. Until then, the only man I belonged to and had to obey was my father. From then on it would be Putti Lal. He was going to be given an eleven-year-old girl to do with as he pleased.

6

It was during the month of Baisakh, a day of summer sunshine and dry, powdery heat – my wedding day.

There were so many faces I didn't recognise that I felt unconcerned by the event. I was lonely and bewildered. I remember being famished, impatient, and tired, but I was also curious. There was music and singing, and the guests behaved in ways people didn't normally behave, but I was the same person as the day before in my blue skirt and blouse. I was no higher than the beard of a billy goat, scrawny as a cat, and nervous as a squirrel in a tree that a crowd of people are trying to force down.

I didn't even see the wedding procession arrive because I was working across the river, digging ditches to irrigate the shoots in our kachwari. The morning passed, and when we finished our chores, Choti and I waded back into the warm water to get away from the mosquitoes that had been trying to bite our arms and legs all morning. The river was low and it was easy to swim back. The water lapped gently at the wide sandy banks and a bird swooped down to catch a little snake from under the surface, making the other birds squawk jealously.

As we played, I saw my mother coming from the village carrying something. I could tell she was annoyed by the way she walked, and she hadn't bothered to cover her head. As usual we had told her we would be back right away and as usual we had disobeyed her. It was fun to splash in the water and try to catch fish with our bare hands, but mother was always afraid that the current would carry us off or something terrible would happen to us by the Pradhan's house. I gathered up my clothes as quickly as I could to meet her on the path.

Choti was cleverer than me: she ran off along the bank to make her way back to the village without being seen. But mother had already spotted me. She seemed more impatient than angry, however, and I saw that she was carrying a beautiful yellow sari.

'I told you not to play in the river!' she snapped. 'Look at you – covered in mud!'

She pulled me by my hair back towards the village. There were so many people along the path that, for a moment, I didn't know where I was. When we reached our little house it was crowded with strangers. All the women from the village were there, chattering excitedly as they examined the presents.

The *baraat* had reached our house and I was covered in mud with my hair in tangles. I didn't know where to hide. I felt awkward around all those people I didn't know. A Pandal had been set up in our yard: garlands of mango leaves hung from a white parasol, and green leaves of a banana palm, wide enough to sit on, lay on the ground.

'Look,' I exclaimed to Choti, 'it's beautiful!'

'Not as pretty as for Rukmini. She had more flowers and more people, and there were more presents.'

I admitted to myself that it was true. Our parents must have had to borrow money to pay the dowry of their second daughter, I realised. What were they going to do for Choti when the time came? Girls really are a curse, I thought, and that reminded me I hadn't eaten anything all morning.

I ran into the house. 'Amma, can I have a chapati? Please, Amma? I'm hungry!'

'No,' said my mother. 'That'll teach you to disappear on your wedding day! You can eat afterwards! First we have to get you washed!'

I had to take five different baths, each with different perfumes and oils. And when that was over, haldi was rubbed on my hands and feet. The wife of the village barber complained that she was having trouble making a ponytail with my hair because it was too short and tangled. When my sister got married, her hair was beautifully thick and long. It had been many monsoons since her head had been shaven for lice the way the heads of us younger children were from time to time.

One of my maternal uncles had brought some bangles that my mother slid onto my wrists and ankles. I was wearing rings on my toes and a silver necklace. The women dressed me in a new blouse and then I discovered that the yellow sari my mother had been carrying was intended for me! I had to gather the loose end of the sari and use it like a shawl to cover my head entirely. After that I couldn't see anything, I could only feel the hands of the women dressing me, fiddling with me, and moving me around.

I was led under the Pandal and made to sit down. Then everybody whispered to me at the same time, telling me what I shouldn't do: don't move, don't make mischief, don't fidget during the ceremony, and don't say a word!

'Even if I'm thirsty?'

Mother shook me by the shoulders.

'No! It's your wedding. Do you understand, Phoolan? You have to sit still and wait for the ceremony to end.'

I was going to have to sit there like the statue of a goddess, without knowing what was happening, without even being able to see anything.

Mother gave me a final warning. 'Now, don't humiliate us!' she said.

Apart from the pangs of hunger, I felt no different from normal that morning. I had hoped that Choti would come and sit beside me but she wasn't allowed to. I sat there alone under the Pandal and it seemed as if I was going to have to wait for ever. I heard voices near me and I knew they were talking about me, but I couldn't see who it was. When I breathed, the cloth over my face stuck to my nose, and I thought I was going to suffocate. My back hurt from having to sit without moving. From time to time, I shook my bangles just to hear them jangling against each other. I had never had so many bangles. But I was annoyed. I hadn't even had the chance to see the necklace before they put it on me.

I decided enough was enough. I lifted my shawl. I was thirsty.

'Choti! Where is Choti? Tell her to come!'

I was told by Nayan, the wife of the barber, who was supposed to make sure I remained still, that it was out of the question. Choti had to stay with the others. Very firmly she said I had to lower my shawl again and sit still. I was the centrepiece of the occasion, but instead I would have preferred to be one of the guests so I could see myself instead, and have something to eat and drink.

At last, I was helped to my feet. I could smell sandalwood burning as I was led by the hand and, though I couldn't see him, I could sense that there was a man beside me. I had to walk seven times around the sacred fire, as the priest chanted a mantra. Then my veil was lifted and a red mark was made at the parting on my forehead. My father and mother took my hand and put it in the hand of this unknown man, whose face I seemed to recognise from somewhere. A big, sweaty hand enveloped my small fingers.

All I wanted was to be able to lift my shawl and see what was going on around me. It seemed as if everybody was

enjoying themselves that day except me. The crown of
mango leaves I was wearing kept slipping against the smooth
fabric of my sari gathered over my head. I thought I was
going to lose it at any moment, and my neck was getting stiff
from holding my head straight. 'No mischief, Phoolan,' my
mother had warned. I had to stand there and not move for
what seemed like hours. I was hungry and thirsty. By the
time the evening came, I needed to pee as well.

Under my shawl I muttered that I had to go to the toilet,
but there was so much chatter and music I wasn't sure anyone had heard me. Finally, I was taken by the hand but
instead of being led outside to relieve myself I was brought
back to sit under the Pandal. From behind the yellow cloth
of my sari, I could make out the shape of a man sitting in
front of me. Then someone lifted my veil and I saw the dark
eyes of a man examining me.

I was handed a metal tray of rice and petals and told to
throw them over his head. Then I remembered where I had
seen that look before. It was the man who had come to our
house, the one who had said to my parents, 'This girl is
suitable.'

I was married to Putti Lal.

I threw a handful of rice over his head, and as I did, I
noticed that his hair was already turning grey. He wore a
white dhoti and the buttons on his kurta over his pot belly
looked as though they were going to burst.

I had to tell Choti! I turned around and there she was
behind me. 'It's him! It's the same man who came to the
house before!'

Choti laughed behind her hands. 'He looks old enough to
be our father!' she tittered. 'You have two fathers now!'

He had a thick black moustache and skin as dark as mine.
And he seemed enormous to me! I had to tilt my head back
to see him as he hauled himself up, covered with rice and

petals. He wasn't handsome like my brother-in-law Ramphal; he smelled of tobacco and, from below, I could see all the hairs in his nose.

With his palms together, he bowed low in front of my father; then he bowed in front of my mother, my uncles and the rest of my family. Then he left.

It was over. I was free!

I took off my sari, put back on my old skirt and blouse, thankful to be able to see my feet again, and ran to the field to relieve myself. Things were back to normal, except that along with Choti, a number of women followed me to make sure I didn't lose any of the jewellery I was still wearing. Meanwhile, the Putti Lal and his family went to dine in the tent that had been set up outside the village.

Back in our house, I was at last given food and something to drink. Someone explained to me that it was the custom for the bride to fast until the ceremony was over. With all the jewellery that everyone wanted to marvel at, weighing up how much it was worth, little Phoolan became the centre of attention. I had never been treated so nicely before. The women asked me if I was happy. I wasn't sure. 'You'll see,' said one of them. 'Your life's going to change now that you're married.' I had no idea what she meant, but it sounded promising. Would I be able to keep the bangles? I wondered.

It grew late, nearly midnight, and the women of the village were still chattering to me. 'Choti, why are they doing all these things?' I whispered to my little sister. 'All this nice food to eat? All the smiles? All these women who want to talk to me and touch me!'

I'd had enough. The jewellery, the music, all the sweets, and the people staring at me; my hair was still tied back tightly, hurting my temples, there was haldi all over my hands, and I was becoming irritated by the jangling noise each time I moved my hands or my feet. I was fed up with this game. The entire ceremony had been a game, fun for everyone else but not for me. I was tired, but before it was all over I at least wanted to see inside the Janwasa, the marquee that the Sarpanch had erected for Putti Lal and his guests.

Barefoot in the dark, Choti and I climbed up on to the terrace of our house, where we dried our pots. We could see the marquee in the field outside the village, lit by oil-lamps. A loudspeaker had been tied to a tree to play the music from the tent for the whole village. There were many more guests there than there had been at our house. Some were sleeping on mats, others were talking or playing cards. 'Look Choti,' I gasped. 'There's even someone writing!'

We were fascinated. Like little nightingales perched on the roof we chirped with excitement. Our whole family was there feasting too, and Choti decided she wanted to join them, but I was too tired by then, and since nobody seemed to be interested in me any longer, I climbed down to find somewhere to sleep.

Under the Pandal where I had sat during the ceremony was the carpet of banana leaves. I lay down there and fell asleep in minutes, exhausted from the day's duties, but enchanted by the sound of music and laughter in the distance.

I heard a voice calling me from far away in my sleep . . .

It was morning, and someone was looking for me, but whoever it was, they hadn't thought of looking under the Pandal. Then two little hands lifted the parasol.

'Who's under there?' came my sister's voice.

I rubbed my eyes with my hands, and saw that they had been painted yellow! It was the haldi. I jumped up with a start, suddenly remembering all that had happened the previous day.

'Here she is! The bride!'

I had assumed it was all over, but it wasn't. I was bathed again and dressed in a pink silk sari that glowed like the sunset. Choti grinned and danced like a monkey around me. She told me she had counted all the presents: there were saris and bangles and many, many saucepans. She had been busy. She had found out that Putti Lal had a house with two storeys and land in another village. He had been paid a dowry of five hundred rupees, plus a cow and a goat. 'Not as many rupees as Rukmini!' she noted.

In his white dhoti and freshly ironed kurta, Putti Lal had returned with his father to our house. In the daylight, I saw he was every bit as old as I had thought the evening before. His hair was grey at the temples. He was fat, with thick lips and thick black eyebrows. He seemed less at ease than he had been the evening before.

I sensed there was something wrong. My parents were sitting side by side on a khat outside our house, looking concerned. They were talking with Putti Lal and his father while I waited in the yard with my nice sari and my bangles. I guessed that this was the farewell ceremony and that the man would leave for his village, like Rukmini's husband, to wait for me to grow before he came back for me. I would be sixteen years old by then, I thought. They called me out of the house.

Putti Lal began with one hand to untie a knot that had been tied in my sari that morning. I started to panic, but my mother said it was all right, it was the custom.

As he fumbled with the knot, he said, 'I'm taking her with me.'

Father bowed his head. 'We agreed!' he mumbled. 'She's too young, she can't be a wife to you yet.'

'But I need her now. My father and I live all alone in our house. We need someone to cook for us and do the chores. I want to take her with us now.'

My mother started to cry.

It didn't seem so terrible to me. This man only wanted to take me to his village to do work that needed doing. I had already been to stay in my grandmother's village and the village where Rukmini lived, and I had returned. I assumed he must have had cattle to feed, clothes to wash, the sort of chores I did every day like all the other girls in my village. Why was my mother in tears?

'Don't cry, Amma,' I said. 'I'll be back.'

Then father started sobbing too. He put his head in his hands. He kept on saying I was too young to leave the family home. I didn't understand. Of course I would have preferred to stay in our village with Choti and all my friends; of course I was a bit frightened by this man and his ageing father, but I was less afraid of them than I was of Mayadin. He hadn't come to the wedding feast, but I knew he approved of the marriage. Everybody had been consulted, and they all must have agreed. Mayadin must have thought that once I was married I would no longer be in his way. He was going to find out he was wrong . . .

'Don't cry, Buppa! Don't be afraid! I'll be back,' I said.

My father knew it was against the law for my husband to take me away to live in his house. Taking an eleven-year-old was like taking a slave, with the difference that we were the ones who paid him. But I didn't know any of that. I didn't know what a man and woman were supposed to do once they were married. Nobody had told me how children were made. When I saw the older girls going to hide in the fields to bury soiled cloths, I thought they had hurt themselves and I knew blood was impure and had to be cleaned from the house.

I began to cry too, but it wasn't from fear of this man and what he might do, it was just because I couldn't stand to see my mother and father crying.

It was early morning and in front of our house a nice

painted cart tethered to two big white bullocks waited.
While Putti Lal was still arguing with my parents, one of my
mother's cousins lifted me up and put me on the high seat in
front. A canvas had been strung above the seat from two
bamboo poles to give shade from the sun. I realised I was
hungry again; nobody had given me breakfast. But it was too
late. Putti Lal climbed up on the high seat with his father,
while five women from his family climbed onto the back of
the cart. The bullocks shuffled and with a creak of the
wheels the cart began to roll. I felt my heart suddenly
tighten. Where were they taking me? I turned around to see
my parents. My mother was standing straight with her hands
on her hips, an indignant posture, but I couldn't see her
expression under her shawl. My father was still crying,
standing with his back bent and his head lowered.

Choti and the other children came skipping along with us
for a while and then they halted and turned to walk back
towards the village. For a moment, Choti stood in the middle of the road, squinting into the sun and waving her little
arms in the air to say goodbye. Then she turned and also
began to walk back to the village. I was alone with these men
and women I didn't know.

When we reached the main road, Putti Lal got down from
the cart along with two of the women. They said they were
going to take the bus to their village and went looking for
something to drink. Since we had halted next to a field, I
climbed down too and I was about to scurry off into the
grass to find some grains to eat when one of the women saw
what I was doing and warned me: 'You're not a child any
more, you're a dulhan now! You'll have something to eat
when we get there!'

I had often heard it said in the village that so-and-so was
the dulhan of this man or that. It meant that they belonged
to him. Mayadin had two dulhans, two wives.

I burst into tears. 'Whose dulhan am I?' I asked, trembling. 'Just because my parents aren't here you think you can make me someone's dulhan? It's not true!'

'You're Putti Lal's dulhan, you little idiot!'

The women burst out laughing as I began to cry even harder.

The old man, Putti Lal's father, consoled me.

'Don't cry. I'll give you some nice buffalo milk when we reach the house.'

The Yamuna was low and almost dry where we crossed, but the bullocks could barely pull the cart loaded with all the people. The wheels got stuck in the sand, so two more of the women got down to walk back to the road and return by the bus. As we crossed in the cart, I heard someone say we were going to take the road on the other side in the direction of a village named Maheshpur. It was very hot by then and I was half asleep, rocked by the bumps in the dirt road, day-dreaming of my bamboo khat in the yard at home under the straw roof. Choti would be the eldest now and she would have to do all the work. She would be the last one to eat . . . All day, we trundled along in the cart. The hot season had begun and the land was parched. The grasses had turned brittle and yellow, only the sugar-cane grew tall and green in patches. Now and then, we passed carts and even lorries going the other way. But this dulhan business worried me . . . If someone said I belonged to him I made up my mind I would beat him with a stick! I was Phoolan Devi and I belonged only to my father.

I woke with a start as the cart swayed to a stop. I had covered my face with my sari because of the dust, and I lifted my veil to see where we were, but it was already too dark. Night had fallen and there were no electric stars in the trees of this village either.

A hand pulled the cloth back up over my face.

'Don't do that!' said a woman. 'You must wear your ghoonghat!'

'Why? I want to see where we are!'

'We're at your husband's house, idiot!'

Why was this woman treating me this way? I was frightened. I couldn't see anything.

'I don't like it here. I want to go home!'

'You mustn't say that. This house belongs to your father-in-law and your husband. And you belong to Putti Lal. You are his dulhan! Now shut up!'

'It's not true. I'm not anybody's dulhan!'

The woman dragged me through the door with my head still covered. Once inside, at least I could lift my veil. My mouth was dry from the journey and I was given some sugar-cane juice that instantly made me feel better. As I drank, my father-in-law lit the oil-lamps and I could see that the house was like ours but bigger. I was taken inside and made to sit down. It was a room with a concrete floor and white walls. I wanted to go back outside to see if there were any children to play with but the women wouldn't let me. When I tried to get away from them they chased after me and dragged me back to the room.

'Please . . . I want my Amma, call my Amma!'

'Shut up!'

'Can I have a chapati?' I asked. 'I'm hungry. Please.'

'You'll have to wait!'

I didn't like these women. I had thought they were relatives of Putti Lal, but why wouldn't they give me anything to eat? I tried to guess how far away I was from my house.

'Come, we must go to the temple now.'

It was the custom for newly-weds to go to the village temple to make offerings to the gods, they told me. Before we left, Putti Lal picked me up and put me on his knee. He made a knot around me with the tail of his dhoti. I used to do this with Choti when we played at weddings with our dolls; making the knot meant we were married. It seemed that the game was still going on. I had to dip my hand in white paint and make my handprint on each door of the house. It took a long time, and by the time it was over I was beginning to feel drowsy from hunger. But I knew the meaning of the sacred outline on the doors: if my hand was there on the doors it meant I really was the dulhan. The women had been telling the truth. I belonged to this man.

We went from one temple to the next, the whole night long, performing different rituals and making offerings. When the temples were closed, we performed the ceremonies outside. In the light of the oil-lamp, Putti Lal looked to me exactly like Raavana, the demon killed by lord Rama.

It was morning again by the time we returned to the house. I was so hungry by then that I stood in front of the women and tore off my veil. 'Now I want to eat! Give me a chapati now!' I demanded.

Everybody laughed. 'She's just a child, a little kid!' someone said.

They offered me another sweet drink and I refused. My stomach was groaning for something to eat, but there was no mother in this house and no children either. It turned out that the women were just visiting for the festivities and they would go in a few days, leaving me alone with the two men. The old man called me Beti, meaning I was his daughter. Since everybody addressed him as Buppa, I supposed I should call him father too, but he didn't have the gentle expression of my real father.

If he was my father, I could lift my veil in front of him – but I didn't dare ask him for anything, and this Putti Lal had not yet uttered a word to me. I turned to one of the women.

'I want to go back home now, please!'

'Oh no. You're here for good. Don't you understand?'

She looked at the two men and they laughed.

Putti Lal laughed loudest. 'She doesn't understand any-thing,' he chuckled. 'She doesn't know what you're talking about!'

I said nothing more.

At least they finally gave me some chapatis to eat. After that, I was left alone to sleep on a khat in a corner of the courtyard while the women sang. My body was aching with fatigue, and the bed of woven hemp was almost new. The bamboo legs were smooth and shiny and the frame was straight. It wasn't like the rickety, torn, sagging khats we had at home. This Putti Lal had money, it seemed, but how could that be when he belonged to the same caste as us? Had he become rich like Mayadin, by stealing from his family? There were lots of men at the house, eating and drinking, and I could hear them laughing at me as I lay there in the corner of the courtyard.

Sleep carried me off – and then suddenly I woke again with my heart thudding. It was daytime, but I couldn't be sure which day it was . . .

I looked around and realised it was morning – but it must have been the morning of the next day – and everyone was still asleep. Clothes and bags that must have belonged to the guests lay everywhere. I got up and saw empty plates and cups strewn about. I went to drink and found the large bar-rel of water in the corner of the courtyard almost empty. Some people were asleep on khats, others lay on the terrace or inside on the concrete floor that had been covered with cotton dhurries. I went upstairs to try to see over the wall. Some children were playing in the street outside. Returning to the courtyard, I disturbed one of the sleeping men.

It was the old man, my father-in-law. I tugged at his sleeve. 'Bappu, I want my Amma!'

'It's not possible, Beta.'

'Make it so my little sister Choti can come then. I'm afraid here all alone. Please, Bappu!'

'Listen carefully to me, Phoolan,' he said, raising himself up on his elbow. 'Your father said you could stay in the house with us for a few days. That was what your father agreed. When he comes to get you, you can leave, but not before. Understand?'

I was reassured. If my father was coming, it meant I just had to wait. This old man seemed like the only person I could trust here. The others all laughed at me. I didn't trust this Putti Lal who said I was his wife. I tried to think of any man in our village who lived alone with an ageing father and no women around; no mother, no aunts, no wife, and I couldn't. Why had he no wife in his house? And why no daughters to do the household chores?

'I don't like it here, Bappu.'

He held me gently by the shoulders and leaned close to me. 'This is your home for the moment, Phoolan,' he said softly. 'You'll have to wait until your father comes to get you.'

He drew back and looked at my body. 'Why are you wearing a blouse?'

'I took my sari off to sleep. It was too tight and I was hot.'

He paused and then led me inside the house. The women who had been sleeping inside were awake now, and he handed me over to one of them. 'Do something about this child. She isn't even dressed properly.'

The women laughed. I must have amused them a great deal. One of the women opened my blouse, looked at my chest, and laughed even more.

'She doesn't even have a bust!'

I waited, thinking they were going to give me a bath, but they just chatted among themselves.

'The bride is so young and the groom is so old!' said one.

The pink silk sari I had been given to wear was the first sari I had ever owned. I waited for one of the women to help me put it on, as I didn't know how, but they just tittered. If Choti was here, I thought, we would teach them to mock. I buttoned my blouse. Mother had told us never to walk around with our clothes unbuttoned and I wasn't going to stand there half-naked for these women to laugh at.

'This is your house now, you'll have to learn to bathe on your own,' said one. 'Your father-in-law has prepared the water in the backyard.'

There was a tub full of water and a pitcher and a hole in the ground for the water to drain away. There were no men there, so I put down my sari carefully, took off my skirt and blouse and quickly doused myself. Then I asked if someone would comb my hair. One of the women, a relative of Putti Lal, did it for me. She helped me put the sari back on too. It was too big for me, and I had the impression of being wrapped in a big sack. The only solution was to gather the extra cloth at my waist with two bangles to hold it in place.

'We'll have to find you something smaller,' the woman joked. I would have liked to put my skirt and blouse back on, but she said no. Married women had to wear saris. 'And don't forget to keep your head covered in the house today. The guests are going to come to give money and they'll want to see your face. You can lift your ghoonghat, and then they'll give you the money.'

'Money? For what? I haven't done any work.'

'How silly this girl is!' the woman exclaimed. 'Each guest has to give you a present, or at least five rupees, to see your face. Didn't you know? It's the tradition, *muh-dikhai*.'

They sat me on a carpet in the courtyard and the guests passed in front of me. Each time one of the guests lifted the ghoonghat, all the women giggled. But they had been right.

The guests did give me money, which I quickly hid away in a little black purse embroidered with pearls that my mother had bought for me. It was a pretty purse with a silk cord to hang around the neck. She had given it to me telling me to put all the money I received in it and not give it to anyone, so she must have known. When my purse was full I hung it around my neck under my sari, the way my mother had shown me. I remembered what she had said: 'Be careful. Someone could grab it and run off with it!' Since it was the custom, I decided I would keep the rupees. I didn't know when they would give me money again. But they could laugh at me all they wanted as long as the rupees were for me. I wouldn't give any to Choti, I'd give them all to my father so he could pay the lawyer to win his case against Mayadin.

I didn't know how to count higher than the fingers on my hands but I guessed there were at least thirty rupees in my purse. I was rich, and without doing anything more than showing my little girl's nose to these people!

Whenever Putti Lal entered the courtyard, the woman hurriedly pulled the ghoonghat over my face again. It seemed to me she did it whenever there was an older man there, but not for the young brother-in-law of Putti Lal.

It was a confusing day. They gave me rupees, so I could buy sweets, and then they made fun of me.

'It's a goose hitched to a camel!' I heard someone giggle.

As soon as I got a chance, I took a peek outside, but there was no camel. There was nothing to laugh about.

7

The old man had washed my hair and given me food. He was kind to me. He even said, 'Oh Phoolan, if my wife was still alive, she would do all this for you while we waited for you to grow up, but I'm a widower and there are no women in this household. One day you'll do it for me and your husband.'

That was the hardest thing to grasp. What was a husband? All the women had gone after the festivities so I couldn't ask them. They would only have laughed at me anyway. Rukmini cooked and did the housework for her husband, as she had done for my father. I didn't believe this Putti Lal could be like my father. He didn't talk to me the way my father spoke to me; he didn't ask if I had cut enough fodder or if I had been to the temple to pray. A husband couldn't be like a father; my father had never tried to touch me like that . . .

'Phoolan! Where are you hiding, my little pigeon?'

It was Putti Lal's voice.

'Now that we are married, I'll show you what married people do . . . Don't be scared. I'm going to teach you a new game . . .'

A game? I was wary, but curious. If it was a good game I could teach Choti. There was a glint in his eye but it didn't seem malicious, I didn't think he wanted to hurt me. Nobody had ever looked at me like that before . . .

'Come! To play this game we have to go inside . . . In the beginning you might be a bit frightened but after a while you'll start to like it.'

He gripped me by the scruff of the neck and made me enter the house.

I didn't like to be inside the house. I preferred to stay in the courtyard and sleep on the khat outside so I wouldn't be near the two men. Around the courtyard, as well as the kitchen and the cowshed, there were two rooms for sleeping and a third room behind these from which you couldn't hear a sound. Putti Lal often shut himself away in there. A woman had come to the house a few days earlier and gone in there with him. His father had been annoyed. They had another argument, and she had gone away again.

He forced me to go in that room and there was nothing I could do. I had seen the old man leave so I knew we were alone, but I didn't scream. After all, I thought, it was only a game. Apart from the door to enter there was only one other door in that room, and it led to a store where the clay jars full of onions, grain and oil were kept. What game did he want to play there in the dark? I wondered. He closed the door and made me sit on the ground. There was no concrete on this floor; it was hard, bare earth, and the room was unkempt and dusty, like all the rooms in the house. Putti Lal unbuttoned his kurta and took it off, then he untied his dhoti from around his hips and let it fall to the ground.

He was naked!

Was he insane? I wondered. He was utterly naked in front of me! In our village, we would take our clothes off when we were with our sisters or cousins to bathe or play in the water, but never with men.

All I could think of to say was, 'I want to play outside! Why can't we play outside.'

I didn't dare look at his body. With my head bowed, I tried frantically to guess what he was going to do. He didn't have a stick so he didn't intend to beat me; there was no water in the room so he wasn't going to wash . . .

He came closer and grabbed my arm, then he sat on the ground and looked at me. My eyes had grown used to the dark by then, and I could see the strange expression on his face. He had thick black hair all over his body. His broad chest heaved as he breathed. I struggled as he began to undo my sari, but he just held my arm tighter.

'Keep still!' he complained.

My yellow sari fell in a heap on the ground, and he kicked it away. Then he tried to take off my blouse, but I wrapped my arms tightly around me. I drew back as I felt his hands on me, but he gripped my legs between his knees and I couldn't move.

That was when I felt something slithering against me . . .

It was a serpent. There was a serpent attached to his body! He wanted me to touch this serpent. I was petrified.

Then he started nibbling at my skin, trying to bite me. He was going to eat me! He was a man who ate women!

'Don't touch me!' I screamed. 'Don't eat me!'

He put his hand over my mouth to choke me. With the other hand, he began to squeeze my chest under my blouse, gripping me even tighter between his knees – so tight I thought he was going to break my bones. The demon was so strong I was imprisoned by his hairy limbs. He was sweating now and he smelled disgusting, like a hyena. I thought the hyena was trying to devour my flesh. I struggled desperately to get free but I couldn't. And then he started trying to do things with his nauseating serpent, things that were unimaginable to me. The pain was unbearable. I begged him to spare me. I told him I wouldn't trouble him or eat his food any more. But he put his hand over my mouth and I could no longer cry out.

He shook me hard by the shoulders and angrily twisted me around, and then he pushed me down with my face against the earth.

I felt his weight on my back, heavy as a buffalo. He began beating me in a way I had never been beaten before. I couldn't even scream at the pain of the serpent pressing at my flesh. He was beating me inside! I thought the serpent was going to tear me apart! It tore me and began to devour me . . . The demon carried me to the bottom of a deep dark pit, where I couldn't scream and I didn't have the force left to fight. It was going to eat until it was bigger than me, and I would die . . .

Then he said he couldn't do anything with me, and he was going to get a knife to open my belly to put his serpent in.

I blindly scratched and pinched him as hard as I could, but it was no use. When I saw the knife-blade shining in his hand, I froze. He held it to my belly, playing with it, showing me the part of my body that was making him angry.

'I'll open it a little and then it'll be easier,' he grinned. 'It's a very nice game.'

I tried not to tremble, not to flinch, and I gritted my teeth to stop myself screaming again. He hadn't hurt me enough. He wanted to do something else to me. He wanted something horrifying from me, and I still didn't know what it was.

I had seen the mongoose by the river fighting off a snake. I had seen him doing it, but I didn't know how to defend myself. Silently, frozen with dread, I cried for my mother, I prayed for help from anyone, from any of the gods and goddesses, but none of them heard me.

It seemed to go on for hours. I was like a rag doll at his mercy. I could see his contorted face, his teeth bared as he insulted me. Why? I wanted to know why? His serpent had become a stick that tore into my body. Why did he want to punish me? I had done nothing bad. I hadn't insulted him. I didn't even know him.

I thought I had died from fear – like the old monkey woman, Mayadin's mother – and would never come back to life.

I bit his hand, only to find out if I was still alive, and he groaned.

I realised I was still alive.

He turned me around and punched me hard in the face.

In my mouth I could taste the blood flowing from my nose, and the taste of dirt from the ground. I felt more blows, but my terror of his serpent was greater. He was trying to use it to choke me, to stop me crying out! Suddenly I could no longer feel any pain from his punches and slaps. Seeing his vile dark face in front of me, the thick, slobbering lips and black moustache, I felt my strength returning; I wasn't trapped with my face in the dirt any more. I began to scream, and to fight back.

Still holding me by the arm, he picked up his knife again and held it in front of me, making me stand up. 'You little bitch! I can do whatever I want with you. I'm your husband, your master! Do you hear! Now shut up!'

He was panting and his eyes were wild.

He got up from his knees and brought the knife towards my belly again, but as he did, he heard a sound outside and turned, loosening his grip on me for a second. I ducked between his legs and bolted for the door. I lifted the wooden bar that held it shut, and was through the door before I felt his hand grabbing me by the neck. He dragged me back, choking me with both hands.

This time he put the knife under my throat.

He threw me to the ground again, knelt down and slid the knife across my belly. It was a big knife with a wooden handle and large blade that I could feel pressing coldly against me, right there where he wanted to open me for his serpent.

Bending over me, he showed me the knife again, waving it under my nose.

'I'm going to use this to open you if you don't do what I want!'

Panic-stricken, I jumped up as he spoke, and like a gazelle I was outside in the courtyard before he even knew which way I had gone. He had left the door open so he wasn't able to catch me for the second time.

I shrieked for help, but in the heat of the afternoon, the village was deserted, and nobody heard me.

He was already behind me, panting, trying to catch me again. He missed me by an inch as I scrambled up the wooden ladder that led to the terrace, screaming with all the air in my lungs, 'He's a child-eater! He wants to eat me!'

He climbed up after me, still naked, but I was able to jump across to the terrace of the house next door, and he stopped at the top of the ladder.

Without his clothes, he couldn't go any further.

I jumped from one roof to the next, and the next, from the top of one wall to another, until at last I saw two women in a courtyard. They looked up as they heard me.

'What are you doing?' one of them asked. I hesitated. I knew nobody in the village and perhaps these women would just take me back to the demon who said I belonged to him and he could do whatever he liked with me. But he might be behind me.

'Save me, please! Putti Lal was trying to eat me! He beat me with his serpent!'

They stared at me in fright. My face was covered in

blood, my petticoat was in tatters, my blouse was undone. These women had to save me, they had to take pity on me. I was at their mercy now. From the roof, I looked around to see if I could see the demon approaching, or locate the dirt road that led back to the river. All I could see were terraces and roofs and the branches of trees that were too tall to climb.

In the courtyard, one of the women shook her head.

'It must have been her that we heard screaming just now,' she said. 'Her parents should never have let her marry so young. It's a disgrace!'

More women arrived and, with difficulty, because I was starting to feel the pain again, I climbed down from the roof.

I could hardly walk.

In a few minutes the courtyard was full of women I didn't know. They tried to calm me as I sobbed in their arms, begging them to take me home to my mother. I felt as though my whole body was on fire and I thought I was going to vomit. My legs couldn't support me and I sat down on the ground. They gave me water to drink. 'Don't send me back to that man,' I whimpered, 'he wants to eat me!'

An old woman put her hand on my shoulder.

'Don't be afraid, we're not going to send you back to him,' she said. She smiled gently at me.

The other women stared at me, their faces half-hidden behind the ends of their saris, appalled at the sight of all the blood on my petticoat, my face and my legs.

'He had a serpent,' I stammered.

'What serpent?'

'In his dhoti . . .'

Then Putti Lal arrived. He had dressed now, and was in a bad temper. He came straight up to me and began hitting me and insulting me. The women didn't move. The way they saw it, he had the right to beat me, the way their husbands beat them, because I belonged to him. That, at least, I could understand.

Only the old woman came forward, and, lifting her ghoonghat back from her head, dared to address him. 'The whole village knows you're a wicked, evil man, Putti Lal. Your soul is twisted with vice. Her parents made a big mistake marrying her to you. We all heard her screaming. You promised you would wait and now you're trying to molest her!'

'Get away, you old hag! She's my wife, I can do whatever I feel like with her. And as for you . . .'

He turned to me.

'Why did you run away? Get up! We're going home. Or I'll kill you!'

He started hitting me again.

I heard a voice pleading with him as I cowered with my hands over my head to fend off his blows.

'Stop! If you keep hitting her like that she's going to die!'

It was a man's voice. 'Have patience. If you look after her, one day she'll be a woman.'

Putti Lal hesitated and I took advantage to try and escape his clutches again, but he caught me by the hair and shouted back, 'I'm going to make her a woman, and I'm going to do it tonight! Now let me through . . .'

He dragged me through the streets in front of the villagers. They had all come out to see what the shouting was about, but not one of them tried to stop him. It was the same with Uncle Bihari and Mayadin, but I could always get away from them. I was trapped with Putti Lal. Nobody dared to come between us to defend me. Even the dogs shied away from us. The men just watched, cowards who saw what one of their kind was doing, but not one tried to intervene. They were frightened, like my father. He had never tried to prevent Bihari or Mayadin from beating me either. All he would do was hang his head and weep. In each house that we passed, there were villagers lying on their khats watching this man shoving me and hitting me as I stumbled back along the path to the house. The more he beat me the more I cried and begged someone to help me, but nobody stirred. He could beat me and abuse me as much as he pleased. That was the custom and that was the law.

By the time we reached his house, he was holding me by my hair. I could feel my scalp on fire as he yanked out whole tufts each time he shoved me. He pushed me into the court-yard and shut the wooden door behind him. Then he pushed me into the room next to the cowshed, where he found a cord used for tying the animals and tied my arms and legs to a khat. Then he kicked the door closed behind him and locked it.

I closed my eyes.

There was no more life in me, I had no more strength left to cry or beg for mercy. It was over. He could do whatever he wanted with me: eat me or cut me to pieces with his knife . . .

'I married you,' he barked, 'you stupid bitch! Who said you could run away? You caused a scene! Did you do it just to ridicule me? It's none of their business, you hear?'

Suddenly I heard the voice of the old man.

'Open the door! Open it or I'm going to break it down.'

He banged so hard on the door that it flew open.

Opening my eyes, I could see behind him a crowd of men and women in the courtyard. 'He's going to kill her, Bappu,' I heard someone say. 'You have to stop him.'

The old man confronted his son.

'Aren't you ashamed of yourself?'

'Look at me, Bappu,' I whimpered. 'He tied me up, he beat me, he was going to kill me!'

Putti Lal walked away muttering insults under his breath.

My father-in-law untied me, gave me some water to drink and told me to go and clean myself and put my sari back on. I was so afraid to go back inside the dark room where I had thought I was going to die that I stood at the door in my torn, bloodstained petticoat. Finally I ran in and snatched the heap of yellow cloth from the floor.

In a corner of the courtyard, under the straw eaves of the roof, stood the barrel of water and a pitcher. As the villagers turned away, I began slowly to wash myself. I could see the cows beyond the doorway looking at me with their sad eyes. But my father-in-law was bolting the wooden door. And even if I could flee, I realised I wouldn't know where to go. I wouldn't have known how to find my way back to my village.

As I washed, I watched a bird pecking at a worm in the mud. So that was what being married meant. All the things I didn't know before had become clear to me. The villagers had gone and the two men had shut themselves in the house. I could hear them shouting. My ears were buzzing and the blood throbbed in my temples. It was four o' clock and the sun was still high, but I realised I was trembling. The stream of water from the pitcher made me shiver. I was freezing in the hot sunshine. I was in so much pain that I couldn't wash myself in the places where he had hurt me. He had used his serpent like a wooden stick to beat me inside.

All those dirty, ugly things he had done, I knew, were the danger my mother had warned us of. That was what happened to girls at the bend in the river. And they happened with everybody's blessing when a man like Putti Lal said, 'She is suitable.'

I realised now why my father had been so worried and why my parents wanted him to wait until I was Rukmini's age. She never complained about being beaten by her husband. She said he was sweet and kind, and took care of her.

Where had he come from, this woman-eater with his serpent? Had he been sent to torment me, like the demons Rama had battled?

I would never be able to forget what he did. My parents were following custom, thinking they could trust him and that he would look after their daughter until she was old enough to become a proper wife. They didn't know what everybody in his village knew, that Putti Lal was a drunk and a gambler, that he was wicked and immoral, that he thought only of his own pleasure and he was even capable of forcing a child to satisfy him.

From then on, whenever I saw him, whenever I heard his heavy footsteps in the street or in the house, I couldn't help it, I wet myself from fear.

I slept on the roof terrace or in the cowshed, with the door open, so as to be able to keep watch on his comings and goings. During the day I didn't leave Bappu's side for a second, and when the old man went away to the market or the temple, I climbed back up to the terrace, even in the blazing afternoon sun. I didn't want to ever have to feel his hands on me again. I was afraid of everything, afraid of going to the toilet, of turning my back on him. I was afraid of him grabbing me by surprise when it was dark . . .

One day, when there was a wedding in the village, he tried to eat me again. He thought the noise of the music and the feasting would drown out my cries. But I managed to get away from him, and ran through the streets frantically yelling, 'He's trying to do it again!'

That time, my father-in-law heard me and came back to console me.

Then I fell ill. My body became covered in boils, I had a high fever, and my hair began to fall out. I couldn't eat, and my stomach was so tense I could hardly drink a sip of water.

The demon brought a big woman home and went into the

room with her. Afterwards he had another row with his father and in my fever I heard him shouting at him that it was all his fault.

'Why did you choose a child? I need a woman!'

'You're married. It's a disgrace to bring another woman to your house.'

'You do it, why not me?'

'I'm not married, I'm a widower!'

'Married! With a child like that? She's no use for anything and now she's sick! I hope God lets her die, and then I can get someone else.'

8

I was alone, abandoned by God. I vomited constantly. Even a sip of water made me nauseous, and the fever made me shiver. Images of the torture I had been through swam in front of me, impossible to forget, and worse, impossible to comprehend. I would become a woman, I would belong to this man, and I would have to live in this house, they told me, but I still wanted to know why. Nobody had told me what marriage would be like. I thought I would be protected by my husband, I thought he would be a second father, as Choti had said, who would give me chores to do and food to eat. I expected to be scourged only if I neglected my chores. Instead I found myself alone with my nightmares.

There was no woman there to console me or tell me what to do. My head ached, and there was a sour taste in my mouth. I had the shivers – one minute I was boiling hot, and then I was freezing cold – but nobody took any care of me.

When I heard footsteps in the yard, I shut my eyes tight, fearing I was going to be tortured again.

The footsteps came closer. I could see a shadow under the door.

'Phoolan? Are you in there, Phoolan?'

It was a man's voice, but I didn't recognise it. I curled up even more tightly on the straw mattress and pulled the cotton dhurry over my face.

'Phoolan, is that you?'

'Who are you?'

I felt a hand on my forehead, and immediately I knew whose hand it was.

'My child! I hardly recognised you! You're so thin, and your face looks different. Phoolan, can you hear me? It's your father!'

I opened my eyes. It was my father leaning over me, and he was crying! He sat down beside me and gently put my head in his lap. Tears began to stream down my face too.

'Take me away from here, Pa! Right now! I beg you.'

I tried to get up but I lacked the strength. My father told me to lie still. He stroked my brow, sobbing.

'Your hair has fallen out, my little baby! Somebody came to the village to tell us you were ill and that I ought to come. What happened? Did somebody hurt you?'

'Oh, Pa. That man hurt me. He tortured me. He wanted to put things in my belly. He said he was going to cut it open.'

'Hush, Phoolan.'

'It was disgusting! He had a serpent and then he took a knife because the serpent couldn't go in, and then he did like the dogs in the village. It hurts so much, Pa, I can't even go to the toilet.'

I told him everything. My father hid his face in his hands. They were things he should never have heard, but I couldn't help myself. I couldn't hold back.

He put his hand over my mouth. 'Don't say it, Phoolan, don't say any more.'

When he took his hand away, I only asked, 'Why did you send me here, Father? Why didn't you come to get me sooner? Look!'

I pointed at the *chimta*, the iron tongs for poking the fire and turning the rotis as they baked. 'He used that to burn my behind, to punish me! I didn't do anything wrong! I didn't do anything!'

'Don't cry, Phoolan, I'm taking you home!'

'Promise, Pa? You promise?'

'I promise. Calm down now. Your father-in-law is coming. You mustn't say these things in front of him.'

The old man came to offer my father something to drink. He sat down opposite my father, shifting uncomfortably.

'It was you who wanted to take her,' said my father. 'I told you she was too young and you should wait, but you insisted, you said you needed someone to do your chores. You are the father of her husband and when I gave her to you, you became her father too. Why did you do nothing to protect her?'

'I know. I am ashamed of my son. Please accept food from my house.'

My father hesitated. It was not the custom for a girl's parents to eat in their son-in-law's house.

The old man put his hands together and bowed low in front of my father. 'I want to offer you our hospitality. Please accept . . .'

My father had come with a man from the village, his best friend. He must have been afraid to come alone. My poor father, who didn't even dare to raise his voice. If only he had the courage to beat the woman-eater to death! I wanted him to take me away from there that instant, without even speaking to Putti Lal and his father. But my ever-humble father bowed and accepted the food for himself and his friend.

Impatience gave me the strength to get up from the mattress. I just wanted to leave, to remove the clothes that made me a wife of that man and put on my old blouse and skirt and leave, without their jewellery, without eating their food. I wanted to forget them. But just then, the demon himself arrived, with his bushy eyebrows and a supercilious air. He looked at my father as though he was a rat who had stolen grain from his store.

'What do you want, Devidin? What are you doing here?' His father intervened.

'Leave him alone. You're the one who ought to humble yourself in front of the father of this girl.'

Putti Lal approached my father, but instead of bowing to touch his feet, he slapped him across the face!

'Who are you to come poking your nose into my affairs?' he said.

Father lowered his head in humiliation.

The two men began to argue, going outside to the court-yard to shout at each other. Sitting with my head in my hands, fearing I might vomit again at any moment, I listened to them. The sound of their voices resounded like thunder in my ears. It would soon be night-time and I was worried that my father might give in to them. His friend wanted to leave right away but my father preferred to spend the night there and leave in the morning. He asked my father-in-law if he could sleep near me.

'She doesn't need her father,' interrupted Putti Lal. 'This is her husband's house. He can go back to his village.'

'My daughter is sick,' said my father. 'She must have water during the night to stop the fever drying her up. Her face is covered in spots. She probably has typhoid. I don't want to leave her alone. I can sleep on the ground here.'

'No. You'll sleep outside,' barked Putti Lal.

What right did Putti Lal have to treat my father like that? He was another one who took himself for a thakur. He had a house and some land but he didn't work. He spent his time playing cards and chasing women. It was his own father who said so! He was just like Mayadin; he thought that having land and rupees gave him the right to treat people however he pleased.

My father yielded, as always, and went to sleep on a mat in the courtyard. His friend did the same. I was too weak to take them by the hands and force them to leave. The fever burned in me, and the night passed in a mist like the one that sometimes hid the far shore of the Yamuna. I dreamt I was struggling with Putti Lal, and then I recognised my father's kind face. It reminded me of how thirsty I was; my tongue was shrivelled like a fig in the sand. When the dawn came I woke with burning cheeks, drenched in a cold sweat. I couldn't even remember how many days it had been since I had eaten.

Neither Putti Lal nor his father had tried to do anything for me. They must have wanted me to die. I had dragged the mattress near the door to be able to see outside but each time he passed, Putti Lal kicked the door shut, and I had to drag myself up to open it again. I needed air, I needed to see the sky to remind myself I was still alive. Each movement I made was painful, and with the pain the terrible memories returned. I had washed my clothes by myself, crying as I scrubbed the blood from my skirt. I had cried as I went to the toilet. I had cried and cried, but all I could do was wait for the pain to subside.

The cattle stirred hungrily and I heard my father arguing already with Putti Lal as the sun rose over the courtyard. I could distinguish the timid voice of my father, and the fierce growls of the demon . . .

'I must take her to the hospital. I beg you, please. I'll bring her back later!'

'Why do you want to take her there? She can get better here. If you take her, people around here will think badly of me. They'll say I am not able to look after my wife.'

'But she needs medicine. She could die; you beat her and the fever won't go away. Let me take her to the hospital! They can take care of her; I'll see to it she gets proper nourishment. And when she comes back, she'll be bigger and stronger. She will obey you, you'll see.'

Hearing my father pleading with him I began to ask myself why he was afraid of Putti Lal. Was it because he had paid him a dowry and now he was in debt? He was my father and he alone should decide for me, but he was begging him now the way he always begged Mayadin. I was a human being – not a cow to be argued over by its owner.

Finally, Putti Lal accepted, and my father told me to hurry up and gather my belongings. I didn't want to take anything with me but my father-in-law insisted, laying the yellow sari on the ground and piling my bangles and anklets on it before tying it into a bundle. I had been so proud of all those pretty bangles; I had taunted Choti to make her even more jealous. Now I hated them. I hated everything to do with that man . . .

The old man offered my father and his friend some parathas for breakfast. The smell of the fried pancakes stuffed with vegetables turned my stomach again. I could neither eat nor drink, but I found the strength to dress. As I was putting my pink sari on, the old man handed me a five rupee note. I hesitated. Was this supposed to restore my dignity? I took it anyway, thinking of the money my father needed for the lawyer, and tucked it under my sari. His friend picked up my bundle, my father picked me up and sat me on his shoulder, and we set off.

In the street, the villagers watched us pass. The men sniggered behind our backs.

'What did you think would happen when you married your daughter to Putti Lal?' one of them shouted.

'Hey, don't bring her back!' advised another.

The women muttered to one another: 'Look how sick she is, poor thing, and thin as a rake.'

'He already tortured his first wife to death!'

It seemed they knew everything there was to know about Putti Lal. There were no secrets in the villages. My mother's aunts and uncles, the astrologers and the Brahmins, they all knew when they arranged the wedding. And now they were giving my father advice. Why didn't they tell him before? How could they have allowed me to be dragged back into that house half dead with pain and fear?

My father said nothing. He tried to walk as fast as he could to avoid hearing them. I only wished he would walk even faster, in case Putti Lal changed his mind and came after us.

When we reached the edge of the village, I turned and shouted, 'I'm never coming back. Never!'

Father only frowned. 'Be quiet, Phoolan,' he moaned. 'Don't say a word. Don't embarrass us.'

We had left the village and we were walking along the dirt road. The sun was climbing slowly in the clear blue sky. I could see the perspiration trickling down my father's brow from the effort of carrying me on his shoulders, and it made me feel better. The rhythm of his steps reassured me and the silence of the sky calmed me. The road ran alongside wheat-fields rippling softly in the warm breeze. On my father's shoulder, I felt like a child again, a child who had been res-cued from a deep, dark well.

'Don't be afraid,' he kept repeating as he walked, 'don't be afraid, Phoolan. It's over . . .'

He said he was going to take me to the hospital in Sikandara, and it would be a long walk. After a while, we halted under the cool canopy of a mango tree and my father put me down. We couldn't see the village any more; we couldn't see any houses at all, nor any cattle. The road was deserted except for us. I was safe. I must have fallen asleep, and when I woke the first things I saw were mangoes hang-ing over me, plump and red like the ones at the Pradhan's house the day he slapped me for asking for one. I could almost touch the luscious ripe fruits above me. I wanted to pick one, but my father said I shouldn't eat yet. He gave me some water to drink from the gourd that his friend carried.

Father gazed at me without saying anything. He must have been thinking about what Putti Lal had done, but I hadn't the strength to ask him the questions that were nagging at me. I didn't want to think about what I had suffered.

Slowly, my father trudged along the road with me falling asleep and waking again on his shoulders. After a time we reached a busy main road. Lorries decorated as brightly as temples passed us laden with goods, sounding their fierce horns like angry buffaloes and setting off a storm of dust. A woman in a pink sari passed us, her head invisible under the enormous bundle of mustard flowers she carried on her shoulders. She waved her arms and shrieked at the drivers to steer their bullock-carts out of her way. There was so much life around me and the noise of scooters and buses deafened me.

At a crossroads, Father stopped in front of a woman selling kakri. She had spread her pile of little cucumbers on a cloth, and squatted there fingering the coins and notes she had earned the way my mother did when she sold our kachwari crop. It had been so long since I had eaten that the kakri was too hard for me to chew, so my father crushed it to a pulp in the palm of his hand and fed me like a baby. All I could think of was how much I wanted oranges or mangoes, but he said I couldn't eat any fruits yet. He was right. As I swallowed the kakri, I felt my stomach contract and the nausea returning.

It was the first time I had seen such a large town with so many people. There was everything you could imagine: shops that sold sweets and cakes and ones that sold saris in all sorts of colours folded and piled up on shelves. There was one shop that sold only gold jewellery and another that sold only rubber tyres. There were carts loaded with mountains of peanuts and dried fruits. And carts with heaps of red and yellow flowers, with people squatting by them making garlands for people going to the temple.

It was mid-afternoon by then, and very hot. Some women were selling water from a cart and my father's friend refilled his gourd. At a bus stop, my father asked the way to the dispensary. It wasn't far, and I felt strong enough to walk by then, holding my father's hand. Here in the town, nobody knew us; the cows and dogs slept in the middle of the road and the air was thick with flies and grey with the hot fumes from buses and lorries. I had never seen anything like it! My ears were ringing and I didn't know why at first. Then I realised it was because the streets were filled with people on bicycles all sounding their bells at the same time. My fear evaporated.

The dispensary was a concrete house with a waiting room full of people sitting on benches, not on the floor. Others waited outside under a tree. My father joined the queue and I fell asleep beside him.

When I woke, the doctor was looking at me as he listened to my father explaining that I had a fever and I had been vomiting. He said nothing else, nothing about the pain. That was not to be spoken of. The doctor was wearing a white coat and pair of spectacles. Behind them I could see he had kindly eyes that seemed as tired as those of the people who worked in the village. I had never seen anyone important who worked before. He made me sit on a stool and he examined me: he scrutinised my face, my neck and wrists and he felt my shoulders.

'This girl is undernourished,' he told my father. 'She's too thin.'

My father was embarrassed. He explained that I had been visiting his in-laws and they hadn't taken proper care of me.

The doctor made me open my mouth and stick out my tongue. He frowned and put a metal spoon in my mouth that made me want to vomit again. I was scared that he was going to cut off my tongue. 'Don't be afraid, little girl,' he said. 'I'm going to give you an injection and then you'll feel much better.'

Nervously I watched him prepare a long metal needle. The barber in the village had pierced my nose with a thorn. Because we couldn't afford jewellery for me to wear in my nose, he had to do it again every year as the hole closed after a time. Liquid bubbled from the tip of the needle as the doctor approached me with it. I looked at my father nervously.

'It's all right, Beti, hold still. It's medicine.'

I gritted my teeth. The doctor stung me first in the arm and then he turned me around and stung me in my buttock. Since my father had allowed him to do it, I didn't protest. Then the doctor gave my father some pills and asked him for twenty rupees. Father took some notes from a purse he kept in the folds of his dhoti and counted them carefully.

'Why do you have to pay, Buppa?' I asked. 'He hurt me!'

'You have a lot to learn, Phoolan!' he laughed. 'The doctor was giving you medicine with the injection. I have to pay him for that.'

Outside, the afternoon heat had not yet begun to lift, and we sat down to wait beside the road, under a tall neem tree. Father was exhausted. He had walked for more than three hours with me on his shoulders. He lay down next to me, put my bundle under his head, and fell asleep, and I did too.

The sun was low when we woke. I was thirsty, and would have loved to drink the juice of an orange or mango, but it was forbidden.

'When will we be home?' I asked. 'Do we have very far to walk?'

'We're going to take the bus,' my father announced.

It was crowded with people and the engine made a lot of noise. Explaining that I was ill, my father asked the other passengers to make room for me and I sat down. The smell of the engine turned my stomach. I looked at my father anxiously and the driver said I should sit near the window in case I wanted to throw up. I touched the seat. It was padded and covered in plastic. I sat on it cross-legged, but that wasn't comfortable. Looking around, I saw the other passengers were sitting with their legs down, so I did the same.

I had seen buses passing on the roads, but that was the first time I had ever ridden on one.

From the window I could see across the plains all the way to the horizon. The fields of wheat lay like straw mats, some still green and others pale yellow where only stubble remained. There were fields of sugar-cane growing as high as a wall. Under clumps of trees were villages like mine, with grazing cattle dotted around them, but I couldn't yet see the river. In front of us, other buses came towards us so fast I thought we would collide. Behind, lorries came up and let out a roar to let us know they were there. I wanted to scream with delight in reply. I couldn't wait to tell Choti that in a bus, the world goes faster than you! I thought it was so funny, and then I vomited again.

Father gave me sips of water from time to time, but the journey was long and fatiguing. I felt dried up, my head still ached and the wind that blew in through the open windows left a dusty taste in my mouth. The bus stopped and people got off or got on, and it started again, and it seemed as though this would go on forever. The sun was low over the fields, colouring the dry grass orange, but I still couldn't see our river.

'There's the bridge!' said my father. 'We're getting off.'

The bus crossed the Yamuna, high in the air. It was as

though we were soaring slowly over the river like birds.

We reached the other side and came to a halt in another town. At the bus stop, my father bought me a kulfi. The sweet milky ice lolly made my throat feel better. We set off down the dirt road to our village, five miles away, on foot. I walked between the two men, eager to keep up so we could reach home sooner.

We passed some villages I didn't know.

'That's Shatti,' said my father. 'Where the muslims live.'

'Quick,' I gulped, 'otherwise they'll catch us and eat us!'

The men laughed.

'Muslims are people just like us, Phoolan. The only difference is they don't go to the same temple, that's all.'

As the sun was setting we left the dirt road for a smaller path. We met some people from the village of Divail who knew my father and they offered to let us sleep at their house for the night, but he preferred to continue.

I could see the neems and the jackfruit trees ripe for harvesting, and I knew my village wasn't far off. It was almost dark, but I could smell the familiar odour of the riverbank. I could hear the birds and animals. I was no longer thirsty and my fatigue lifted from me like a crow flying away from a field. Choti would probably be at the kachwari, I thought. I could hear singing and I ran down to the shore, but I couldn't see her. Then I noticed a skirt flared in the grass and someone lying there. It was Choti, sleeping instead of guarding the harvest of watermelons she had brought back across the river! When she saw me, she threw her arms around my neck, almost choking me as she hung there blubbering tears of joy.

'Phoolan! I missed you.'

She ran to get one of the watermelons she was supposed to be guarding and sliced it open with her knife. The juice tasted cool and sweet as it ran down my chin. I took great bites of the soft red flesh of the melon, laughing with Choti as we spat the pips high in the air.

Nothing had changed. I saw Pancham, the boatman, carrying a lantern to go fishing. He held it under my face.

'Your daughter is thinner than a mongrel, Devidin. She doesn't look healthy.'

Choti looked at me with fright in the light from the lantern. She wanted to know what had happened. I just shook my head.

Mother was waiting in our yard, wiping her tears with a corner of her sari. She couldn't even speak, she just held me tightly in her arms. She was still crying as she brought a jug of water to wash my feet. I couldn't bring myself to tell her everything that had happened. It was my father who whispered in her ear the horrors I had recounted. My mother felt my shoulders and my back and then held me away from her, examining me, before bursting into tears again. Her crying woke little Bhuri and Shiv Narayan and, not knowing why their mother was crying, they began to cry too.

Nothing had changed in the house. The same old khats, the same old clay pots. I had the feeling that I had been far from there. While I was away, I had imagined that none of it existed any more, but the washing was laid out to dry in the warm night just as before.

With her head in my lap, little Bhuri fell asleep again and, finally, as she ground wheat for chapatis, my mother's rage exploded. 'I'm going to give that Putti Lal a good hiding! I'm going to take a good stick and beat him. He better not show his face around here!'

She heaped curses on him as she prepared chapatis for me.

'I don't want her to go back!' she said to my father. 'That bastard nearly killed her!'

Father ate the chapatis. I couldn't swallow anything more

substantial than some warm milk and rice, and it soon started to make me feel sleepy.

'She's married now,' I heard my father say. 'I don't know how we can *not* send her back. A wife must live in the house of her in-laws. That is the custom.'

I could see the flames of a torch moving above our wall. It was our neighbours, curious to know what had happened. Mother blew her nose and straightened her sari, then she looked at me purposefully. 'Don't say anything about this to anyone, you hear? You'll get a bad reputation. You were sick, you were given nothing to eat and nobody looked after you, that's all. You hear?'

The neighbours entered and began to talk with my parents. Some of them said I ought to go back because it was dishonourable for a wife not to live with her husband. Others thought I should wait a few years at least. They all stared at me as though I had changed somehow in their eyes, and they were trying to work out what it was. I thought they couldn't have known of the tortures I had been made to suffer. But I obeyed my mother and said nothing, without understanding why it would be me who would have the bad reputation, while he was the one who beat me and tortured me. To our neighbours, my parents expressed their indignation but I sensed the same frustration behind it as when they complained about Mayadin stealing our tree. Their rage was never sufficient to fight those who held bundles of rupees in one hand and long sticks in the other. But I knew one thing: I was never going back to the woman-eater.

I went inside the house to lie down with Bhuri and Shiv Narayan. My mother followed me and lay down near us. I fell asleep at once, a sleep deeper than the deepest well.

The next morning, my fever had almost lifted. The twenty rupees for the doctor had been well spent. All I needed in addition was to go and bathe in the Yamuna with my friends, and let the sacred water carry away my secret shame.

My mother warned me again before I went to the river: 'Don't tell them, don't say anything to anybody about what Putti Lal did to you.'

The mention of his name made me quiver, and I had to concentrate to chase the memories from my head. I wanted to drown him, choke him, bury him in the sand and let the monsoon rain submerge him! The days passed, and I still couldn't forget, but the peaceful rhythm of life in the village helped me to recover my strength. It was only at night, in the dark, that I was afraid. That was when the nightmares returned. But the nights turned into days again, and the days turned into months . . .

It was during the month of Ashad. I was out in the fields, minding a cow, when Choti came running up to me.

'He's here, Phoolan,' she panted. 'He's come to get you!'

I ran like fury towards the temple to climb the tallest neem tree in the village and hide among the leaves. My mother was yelling at him so loudly all the village could hear.

After a while, Choti came and told me what was going on. 'He's all red,' she said, 'he's spitting and insulting everybody! Amma says he tortured you and nearly killed you! She wanted to send him away but Buppa made her give him food!'

I tried to think of a plan. I scrambled up to the highest branch, disturbing the monkeys who cackled hysterically in my ears, but everyone knew about my hiding place in the big tree on the road to the temple. When I was smaller, I used to spend hours up there trying to catch baby parrots as they flew back to their nests. Once when I put my hand in a nest, I had felt something cold – a snake! I had let it fall with a shriek on the children below.

The memory made me shudder.

Choti returned. 'Amma has thrown him out,' she exclaimed. 'He was furious, but he went. I saw him going along the path on a new bicycle, a black one. He bought it with the dowry.'

I climbed down warily and returned, waiting at the corner by Mayadin's house and listening in case I could hear him. He had gone, as Choti said.

I had a suspicion that Mayadin was behind his visit. Mayadin thought he had got rid of me, and it had annoyed him to see me in the village again. He was worried about his field of hora. I had heard him asking my father, 'What's your daughter doing here?' He had intimidated my father with his usual superior tone. 'She is married. She ought to respect tradition like other girls.'

A few days after Putti Lal's visit, my mother went to her family village for a few days while my elder sister Rukmini came home to look after us – and sure enough, he was back on his black bicycle. It had to be Mayadin who told him my mother had gone away.

I ran to climb my tree again but it was Rukmini who came to get me this time.

'Get down from there, Phoolan, your husband wants to see you!'

She said that I had to go to live in my husband's house, but she didn't know what it was like there. No one knew. I had told them nothing. When I said I wouldn't come down, she left to get my father and I decided to find a new hiding place. I knew that without my mother there, if my father and Rukmini agreed I should go, there would be nothing I could do.

I hurried down to the riverbank and hid between the big wooden boats hauled up on the sand for repairs.

But Father and Rukmini found me and dragged me back

to the house. Rukmini insisted I wear my sari and my ghoonghat. 'That's enough, Phoolan,' she said. 'You have to greet your husband.'

They tried to force me to go into the room where the monster was waiting, but I struggled desperately. They didn't understand why I was afraid, they didn't know. If my mother was there, she would have known; she understood what I had told her. Father had covered his ears, he hadn't wanted to hear, but she knew the danger I was in.

'We're not going to send you back to him,' said Rukmini. 'But you have to greet him.'

I gave in, entering the room with my head bowed so as not to have to look at him. I tried to stop myself from trembling, but then I heard my father say, 'Putti Lal's house is your house, Phoolan. You should be living there now.'

'You must do as I do,' said Rukmini. 'I live with my in-laws and I come back to see you. You'll get used to it, Phoolan. Please, don't make a fuss!'

Don't cause trouble, don't make a fuss! By the end of the day, in any case, they had decided for me. Putti Lal went on ahead to find a boat and my father and Rukmini brought me to the river. They put me in the boat with the ferryman on one side of me and Putti Lal on the other. They must have known that I would have jumped in if I had the chance and swum away with the current, even if it carried me to the bottom of the river. I had heard of women who committed suicide, leaving one life to be reborn in another.

Putti Lal turned to me as we crossed. 'If you resist me, I'll beat you. You remember how I beat you, eh?'

I was so panic-stricken by the time we reached the far side that I jumped out of the boat and raced along the river-bank, not knowing where I was going. The demon followed behind on the black bicycle that had cost many hundreds of rupees – as much as the price of a cow. I ran like a deer fleeing a tiger, afraid I would be eaten, until like a deer I could run no more. He snatched me up and sat me on the cross-bar in front of him, trapping me between his arms and pedalling furiously to pick up speed. I could smell his sweat and feel his breath on my back. If I tried to move, he pinched my arms and insulted me. 'If you keep telling people tales like the ones you told your parents, it won't be you,' he threatened, 'it'll be your corpse that goes back to your village to be burned!' He didn't stop pedalling until we reached his village.

It was evening when we arrived, and his father was dozing on a khat in the courtyard. I ran to him and touched his feet in supplication. 'Keep me here with you,' I begged. 'I won't go inside with him! I won't.'

'Be a good girl, Phoolan,' he said. 'This is your house. And Putti is your husband. Don't be scared. I'll sleep near you.'

But he didn't do as he promised. After they had eaten, the old man went to the room where he slept, leaving me alone with the demon.

'Come and lie down.'

'No,' I said. 'I'm staying outside! I want to sleep here.'

He slapped me.

'Do you want to be a wife or not? You're going to grow up if I have to force you. You aren't leaving here until you've given me three or four children at least!'

I bit his hand, but he had no difficulty forcing me into the room. He simply picked me up and, holding me to his chest, carried me in. I kicked at his knees but it was no use. I was in his torture chamber again, with his serpent.

I tried desperately to think how I could give him a child, so he wouldn't beat me again . . . I remembered my mother's belly swelling and how she had come out of the room with baby Bhuri, but I didn't know how children were made.

He slapped me and forced me to hold his serpent. I could still hear my father and my elder sister telling me I had to obey him, saying he was my husband. I wanted to turn to stone like the statues in the temple, to have no more thoughts in my head, to hear nothing and see nothing more.

The next day, he decided to punish me because I dared to complain to his father about how he hurt me. He broke a fresh branch from a neem and held me by the arm to cane me.

'You shouldn't say those things to my father. It's degrading for me!'

He whipped me until the skin peeled from my back and I swore to him I wouldn't say anything more.

He left me alone for the rest of that day, and the next, and then he dragged me again into his torture chamber.

When I emerged in the daylight, there was blood all over my behind and a horrible, searing pain in my belly.

I used any pretext to get away and hide. I hid in the fields or at the back of the cowshed or behind the big barrel of water in the yard, but he always managed to find me, and hurt me again. There was nothing I could do to stop him. But I swore to the goddess Durga who drank the blood of demons that he would pay for the pain he caused me. I swore I wouldn't spend my life cowering behind doors in the dark, or flat on my belly in front of this man. He had said himself that I would grow one day. So I vowed that I would survive, and I would have my revenge.

9

The house was deserted when they came for me.

I was hiding by the water barrel in the courtyard, dreading the moment I would hear Putti Lal's footsteps approaching. I had been there for weeks, mistreated and abused by him with no one to help me. They waited until it was quiet and then climbed over the wall: my maternal uncle Tara Chand and his son Kallu.

I let out a cry of relief! Bless the goddess! My mother had sent someone to rescue me!

'Ssssh!' whispered my uncle. 'Your mother and your aunt have decided you can't stay here. We're taking you to our house.'

They told me to get my clothes and jewellery, and they helped me scramble over the wall behind the house at a place where it had partly fallen away. Nobody heard us. We hurried through the streets and into the fields, and soon we were out of sight of the village. I ran, jumped and shouted for joy. The others could barely keep up with me, but I feared Putti Lal would catch us. I refused to slow down.

'Don't worry,' said cousin Kallu. 'If he follows us I'll give him a good hiding!' My cousin was older than Putti Lal. He was a big man and that made me feel better.

To avoid taking the road, we crossed the fields all the way to Sikandara, the town where I had seen the doctor with my father. It was night by the time we arrived and my uncle struck a deal with a lorry driver to take us on to Kalpi. From there, we could reach their village on foot. Normally, the driver wasn't allowed to carry women, but when he saw me, he shrugged. 'She's so young, if the police ask any questions,' he said, 'I'll just tell them she's my daughter.' His lorry bounced uncomfortably and the noise of the engine hurt my ears but I didn't care. I was imagining the look on Putti Lal's face when he found out I had gone!

When we reached my uncle's house, I rushed into the arms of my aunt. Tears fell from me in a burst of relief.

'Mausi, do you know what he did?'

She put her finger to her lips. 'I know, Phoolan. I know.'

My aunt, Khiniya, resembled her sister, except she was plump and contented, while my mother was skinny and irritable. She was older than my mother and her hair had already started greying, but when we stayed at her house she always greeted us with a smile and had nice things ready for us to eat, not a stick to discipline us with like my mother. Her husband was about the same age as my father, but he was more cheerful too, though he frowned now as he studied me.

'Your father should never have made you go. If you were my daughter,' he said, 'I wouldn't have married you to that man.'

I felt safe with them and, as my fear left me, my appetite returned. I was given warm milk to drink and some chapatis to eat. Their house was like ours, with two rooms around the yard for them, their five sons and three daughters. The married sons slept inside with their wives and I was to sleep outside with my aunt and uncle. 'Sleep,' said my aunt softly. 'You need sleep at your age . . .' It was the first night I had been able to sleep for weeks and I slept for two whole days and nights after that.

When my mother arrived, exhausted from journeying alone on foot, I was still asleep. It was hearing his name that woke me.

'Putti Lal has complained to the police,' my mother was saying. 'He told them his wife has been kidnapped by our family and they came to our village looking for her!'

I wanted to hide but my mother said there was no point, the police would come looking for me here and my uncle would only get in trouble. There was nothing else to do but return to our village. She told me she wasn't going to let Putti Lal take me again this time. She was going to complain to the police too.

We said goodbye to my aunt and her family and left.

As soon as we reached our village, it began again. The whole village had been talking about nothing else since morning. By the time we arrived in the evening, all our neighbours were there outside our house, airing their opinions. They told my mother to forget custom, they told her she shouldn't send me back to my husband's house. While Choti, Bhuri and my little brother jumped up to greet me and hung from my neck, delighted to see me, the whole village was busy deciding my fate – as though I belonged to all of them.

Mother shouted over the chatter. 'She shouldn't have gone with him for at least five years. Putti Lal agreed when we made the arrangements. Mayadin was behind it all. He was the one who persuaded Putti Lal to take my little girl with him. We weren't the ones who didn't respect tradition.'

Father tried in vain to stop her from telling everyone the truth. He was angry because he hadn't known anything about what he called my kidnapping. He had been extremely worried, but not only that, he didn't agree with it – he never agreed with anything that went against custom. I knew my father loved me, but I hung my head in sorrow when I heard him say to the villagers that he had allowed Putti Lal to take me away because Putti Lal wanted it.

We were no sooner inside our house than Mayadin came marching up with Putti Lal and some men from his village. 'Send the girl back with them immediately!' Mayadin commanded. The men barged into our tiny yard, followed by a throng of villagers. Among them were the panches, and there were more villagers outside.

Putti Lal had convened the Panchayat; he had demanded that we should be expelled from the village, accusing my family of kidnapping his wife. He said the men he had brought with him were policemen, and he threatened that he was going to press criminal charges against my parents.

Mayadin seized my father by the hair and forced him down on his knees.

'Devidin,' he barked. 'Your daughter has blackened our family name in front of the whole village. She is a delinquent. Send her back to her husband immediately!'

'It's the law,' Putti Lal added. 'Phoolan Devi must do as her husband says.'

It wasn't the law, it was *their* law. Because they had rupees, they could make up the law to suit them. I ran to the cowshed and crouched in the dark behind the animals, burying myself in the straw. It seemed as though the entire village had gathered in our yard. Some of them had even brought their own khats so they would be able to lie there debating the rights and wrongs of the affair.

Suddenly a hand grabbed me by the scruff of the neck and dragged me out into the yard. Putti Lal was holding me in his hairy paw like a bear toying with a cat. It was dark outside now and menacing shadows thrown by the flames of the oil lamps flickered on the faces of the villagers as they stared at me in silence.

Then everyone began to shout and argue again.

'Take her,' my father told Putti Lal. 'Lock her up until she dies. Kill her if that's your right.'

My father was so resigned it was all he could bring himself to say, but my mother wasn't going to give in. 'She's my child,' she sobbed. 'I brought her into this world. Whoever harms her harms me too!'

And then my mother and father began to argue too.

'I want to die. This is all your fault, Devidin!' said my mother.

The men who had come with Putti Lal said they were policemen from his village, but they wore no uniforms, only bush shirts. They threatened to take me and my sister too.

Mayadin laughed, twiddling the end of his moustache. 'Yes. Take the entire litter of these bitches! They'll look after your houses too.' He winked at Putti Lal . . . 'Take the parents too! You can put them to work to reimburse your expenses!'

My mother had been right, I was sure now. Mayadin had wanted me out of his way ever since the Panchayat had decided we had the right to the hora from his field. He took pleasure in knowing that Putti Lal was torturing me.

Mother snatched me away from him and held me against her with her arms around my neck. She was holding me so tightly I thought she would choke me. 'She's never going back to that man,' she hissed. 'If it's her death you want, I'm going to kill her with my own bare hands!'

She really was trying to choke me! But what else could a woman do? What could a mother do in our village to defend her daughter from these men? No matter how viciously she chastised me at times, I had always believed my mother could protect me from danger. But I saw in that moment that she was alone. She was powerless before the man I still couldn't even bring myself to look at. I begged my father to help us. He was the head of the family, he was supposed to be our protection against the world, but all he could do was weep hopelessly, harassed from every side. I begged all the other villagers who were watching us, but they just fell back as Putti Lal wrenched me from my mother and started to barge his way through them.

He was taking me away again! He was holding me like a sack of grain under his arm. My terror of him was so great that I wet myself.

My mother leapt at him, pulled me away from him, and spat in his face. 'You aren't taking her! You're not married to my daughter! I renounce the marriage!'

'Then give me back all the jewellery I gave her!'

He thought he was going to be able to sway my mother with a few silver bracelets.

She took me back inside, put me down, and found a large tray, the same one I had used to shower him with petals. She flung the jewellery on it and went out again. In the yard, she crouched down and began to brandish the objects in front of Putti Lal and the rest of the villagers.

'Look, all of you, look! You're all witnesses! I'm giving him back this silver necklace, and this silver bracelet, and this anklet and these ear-rings. I'm giving it all back to him! There's not even five hundred grams of silver here. I'm giving it all back! I'm going to have it written down on paper, so that everyone knows that Moola Devidin gave Putti Lal back his jewellery. Let him give it to another wife!'

She gave the pieces of jewellery to him one by one, waving each item around for everyone to see before she pushed it into his grubby hands. His eyes were burning with fury.

Some of the panches began to murmur. 'She's right, she's right!' they said. 'He shouldn't have taken her.'

Mayadin was sweating. From inside the room, I could see his nostrils flaring as he snorted in anger. In the light of the lanterns he looked like an evil bullock.

'You'll never be able to marry any of your daughters again, Devidin,' he threatened. 'You're a disgrace to the family!' he said to my father, nervously twiddling the ends of his moustache, but the panches agreed that since my mother had given him back his jewellery, I didn't have to go back to Putti Lal.

He was left with only two allies on the village council – Mayadin, and the head of the council, the Sarpanch. Everyone else in the village finally sided against him.

I lay down on a khat against the wall of the house, covering my ears so I didn't have to hear the sounds of their voices. I was bewildered. My hopes of being rescued from the torture had lasted only a few days, and now I didn't know what was going to happen. It seemed that anyone could decide for me. I was exhausted and saddened by my father's timidity and I had begun to realise that, no matter how strong I became, the power of men was something that would always be beyond my reach. And with mounting fear I began to sense it wasn't a game any more, like hanging on to the nose of Mayadin's bullock or stealing his lentils. It was a battle that was just beginning, and I knew instinctively it would be daily, cruel and terrible. Even if my mother's wrath succeeded in winning one battle, I would be a girl without a husband in a village like all the other villages where such a girl was fit only for abuse.

I fell asleep listening to them outside, still talking, still trying to decide what was best for me.

They were back the next morning. I hid inside the kitchen doorway. I could see Putti Lal with his hands on his hips and his eyes rolling in frustration, demanding that my parents return his wife to him. This time there were four policemen with him, wearing uniforms and carrying rifles. The men who were with him the night before were not there. He said he had gone to fetch these policemen from Sikandara. One of them even had stars on his shoulders.

The policeman with the stars hit my father with his lathi. 'How dare you kidnap your daughter,' he bellowed at him. Another policeman grabbed my mother by the hair and shoved her into the house, ordering her to fetch her daughter.

My mother made me come out of hiding and, holding me by the shoulders, stood me in front of the police officers.

'Here she is,' she said. 'This is my daughter, Phoolan Devi.'

The police were confused. They looked at my mother in disbelief, and then turned to Putti Lal.

'Is this your wife?' asked one.

Putti Lal was nervous now. He was sweating, as though he couldn't wait to get his filthy hands on me.

'She's just a child,' said the policeman with the stars.

My mother drew herself up and adjusted her sari when she heard this. She began to accuse Putti Lal.

'He tortured her! He took advantage of us to procure himself an innocent child. Well, she's not married to him now! He broke the contract by taking her before the day of the *gauna*. Let him find himself another wife.'

The police turned to go, leaving Putti Lal with a warning. 'You brought us all this way for an infant! Look at her. How old is she? Ten, eleven maybe . . . It's illegal to take a bride under the age of eighteen. If you come to us with any more complaints, *you* are the one who will end up in prison!'

When I heard this, I breathed again. My ordeal was over at last.

The police made Putti Lal leave our house with them, and my mother bolted the door. He returned later, and shouted for us to come out, but my mother said we were not to answer him. All day long, he banged on our door. He went away and came back and banged on it again. But as the sun began to set, he gave up.

There was silence outside.

I fell asleep again, and for two years, we were left in peace. But it was a fragile peace, and I was right not to believe it would last.

10

After the demon had departed on his black bicycle, taking his trinkets, Mayadin tried at first to terrorise us. For a while we were unable even to leave the house. He invited some thakurs from a nearby village to stay with him and put a khat right in front of our house for them. My mother fretted about our safety as long as these men were there. She wouldn't let us girls go out to the fields to relieve ourselves, and we had to use a pot. They were big, fearsome men who sat on their khat all day talking, eating, drinking tea, and watching to see when we came out to empty the pots. Whenever they saw us, they would taunt us. Finally, my mother sent me to live with my aunt for a while, and after that, with my grandmother.

She was my mother's mother, and I loved her very much. My grandmother's love and kindness helped me to play games again with my little cousins, and I buried somewhere deep in my mind the horrors of my eleventh year. I learned not to fear the dark any more, though from time to time the nightmares returned . . . I would dream I was being buried alive and I could no longer see the daylight; or I was at the bottom of a well, screaming for someone to save me. Then I would feel grandmother's hand on my shoulder, and when I opened my eyes, I would see her frail body on the khat beside me, and everything would be all right again.

When I was a little child, my mother sometimes used to take me to stay with her when the rains flooded the village. My grandmother had a broad, gentle face. She had seemed to me much bigger once, with strong arms, but old age had somehow withered her, though I had no idea how old she really was. Nobody knew the real ages of the women of our villages. There was nothing to mark the time apart from the lines that formed on their faces. Their teeth turned yellow, their skin became as dry as an old banyan tree, and their bodies became stooped and rounded – or their bodies changed and grew, like mine . . .

While we were playing at my grandmother's house, one of my cousins pinched me and it hurt very much. Rubbing myself to ease the pain, I could feel something in my chest. I ran to my grandmother wondering if it was normal or if I was sick. When I showed her where the swelling was, she began to laugh. 'There's nothing wrong with you, that's just your bosom growing at last! All women have a bosom one day.' She warned me never to let myself be seen without a blouse, and said that if she caught me playing with older boys, she would slap me. But she was always kind to me. She told me stories, and hugged me tight when I shivered with cold in the middle of the day.

Eventually, I returned to my village and, heeding my mother's warnings to stay out of trouble, busied myself with my old chores: fetching water, minding the animals, gathering and crushing the fodder for them; and my old pleasures: bathing in the Yamuna with Choti and my friends. One monsoon passed, leaving the village muddy and the rivers swollen, and then another did the same, and I must have been thirteen years old when the rumour reached our village that Putti Lal was living with another woman.

Hearing this, my mother decided that she was going to set about finding me another husband. And, as she did,

Mayadin began again to torment us, waiting for my mother as she went to the well and telling her in front of all the women of the village that her daughter was the shame of his family, and that a decent girl would be living with her husband by now. Mayadin protested to my father that marrying me to another man would be a stain on his good name. When it came to land, we weren't part of his family, but when it came to the disgrace of being a woman without a husband, I belonged to his family again. The men made the decisions and the women could weep however much they liked, their fears and hopes would always be carried away like the walls washed away by the rain.

I had grown perhaps an inch or so in height, and my chest was a little bit rounder, but I didn't feel like a woman. I wasn't ready to face Putti Lal and his serpent again. I used to watch the married women of the village with their saris pulled up over their heads. Some of them had a quiet, submissive air, awaiting the day they would go to live with their husbands, unaware of what lay in store for them. Others carried their naked infants in their arms, proud of their sons, but already barking at their daughters. You could read the different destinies of the boys and girls of our village in their eyes. The boys' expressions were arrogant and demanding, while the girls looked scared and mistrustful.

The only man who had ever been kind to me was my father. He was kind to us all. Often it was my father who picked the lice from my hair as I fell asleep with my head on his lap alongside Choti and the two little ones: Shiv Narayan, who was already going to the village school, and little Bhuri, who was still too small to help with the chores. If only he didn't have to struggle all the time, I thought; if he just had a few bighas of land to be able to feed us, then we would be able to live happily and peacefully . . .

He was always praying that the court would give us

justice, so that year, I went with him all the way to Orai, to
see this court he put his trust in. When I was little, I used to
think there was a god living at the court and that he would
decide when to give us our land. I imagined the court to be
a sacred place, like a temple, quiet and without any people.
I was eager to speak to the god who lived there, and I
thought I would be able to put my faith in him the way my
father did. But what I saw after we had walked the whole
day long to get there was a large house of yellow concrete
full of men arguing. My father gave the lawyer a bundle of
rupees and we had to wait for hours for another lawyer
wearing town clothes – a white shirt and black trousers –
and carrying a leather case to come to speak to the first
lawyer. And then we returned home with nothing. There
was no god at the court in Orai, I realised, just men who
measured their importance in rupees. It was even more for-
bidding than the Panchayat in our village, but at least I
knew after that why our father always returned poorer than
ever from the court, and without a single bigha of land to
grow lentils.

I was still determined, however. 'You have to win your
case against Mayadin,' I told my father after we returned
from the court. 'You let him insult you! You let him beat
your wife and daughter!'

He stared at me in wonder. 'Look Moola,' he said, 'it's as
if my own mother has come back to fight for me!'

Then the smile went from his face. Father was so gentle,
so different from men like Putti Lal. He was a simple man
who only ever complained about the land that had been
stolen from him by Bihari and Mayadin, but he was too
scared to confront them. He told me he needed more rupees
to win the case and my mother didn't want to ask her family again. He was working as hard as he could, he explained,
shaking his head, but we hardly had enough to eat as it

was. There was a girl in my village who had helped her father to win a case like ours with rupees from her in-laws, my father told me, and Mayadin must have been afraid I would do the same thing. That was why he had insisted I go to live with Putti Lal. And why he began to harass my mother again after she said she was going to find someone else to marry me.

Mayadin didn't like it one bit when he found out I had gone to the court with my father. He let Putti Lal know I would soon be fourteen years old, and he could come and get his wife. All I wanted to do was stay where I was. But no one cared about the wishes of a girl, nor the wishes of her parents if they were poor and belonged to a lowly caste.

The atmosphere changed in the village. I heard whispers as I passed. 'It's such a shame her husband abandoned her just like that,' someone said. Tradition had to be followed. There was no other road. My grandmother had told me a girl ought to be married and should go to live with her in-laws before her periods started, so that there would be no doubt about her chastity. I had not yet had my first period, so I was still chaste in their eyes.

It was my mother who said it, on a cold winter morning. 'You have to go. I've tried everything, but you're grown up now. We can't keep you here and I don't have the right to marry you to someone else. We have to do what he says.'

To make sure I didn't run away to hide with my aunt or my grandmother, Mayadin insisted that I come to live under his roof, in the big concrete house with two floors that his father built with the proceeds from selling my father's land. I feared he would try to beat me. In his house, I wouldn't know where to hide. I had never been inside it before. There were eight or ten rooms – I couldn't even count how many – each for a different purpose. There was a room for storing grain, oils and dried fruits, another for keeping the farming tools, one for the cattle, one for the servants, and more rooms for sleeping in winter. With my head covered, as was the custom for married women, I was led to the room where Mayadin's first wife slept.

I was grateful for her company at least. She had often aided us in the past without telling her husband. She used to stop by our house on the way to fetch water from the Nadi with her clay pot. Water from the river was better for cooking than water from the well. It was softer and the lentils and potatoes cooked more quickly. The pot she carried down to the river should have been empty, but in it sometimes there were lentils or some wheat for us. She did this often, without Mayadin finding out. In any case, she told us, she didn't care if he did find out. He didn't need an excuse to beat her, she lamented, he beat her anyway.

Bhabhi always wore a plain cotton sari and she wasn't ashamed to speak to my mother. Mayadin's second wife was younger and much prettier. She wasn't thin and underfed like Bhabhi; she was chubby, with nice light skin. She wore saris made of satin, and plenty of bangles. Like Mayadin, she behaved like a thakur, and made the villagers touch her feet if she was charitable towards them. She once asked me to come and delouse her head, but I refused. My mother didn't want me to either. And we were both beaten by Mayadin for it. After that, she never spoke to us again.

I was locked in his house. I had to eat there, sleep there and wait for him to decide how to dispose of me. My mother couldn't do anything about it, despite her hostility, nor could my father. I crouched in a corner, dreading what lay ahead.

'Don't be afraid,' Bhabhi told me, trying to console me. 'This Putti Lal has another woman now, he'll leave you alone.'

She explained that Mayadin was only interested in his younger wife. Even if he beat her, at least Bhabhi didn't have to go to his room any more. 'He thinks I look old, and I'm only good for doing the cooking. His new wife has time to make herself beautiful for him.'

'But people say the woman who is living with Putti Lal is older than me! She's his age.'

'If he chose her, he only wants you as a servant. You're still too young to go with a man, believe me.'

If only Bhabhi knew . . .

But I couldn't tell her. My mother had forbidden me ever to say anything; she didn't want anyone to know. I was alone with my fears.

'Where are all your bangles?' asked Bhabhi.

'My mother gave them all back to him.'

Bhabhi sighed. 'Jewellery isn't important, Phoolan,' she said. 'Look, I don't have any either.'

Before I was married, I thought the sound of bangles jangling on my forearms would be delightful. I looked forward to being able to wear bells around my ankles and silver necklaces around my neck, but not any more, not since I had learned what they represented for the man who gave them. A necklace was no prettier than a piece of rope that ties a goat to a tree, depriving it of freedom.

I had been there for eight days when a servant came running into Bhabhi's room. 'Putti Lal is here,' he said.

This time, it only lasted for two weeks, and Putti Lal didn't try to torture me with his serpent. 'Just understand one thing,' he told me as we approached his village again, 'it's because you left that I took another woman. Now you'll just have to get used to her. If she beats you, it's her business.' He said I had to show her respect; I had to touch her feet. 'And if you get any ideas about running away,' he warned, 'your

parents will be in real trouble next time. I'll go to your village with my friends and give them a good hiding!'

He didn't even beat me – she was going to take care of
that.

Her name was Vidya, and even the old man, my father-in-
law, said he could do nothing about her. She was the one in
charge now. She had borne a baby girl for Putti Lal and
taken over the household, complained my father-in-law. She
had a narrow, pock-marked face and walked with a limp. As
soon as she set eyes on me she immediately sent me to sleep
in the cowshed. It hadn't been swept out in a long time.

The next morning, I was woken at dawn and told to do all
the cleaning she had neglected. The kitchen was even worse
than the cowshed. I worked from dawn to dusk like a slave,
cleaning, washing, feeding the animals, filling the pots. I
saw the baby inside the house, but she wouldn't let me
approach the cot. She barred my way as though I was a
leper.

'Stay out of this house,' she hissed. 'It's my house now,
you have no business here.'

I was kept outside, with the animals. I was not to come
into the house except to do the cooking. I had to prepare the
chapatis and then watch her, Putti Lal and the old man stuffing themselves. Then I had to wash everything and wait for
her to decide if I could have a chapati. I was not allowed to
eat cooked vegetables, only salted peas. And I had to eat
alone in the cowshed in the dark.

I wasn't allowed to bathe either, and I began to feel that I
was being devoured by insects. I thought I was going mad. I
couldn't concentrate. All I could think of was the river, or a
jar of water. By depriving me of food and baths she was
depriving me of life; as though she purposely wanted to
make me ill and repugnant, as though she wanted me dead.

While I was doing the chores she would call me to come

and massage her or delouse her head. She was much older than me, and her skin was as dry as her heart; there was no maternal kindness in her hard eyes, just jealousy and bitterness. If I fell asleep from exhaustion as I massaged her feet, she would just snap at me to get on with it, calling me a lazy little bitch! I worked like a donkey, and if she wasn't satisfied, she would thrash me with her stick. I soon realised she was never going to be satisfied. She would beat me on any pretext, or for no reason at all. And when I protested, Putti Lal joined in. He brought a rope and trussed me up like an animal for her to vent her bitterness.

This time, the people of Putti Lal's village responded to my howls. They pushed open the door and came into the yard.

'Look at her,' said a woman. 'You made her sleep in the cowshed. It isn't right. Is she your wife or not?'

'Who is this woman that she can run your house like that?' one of them asked Putti Lal.

'Are you crazy?' asked another. 'Why are you beating her every day like that. If you kill her, we'll all be accomplices.'

Some women came to untie me and dragged me out right under Putti Lal's big nose.

'She's good for nothing,' he barked. 'She breaks everything, and I'm supposed to feed her and console her?'

'They had a whip,' I told them, 'and they were going to beat me to death! One night they wanted me to come into their room with them!'

The women belonged to a caste of shepherds called gadariyas. They were poor like us mallahs, but they stood up for me. They told me I didn't have to go back. The old man, my father-in-law, had gone to get help from his brother, Putti Lal's uncle, who came and said I could stay at his daughter's house. I thought I had been rescued again, but the next day, the uncle told me, 'She's just his concubine, you're his wife. I'm going to take you to the police to make a complaint. You have your rights!'

I told him I didn't want to be Putti Lal's wife.

'Putti is doing everything he can to get rid of you,' he said, 'but it's humiliating for a woman to be rejected by her husband. Your life will be ruined,' he warned.

Meanwhile, the Panchayat of Putti Lal's village had met and decided that I had to stay in my husband's house, and that if he beat me in future, he would be taken to court.

The next morning, before the sun had risen, Putti Lal came to get me from the cowshed, and speaking softly to me, told me to get my things, he was taking me home. He had never spoken to me nicely before and I was suspicious but I went along with him. He sat me on the crossbar of his black bicycle and we set off. He even stopped by the roadside to get fruits, and gave me some to eat.

When we reached the Yamuna, he said, 'Take your bundle of clothes and go. Your village isn't far.'

'No,' I protested. 'I don't want to go alone. People will think I ran away. They won't know why I came back alone. Mayadin will try to beat me, and my mother too! You have to tell them!'

He shook his head in vexation and left me on the banks of the Yamuna with his bicycle, saying he would go and find a boatman to take me across. Surely he wouldn't leave the bicycle he had bought with the dowry my father paid him, I reasoned. It was worth more than me! But the hours passed and by the time night fell, there was still no sign of him.

It was cold and I curled up in the sand covered by my pink sari. The sky turned a deep blue and then black, and the wind began to moan along the slopes by the river. I could hear stirrings in the bushes and feared that a hyena or a tiger was waiting out there to eat me. I prayed to God to make Putti Lal come back, to spare me from being eaten, or being humiliated. No one came. Spirits haunted the river, and I feared they would drag me by my feet into the water. I dug myself into the sand and held tight to the bicycle because I knew that iron had the power to ward off evil spirits. The river was so high, I couldn't cross it alone. I lay there shivering with cold and listening to every noise in the dark, starless night. There was not even a glimmer of light to reassure me.

In the dawn, the dark shadows disappeared and left only a mist floating on the river. I could hear voices, and I saw a shape coming out of the mist towards me. Then I saw the lanterns. It was a boat.

'Who's that?' cried a man's voice.

I recognised him. It was the village barber. Then I heard women's voices. I recognised one of them.

'Mother. It's me, Phoolan!'

She climbed out of the boat and ran to me, hugging me in her arms.

'He left me here, mother. He's gone!' I told her.

She cried harder than I had ever seen her cry before. And I saw my father too behind her. They must have been on their way to the kachwari. He put his hands in front of his face and began weeping too.

'Oh God!' he said. 'What have you done now to my little girl?'

'I don't know what star it was you were born under, Phoolan,' said my mother, shaking her head. 'I don't know why God has abandoned you like this.'

My teeth were still chattering from fear.

'Amma, I'm hungry,' I said to my mother.

'Come, come back home. I'll make you some hot milk.'

'Oh no, Moola,' shouted a voice. 'Don't take her home, take her to Mayadin. He was the one who forced her to go.'

There were a dozen or so villagers in the wooden boat,

and they all agreed. One of them said that when they had seen me lying there, they thought it was the corpse of some woman who had been beaten and thrown in the river.

I was going to find out that, without a husband, I might as well be a corpse floating in the river.

11

It wasn't long before some members of Putti Lal's family brought news from his village. Putti Lal had told everyone that he had taken me to stay with a cousin of his. Seeing me back in my village, they realised he had lied, and told my mother she should complain to the police. They said she should make him take me back. My head began to spin when I heard this. My whole body stung from the yellow haldi my mother had rubbed on me to heal my wounds. Not again, I prayed, not again! But my mother refused to go to the police. She wasn't going to force Putti Lal to take me back, she told them, no matter what. If I became the shame of the entire village, that's how it was going to be. She was going to feed me and look after me.

Mayadin was furious. From that day on, he harassed my mother whenever she passed his house on her way to the well. He called her all sorts of names, and threatened her with all manner of punishments, but all he ever got back was the growl of a tigress: 'Go to hell! Leave us alone!'

So he turned on my father, my poor humble father, and cornered him in the square outside the temple, in front of all the other men of the village. 'It's not right to keep a daughter at home once she's married,' he would shout. 'Send her to her husband. She's a stain on your house.' My father would stoop even lower, without replying, and scurry off to his labours.

When I had recovered enough strength to go back to work in the fields with Choti and the other girls, I was the one he picked on: 'Tell your father to stop his law suit or I'm going to make life unbearable for you!' he threatened.

One day, I became so annoyed, I shouted at him in the middle of the village. 'What belongs to you belongs to me. That's what you can't stand!'

'You're going to lose,' he threatened. 'I'll make sure of that.'

'How can we lose,' I taunted him, 'when we have nothing to lose?'

As the weeks went by, he changed tactics, just as he had before. Instead of threatening my mother, he tried to tempt her, saying he had found a good husband for me.

He brought more widowers to the house looking for young brides, and married men looking for second wives. My mother just threw her shoulders back and told him he was the one who should be ashamed of himself.

'Can't you leave her alone?' she snapped at him. 'Haven't you ruined her life already?'

The scars slowly healed. I toiled with my father gathering firewood, and carrying it to other villages to sell along with the cucumbers and watermelons from our kachwari. I began to take the initiative for my father. I was the one who did the bargaining for wheat and salt.

After the monsoon, when the autumn harvest was done and the cold season was on its way, Choti and I joined him when he went to work as a mason repairing walls and houses that had been damaged by the rains. We had to carry the bricks and sand to him as he built the walls. He was paid twelve rupees a day and we were paid two-and-a-half rupees each. We laboured from dawn until the sun went down, and the work changed me.

As my strength returned, my confidence grew. I was no

longer the submissive young girl who accepted whatever others decided. Climbing up and down the wooden ladder with my sack of stones all day long, I thought about my fate. I stopped caring that tradition had left me abandoned. All that mattered was to earn enough to eat. And that meant getting paid for our work. All too often, thakurs who hired us forgot to pay us. 'Come back tomorrow,' they would say, waving us away. And when we returned they said they had already paid us with food, or that we hadn't worked on certain days, and they would deduct it from our wages. They had kept an account, they said. I told them we *had* worked, we had done what we were asked, and we hadn't done it in the hope that God would pay us one day. I started asking for my wages day by day, to be sure.

'I worked today,' I would tell them, 'and I want my money today!'

My father was afraid of this sort of talk. He would tug me by the arm and whisper to me to be quiet and not to say such things. But more often than not they gave in and paid what they owed. And if they refused, I found ways to blackmail them. Choti and I would sneak up on their cows or goats, untie one and set it loose in the fields. Or else I would lead the animal back to our house, then go to see the owner.

'Are you going to pay now?' I would say to him, 'or shall I keep your goat?'

People threw me out, calling me insolent and saying I had been raised badly. They complained that I used bad language. But as far as I could see I was doing nothing wrong, simply requesting the money I was owed for my work. It wasn't bad language to ask for it loudly, with my head held high, and without fear.

I had been through so much, I had been so often in the grip of terror, that I had nothing to fear from them. I don't think I was afraid of fear even. I certainly wasn't afraid of

confronting them. I couldn't be belted or whipped or hurt
any more than I already had been. Choti was afraid. She ran
off as soon as someone threatened us. Perhaps she had seen
me being beaten too often. But I stood my ground, ready to
fight. If a woman twisted my arm to throw me out, I would
twist her arm too. If she slapped me, I would slap her back.

When he heard about these confrontations, my father
complained about my attitude and told me to behave with
respect, but my mother often took my side. 'Phoolan is right,'
she told him. 'We work hard and sweat blood for them, so
they should pay us.' And if someone who owed us money
came to complain about us taking his animals, she would say,
'God is punishing you for not paying my daughters. You'll get
your goat back when you've paid what you owe.'

Spring came around and then the hot season. The monsoon was on its way again and, before it arrived, we helped
my father to build a house for someone. It was a little house,
just two rooms, as he wasn't a very rich man. Father built the
walls brick by brick without help. All that was needed to finish it was the straw and tiles for the roof. My father asked to
be paid, but the man told him to come back the next day
when the job was finished.

'You told us we would be paid after eight days,' I
reminded him, 'and it's the end of the week now.'

'Tomorrow,' said the man.

As we left, I whispered to Choti, 'Wait until it's dark.
We'll teach him a lesson. No rupees, no house.'

It was eight o'clock, still light, but the rains had started to
fall so heavily that everybody was inside. The water fell in
torrents from the sky, shaking the trees, drumming on the
roofs, and flushing the excrement from the ditches. The rain
made so much noise Choti and I were sure nobody would
hear us as we set about demolishing the half-built house.

We climbed on to the walls and began to stamp on them,

kicking the bricks off. The clay that held the bricks crumbled, turning to mud, and steadily the walls were reduced to nothing. All that was left was a heap of red mud with two red devils dancing on it in the rain. I was filled with a sudden, malicious joy; each kick, each brick that fell or crumbled, filled me with glee. I felt that I had a physical power over something for the first time in my life, the power of destruction, the dark force of Durga, the goddess. It had taken eight days to build the walls and just two hours to demolish them, helped by the monsoon that fell in great squalls. The storm was directly above us, filling the grey sky with thunder and lightning.

With our work done, it was time to return home. To get the mud off us we stood under the gutter letting the rain splash on our faces, rubbing our legs and arms, and then we rinsed and wrung out our clothes before putting them back on and going inside, still dripping wet.

'Where have you been?' snapped our mother. She had been waiting for us and she was in a bad mood.

Choti and I lied, as we had agreed. 'We went to the toilet,' I said.

'Oh no, I don't think you've been peeing in the rain for two hours. Come here, you . . .'

She grabbed me by the hair and twisted my head.

'Tell me the truth!'

There was no way she was going to get the truth from me. In any case, we knew all along we were going to be slapped. We told her nothing.

The next day, we found the man walking around and around the ruins of his house, lifting his arms to the sky and looking up in despair.

'The rain! My house is ruined!'

'You said you would pay us today. Give us our rupees.'

'Get away from me! Can't you see my house is ruined.'

'It's because you didn't pay us that your house was ruined,' I told him. 'God sent the rain last night just for you! And God will make the house you're living in now fall on your head unless you pay us what you owe!'

The people in our village were superstitious. Omens from the sky filled them with dread. The man paid us without another word. But father looked at me suspiciously when I gave him the rupees.

'How did you do it? he asked.

'I told him God was punishing him.'

'God destroys the houses of those who don't pay now? Which demon gave you that idea?'

'It wasn't any demon. It came into my head, just like that. I told him that God had answered my prayer.'

Later, I told my mother the truth and she slapped her forehead, swooning as though she was going to faint from disbelief. 'It's wrong to destroy things, Phoolan. If anyone had seen you, you could have been killed for doing something like that,' she warned. 'It was a crime. Don't ever do anything like it again.'

But I felt justified when I told my friends about it. They laughed and said they would do the same thing themselves next time. They too were girls who had to carry bricks up and down wooden ladders all day long while their fathers or their husbands built the walls. They liked working with me, they told me, because I knew how to make sure we were paid. From then on, we warned anyone who hired us that if they didn't pay us, the thunder and lightning would come, and their houses would fall on their heads.

I was discovering piece by painful piece how my world was put together: the power of men, the power of privileged castes, the power of might. I didn't think of what I was doing as rebellion; it was the only means I had of getting justice. But it was then that my rebellion began, when I was fourteen or fifteen years old and struggling to survive by any means I could. I was a woman who belonged to a lowly caste. Faced with power and rupees, I used any trick I could. I encouraged the other girls to sabotage the crops if the landowner wouldn't pay us. I reminded the landowners that we were the ones who ploughed their fields, we spread the manure, we sowed the seeds and gathered the harvest, and they had to pay for our backbone and sweat. I warned those who refused to pay what we asked that they would see nothing growing on their land the next season. I didn't realise that by doing this, I was making many enemies.

I had found a strength in me that I hadn't suspected, a force I drew from my mother. 'Stand up straight,' she always told me. 'Be proud of yourself. If somebody slaps you, slap them back; if someone throws a stone at you, throw one back; if someone beats you and you don't fight back, then I'll beat you.' And she always added, 'Be fair; don't steal anyone's fruits or crops; be honest.'

With my father, though, it was always, 'Be humble, and be sure to touch the feet of anyone who gives you work.' If I devised a way to make sure I was paid, he would ask which demon had put the idea in my head. When someone refused to pay me for working his lands, saying the harvest wasn't adequate, I would buy wheat from his wife and tell her I would pay her later. When she asked for the money, I would tell her to ask her husband for it. It wasn't a bad idea that came from a demon, but a good idea that came from Phoolan Devi, so that her family would have enough to eat, and her father would have enough rupees to pay the lawyer, and to pay Choti's dowry.

The winter passed and it was spring again, and we were working in someone's field planting watermelons when a woman passed and smiled pleasantly to us. She had come

from the village where Rukmini lived looking for marriage-
able girls, she said, and she asked us where we lived.

We followed her back to our house.

'I would like the eldest one for my son,' she said to our
parents, 'the one with the lightest skin.'

Choti's skin was darker than mine. She meant me!

'Unfortunately, Phoolan is already married,' said my
father. 'She was abandoned by her husband and her in-laws
sent her back to us.'

The woman left, but returned the next day with her husband. She was short, with dark skin, and her husband was
very tall. He had a bushy moustache and a bald head with
white hair at his temples like wisps of cotton. Choti and I
hid by the wall outside the courtyard, giggling like little
children as we listened to the couple talking with our parents inside.

'We're poor like you,' we heard the woman say. 'We have
five sons and two daughters, and not much land, but we
work hard and my sons earn enough to live. My son says he
wants Phoolan, but we think it should be the youngest.'

'It's for you Choti!' I exclaimed. 'It must be the boy who
was watching us in the field. Remember, we nearly hit him!'

He had kept on coming back day after day, and finally we
had told our parents.

It annoyed me to hear them say he preferred me to Choti,
because I thought she would be angry with me. And I didn't
like the way he had looked at me. Later, I told my father I
would slap him if he looked at me like that again.

'You mustn't do that, Phoolan,' said my father, waving his
arms. 'He's going to be your brother-in-law!'

The preparations for the marriage began and, six months
later, Choti was married to a sweet-looking boy of fourteen,
hardly older than her, without any trace of a moustache on
his upper lip.

The dowry cost us much hard work and sacrifice. Father sold all the silver jewellery that my mother had left. We had to stockpile food, especially wheat, which was expensive. We were going to need plenty for the festivities. But I was glad that this young Baboo, who seemed to me kind and honest, was going to be Choti's husband. They were the same age at least, and had the same innocence. I didn't have to fear that my little sister would have to go through the same ordeals as I had.

The time was soon to come when my mother would go from village to village, asking, 'Is there anyone who will marry my daughter Phoolan? Even someone lame or blind?'

But there was no one.

12

She was one of the Pradhan's daughters. She liked to bother us at any time of the day, whatever we were doing, to give us chores. And of course she didn't pay us. She wouldn't even give us anything to eat.

That day, we were all walking back from the river to the village, my mother and father ahead, and the rest of us behind, joking and laughing. It was a day when everything was going well for us. I could feel the sunshine warming the earth under my bare feet. I heard a parrot squawk above me and fly from the branches of a neem like a flash of green lightning.

Suddenly the girl blocked our way. 'Hey, you there!' she barked. 'I need you.' She pointed at a row of roof tiles outside her courtyard that had just been baked in the kiln. 'Wash them carefully and put them to dry on the roof,' she said.

My mother replied that first of all, she shouldn't speak to us in that tone of voice, and secondly, we had work to do and we would see to her work later.

The girl picked up one of the tiles, lifted it up over her shoulder, and hurled it at my mother. It hit my mother on the side of her head and she fell backwards bleeding. Choti ran forward to help her, and I lunged at the girl and punched her hard on the arm.

'Stop, Phoolan,' yelled my mother. 'Don't hit her! They'll only beat us!'

'So,' I said. 'She was the one who started it!'

'Look, they're coming!'

I turned and saw the short round figure of the Pradhan approaching. I feared he was going to beat my mother and father.

'Run, Father! Take Amma and cross the river. Run!' I told them, looking around for a place to hide.

Nearby was a little hut where we stored firewood. We headed for it, but as we climbed on to the wall of the hut, I realised he had seen us. I could hear him from a distance insulting us and shouting that he was going to kill us this time, he was going to beat us to death.

By attacking a girl from one of the families that ruled the village, I had seemingly committed a crime. The Pradhan wasn't going to let anyone get away with defying his authority. As he came nearer, I realised the lathi he had in his hand was tipped with iron. Behind him were his two sons and two more men who worked for him guarding his crops, and behind them were four of his servants. They all had sticks in their hands.

Choti tugged at my arm. 'This way.'

'What's the point? Stay where you are.'

There were trees around us and I saw a branch hanging low enough to break off. Now I had a stick too, almost as long as the Pradhan's.

'Don't do that, Phoolan,' Choti pleaded. 'Don't do that! It would be better not to hit him back if he beats you.'

Standing on the wall with my stick in my hand, I waited for them to come up and get me. The Pradhan's sons got there first, followed by their father and they were all armed with lathis. The Pradhan looked around at his sons and his men and then climbed up onto the wall and gave me a slap.

I recoiled, and tried in vain to explain.

'I only hit your daughter because she hit my mother!'

He slapped me again.

I lost my balance and fell to the ground. He jumped down and started beating me with his iron-tipped lathi. I tried to grab his clothes, knowing that if I could tear them off he would run and hide. He was wearing a white kurta and a dhoti tied around his waist. I reached out but I couldn't grab them, and he was hitting me harder and harder. He was spitting insults at me, calling me a whore, a bitch, and every ugly name he could think of. Finally I caught hold of something. I wouldn't let go, even when one of his sons tried to help him by striking me hard on the back.

In my desperation to resist the Pradhan, I had grabbed instinctively at his serpent! I had a good grip on it, and the more he screamed and tried to beat me off, the harder I hung on to it, until he was yelling in pain.

'Help! Save me! She's going to kill me! The bitch is going to kill me!'

His sons tried to pull me away, but I hung on.

'Hit him, go on!' I yelled to Choti. 'Go on!'

'No, no! Let him go, Phoolan. They've got our Buppa!'

I could see the Pradhan's eyes brimming with tears, so I knew he must have been in great pain. but then I saw that the Pradhan's guards had started caning my mother and father with their lathis. My father was on his knees, holding his arms over his head to fend them off, sobbing and begging them to stop.

Some villagers stood there dumbstruck.

'Help us!' he groaned. 'They're going to kill us!'

I could never stand to see my father crying.

I let go, and the Pradhan staggered back, doubled up in pain. I took advantage of this to grab his iron-tipped lathi.

My mother had managed to get away from the guards

and she was fleeing in terror towards our house. My father was behind her. The men who had been beating him were coming for us now.

It was all I saw before the Pradhan's sons fell on us and started to batter us. They were beating poor Choti so hard, all I could think was that she was to be married in two weeks, and they were going to disfigure her. But she managed to dodge out of the way of their sticks and run away, and they turned on me.

'You little bitch. How dare you? You little whore! How dare you try to embarrass the Pradhan!'

There were four of them around me, snarling with menace. They beat me so hard I couldn't see for the blood streaming over my eyes. I fought back blindly twisting and turning to avoid their blows. They were thrashing at me so wildly that they missed me more often than not. They were beating me with such fury they couldn't even see what they were doing, and I managed to slip between their legs and run back to our house.

The rest of my family was already inside. I was the last. Father shut the wooden door behind me, panting for breath as he drew the iron bolt across. He turned to look at me with his back against the door and when he saw me, he started weeping again. There was blood all over my face, all over my arms, all over my back and my legs.

He brought me a bowl of water and helped me to drink it. I choked as I sipped – my lips were torn and bleeding. He brought another bowl, pouring the water slowly over my face to wash away the blood from my eyes. Outside we could hear the villagers shouting. My little brother cried out for help; he didn't realise that this time it wasn't our neighbours shouting, it was all the rich people of the village in an uproar about us.

I had only been trying to defend my mother, and I was

only doing what she had always told me to do. If a man tried to attack me, she said I should hit him or twist him as hard as I could down there, and that would give me enough time to get away. Instinctively, I had done it to the Pradhan, and the beating I received was worse than if I had stolen a cow from him. Where was the justice for us? His daughter had no right to speak to us the way she did, nor to throw the tile at my mother. His sons had no right to beat us half to death. But now my mother was angry with me! It was always me who started the fight. I shouldn't have attacked the girl. I was the one in the wrong!

'Should I just put up with it? Even when she hit you?'

'Phoolan, when will you learn that we can't fight them?'

I didn't believe her. First it was Mayadin we couldn't fight, but in the end he hadn't been able to make me go back to Putti Lal. Then it was all the people who refused to pay us, and I had been able to scare them. I wasn't going to stop now.

'But nobody in the village is going to help us this time,' cried my mother. 'You heard them! They could kill us if they wanted to!' she howled. 'There's nothing anybody can do.'

We heard noises outside the door . . .

'You see,' she said, 'they're shutting us in. We're trapped!'

There was a scratching sound outside the yard, like a pack of wild dogs tearing at the wooden door.

'Bitch! Come out!'

Father turned on my mother. 'It was your fault! Couldn't you have gone back another way? Now look what you've started!'

'It was your daughter! She was trying to defend me and they attacked her.'

'Phoolan, you shouldn't have done it,' groaned my father. 'Attacking the Pradhan is a serious crime.'

'He deserved it,' said my mother. 'Look what he did to our girls: he beat them bloody! She was right!'

'You're crazy, both of you!' I shouted at my parents. 'What are we going to do now?'

I already knew what I was going to do. I had forgotten the pain, but the rage in my head hadn't subsided. I climbed up on the terrace where we dried our clay pots, and began to throw them one after the other at the crowd outside. Choti climbed up and joined in with me.

'Get down from there,' said my mother. 'If you keep on provoking them they'll set fire to our house!'

As they drew back to avoid the pots shattering around them, some of the villagers went on insulting us for being so disrespectful; others who had come just to spectate began to laugh and encourage us.

'Look at those girls! Look at them!'

I picked up the last pot with a sigh and heaved it over my head. Then I began to laugh too, despite the pain, and the blood that covered me. I felt better: retaliation had delivered me from my rage.

'Stop!' shouted my father. 'Are you crazy? Stop!'

I climbed down and fell with exhaustion on the dirt floor of our yard. Mother brought some water and began to clean our wounds, before she put bandages on them. Finally the night came, and with the dark, calm returned to the village, but we continued to listen for every sound, barricaded in our own house as though it was a prison.

When the villagers had started laughing, the Pradhan and his sons had been the first to leave. It was a glimmer of victory for me.

The Pradhan behaved like a rajput towards the poor people in the village, and his sons were even worse. Ever since I was a child they had acted as though it was their right to

abuse us. 'Come here, do this, do that, get out of our way . . .'
We were supposed to avoid their house and say nothing to
them if they made dirty remarks to us.

Perhaps it was because we ignored them that the
Pradhan's sons had started to pick on Choti and me. They
were pompous, arrogant boys who believed that because
their father was the head of the village federation, they had
the right to do whatever they pleased with village girls. My
mother always warned me that if one of those boys ever cornered me, other boys would find out and try to take
advantage of me. I had lost count of the number of times
they had tried to catch me.

After what had happened, my mother wanted to go to the
police. It would have been the first time anyone in our village did that. They could beat us and even kill us without
anyone daring to accuse them. Even when the poor blacksmith died after being beaten by the Pradhan's men, no one
had uttered a word. Two of our neighbours had managed to
get in to our house over the back wall. They too thought we
should go to the police, but Father said no. He wanted to get
advice from the lawyer in Kalpi in charge of his case. 'I'm
worried that something might happen to Phoolan after what
she did,' he said. 'If we go to the police, the Pradhan will be
let off, and Phoolan's the one who will go to jail. The only
person who can help us is the lawyer.'

He decided he would stay there with Bhuri and my little
brother while the rest of us went to Kalpi. It was midnight by
then. The crowd had dispersed and the dark and the silence
brought my fears back. Kalpi was six miles away, but my
mother set off barefoot along the road in the dead, still night,
and Choti and I followed. On the way, she warned us to be
wary. 'When we see the lawyer, don't tell him it was the
Pradhan. Just say you were beaten.'

'Why? He and his sons were the ones who beat us!'

'Phoolan, don't make things more complicated. We'll say the villagers beat us and that's that.'

Choti was limping, and I was covered in blood-stained bandages, but we weren't allowed to say who had done it.

It was two o'clock in the morning when we reached the lawyer's house in Kalpi. Mother sat us down on the ground outside and went in alone to speak to him. The town was more intimidating in the night. The shops were closed and dogs snuffled at the scraps of rubbish under the pale electric lights. While our mother was inside, Choti and I counted our bruises, as we always did after a beating. I felt wretched and filled with despair. I unwrapped my bandages slowly and saw that my limbs had swollen.

All of a sudden, a little monkey jumped up in front of us and started playing the fool. He sat down, lolled his head, grinned and started imitating us, pretending to count his bruises too. It was so funny that we forgot our sufferings and started to play with him. When I cried, the monkey cried. Choti laughed, and he laughed too, baring his white teeth and pink gums. Mother was still inside when we heard the noise of an engine. The monkey fled, and I saw the lights of a car. Some men were getting out.

'It's them!' I warned. 'It's the Pradhan and his sons!'

Choti began to wail. 'They're going to kill us, Phoolan!'

I wondered who had told them where we were.

'If they try to beat us, here at least we can shout for help,' said Choti, and the idea that we weren't alone there in the town gave me courage. I called to our mother.

She came running out with the lawyer at her side. The lawyer said his name was Santosh and he asked the men to identify themselves.

The Pradhan hesitated.

'Don't lay a finger on them!' he said. 'If you start a fight here, I'll have you put in prison, however important you think you are!'

But the Pradhan approached calmly, with a smile on his face. 'There's no need for that . . . We don't mean any harm. We went to their house to discuss the matter and their father told us they were here. We've simply come to talk, that's all.'

He bowed down in front of my mother and touched her feet.

'Please forgive us!' he said. 'Your daughter embarrassed me and I became a little angry, that's all. I've always treated her like one of my own family, and look what she did to me!'

He pointed down at his dhoti with a grin. Then he turned to Choti and I, and bowed down and touched our feet too! Never before had he done a thing like that. Our mother was amazed, and I could see that she drew herself straight, proud all of a sudden to have the Pradhan at her feet, as though she was somebody important.

He continued to plead with the lawyer, apologising for what had happened and speaking of us as though we were children he had fed and raised with his very own hands. I didn't know what to think, except that the threat of complaining to the police had worked, and that perhaps we really had won our first victory.

It was getting late, and we decided to set off home. I wasn't satisfied; I wanted my mother to show me the police station, even from afar.

'Where is it?' I asked, pulling her by the sleeve.

'That's enough, Phoolan. The Pradhan has said he was sorry.'

He had been outraged enough when I held his serpent, and now he had demeaned himself even further by touching our feet. Something wasn't right. As soon as we were out of view of the lawyer's office, the Pradhan turned to my mother.

'You ignorant bitch!' he said viciously. 'You're not going to get away with this. You're going to regret the day you were born.'

That night at Kalpi, he had behaved like the little monkey, grinning in front of the lawyer and touching my mother's feet. Now he was spitting in her face. He was a rich landowner, head of the federation of twelve local villages, the most important man in our district, and he was friends with the Sarpanch and the police. Phoolan Devi and her family of poor landless mallahs wouldn't be able to fight him on his territory.

He climbed back into his taxi to return to the village with his sons while we trudged slowly home, Choti limping and me in my bandages, up and down the hills along the banks of the Yamuna where the vultures waited in the dark.

13

The hypocrites had sniggered when I was pulling on the Pradhan's serpent, and they thought it was funny when I was throwing the pots from the roof, but afterwards they pointed at me in the street. 'She embarrassed the Pradhan!' they said. 'She humiliated him in front of everyone. That girl really has no shame!'

I must have been fifteen years old by then. All the other girls of my age were married and living with their in-laws, but not me. I no longer had the red mark on my forehead, and I was always forgetting to cover my head with the end of my sari. I didn't realise it, but I had become a disreputable girl in the eyes of the villagers, someone the young men thought they could treat how they liked because she belonged to no one, she had no husband to protect her.

Choti had gone to live with her in-laws and only returned to see us occasionally. My little brother Shiv Narayan was too small to defend me. There was only little Bhuri. She was about five years old, with a little round face and big black eyes. She followed me around like a puppy. 'If you see anyone trying to hurt me,' I told her, 'run and hide if it's a woman. But if it's a man, run and tell Amma as fast as you can!'

I avoided replying to the young men who ganged up and tried to corner me on my own, especially their leader, the

Sarpanch's son. He was much bigger than me, and much older, but he was always teasing me. Once, he had sent a boy to our house with a message that his wife wanted me for something. It was dawn and we had just woken up, but my mother said I had to go if the Sarpanch's daughter-in-law was asking for me. The Sarpanch was the head of the village council. I followed the boy, thinking she had chores to be done and wondering if she would pay me, but once we reached their house, the boy ran off shouting, 'Here she is. It's Phoolan!' It was a trap. His wife wasn't there, of course, but the Sarpanch's son wasn't alone; there were a dozen rough-looking young men with him, some I didn't recognise from our village. I took off at lightning speed with them roaring with laughter behind me.

After that, he wouldn't stop pestering me. He and his friends – who included the Pradhan's two sons, the ones who had beaten us – used to block my way and then take rupees out and wave the notes at me. If I managed to dodge them, they threw stones at me. There seemed to be nothing I could do to stop their bad behaviour.

I tried to make sure Bhuri never left my side, so I could send her to tell my mother, but she wasn't with me one morning as I was on my way back from the river and I didn't see the Sarpanch's son until it was too late.

He grabbed me and started touching me all over in front of his friends. Before, he had contented himself with saying dirty things as I passed, but that time, there was an evil glint in his eye. It was a look I instinctively knew meant danger for me. I panicked and slapped him hard. He let go of me, and his friends pelted me with stones as I ran away.

I wasn't hurt, but I was furious nonetheless. 'Why are they always after me?' I moaned to my mother.

She sat me down. 'It's because of your . . . situation.' She hesitated. 'God knows, you don't even look like a woman!'

Childbirth was still as deep a mystery to me as it had been when Bhuri burst from my mother's belly. Despite how small and cramped our house was, we never saw our parents together. And I never talked about it with my friends. Just before Choti's wedding, my periods had started, but I had been too busy grinding all the wheat for the feast to give it much thought. All I knew was that I had become like the older girls in some way. What had happened with Putti Lal and his serpent I thought of as a vile and undeserved punishment. No one spoke of it, and I had tried simply to forget it. I still only vaguely associated it with what men would do if they managed to get a girl away from the protection of her family, the great danger I sensed around me constantly.

For the past two years, men had been trying to lure me aside. I was the black sheep of the village, I was nasty, twisted and spiteful. I lived in permanent fear of being caught by someone because, whatever happened, I knew I would be the one who got the blame.

I urged my mother to complain to the Sarpanch about his son. I had had enough of the rule that made women silent victims who had to accept the will of men. And the sons of the rich especially could do whatever they wanted it seemed. I certainly wasn't the only one. We girls knew about women who had been caught by men, sometimes by two or three or even ten men at a time, and nothing happened to the men, nobody punished them. It was always the daughter or the wife who had to bear the shame; she was the one who was punished. Sometimes her parents or her in-laws would throw her out into the night; if they were kind, though, they would try to marry her to someone, or to anyone at all. I asked my mother why all this was so, and she couldn't answer.

She agreed to go to the Panchayat and complain.

This time she was very polite and she didn't insult anyone.

'That young man behaved improperly with my daughter,' she said to the Sarpanch. 'He keeps on teasing her. Why do you allow it? If he wants her, all he has to do is marry her, otherwise he should leave her alone.'

She knew that he didn't want to marry me. A girl like me had no hope of being married suitably. Though I didn't know what I had done, my 'situation' as she called it made me a woman no man would want to marry.

The Sarpanch threw my mother out of his courtyard. 'Get rid of that girl,' he shouted. 'Tell her to shut up with her nonsense! She brings dishonour to the village!'

That same night, like the thunder exploding, I learned what the great danger was, not by the bend in the river, but in my own house.

It must have been past midnight. My mother and I had been talking all evening about what had happened that morning with the Sarpanch's son. My father told us not to say anything about it in the village. I was the one who would have to watch out for myself in future, being careful not to cross his path, and to cover my head. It was as if I was supposed to dig a hole to hide myself. My mother and I went to sleep in the room where we stored the hay. We spread a cloth over it to make a soft mattress, and lay down. Just before I dozed off, a shiver ran through me.

I sensed someone there in the dark. I thought it was a spirit. My mother stirred – she had heard it too. She stood up, and then she froze.

Someone pulled the blanket from me. I felt a hand over my mouth preventing me from crying out.

'Wait, Moola!' said a voice. 'Stay and see what we're going to do to your daughter!'

There was a gang of them: the Sarpanch's son, who had a rifle in his hands, and another man I thought I had seen before, but in the dark, I couldn't recognise the others. I shut my eyes in terror.

Flattened against the ground with one gripping my hands and another holding my feet apart, I heard them slapping my mother and insulting her, telling her to watch. And I heard my father, crying and begging: 'Oh sir, don't do that! Please, sirs, I beg you, spare my daughter. We will take her away tomorrow. We will leave this village and take her with us. Please, don't do it . . .'

My spirit flickered like a lamp and began to fade. All the cries and grunts and all the insults seemed far away. Two bodies; two hurried rapes. I shut my eyes tight and gritted my teeth so hard my gums bled.

'See what will happen, Moola, if you ever say things like you said today. Let's see you try to ruin my life now.'

They left the way they had come in, over the wall, without saying anything else. I ran into my mother's arms.

'Amma! Help me,' I pleaded, 'I want to die! Throw me in the well!'

Bhuri and my little brother were sobbing in a corner.

'They hurt Phoolan,' said Bhuri.

It was too dark for them to see what had happened, and they were too small to understand. But my mother and father had seen everything . . .

It had taken place right in front of them, in their own house.

My mother looked at me and shook her head. 'What did I do to deserve a daughter like you, Phoolan? Why did I bring you into this world? I'm ashamed!'

Father closed the door carefully and told her to shut up. We would all have to shut up and say nothing, not make a fuss.

I couldn't even breathe. I was choking with pain and humiliation. What had happened to me as a child with Putti Lal had been dreadful, but it wasn't a public dishonour for anyone, not even for me, because I was married to him. I belonged to him and that had meant he could do as he pleased with me. This time it was different. Now I understood what the great danger was that my mother always warned me about, and now my life was ruined. The only course left to us was to keep silent, to close the doors, cover our heads, and say nothing. But I didn't know how I was going to keep quiet, or how I was ever going to be able to sleep . . .

'Amma,' I wailed. 'I want to die!'

'Shut up! Shut up!' said my mother. 'Do you want the whole world to know what happened to you?'

I didn't hear her. I just kept on sobbing with helpless rage.

'Why me? I want them beaten. I want them to be punished. I want to kill them!'

It was impossible to sleep. I thought about it the whole night, and my dark, terrible thoughts always ended with the same faint glimmer. I had to find someone to help me. I wanted revenge on them. I wanted someone to do the same thing to *their* wives, so *they* would know how it feels to suffocate from shame and humiliation. I knew I wouldn't be able to sleep until I found someone, because I knew I couldn't achieve what I wanted alone. Then I remembered my cousin Kailash . . .

He was the son of one of my father's sisters, a mallah like us who lived in a village called Teonga, the other side of the Yamuna. My father didn't like him very much. He said Kailash came to our house a bit too often. He was always hanging around me, but I thought he seemed friendly enough. One day he had said to me, 'If anyone hurts you, tell me, and I'll see to them for you!'

Before dawn, before my mother realised I had gone, I ran down to the river. The boatman was half asleep and didn't even ask me where I was going. I crossed the Yamuna and ran all the way to Kailash's village. I immediately told him what had happened. He looked at me excitedly.

'Right, three of us will go there and see to them. We'll go tomorrow. Now, sit down here beside me.'

'No! We have to go right away!'

'Tomorrow, I said. Stay here today with me and we'll go tomorrow.'

He patted the khat beside him.

'You're all the same!'

I cried all the way back to the river. I was still crying when my mother grabbed me by the hair as I entered our yard.

'Where have you been? I told you not to leave the house.'

'I went to see Kailash, to ask him to help me.'

'Nobody's going to help you! Nobody's going to do us any favours. What did you think he could do for you?'

'Nothing,' I said. 'You're right. Nobody's going to do anything for us.' I moved towards the door.

'Where are you going now?'

'I'm going to cut some grass. I can't stay here locked up.'

'You're not going alone. Kunjan can go with you.'

Kunjan was the daughter of a neighbour. The day before, when we told everyone how the Sarpanch's son had grabbed me and tried to touch me, her mother was the only one who didn't say that we shouldn't make a fuss, and that there would be nothing we could do about it. She even mentioned a man, a thakur, who lived in a village called Narihan, who might be able to help us. I didn't really understand who he was, but I knew he was somebody rich.

Thakurs were more powerful than mallahs, I knew that. I had to find him!

Kunjan took me to her mother. The name of the man they knew was Phool Singh. He was a *mukhiya*, a village chief who belonged to a caste higher than ours, and Kunjan's mother said he had some kind of quarrel with the Sarpanch of our village.

Without saying a word to my mother, taking my sickle as though I was on my way to the fields to cut some grass, I set off with Kunjan for his village. To get there we had to follow the Yamuna for a mile or so. I marched along the path with my teeth clenched. My anger would not die down. I had neither eaten nor slept nor bathed, I hadn't even washed my face since it had happened. There was only one thought in my head – revenge. And I knew that on my own, without any help, I wouldn't get the justice that I wanted.

Reaching the village, we saw a group of men gathered by a large wooden grain silo. We told them who we were looking for.

'I am Phool Singh,' came a booming voice. 'Who are you?'

He was thin and tall – a thakur. I kept a respectful distance, but found I couldn't speak. I could hardly utter my name.

'Where do you come from?' he asked.

'Gurha ka Purwa.'

'And what do you want? Is it work you're looking for? Because if it is, there's no work here for you.'

I collapsed in tears, shaking my head. His tone changed as he told me to come closer. I bent down to touch his feet, and then I began to tell him what had happened. My voice was frail at first, but telling someone about it made me feel better. I overcame my hesitation. He listened to me but said nothing. I told him all the things that girls in disgrace are forbidden to tell. I told him who led the gang, and what he had threatened to do if we complained. The thakur seemed shocked.

'Go back to your village,' he said. 'I'll deal with it tonight.'

'Please can I stay here until you come? My mother says we're too poor for anyone to help us.'

'You cannot stay here. You have to return to your village. I told you I will come tonight!'

His insistence frightened me, but I still didn't believe him. I was sure he wouldn't come. Why would he do anything to help a poor mallah girl like me? I thanked him politely and we hurried back along the path by the river, cutting some grass as we went. If my mother found out I had even spoken to him, let alone what I had said, I would get a slap.

I was still thinking about it as we gave the grass to the animals in the stable. It was as if my mind refused to accept what had happened. I still couldn't sleep, I couldn't sit down, I couldn't be silent. My mother was right, I wasn't like other girls. I couldn't let myself be beaten and humiliated without even a whimper of protest. My sister would probably have killed herself. She would have obeyed the rule of silence. Not only did I have no respect for any such rule, I didn't believe anything anymore. I was sure the thakur wouldn't come. He looked down on people like us. What had happened to me was of no matter to him, I realised, and decided I had to try something else.

'Where are you going, Phoolan?'

'Nowhere! Just out in the yard.'

I flew like the wind down to the banks of the Yamuna and across again to Kailash's house.

'I'll do whatever you want if you come with me right now!' I said.

He tried to force me into the room where he slept. I began to sob again, I couldn't help myself. I had to bite my lip to contain my anger. They had done it in front of my mother and father and I wanted revenge. Kailash had been drinking and could hardly stand up. I pushed him to the ground and ran off.

'Dogs!' I shouted. 'You're all dogs!'

It was already night and the boatman was looking at me strangely too. It was the second time that day I had asked to be rowed across to Teonga, and my appearance must have frightened him. It was nearly the end of October and it was starting to get cold, but I felt nothing, neither hunger nor cold nor fatigue. I felt dirty, that was all, I felt humiliated. I wanted to throw myself in the river to wash away the terrible stain for ever. I wanted to tie my hands and feet and drown myself. At the bottom of the boat, under my feet, I could feel some rope and I started tying my feet with it in the dark. Nobody wanted to help me, they all wanted to hurt me. Either they wanted to beat me, or humiliate me or chase me from the village like a dog.

'What are you doing there with that rope?'

The voice of the boatman snapped me out of my dark thoughts. I found myself wondering how I would have been able to tie my hands . . . Anyway, I reasoned, if I was dead, I reasoned, I wouldn't be able to have my revenge. Even if I had to die afterwards, I decided I would have my revenge first. Nothing was going to change anyway, I realised. People would still think of me as a wicked girl, I would still be beaten by my mother, and the young men would go on calling me names and following me around the village. But I was going to kill him first! I was going to go home, get my sickle and kill him . . .

My parents were waiting for me as I came up the slope from the river. When I saw their faces, I thought someone had been beating them again. They were pale with shock.

Mother grabbed me by the hair again. 'Where have you been?'

I told her I had been to see Kailash. I didn't care what she thought. I wanted vengeance. I told her I wanted someone to do the same thing to his wife.

'Don't talk so loud!'

It didn't matter to me who heard us.

'Get inside!'

Something had happened. I thought my mother would slap me, but she ushered me into our yard, and then father hurriedly bolted the door.

'Where did you go, Phoolan? Tell me the truth: you went to Narihan . . .' Then she slapped me. 'I knew it,' she said. 'There was a tall man here, a thakur. There were about twenty of them, on horses, and they had rifles. He was the one you went to see, wasn't he?'

They had come, and I wasn't here!

'Why did you do that? What's wrong with you?'

Father stopped her from slapping me again. For once, he took my side. 'Stop hitting her, it's all you ever do to her. She has been hurt enough.'

'What happened?' I asked. I was itching to know.

'It means more shame for us. The whole village is talking about it. Couldn't you keep quiet? Why don't you ever listen to me, Phoolan?'

My mother was a mystery to me sometimes. She would encourage me to fight back at times and at other times she would just tell me to cover my head. The humiliation I had suffered was hers too; the danger she had tried to protect her daughters from for so long had happened. I wanted to shout out the name of the man responsible for this crime, and she wanted me to remain silent. But for me, the shame was harder to endure in silence.

The only person who would tell me what had happened was little Bhuri. I listened as she whispered excitedly in the dark.

'Someone came to the village, that's why Amma was angry. They went to the Sarpanch's house, and everybody from the village came out. The Sarpanch and his son weren't there, so they beat the women and they took off the sari of one of the women while everybody was watching! And then they shouted insults at them.'

The next morning, I heard from the other girls that the woman whose sari had been ripped from her by a thakur was the Sarpanch's wife. He had warned her that if her family continued to mistreat the poor women of the village, he and his men would come back and do the same thing to her!

I was joyful, a joy I had never felt before. I had been avenged, I was delivered from my shame. I ran through the village to the Sarpanch's house.

'Are you going to misbehave again now?' I shouted.

It was the Sarpanch himself who came out. 'Get away from here! If I see you here again I'll fetch my rifle and shoot you!'

'Oh, you're going to shoot me? It's your son who should be shot for what he did!'

My mother arrived in a panic and snatched me away. 'What are you doing now?' she said, dragging me back to our house. 'How can you talk to the Sarpanch like that. They'll start again.'

And again, I was the one who got the hiding.

My mother locked me in. 'Wash yourself, comb your hair; eat something. You look like a madwoman.'

I began to cry, but this time, my tears were tears of relief. I didn't stop until the night came. One minute I was laughing with satisfaction at what the thakur had said to those women, the next I was angry again because it wasn't enough for me, and the next I was terrified by the difference between me and the other women of the village. I realised the other women were afraid of me, because I wouldn't put up with the things they would put up with. But I still hadn't been able to find the courage to shout the name of the Sarpanch's son out loud.

I hadn't broken the silence, after all, but as the joy of my triumph began to wear off, I realised I had done something worse. I had gone to ask for help from someone of a higher caste. I had betrayed my caste, and it only really dawned on me then that the thakurs from Narihan had taken my side purely because it was to their advantage. I remembered what Kunjan's mother had said about Phool Singh having a dispute with our Sarpanch. If they had come, I realised, it wasn't for my sake. I had just given them an excuse. But there was one comfort, at least. I had prayed so hard to the goddess, asking her to give me revenge, and this time she had heard me.

The very same evening, there was a meeting at the Panchayat, and a villager came to tell my parents they should attend. I was the subject of the meeting. They were going to decide on my fate, and of course I wasn't invited, but I went anyway to hear what they were going to do with me. They would probably try to drive me from the village somehow. They had been wanting to do that for a long time. I didn't even care any more.

The members of the Panchayat had gathered outside the house of the Sarpanch, under the big neem tree. I could see them in the light of the oil-lamps as I crept up from behind, pressed against the walls of the houses. I came all the way up to the platform around the tree and, crouching under it, listened to what they were saying.

They were talking about an old man named Sonelal, whose wife was dead, and who owed a favour to the Sarpanch.

'We could marry her to him.'

I ran away, my anger flooding back. What right had they

to decide for me? These men were never going to leave me alone; they wanted to marry me to some old man now who would take me far away to beat me in his turn. I pretended to be asleep when my parents came back, but I was still wide awake, trying to decide if I should flee before they came to get me. My mother was in despair; father looked crushed. Had they even tried to defend me? I wondered.

'Phoolan, they've made up their minds, they're going to marry you to the Sarpanch's servant. There's nothing we can do now. You brought it on yourself.'

'I'll hide.'

'Where? Nobody will help you. It's night. Where will you go all alone?'

'I have to think.'

I went out of the room and climbed up on to our little roof terrace, under the stars. From there at least I would be able to see if anyone came to get me. It took a while for me to persuade myself they weren't going to come that same night. I listened to the sounds from the village: the noises of the animals and the wind rustling the leaves. Hiding in the village was too dangerous, there was nobody there I could trust. Even someone like Kunjan's mother would end up having to tell on me. It would have been better if they had decided to ban me from the village rather than marry me to an old man who used to be the Sarpanch's servant. It was as good as handing me over to the Sarpanch, his son and their men. My vengeance had been a sham. I began to see that they still had the power of life or death over me. I had only one hope left: go to Rukmini's village. It was far away, and I told myself that nobody would come looking for me there. Rukmini's in-laws were prosperous. Uncle Bihari had been afraid of them. With luck, I would be safe there.

But I would have to borrow five rupees from my mother and leave alone. I resolved to do it. I was no longer safe in my house. My parents couldn't protect me any longer. They had suffered the ultimate insult. Their daughter had been humiliated in their own house, right in front of their eyes, and they couldn't even complain. Who was there to complain to? Not the police. What had happened was too common, and too shameful. Women who had been humiliated like me had to obey the rule of silence to save their lives, and for the honour of their families. There was no other way. The police would never take my side. I didn't have any rights in their eyes, I was just another low-caste woman, without even the protection of a man.

The night was long. I hadn't slept the previous night, and I still couldn't sleep now. I wanted to rid myself of my body. It disgusted me.

The next day, as usual, at midday, I had to go and fetch my little brother from the school. Before I did, I went to my mother to ask her for money, something I had never done before.

'What do you want five rupees for? What are you going to do with five rupees?'

'Nothing. Don't worry.'

She looked at me suspiciously for a moment. But then she gave me the rupees and I tucked them carefully under my sari around my waist. She had understood, otherwise she wouldn't have given them to me. She knew that fleeing was the only possibility left to me, and though she couldn't make the decision for me, she could decide to let me go. I would take the stain with me, purging the village of my presence.

I met Shiv Narayan by the school and knelt down in front of him. 'Listen to me carefully,' I said. 'You must go home on your own and tell Amma that I had to go somewhere.'

He began to cry. 'You're going to die, Phoolan!'

'No, I'm not going to die! Don't be afraid, just go back home.'

I thought that he must have heard someone at school talking about suicide, and he was afraid I was going to kill myself. But I wasn't going to do that. I was determined to survive.

14

'Who's there? What do you want from us at this hour?' It was Rukmini's voice.

'It's me!' I said.

It had taken me all day and half the night to get there. The bus had cost twelve rupees; I had given the driver my bangles. The bus was full of men. Whenever one of them looked at me, I shuddered. Then I had walked through the forest in the dark, terrified that I was being followed, afraid the trees were reaching out to grab me.

The door opened and Rukmini held up a lantern.

'Phoolan!' she exclaimed. 'What are you doing there? How did you get here all alone?'

She let me in, studying me from head to toe. I hadn't slept for two nights, my sari was torn, my feet were black. Rukmini called her husband. 'Look at her! Look at the state she's in!'

They wanted to know what had happened, but I couldn't stand up a second longer. I collapsed on the straw in their yard, sobbing with relief. All day I had been sobbing, out of panic and fear. I had feared most of all that Rukmini wouldn't let me in – for fear of reprisals against her family. I held on to her and wouldn't let go, profoundly thankful to be given security, compassion and peace.

Her husband poured some water in a basin and brought it

to me. Ramphal was tall, with a sharp nose and a wide fore-head. 'Poor Phoolan,' he said in his sweet, considerate voice, 'wash your feet, it'll make you feel better.' My sister gave me a chapati and some lentils to eat.

Only after I had washed and eaten, and drank some water, was I able to tell them what had happened. As I did, I realised what I had done by running away. My parents would be worrying about me, and the Sarpanch, Mayadin and the rest would be furious when they discovered I had defied them and escaped from their clutches.

The next morning, Rukmini asked a favour from me. She had four children already, three boys and one girl. The youngest was only six months old, and she told me that she was expecting another baby. Though his family was better off than ours, Ramphal was poor. He belonged to the same caste as us. The walls of his house were covered with mud, like the walls of our house; that had made it easy for me to recognise it when I arrived in the dead of the night as all the other houses were built of bricks and concrete. Rukmini was worried that they would not have enough food to feed another child. They didn't have enough clothes for the children already, she explained, nor enough khats to sleep on.

'I'm going to have an abortion. Since you are here now you can come with me to the clinic . . . Ramphal is against it, he wants us to keep this one, too, but I don't know how we'll be able to feed another.'

'Keep the baby,' I said. 'Please, you'll manage!'

'You don't understand, Phoolan. If this baby is another girl, she'll die of starvation. Now I know why Amma used to complain all the time!'

Rukmini had made her mind up. She had heard of a clinic in Etawah, a big town, where the operation was done for free, and she said she could be sterilised at the same time, so she wouldn't have any more children. She wanted me to come with her to take care of the baby while Ramphal stayed and looked after the other three children. Because Rukmini was happy with her husband, I had never imagined that they might be poor, but they were. I began to see how hard life was for them. My sister had nothing. Even finding the money for the bus fare to Etawah was a problem for her. She counted and recounted the rupees before knotting them in her sari.

Rukmini was relieved to be on the bus. She wasn't worried about the operation. She told me the doctor was a woman, and the government had been running a campaign in that district to persuade women to have fewer babies.

While my sister was admitted to the hospital I was left outside to take care of little Chunna. It was cold, and the baby wouldn't stop crying, but I didn't have a shawl to cover us. I was shocked to feel how thin he was in my arms. In the hospital they gave me some powdered milk and water and I spent the rest of the day dipping a piece of cloth in the milk and giving it to him to suck.

I remembered when Bhuri was born, and our mother decided she wouldn't feed her. Rukmini must have been twenty years old by now, and she already had four children to feed. The little baby was so small and thin that I wanted to cry as loudly as he did as I went to sleep on the floor in the waiting room.

Ramphal came to relieve me the next morning. He told me he was taking me back to their house with the baby, and afterwards he would return to the clinic to be near Rukmini.

I had my hands full for eight days. I had to wash, wipe and feed the children, and rock the youngest one to sleep. He seemed to be getting thinner every day, and he wouldn't stop crying. I was so busy I didn't have a second to think about what might be going on in my village. And if I had thought about it, I would never have imagined that, while I was looking after my sister's children, I had become a criminal . . .

'Have you been anywhere, Phoolan?' asked Ramphal when he returned from the clinic with Rukmini. 'Did you leave the village?'

'No.'

He seemed doubtful. 'Are you sure? You didn't go anywhere, you didn't see anyone?'

Where would I go, I wondered, with four children hanging on to my sari? Ramphal turned to the children and asked if I had left them somewhere, or with someone, even for a moment. They said I hadn't.

'What is it, Jeeja?' I asked Ramphal. 'What's wrong?'

'They're accusing you of being a dacoit!'

'Me? A dacoit!'

I had heard the word before, but I didn't know what it meant. Our father had always told us never to go into the forest because of dacoits and I had always imagined dacoits to be terrifying demons. Ramphal said that the Sarpanch and Mayadin had been the victims of a dacoit. I thought it was no more than they deserved.

'They must have been very scared,' I said hopefully.

Ramphal raised his arms and shook his head in exasperation. 'Phoolan, are you pretending to be stupid or do you really not know what a dacoit is?'

Rukmini came to my defence. 'Leave her alone!' she said. 'How is she to know? She thought it was the name of a creature that lived in the jungle, with four arms, four ears, a massive jaw and long teeth!'

'A dacoit is a bandit, a thief!' said Ramphal. 'The Sarpanch and Mayadin have accused you of being a criminal! They're saying there was a robbery in the village; that you looted

Mayadin's house. It's very serious. Everybody's talking about it there.'

And that was how, for the first time in my life, on that winter day as I approached the age of sixteen, I found out what a dacoit was. The monsters my father had warned us about to frighten us from going into the wild were bandits. I had no idea what I was supposed to have done, but this false accusation was going to be the turning point of my life . . .

Ever since the thakur had come from Narihon to threaten the Sarpanch and I had run away, I had become a dacoit in the minds of the elders of my village. It wasn't enough for them that I had been rejected by my husband and then humiliated to the very depths of my being, they were going to brand me a criminal. I should have thrown myself down the well, and when I didn't, they tried to marry me off to an old man to get me in their clutches. But I still didn't know what I had done to make them hate me so. I knew little of the world and its laws. I had refused the fate marked out for me by my birth; I had fled my village, my family and my community. That was my only crime. Now they wanted to crush me, eliminate me for good.

A few days later, I learned that my parents had been arrested. I decided I would have to go back to my village; I would have to face their accusations if I didn't want my parents to have to pay for a crime I didn't commit.

Ramphal came with me on the bus. On the road back to my village, we stopped to drink at a water pump and Ramphal cautiously asked a local farm hand if he had heard anything about a looting that had taken place in the area.

'We heard some shots, some explosions, and people said it was a dacoit, that girl who ran away. They made a big fuss about it, and now they're after her!'

Ramphal wanted to turn back. 'They'll arrest you,' he warned, 'and I won't be able to do much about it.'

But I had already made up my mind to go back. Some people in the next village advised us not to follow the river but to take the road that ran by the foot of the hills. They said they had heard about dacoits in the area. The dacoit, I realised, was me. Ramphal was worried that if he took me all the way back to my village, they might arrest him too. He couldn't risk having to leave Rukmini and the children alone.

In the end, he put me on a boat and told me I had to go the rest of the way alone.

As we crossed, the boatman studied me carefully.

'You were the one who did the pillage, aren't you? If you go back the police are going to arrest you.'

'I know,' I said.

The Yamuna shone in the winter night. I quivered as the boat tossed in the freezing wind. I laughed to think that Phoolan Devi, the so-called dacoit, was returning to the scene of her crimes. I chuckled nervously in the cold.

15

'Who are you?'
'Phoolan, Devidin's daughter.'

The boat came up on the banks of the Yamuna by my village and my feet had barely touched the sand before the men waiting there grabbed hold of me. They tied me up like a bullock, with a rope between my ankles, and sent someone to fetch the police from the station at Kalpi.

Then they lit a fire with some driftwood that made a thick smoke, and settled down to wait.

They were wearing bush shirts, but although they had tied me up, they didn't scare me. It was almost as if they had tied me up for their own safety. On my way to Rukmini's village, I had been stopped by policemen wearing uniforms and carrying rifles who wanted to know what I was doing all alone. It was the first time policemen had ever spoken to me and I was frightened of them. They used bad language, like men in the village hired by the rich to guard their crops, who find themselves with power over the poor. These policemen, if that's what they were, must have been hoping for a reward for capturing me.

'Is she really the dacoit?' one of them asked.

'You wouldn't believe it, would you? Capable of looting Mayadin's house at her age!'

'It wasn't me,' I told them, 'I didn't steal anything! What am I supposed to have stolen?'

They didn't know. They had simply been told to watch the river, check all the passengers in the boats, and arrest Phoolan Devi, the bandit.

'The whole village knows you were one of the gang that raided Mayadin's house. The Sarpanch says you were with them. You're a dacoit!'

I stared into the fire, trying to ignore the shadows all around me, and the rumblings of hunger and uncertainty in my belly. I was being held at bay from the village, tied up like a wild animal. I spent the whole night there on the banks of the Yamuna, wondering where my family were, fearing they had been imprisoned.

The sun had not yet risen and it was still dark and misty when four more policemen arrived. These policemen wore khaki uniforms and heavy boots, and they were carrying lathis and rifles. Right away, without even saying anything, they set about beating me with their lathis, two of them in front of me and two behind. The batons were made of hard bamboo with iron tips. They beat me on my arms and my legs, and when I tried to lift myself they shoved me back down and insulted me. They kicked me and beat me without letting up.

'It wasn't me!' I cried, trying to fend off their blows. 'I wasn't there! I didn't do anything! I was with my sister at the hospital . . .'

Because I didn't know how to sign my name, I had made my thumbprint in the hospital register when my sister was admitted, and they wrote my name above it.

'Ask Rukmini! Please, ask the hospital!'

It was no use. I could cry my innocence to the wind, the policemen didn't care. When they had finished their morning exercise, they made me stand and start walking towards the village. They led me directly to Mayadin's house, where they started caning me again, in front of his door. They caned me harder this time, flaying the skin from my arms and legs. My limbs were raw and streaming with blood. I screamed in pain but nobody dared to stop them. The villagers came out and huddled together in the chilly morning air watching from a safe distance. A beating was a common enough spectacle for them, and they had seen me beaten before.

I could see my little brother sobbing and hiding his face a few yards away from me. 'Leave my sister alone,' he shouted, 'Let her go!'

And then in my fog of tears I saw my mother and father cowering in front of one of the policemen.

'Bastard dogs!' said the officer. 'Couldn't you discipline her?' And he started to beat them too with his lathi. 'You let her get mixed up with dacoits! She looted Mayadin's house!'

I couldn't even cry out, I had no voice left. I couldn't even feel the blows from the batons or the kicks from their boots. My sari was torn. My bones felt as though they had been broken.

They dragged me to my feet and pushed me forward with their rifle barrels.

'Walk, you bitch! Walk!'

I stumbled forward, with two of the policemen in front of me and two behind. They ordered my father to come with us. He walked alongside, not uttering a word, mortified with shame. He didn't even look at me as we left the village on the road to Kalpi.

The police station at Kalpi was full of people. There, chatting with the Chief Inspector, drinking tea and looking right at home, were my accusers: the Sarpanch, the Pradhan and Mayadin with his second wife. They were telling him I had stolen some valuables from Mayadin's house.

Mayadin's wife – the one who walked around the village

with her nose in the air, the one I had refused to delouse – said she was sure I was the one who had done it.

The policemen turned to me.

'Talk!' said one of the officers. 'Where's the rest of your gang? Give us their names.'

I froze.

'Who do you think you are? We've dealt with tougher ones than you.'

They started beating me again, in front of everybody.

I begged them to let me speak, but they wouldn't. They only wanted to believe Mayadin; they refused to believe anything I said.

'Get her to own up quickly so we can all go home,' he said. He was enjoying it. He was grinning like a baboon to see the police beat me because he ordered it.

'Do whatever you have to so we don't have to see her again, do whatever you like. She's just a dirty little slut!'

I had nothing to confess. The only crime I had committed was to be born into a poor family, and to have fought with Mayadin over the land that his father stole from my father – my poor father, who was crying alone in a corner. He had never been able to defend me from the men who wanted to hurt me and punish me. I was the one who was helping him now, and Mayadin didn't like to see me going to court with my father and working with him.

When my father finally tried to speak, he was beaten too.

'Confess, you little bitch! Tell us what you stole!'

It went on like that until the night, and then my father and I were locked in a cell.

The walls were made of concrete but the ground was hard, bare earth, like the floor of our house. We clung together, squatting in a corner.

'Amma has gone to get the lawyer,' whispered my father. 'She'll come soon.'

He closed his eyes and started to pray . . .

The next morning, I was taken from the cell without my father. There was no lawyer, only more policemen. Mayadin's short-sighted little brother-in-law, Mansukh, who worked for the police, had brought them from other villages. There must have been at least a dozen of them. There was one in particular, a fat Chief Inspector who made horrible suggestions about me. Mansukh squinted at me for a while and then said, 'She's not dangerous. You can do what you like with her, the little whore won't say a thing.'

He was right.

I never breathed a word about what happened during the three days and three nights that I was in that police lock-up with those men. I was too ashamed, too degraded by what they did to me – and too afraid. They said they would arrest my whole family if I told anyone . . .

They returned me to the cell. My father was squatting in a corner with his hands over his face. I slumped down in the opposite corner, defeated by the insults and the blows, still not knowing that the humiliation I had been forced to endure two weeks before in my own house was about to happen again. But my father knew. He crawled towards me slowly on his knees and whispered, 'Don't let them take you, Phoolan. Don't let them take you anywhere else except this lock-up.'

They didn't take me anywhere. They stripped me right there in the cell, tearing off my sari, my blouse and my petticoat. They made me stand there naked in front of my father . . .

He shut his eyes and turned his face against the wall.

They pushed me to the ground and began to beat me again.

'Admit it was you! Say it! Damned bitch! Say it!'

This time I said what they wanted to hear.

'Yes, sir! Yes, sir.'

'You were the one who committed the robbery?'

'Please, sir, don't beat me any more.'

'You are guilty. You are a dacoit.'

'Yes, sir.'

My father was doubled up in shame, his arms over his head. I was the one being caned, but he was the one who cried. I could see his shoulders jerk with his sobs.

Then the officers dragged me naked out of the cell and down the corridor into another room. They flung me to the floor. It was a cell like the first with a small, high window, concrete walls and a dirt floor. There was nothing in the room. I heard the heavy iron bolt slide shut outside. I was alone, sitting there with my knees drawn up and my arms wrapped around me to hide my nakedness. I was trembling so violently, I could hear my teeth chattering, but something prevented me from crying.

Then the policemen returned, carrying chairs. The bolt slid shut again with a terrifying screech. I closed my eyes.

They put my hands under the legs of the chair, and one of them sat down on it. Some of the others stepped on my calves with their heavy boots.

I couldn't say how many of them there were. They didn't see my face and I didn't see their faces. My eyes were shut like stones. I was a stone.

The next day, when I opened my eyes again, I found I was still there, naked and alone. Then I heard them returning . . .

One of them was carrying a bowl of water. They gave me back my petticoat and my sari, torn and covered in blood. They told me to wash my clothes in the bowl.

'If you say anything, we'll come and set fire to your house! And we'll do it all over again. Do you hear?'

'Yes, sir.'

I was still shivering with cold. I trembled so much I could hardly stand up. If I could have escaped from there at that moment, I would have thrown myself down the first well – or found some petrol in the first house and burned myself alive. The horror and humiliation had left me with just one thought in my head . . . I wanted to die. I didn't even care about vengeance this time. Revenge was utterly beyond my grasp. They wouldn't even let me out to go to the toilet. I had to relieve myself right there in the cell, like a dog. And now they were making me rinse away the evidence of their torture. I wanted to die. That was all.

When I had wrung out my clothes, one of the police officers picked up the bowl and poured the water over me.

'Cover yourself with this.'

A policeman handed me a blanket that I wrapped myself in as I waited for my clothes to dry.

My eyes were swollen from being squeezed shut and my body was covered in bruises. The skin on my calves had been rubbed raw by their boots and I could no longer move my hands. I held them in front of me like two useless gloves. They were blue and swollen, and they would never cease to ache, to remind me of the chair, and the fat policeman sitting on it.

They took me back to the same cell as my father. As soon as they had gone, he wanted to know what they had done.

'Nothing, Buppa, nothing,' I said. 'They just asked me questions, and beat me. Nothing.'

'Tell me, Phoolan. They hurt you. I can see your eyes.'

'No, Buppa, nothing . . .'

They had warned me that if I screamed or cried for help, they would put hot peppers up me, and then I would really scream. And they had all laughed. But my father wouldn't stop asking me what they had done.

'Nothing,' I kept saying, 'nothing.'

I must have looked like a madwoman.

'Nothing,' I kept repeating. I wasn't crying. I couldn't feel anything. My body no longer had any existence for me. It wasn't part of me, it didn't matter to me, it didn't belong to me . . . I don't know how it managed even to stay upright. It was moving without me, walking around and around the cell, sitting down, getting up and walking around again . . .

'Calm down, Phoolan. What is it? What did they do to you? Tell me, tell your Buppa . . .'

Nothing . . .

But I couldn't keep still. I banged my head against the wall on one side of the cell and then I banged my head against the other wall, and then I did it again. I did it because I was beginning to remember what they had done to me. I began to remember who I was, and what my body felt like. One by one, the memories returned: the pain, the groans of the policemen, their insults. I wanted to see them roasted alive! I wanted to hear them beg for mercy.

'Don't you dare set foot in the village again, bitch! Don't you dare go into Mayadin's house. Don't you dare insult the Sarpanch!'

'I won't, sir.'

When my mother arrived at last with the lawyer, I ran into her arms. Finally, the tears came to me, and it was as though they would never stop. I didn't scream or wail, or say anything, I just cried and cried, ridding myself of a suffering I couldn't describe.

'Why did you bring me into the world, Amma? You should have killed me. I'm not ever coming home. I would rather be a beggar than come home now.'

The lawyer tried to calm me. He too wanted to know why I was in such a state. I was terrified, nearly hysterical. He wanted to know why it was I had marks all over my body and my clothes were in tatters.

Nothing. I said nothing, because I could see them there behind the lawyer, listening to what I would say. And in my head, I could hear them saying, 'We'll hang you, we'll stuff hot peppers up you, we'll burn your house . . .' So I said nothing. I just cried and cried, until the lawyer gave up his attempts to get an answer from me and my mother began to shout at my father.

'They beat her! You were here and you did nothing about it! You just cry like her!'

My poor father. I was so ashamed of what had happened to me in front of him, so ashamed of what he had been made to see. He had not been left with even a scrap of the dignity due to a man. I wanted to douse them all with petrol and light the match. I would watch them all burn, and then I would burn too.

While my father had been cringing helplessly in the corner of the lock-up, my mother had been busy. She had been to the hospital where she had been able to get a copy of the register with my thumbprint. The police changed their attitude when they saw this piece of paper. Mayadin immediately said it was a fake. He accused my mother of forging it. But it obviously bothered the police officers, and they didn't like it when the lawyer started asking them what had been going on.

'Who is this officer? What's he doing here? And this one?' he asked. 'This isn't their district! Who told them to come here, and why? Who is on duty here? My name is Santosh Tivari, I'm a lawyer at the bar, and I have proof that this girl was elsewhere at the time of the alleged crime. Now, who are you? What have you been doing? This girl has been mistreated.'

The fat Chief Inspector – the foul, squalid one – looked around at his cohorts before replying carefully to the lawyer.

'Ask her yourself if we mistreated her,' he said calmly. 'Nobody beat her. I didn't lay a finger on her. Ask her if she's guilty or not. She has already confessed that she took part in the robbery.'

As he spoke, I could still hear him saying, 'First of all we'll do this, and then that, and then she'll tell us the truth!' Now he was trying to be clever. He even turned to Mayadin and warned him: 'If you're accusing her falsely, you'll be in trouble. It would be better to let her go now – now that she understands what could happen to her if she continues . . .' But Mayadin refused. He said he wanted me to stand trial. He was enjoying it. What they had done to me wasn't enough for him. He wanted to see me sent to prison.

The police brought me a chapati and plate of dal and forced me to eat. They gave me a cotton sari that one of them had gone to fetch from his house. Then they took me outside. When we were out of sight of the lawyer for a moment, one of them whispered in my ears, 'Remember, if you say anything to the judge, we'll get you . . .' They made me climb into the back of a covered lorry and then some of them climbed in behind me. It was late afternoon and the sun was going down, staining the sky crimson like blood.

As the engine started up, I caught a glimpse of my mother standing in front of the lorry, waving her arms and shouting.

She was trying to block the lorry, but they pushed her aside. As they did, my father came up and slipped something into my hand, and then the lorry moved off. It was a five-rupee note.

I sat there surrounded by policemen. I was still a child, just sixteen years old, an uneducated, illiterate peasant fit only for minding cows, collecting dung and wiping the bottoms of my nieces and nephews. Why all this violence and hatred towards me? As we drove and I watched the night fall, surrounded by all those policemen, I began to wonder if there was some force in me they were all trying to crush, a force that made me retaliate, a force that drove me desperately to survive. I tried to comfort myself with the thought that being beaten and humiliated was better than suffering in silence, like the women in the villages I could see lit by lanterns in the fields around me. I resolved to hang on to this force that was a gift of Durga. I was still tearful and afraid, like a child. There was pain and dread in my body. I still needed my mother, I wanted tenderness and protection, and it seemed as though all I got was more violence. But I was learning to survive; even as I wished I was dead, I knew I would survive.

16

I almost laughed when I was shown the evidence of my crime: a piece of clothing that looked like an old towel, and some bangles and anklets. That was my booty.

The police were taking me in the lorry with my feet in chains to the court in Orai.

'There's a judge there, an important man. If you confess,' one of them said, 'he'll let you go. Do you understand? Just tell him that you stole from Mayadin's house. And God help you if you say anything else.'

In his mirror, the lorry driver saw the policemen punctuating their warnings with slaps and blows.

'Why are you beating her like that?' he asked, turning around. 'What has she done?'

The police ordered him to stop the lorry and get out. They beat him with their lathis too, there by the roadside, and he didn't turn around again after that. He just stepped on the pedal and sounded his horn when they told him to hurry up. It was dark and the police were worried the court would be closed. We drove for two hours in the lorry. They kept telling me that I had to confess. 'You say you ran away and became a dacoit and then you came back to rob Mayadin's house, and that's all.'

The lorry came to a stop on a wide road lined with neems, in front of a large concrete building. I recognised the peeling yellow paint. It was the place I had visited with my father.

My heart sank as I was led into the grounds. I knew there was little hope of justice here.

The court was still open, and there were people everywhere, police, lawyers, witnesses and prisoners. I thought the court only dealt with cases like my father's dispute with Mayadin's family. There were always disputes over land in the villages, or between landlords and tenant farmers, and many poor people had to do as my father and give most of what they earned to lawyers in the hope of one day receiving justice. Even for uneducated people like us, the court was a familiar place. But I didn't know until then that the judge also dealt with dacoits.

He was sitting high up on a platform behind a long table, and I had to lift my head to speak when the policeman brought me in front of him.

He asked my name.

'Phoolan Devi,' I answered.

'And what have you done to find yourself in here?'

'I don't know.'

There was a ripple of laughter from the other judges and lawyers at the tables around me, and one of the policemen guarding me kicked me on the ankle.

'You have no idea why you're here?' asked the judge.

'No.'

The policeman trod on my bare toes with his heavy boot. I reddened with pain and I felt tears welling in my eyes but I kept them fixed on the judge. He wore a simple woollen waistcoat and spectacles. His modest clothes and kindly eyes made me hope he might have some sympathy for me.

'Don't be afraid,' he said. 'Now, tell me what you did.'

'I'm a bandit!'

This time the other ones didn't try to hide their laughter.

'A dacoit!' exclaimed the judge. 'Do you know what that is?'

The policeman hurriedly intervened. 'We caught her red-handed. She knew the house well so she knew where the valuables were kept.'

'I'm not talking to you,' said the judge, 'I'm talking to this young girl . . .'

The judge studied me through his spectacles, as though he was wondering whether to believe me. I heard murmurs in the court: nobody seemed to think I could be a dacoit. When the judge spoke again, it was to ask me why I was in such a condition. He must have thought I was stupid, because he didn't even wait for an answer. He turned to the policemen instead.

'When did you arrest her?'

'Yesterday, sir.'

'Has she been mistreated?'

'No, sir. Nobody laid a finger on her.'

'This young girl seems disturbed to me. She needs something to calm her nerves. Let her have a rest and then bring her to me.'

He made some more comments in English to the other judges that I didn't understand. Even in my own language, he spoke too well for me to understand much of what he was saying.

The policemen took me from the courthouse into an adjoining building where people were eating and drinking. I had never been inside a canteen before. There were drinks in bottles and all kinds of food and provisions. I was given a small tin of condensed milk to drink by the policemen. 'Are you going to do what we told you or not? If you tell the judge any tales we'll come to your house and it'll start all over again.' They glared at me, and when I had finished drinking, they brought me back in front of the judge.

'Do you feel better now? Good. Do you know that you've been brought here because you're accused of a crime?'

'Yes, sir.'

'Are you guilty of this crime?'

'Yes.'

'Do you understand what it is you're saying? If you plead guilty you'll get a seven-year sentence. Tell me what really happened . . . You committed this theft all alone?'

'Yes, I'm a dacoit.'

The judge became impatient. 'The girl has lost her senses! Take her away.'

He must have suspected something. He couldn't have failed to notice my tangled hair, my puffy, swollen face, and the awkward way I held my injured hands together in supplication to him.

I was put into another lorry with other prisoners, to be taken to the prison along the road. When I saw the huge iron bolts on the gates, I shuddered, dreading what they were going to do to me next. I didn't know what a seven-year sentence was. I didn't even know what a prison was. When I saw the high walls, I thought it was a bigger and even more terrifying police station.

A guard opened the heavy double gates and then shut them again behind us. We were taken from the lorry into a room where the policeman said something to another man who was sitting behind a large table. Even though they spoke my language, I could only understand half of what they said. The man at the table wrote my name and my identifying marks in a big ledger, then he took my hand and with a rubber stamp printed a circle on my wrist in blue ink. Then a woman dressed in a sari came. She took me out and told me to sit down and wait.

I squatted against the wall, listening to her voice echo down the long hallway. I could see many doors and I didn't know what might be behind them, but I was relieved at least to see there were women in the prison. She came back with a grey blanket and told me to follow her. 'Don't be afraid,' said the woman. 'They're going to let you out in a few days.' I burst into tears. I didn't believe her.

'Please don't leave me alone with the police,' I said. 'They'll hurt me!'

'Nobody's going to hurt you. This is a prison. There aren't any police in here. There are only women here, and nobody's going to harm you.'

I was led through a door into a courtyard and then through an enormous metal door with a heavy handle. I saw the toilets, and asked if I could use them. The smell was disgusting, and there was no water anywhere.

The woman in the sari seemed to be in charge. She led me afterwards into a large room full of women. As soon as we entered, they all came over from where they were sitting and started speaking to me at the same time. They wanted to know who I was and which gang I belonged to. They made me turn around, inspecting me. 'She's so small!' one of them exclaimed. Then the woman in the sari pushed them aside to search me. She asked me in front of the others if I had any money. I showed her the five-rupee note that my father had slipped into my hand before I was put on the lorry. She said I wasn't allowed to have money in there and she took it. The other women seemed to lose interest in me after that and I went to sit down on the floor with my blanket, like everyone else, near two women who scared me less than the rest. One was very old, and she asked who had beaten me. When I told her how I had been tortured by the police, she didn't ask which gang I was with or which robberies I had done, like the other women. She shook her head and said it was what some policemen did whenever they arrested a woman, whether she was a criminal or not.

For the first few days I was unable to eat or drink. Nobody came to see me. When I cried for my mother in the night, the women just made fun of me. 'Don't be afraid,' said one, 'your mother's going to rescue you. She'll fly over the walls by magic and take you with her!' Only the old woman told me the truth: 'Nobody's coming to get you now. Your lawyer will appeal and you'll have to wait for the judge to decide. Be patient. It takes time.'

The chief guard warned me it wouldn't do me any good going on a hunger strike; I was going to need my strength to work. I would have to clean the latrines and repair the walls where the mud had fallen off. He tried to explain to me what I should say when I went before the judge again. 'Those policemen lied. You mustn't worry what they said. Don't tell the judge you're a dacoit, or you'll be here a long time. Eat now! I want to see you eat!' He watched as I ate. He wore a khaki uniform like the policemen, and I was wary of him. I thought he was a police inspector of some kind and I obeyed him without a word. I ate, I drank, and I worked in silence.

Finally, after I had been there a week, my mother came to the jail. I begged her to get me out of there. I had not been beaten, but it was the concrete walls, the locks on the doors, and the uniforms that scared me. I had been unable to sleep, dreading that the violence would start again. As soon as he heard that my mother was there, the chief guard came to speak to her.

'Tell your daughter that she mustn't say she's a dacoit. The judge will give her a seven-year sentence.'

My mother shook me by the shoulders. 'Phoolan, why did you tell the judge you did it? Why did you lie to him? What got into you?'

But the guard was there in his khaki uniform, just like the others, looking at me . . . 'We'll burn your house,' I could hear them saying. 'We'll do it all over again . . .'

An hour later I found myself on a lorry with other

prisoners, returning to the courtroom. The other women prisoners were talking and making jokes but I was paralysed with fear: there were two policemen sitting opposite me. The sight of their police uniforms made me shiver. They were staring at me, making obscene gestures and winking. The women giggled. 'She's lost her mother again,' said one.

In the courthouse we were made to sit on the floor in a big waiting room. My mother tried to come in too but the guards wanted a bribe from her. Since she had no money, they pushed her out. 'You'll be able to see her when she's back in jail,' they said. I waited for what seemed like hours in that room full of policemen and prisoners. There were men and women in there. Everybody used bad language and some of them said disgusting things to me. Even the police who had brought me from the prison, whom I had never seen before, laughed and told me to come and see them when I was released.

Outside I could see my mother, alone, walking back and forth between the neems along the pavement. She was crying. She had managed to tell me in the few moments we had been given that she had paid five hundred rupees to a lawyer in Orai to represent me. She had told me not to say I was a dacoit and not to say I had robbed Mayadin. But around me, all I could see were policemen.

It was the same judge as before. He smiled at me over his spectacles.

'There you are again! Have you changed your mind?'

I didn't reply. My knees were trembling; I was convinced he was going to send me back to prison. But he turned to speak to a young man in a white suit with black shoes. He must have been the lawyer my mother told me about. They spoke in English, and I couldn't understand what they said. The judge shrugged and then turned to me, speaking in Hindi.

'Your lawyer is asking me to set bail so you can go home, but *you* want me to send you to jail for seven years like a dacoit. Tell me the truth, Phoolan. Were you beaten? How long were you held at the police station.'

I began to cry again, and the lawyer spoke for me. He explained that it was all to do with a dispute between my father and Mayadin – that I hadn't stolen anything, and that he had proof I was with my elder sister at the time. Then the judge called my mother. She told him I had been locked up for three days in the police station and that I was beaten and tortured in there. She said they had forced me to confess to something I hadn't done.

'Tell me the truth,' the judge insisted, looking at me sternly. 'Did you steal anything from this Mayadin?'

The policeman behind me didn't kick me or pinch me. He just stared ahead. He was from Orai, not from Kalpi. Perhaps he wasn't evil like the others, I thought. In any case, my mother had told the judge the truth so there was nothing left to lose.

I told him. I said I wasn't a bandit and I hadn't stolen any-thing. About the rest, the torture and the shame, I remained silent.

It was all over. The judge uttered a few phrases, and I heard him say he was fixing bail, though I didn't know what that was. I was going to be taken back to the prison, the lawyer explained, but I would soon be released. The judge had said I was free, he had written something on paper, so why was I on my way back to prison? It seemed that words on paper and reality were not the same thing. Another five or six days passed before the chief guard said, 'Bail has been posted for you. You're leaving today.'

They took my fingerprints, and wrote more words in the big ledger, but when I asked for my five rupees back, the woman who had taken my money just looked at me. She had taken the rupees in front of the other prisoners so they would leave me alone, I had realised afterwards, but now she was keeping them for herself. Meanwhile, the guard went out to ask if anyone was waiting for Phoolan Devi.

The lawyer came forward, with another man. They said that my mother had gone home to her village and they were going to take me there.

'Do you know these men, Phoolan?' asked the woman.

'No.'

The lawyer looked at me in surprise.

'Of course you know me.'

'No. I saw you at the courtroom but I don't *know* you. And I've never seen him before.'

The guard sent the two men away, and I had to spend another night in prison. The next morning, he called the woman who had taken my money and told her to put me on the bus for Kalpi. She gave me some rupees for the fare and I asked her again about my money. 'You little fool! If you mention it again I'll slap you!'

She left me at the bus stop.

In Kalpi, I had to ask my way several times as I couldn't remember the road back to our village. As soon as they realised I was alone, men tried to take me aside. One of them threatened me with a knife, and I ran until I was out of breath, fearing that at any moment, I would turn the corner and see the red and blue sign of the police station again. Only when I was sure I was not being followed did I stop to wash my face at a tap before going on, walking between the carts and among the cows so as not to be noticed. Whenever a man in a uniform passed, I moved closer to the animals, fearing I would be kidnapped, beaten and tortured again. I couldn't think why my mother hadn't been waiting at the prison, and why those two men were there instead.

When at last I reached home, I found out why I hadn't

been released right away. My mother had sent the lawyer to get me, and the man with him was the person who was lending us the bail. She explained this was money we had to give the court so I would be released. It was expensive to borrow from him, but my mother said she had had no choice. It had taken her a week to find someone to lend us the money. Everyone in our village was afraid of what the Sarpanch or Mayadin would do to them if they had any dealings with us.

All the people who knew how to read and write and speak English had been right to laugh at me in the court. Compared to them, I was like an animal, startled and terrified, like all the poor people of my caste. All we had to protect us was our fear and mistrust. Ignorance, I realised, could be every bit as cruel as hunger.

17

None of the animals had been fed while I was gone, and my bullock looked sad and fatigued. When he was young, I was the one who fed him, mixing the bran left over from milling the wheat with water to make a porridge, so that he would grow strong. His eyes filled with tears when he saw me return – big watery tears that ran down his snout as he licked my hand. He seemed to know I had suffered. He had suffered too. Nobody had taken care of him, and now he was so weak that all I could do was rest my cheek against the rough hairs of his neck and cry too.

Before I did anything else, I brought him something to drink and went to cut some grass for him. I didn't have the courage to face anyone else. People disgusted me. The villagers who had seen me arrive hadn't been able to keep their noses to themselves.

'Look how she's changed!' someone said.

'God knows what they did to her! Tell us, Phoolan. What was it like in prison?' they asked.

'Do you like men now, Phoolan?' one of them had jeered at me. 'How many did you sleep with?'

I just stared straight ahead. Their curiosity was sickening. I was a loose girl in their eyes. The beatings, the prison, everything I had endured had gone the rounds of the village. My friends avoided me. They lowered their heads and wouldn't talk to me. But they loved to gossip about it, especially the women.

My bullock didn't ask me anything. He had been waiting for me in tears, without any judgements.

As I tried to make him eat, I heard my mother shouting in the other room. 'Why should we have to pay? Everybody has a right to water from the well. It's Mayadin's fault she was in jail. Why should we have to pay for her?'

She was arguing with Buldi Seth, a shopkeeper who was one of the village elders. He was telling her that, because their daughter was impure, the Sarpanch had decided they would have to pay a deposit to let me draw water from the well. Buldi Seth wrung his hands together and said he was sorry, but that we would have to pay eleven hundred rupees! He had come to propose to lend us this sum, knowing as the Sarpanch did that the interest payments would bankrupt us. My mother threw him out of our house. She screamed at him all the way back to his little shop.

'I don't care what the Sarpanch said, we aren't paying anything.'

She screamed so fiercely that the villagers scurried back inside their houses to hide.

It had taken my mother days to find someone to lend us the money for my bail. Mayadin had given word that nobody should help us. Finally she went to see Phool Singh, the thakur from Narihan who had threatened the Sarpanch's wife. Even if it was for his own reasons, he was the only one who would help her. All this time, she hadn't been able to look after the animals, nor even take care of my little brother and sister. Shiv Narayan and Bhuri had fended for themselves, with only rice and water to eat. My father had fallen ill, and wouldn't stop whimpering. In his fever he moaned with terror that I was cursed. It really was a curse. We no longer had access to the well.

From the very next day, the women began to chase me away when I went to fetch water. 'Don't come near our well! You've been to jail. You're unclean!' they screeched.

I dropped my pot and the rope and ran back to the house. From then on, I hardly dared to open the door to sweep the dust out of our yard. I had become a pariah.

That evening, when my mother came back from working in the fields, she was cross with me for not doing the chores she had given me.

'Amma,' I told her, 'they say I'm dirty . . . and the whole village will be polluted because of me. Wherever I go they say things behind my back.'

They had accused me of sleeping with men in prison, and said that by coming home, I was bringing shame on the whole village.

'They want me to go, to disappear from the village forever. Send me away, Amma, or I'm going to throw myself in the well!'

'If you kill yourself, everybody will say it was because you were pregnant. You must show them you didn't do anything wrong. You can stay here and eat here at home with us. You're our daughter, we love you.'

My poor father, so feeble with sickness and fear, told me he loved me too. 'Phoolan,' he said weakly, 'nothing and nobody is going to take you from us – as long as you don't do anything that will bring more trouble.'

We couldn't survive without water from the well, but the villagers were determined to chase me away like an evil spirit. The next day, they came to our house and told us again that the Sarpanch had decided we had to pay if we wanted water from the well. 'We're poor, we can't pay so much,' my father pleaded. He tried to explain that the lawyer had cost five hundred rupees, and offered to pay them six hundred, but they wanted more. My mother shouted at them to leave us alone. 'We will never pay! Never! Phoolan will go and fetch water from the Yamuna.'

But it was exhausting carrying a jug of water on your shoulder all the way from the river, and people said vicious things as they went by on the path.

'Why don't they just put her in a cart and dump her far away?' they said.

'Or tie her up and leave her by the road.'

After a few weeks, my father recovered from his illness, and went looking for work, but nobody would rent him their field, not even to take the lion's share of the crops when the harvest was in, and nobody wanted him to make doors or chairs for them. So he went to pray at the temple, but God wasn't listening to him.

I was terrified. I hid at night, sleeping between the hooves of the cows or on the little roof terrace. During the day, I heard everyone around me whispering:

'*Get away . . .*'

'*She's unclean . . .*'

'*How many men?*'

Little Bhuri fought with the other children after they spat in her face. Even the old fisherman who lived next to us, and who was so poor that we often gave him food because he had no family to help him, avoided me.

'Don't come near me, Phoolan,' he said. 'If you talk to me, they'll want to chase me from the village too.'

It continued like this for six months, all through the summer and the hot season, until the monsoon. We were shunned by the village.

Finally, my mother decided that I had a right to be able to go to the well like everyone else. 'It doesn't belong to Mayadin and his kind. Go and fill the jugs.'

There were three policemen guarding the well. I had

gathered my courage and told myself that if anyone tried to stop me taking water, I would throw myself in. I lowered the rope with the bucket and started to bring it up slowly. The policemen were sitting under a tree, watching me. Just as I was about to leave with my rope and bucket, Mayadin came with his servants.

'Look at that girl,' he bellowed at the policemen. 'She has no shame! She dares to come and fetch water here!'

The policemen got to their feet and came towards me.

'Get lost!' they barked at me, raising their lathis as though I was a stray dog.

'Why?' I protested. 'Why should I?'

'How dare you show your face in front of a respectable fellow like Mayadin! Get away from here or you'll get a bloody good hiding!'

I put my bucket down, and turned to my so-called respectable cousin.

'Why do you need the police to deal with me, can't you take care of it yourself? You have land because your father stole it, but you'll never be in peace as long as I'm alive. I'm warning you like you warned us, I'm going to make your life unbearable!'

'Listen to this, listen to how she speaks to me!'

'If your sipahis touch me,' I said. 'I'll throw myself in the well!'

I turned and walked away, shaking my head.

The rich only wanted one thing from us: they wanted us to be their obedient slaves. They had provoked my rebellion, and now they were turning me and my family into pariahs because of it, with no wheat, no work, not even any water. They could sentence us to our deaths simply by denying us a place in our community. My father used to tell me it was our destiny, and there was nothing we could do about it. We were born to serve others. 'Why is it my destiny?' I argued.

'They're no different from us, they have the same blood in their veins. We have our pride, and they have theirs, so why us?'

We shut ourselves in the house, fearing the police would come. But when the knock came, it wasn't the police . . .

'Open up! Where is Phoolan? We want to see her!'

I hid in the stable while Bhuri answered. 'She's gone with my mother.'

'She's supposed to be here when we come. She's on bail!'

They said they had a summons with the date of my hearing, and they had to hand it to me in person. My mother told me to come out and my father opened the door. It was dark and he couldn't see them clearly.

There were more than a dozen of them. Some of them were well-dressed, and at first I thought they were lawyers who had come with policemen, but then I realised they were thakurs . . .

'Where have you been hiding? We called for you and you wouldn't come,' said one of them.

He was an old man I recognised, one of a gang that pestered us mallah girls in the fields, trying to catch us and molest us. Thakurs thought they were maharajas. They lounged around all day giving orders for fields they never even went to inspect. And if they had no lands, they would do anything rather than toil in the fields. I had seen gangs of them waiting at the marketplaces and at the bus stops.

'Who do you think you are?' the old man asked me. He tried to grab hold of me. 'Girls of your caste are only good for one thing,' he sneered.

It happened again. I was beaten, assaulted and humiliated – and again my parents were forced to watch.

I was less than a dog, one of them said.

When my mother and father pleaded with them to stop, they were beaten too.

It was the middle of the night when they dragged me half-naked along the street to Mayadin's house.

He must have been the one who put them up to it. He must have told them to frighten me, but when he came out of his house and saw me, he was uneasy about what they had done. He told them I was his cousin and the quarrel between our families was our concern. He said they shouldn't have got mixed up in it.

'It has nothing to do with you thakurs,' he said.

I couldn't believe it! He was embarrassed because the men who had beaten and violated me were thakurs, and we were just mallahs, even Mayadin. Because he had land, he thought he could behave like a thakur, he thought he could use them to scare me and my parents. But he was also afraid of them. He was twiddling his moustache and pretending to be annoyed at what they had done. He must have been fretting that if anyone heard them, he might be implicated. He needn't have worried.

I cried out, I howled and yelled, but nobody came out of their houses, not even to see my new humiliation, not until they were sure the thakurs had gone. Then they came out. They had all been afraid they would be called as witnesses.

When the thakur jackals were beating my mother and my father, I had heard them saying it was no more than we deserved. 'If you had shown respect and done as you were told, we would have left you alone,' they said. We were nothing to them. They said it was our duty to serve them. I had a bad reputation, and they knew they could do what they liked with me; nobody would come to help me. One of them even congratulated my mother for giving birth to such a pretty girl.

'She was a lot of fun,' he said as they left the village. 'Don't forget to send her over to see us from time to time.'

It was the worst of all insults. By saying it as the villagers finally came out of hiding, he was branding me a fallen woman, in their power.

I was beginning to realise it was not just our poverty that made us victims, it was being born in a lowly caste. I couldn't accept it. They had dumped me outside the house as they left and my mother came out but instead of taking me in her arms she started beating me with her fists, yelling and cursing hysterically. 'It would be better if you died this time!'

But I wasn't going to die. No matter how terrible I felt, I knew I wasn't going to jump in the well this time. I knew she didn't want me dead, she was only beating me because she was powerless. It was all she could do. I was the only person she could beat and curse.

'Leave her,' said my father, lifting his head.

'We're going to the police tomorrow,' she decided.

I didn't know if I was more frightened by what had happened or by the thought of going back into the police station at Kalpi.

Why were thakurs better than me? Why was it me, always me, who was the one who was beaten and defiled in front of the whole village?

'Why me?' I wanted to know.

'It's our destiny,' said my father, lowering his head again. 'We have to obey people of a higher caste.' He told me about a girl who had been taken away by thakurs who made her go from house to house, to serve them with her body.

Would I too have to become a girl who belonged to them like an animal?

This time, I couldn't just go and bathe in the river and let the holy waters wash away my rage. The pain had become a part of me.

My mother made me go alone to the police station in Kalpi

to complain. No one in the village would come with me as a witness. They were all out there in the morning brushing their teeth and washing, shaking their heads and pretending they had seen nothing, and that they couldn't be sure about what they heard. They were afraid of reprisals. I was too. I didn't know how to tell a good policeman from one who beats and rapes, but my mother promised me nothing could happen to me there. All I was going to do, she said, was make a complaint. I had a right, she said.

The policeman on duty at the door of the yellow concrete building recognised me. He asked me what I was doing there and I told him what had happened in the village: how I had been forbidden to use the well; how the thakurs had come in the night . . .

He went to get his superior. I was relieved to see it wasn't the same fat chief inspector as before, but a deputy superintendent. He asked me for my name, and the first policeman began to type a report while the deputy superintendent asked me questions. But when I started describing the thakurs and telling him I had recognised some of them, the superintendent stood up and slapped me.

'Even if they raped you, so what? Don't you have any shame at all, coming here to accuse them?'

He had me thrown out into the dusty street.

'How dare you try to blacken the names of respectable citizens. Thakurs do a good job of keeping people like you in line, now go home and shut up.'

I could hardly breathe. I was choking. It was as if I wasn't even allowed enough air to stay alive, I didn't exist. The dirt road back to our village ran up and down the hillsides along the Yamuna and it was a tiring walk. When I met my mother coming from the village to see what had happened, I sobbed to her that it was no use. I just wanted to die.

'I won't let you. You aren't a pariah!'

She said we were going back to Kalpi to see the lawyer, Santosh Tivari, who had defended me when Mayadin accused me of stealing his wife's trinkets. But without even telling him anything of what had happened to me, my mother just asked if he could find me a husband. He said he didn't know anybody who was looking for a wife. We returned to the village. My parents asked everywhere. Anybody, of any caste, would do: ugly, lame, blind or deaf, young or old, anybody to get Phoolan out of trouble. Nobody wanted me, not even the undertaker. I had become a fallen woman since the thakurs had put word around that Phoolan Devi was born for their pleasure.

Many times after that, men came to the house asking where they could find me. When my mother asked why they wanted to know, they laughed with surprise. 'She's asking us why we want her daughter!' As if we didn't know.

Usually, they were thakurs from other villages. They came to our house, five or six of them at a time, and threatened to beat my mother or my father to find out where I was hiding. But my mother never told them and my father just said, 'Find her yourself. She's gone.'

We kept our front door locked. I had to hide all the time. I could no longer sleep at my house. I used to sleep in a tree instead, hidden up in the branches among the monkeys and birds, with fear knotting my gut and tears constantly in my eyes. There were so many thakurs coming around looking for me that the villagers began to worry about the safety of their wives and daughters and I was the one who was blamed. The whole village was out to get me. Hiding became my daily routine. I was always changing my hide-out, climbing trees and sneaking about close to the walls so as not to have to hear the villagers sniggering, not to have to see them pointing at me and saying, accusingly, 'It's her.'

I tried to work, but nobody would hire me to labour in

their fields or mind their cows. Even if all I did was help my father when he was working in another village, the people who employed him would use me as an excuse not to pay him, saying that because of what I had done, he didn't deserve to be paid. We worked hard all day, but when the time came to distribute grain to the labourers, we were given nothing on the pretext that my presence brought shame and dishonour. It wouldn't stop; each day, there was another indignity.

One day, all of this put me in a foul temper. My father and I were exhausted after harvesting millet for someone who then refused to pay us. The man said Mayadin had told him to withhold our wages. I gripped my sickle and started to scream. 'You bastard dog, you're going to pay us. How dare you give our wages to Mayadin. We're the ones who did the work, not Mayadin. Pay us or I'll cut you to pieces!'

I was really going to do it! I knew I would have been sent back to prison, but at least there I could live in peace with all the other pariahs.

By chance, Mayadin's sister had seen what happened. She stood there staring at me as though I had gone mad.

I waved my sickle in her direction. 'And I'll cut you into pieces too!' I warned her.

She ran off screaming, while my father tried as ever to calm me. 'Don't do that, Phoolan, don't say anything!'

I didn't care. It was the first time in my life that I had wanted to kill someone, really wanted to kill. I could feel the sickle in my hand and I felt the anger like needles in me, flooding me with new force.

The man held his palms up. 'Wait, okay.' He gathered up a big bundle of grain and put it down at our feet.

We brought the sheaves of millet back to our house and went together down to the river to wash them. I was still enraged but I felt triumphant too. I decided I was going to bathe in the river. My mother told me to be careful, the currents were strong. I told her I wasn't afraid of anything any more. I took off my sari and leapt into the water with my mother running after me. She must have been afraid that I was going to drown myself. But as I swam, I was filled with a delirious feeling of happiness. The water was warm in that month of Ashad, the sky was bright with stars, and the sand was still hot.

Because they lived in fear, I realised, all you had to do was frighten them! Because they used violence, you had to be violent too!

The next morning, I went to Mayadin's house and yelled his name until he came out. 'I'm going to get a rifle and I'm going to kill you! Go and make a complaint now! Go on! Make them put me in prison! Go and tell your sipahis to come and arrest me, I'll get out and I'll be back for you!'

He scurried back inside, bolting the door behind him.

Then I went to the Sarpanch's house. One of his servants was outside, alone. 'Open this door!' I ordered.

I knew the Sarpanch's son was inside. The one whose name I was too afraid to say aloud before. But now I was able to.

'Suresh,' I shouted out.

'What shall I do, master?' the servant asked timidly. 'Phoolan is here.'

'She's alone?' asked Suresh.

'Yes.'

'Let her in. I'd like to see her again.'

The whole family was there: his father the Sarpanch, his mother, his wife, his cousins. They all came out of the house into the courtyard. I marched up to Suresh and stood facing him.

'You're coming with me, Suresh, and because of what you did to me, we're going to get married, right here in your courtyard! And if you don't, you know what I'm going to do? I'm going to cut it off! You won't even be able to pee through it!'

I laughed to see the startled looks on their faces.

'From now on,' I added, 'I'll be watching you. I'm not going to take my eyes off you for a second.'

Suresh went pale. 'What are you talking about?' he protested. 'How dare you say such things and threaten me like this! . . . Anyway, I'm already married!'

'Yes, you're married. And from now on, stay with your wife, don't come near me again. I've got a rifle!'

'Calm down, Phoolan.' It was the Sarpanch speaking this time. 'He isn't going to do you any harm – and you can use the well.'

'Go to hell! I don't want to use your well. I can drink water from the river!'

I stormed out of the courtyard after telling them to go and tell the police if they liked, that even if they put me in prison, I would be back for my revenge; I would be back to kill them all!

From that moment on, I began to breathe again. I walked through the village without shame. I went to the river to bathe whenever I wanted. I had no more fear. I told my parents their daughter was dead. My father was alarmed. I told him not to worry, I wasn't going to drown myself.

Some policemen came to complain to my mother that I had been 'aggressive', I had 'misbehaved', I had even threatened people with a rifle. They wanted to punish me. There were fifteen of them and they ransacked the house searching for me everywhere. They climbed on to the terrace and overturned all the hay in the stable. When the Inspector found me behind the cows, he began to insult me and raised his lathi to strike me. In the past I would have screamed in fright at the beating I was going to get, but that day I shouted back at him. 'Don't try to beat me! I haven't done anything and you have no right to speak to me like that. What do you want to do, lock me in the police station like before? I'll get out, and I'll come back and kill Mayadin. All you can do is lock me up and torture me.'

The villagers had come to see what was going on as usual and they heard everything. The police could do nothing in front of so many witnesses.

'Let's go,' said the Inspector, turning to his men. 'She's crazy!'

I wasn't mad. I had nothing left to lose. There was no more humiliation they could threaten me with. I threatened them instead.

One day, an old man came to the village, a thakur. He must have asked where I was and been told I was working in the field with my mother. He came up to us and spoke to me without realising who I was.

'Do you know where I can find Phoolan Devi?'

'Why do you want her?'

'Oh I must have that girl! I've heard all about her and I want her!'

'And then what are you going to do? Are you going to marry her? Or are you going to torture her and do dirty things with her?'

'I've heard you can do whatever you like with her!'

He was old, his face was dark and lined. He looked pompous in his white kurta with a turban on his head.

'You must have come a long way,' I said. 'Have a rest. Phoolan has a lot of visitors. All the thakurs want her. I'll go and tell her you're here.'

I snapped a nice strong branch from a tree and I removed the leaves, testing it against my hand. My mother saw me from a distance and looked puzzled for a moment, then went back to work. She must have thought I was going to use it to drive an animal out of the field. I crept back to where the old man was lying and began whipping him as hard as I could.

'You wanted Phoolan,' I screamed, 'you've got her!'

I kept whipping him.

'Go on! Take her! Do whatever you like with her!'

My mother came running over and helped the old man to his feet. He ran off and I sat down under a tree, exhausted but doubled up with laughter as I watched him disappear across the fields. He had been so surprised, he hadn't even cried out for help.

I had changed. My whole being had been fired with rage and rebellion by the nerve of the thakurs, by their contempt for us. For a while I worried that more of them would come to avenge the one I had beaten. I was on my guard at all times, and I worked out a plan in my head. I would get my family out of the house, pretending I was going to do what they wanted. I would invite the thakurs to sit down, telling them to make themselves at home, that I was going to attend to them all . . . Then I would bolt the door and set fire to the house!

I thought about it all the time, imagining the scene . . . I was almost disappointed when the days passed and nobody came. I knew the name of the old man, and where he lived. I had heard that he had done what he wanted with at least two hundred girls; just like that, because they were poor mallah girls like me who were born to serve him.

More than a fortnight after the old man fled with his dhoti on fire, two thakurs came to the house looking for me. 'You want to know what my daughter can do,' my father replied. 'Ask her yourself.' It was as though he no longer even had the strength left to be embarrassed anymore. He called me out into the yard.

I calmly asked them their names and what they wanted.

'Do you have wives, or sisters or daughters?' I enquired.

They looked confused. 'Would you like someone to do to them what you want to do to me? Get out! Go back to your wives! If you set foot in here again, I'll kill you!'

They were amazed.

'You must be crazy to talk to us like that,' one of them said. He told his friend, 'She must have someone behind her.' They decided to leave. It hadn't been necessary to set fire to the house. All it took was courage, and the threat of violence. My mother had heard what happened and came out in tears to tell me off. 'You threaten everybody. You keep talking about your rifle but you don't have a rifle!' It was true, but word had got around and everybody was afraid of me now. Nobody from the village bothered me and nobody came from other villages to demand vile things of me. They lowered their voices now when I passed. Perhaps they imagined I had been given a rifle by my uncles, but it was only a phantom rifle that I had. The villagers were scared of a phantom. If they had been on my side, nothing would have happened. They were afraid of Mayadin too. They believed that because he was rich, he could crush them all.

I was kept at bay like a wild dog and feared now too, and I began to distance myself too – even from my family. I hardly spoke to my father unless it was to ask him why he brought me into the world, in such a poor household. I couldn't stand their presence, neither my father nor my mother. In the past I had always been afraid of my mother, terrified by her temper that was so like my own, but now if she lifted a hand to slap me, I threatened to slap her too, and she would back down. Sometimes I wanted to pull her by the hair and knock her head against the wall. I never did it, but I wanted to. And I kept out of the way of my little brother and sister. They too had started to annoy me.

Sometimes, while I was just eating quietly near the fire, or resting on a khat, everything would suddenly come back to me, all the things that had been done to me, all the horrors. I would get up and run to Mayadin's house. 'Kill me!' I would scream like the madwoman they thought I had become. 'Come on! I'll kill you too, and it'll be over.' Or I would wake in the middle of a nightmare and run to his house in the dark. He would be so worried, he wouldn't even show his face. He would call his servants to defend him, and the next day he would go and see the Sarpanch to discuss what they were going to do about me. They all thought the only reason I had the nerve to behave that way was that I was under someone's protection. I used to howl with laughter to see them cowering from me.

I was afraid too, but I didn't show it. I was afraid of what they would do to my parents. Nothing they could do to me now could be any more terrible than what had happened already. They had done their worst. I was still alive. That was all that mattered. They had beaten and violated me, but I would have my revenge . . .

The month of Ashar passed, then the monsoon was due. My father was so worried about my safety that all he said to me was, 'Don't talk like that, someone will come to kill you.'

Phool Singh, the thakur from Narihan, the only thakur I had any trust in, came to see my mother. 'If someone of my caste or even of my family comes to your house,' he warned, 'don't let them in . . . I can't help you any more.'

My mother asked him why not.

'I can't take on my entire caste. Hide your daughter, lock her up! The men of my caste are like dogs.'

He didn't even trust his own sons. We had heard that he helped other poor people, not only girls like me, but people of other lowly castes, and muslims. But men were all jackals to me. They all wanted to eat me, cut me into pieces. They lurked in the dark like tigers slavering for my flesh.

*

The eyes of my bullock had become dull and empty. He had caught a chill with the monsoon and, for a while, he seemed to recover but now he was ill again. He began to tremble and then he started to vomit. I went to get some water for him and I brought him into the house so he would be warm. He lay down, and I held his head close to me and caressed his neck as I talked to him gently. We stayed like that together all through the night.

In the morning, he was dead. He had died without a moan, listening to me tell him about all the things we were going to do together.

The monsoon rains were still pouring down. The sky was grey and the path outside our house had turned to mud. Nobody would help us take the carcass out of the house, but it had to be done somehow. Finally, after we had begged and begged them, some sweepers, the poorest people of our village, helped us to pull the dead animal out of the house and heave him up onto their cart. They took him to the Yamuna and threw him in.

Away with him in the rain went my tears . . .

18

I had slept badly, as usual.

For days, the monsoon rain had been falling heavily. It had finally let up that morning, leaving everything fresh, but there was no peace for me in the coolness. In the air that had been washed clean of dust and heat I could sense only menace . . . My instincts had been sharpened from always being on the lookout.

When I was out spreading manure in a field, I saw a man coming from afar. As he came closer, I recognised his yellow teeth and odd-shaped nose. He was the Sarpanch of a nearby village.

He didn't recognise me. He asked me the usual question. Did I know where Phoolan Devi lived?

Warily, I pointed at Mayadin's house.

'She's living there now?'

I asked him why he wanted to know.

'They're coming to get her tonight,' he said.

'Who is? Why? She hasn't done anything wrong.'

'She's dangerous. She's mixed up with dacoits.'

He asked my name and I told him it was Bhuri. He narrowed his eyes at me and left. I hurried home as soon as I could.

My mother refused to believe my story. I had to beg her to go with me to the police station in Kalpi to ask for protection, and she only came in the end because she needed help to carry sacks of seed back for planting after the rains. When we reached the building with the red and blue sign, she let me do the talking. But it was the same deputy super-intendent who had thrown me out the last time, and he just laughed and said he had heard enough of my complaints.

'One minute you're accusing them of assaulting you and now you're saying thakurs are coming to kidnap you. Who would want to kidnap you? Go home. They'll find someone to marry you in the end.'

There was nothing else to do but buy the seed and return. Each sack weighed thirty pounds; I carried one on my head, and my mother carried the other. As we passed the outskirts of town, it started to rain again. We trudged on and very soon it was raining so heavily we could hardly see in front of us. I told my mother we should have stayed in the town, where I felt safe. I was tired, and the cold rain made me shiver. I would have liked to sit down somewhere in the town, somewhere nobody knew me, and never get up again. But my mother had wanted to get back.

We had to cross a small river in the gusts of rain with the sacks on our heads. The waters were high and the currents swirled around us. My sari clung to me, dripping wet in the gusts of rain. It was late when we finally reached home, exhausted from carrying the sacks, but there was still work to do. In the dark I had to round up the cows and feed them while my mother cooked chapatis for us, but by the time I had finished, I was so weary I couldn't eat.

'Don't worry, Phoolan,' my mother said. 'Take your sari off to dry and go to sleep.'

I was even more afraid of thakurs than I was of the police. When I had asked the police to keep me in the lock-up, they had just joked that they would be only too pleased to keep me there . . .

There was only one person who could protect me from fear and indignity – the husband I didn't have. Without a husband, I was like a rabbit under the paws of a tiger.

I begged my mother to hide me somewhere.

'Hide you where?' she asked.

What would they want to kidnap me for? What men always wanted from me, I thought. They would want to hurt me and humiliate me, and perhaps this time even kill me . . . But the sound of the rain falling steadily on the straw roof helped me forget my dark broodings – until a loud noise woke me with a start.

The courtyard wall shook so hard I thought it had collapsed and the house was about to be carried away by the rains. This happened sometimes to houses at the edge of the village by the river like ours. But the wall didn't break. The wooden door flew from its hinges and I saw the silhouettes of men in uniforms. They burst in and seized my father, who was sleeping inside the doorway of the stable.

I could see the startled look on his face as one of the men picked him up by the shoulders and bellowed, 'Where's the little whore? Where is Phoolan?'

'She's asleep. I don't know where.'

In their khaki uniforms they looked like policemen, not thakurs. The light from their torches illuminated the sheets of rain, and I saw they were carrying rifles. Some of them flashed the beams of their torches around looking for me while others rapidly tied my father with a heavy rope. My mother ran out into the yard with a lantern to face them.

'I can't stand it any more,' she shouted defiantly. 'How dare you barge in here in the middle of the night like this?'

But what use were the screams of a woman? My mother too must have thought they were policemen sent by Mayadin or the Sarpanch. I was taking no chances. I slipped to the back of the house where, with luck, I would be able to climb over the wall into the next yard. Glancing back, I saw the men battering my mother and father.

'Where is she? Tell us!'

I was about to scramble over the wall when I saw lights everywhere outside too. They had surrounded the house. There must have been at least a dozen of them at the back and I guessed there were probably more in the street. I let myself drop down and crept back into the kitchen. I saw the bundles of grass we dried to use as brooms to sweep our yard and I thought I could try to hide under them, but it was no use. I picked up one of the bundles. It was all I had to defend myself against their rifles. They had surrounded the house like an army and invaded the yard. I could hear them in the kitchen kicking over the pots and smashing everything with the butts of their rifles.

Then I heard my little brother screaming for help.

'We'll take this one instead!' one of the men shouted. 'Tell her she can come and get him whenever she's ready.'

If it hadn't been raining so hard, I would have been sleeping on the terrace where I always slept when I felt endangered, and perhaps I would have been able to escape them. But perhaps my father was right and you can't escape destiny. I let the broom fall from my hand and walked out into the beams of their torches.

My father was still tied up like an animal for slaughter and my mother was on her knees in the rain in front of the men, pleading with them to let Shiv Narayan go.

'I'm Phoolan Devi! Kill me if you want to, but let him go.'

The men turned to me, and one of them stepped forward, fixing me with his stare like a snake preparing to strike his prey.

He gave me a vicious slap. 'Get away from here! You think you can have us believe you're Phoolan Devi? You're just a little shit!'

'But that's Phoolan!' my mother shrieked. 'Take her, but leave my son!'

The man who had slapped me approached me with his torch. He held it under my nose, then inspected my blouse and my petticoat, pointing the beam all the way down to my naked feet. Then he brought the light back up to my face.

'You are Phoolan?'

He must have been expecting someone bigger. He looked at me as though there had been a mistake, and I was wasting his time. I couldn't see his features clearly in the dark, but he was thin and not very tall, and he had a deep voice.

'Yes,' I stammered. 'I'm . . . Phoolan.'

The man turned to my mother. 'Is this a trick? She's too young to be a dacoit.'

I still thought they were policemen who had come from another district. There seemed to be two of them in charge: the thin man who had slapped me, and another one, taller and more heavily built, who spoke crudely to the first man.

'Are you going to use her or shall we kill her now? We've come all this way for a bloody girl. We can't just leave her, people won't take us seriously. Go on, Vickram! What are you waiting for?'

'Don't rush me. We'll do what I say.'

'Hey, she's a mallah like us,' called one of the men from the shadows. But the tall one kept on trying to incite his companion.

'Let's do the job we came to do. If you don't want to use her, I will. Make up your mind.'

The one with the deep voice studied me a moment longer, and then he straightened. 'We're taking her. Release the boy!'

My mother had guessed that the one named Vickram was a mallah, like us. She threw herself to the ground before him and touched his feet. 'I beg you, leave her here, leave her in peace! She hasn't done anything wrong.'

'I can't leave your daughter.'

The men in the gang began to murmur behind his back. Vickram stepped back to talk to them, and I couldn't hear what they were saying. I stood there frozen with dread, convinced they were planning to kill me.

'Amma, help me, Amma!' I whimpered.

My father took up the cry, hoping to wake the villagers. People started coming out of their houses with lanterns to see what was happening, and the men turned around and aimed their rifles at them.

'Don't come any closer,' one of the men warned. 'Get away from us.'

The tall, broad-shouldered one shook his head slowly and spat.

'I am Baboo Gujar Singh! And I swear I will kill you all!'

Suddenly there was a commotion all around me. One of the men was pulling me by the arm and another was shoving me forward. I heard rifle shots. They were shooting in the air to scare off the villagers, and I was being carried along barefoot by the two men, unable to struggle free. In a few moments we were beyond our little row of houses and heading down to the river. Behind me I could still hear rifle shots exploding in the night and my father yelling for help.

I was certain they were going to kill me. Any second now, I would be dead. The fear of death was a strange sensation. It was a fear I felt in my throat as I stumbled down the slope towards the bank of the river, half-carried, half-shoved by the two men like a piece of straw in a stampede. I found myself praying only that they wouldn't rape me before they killed me.

They had switched off their torches and I could no longer hear the cries from the village by the time we reached the river. I was surrounded by phantoms. They were untying a boat.

'Why go any further? Let's use her here!' one of them

said. 'That way we won't have to take her with us.'

'Nobody touch her! We'll do what I say,' another replied.

They lifted me up and threw me in the boat. 'Watch out,' someone shouted. 'She's a mallah's daughter, she knows how to swim.' The phantom men were real enough. They surrounded me in the boat, blocking me on all sides so I couldn't jump out. I couldn't even see the river behind all their thick necks and wide shoulders, and their rifles. All I could see was the rain coming down in raging torrents as the lightning flashed.

We reached the far side, and someone pushed me out.

'Get going! Hurry!'

'Go on ahead, that way. If you try to run away, we'll shoot you down.'

I stumbled along the path that ran by the river, my bare feet sinking in the muddy ruts made by the carts. They were right behind me. I couldn't see them, but I could feel their rifle barrels prodding my back when I stumbled. I had to lift my petticoat to my knees to straddle the puddles of water. The rain was stinging my eyes, I could feel my legs being scratched by thorns and my heart pounding as though it was going to explode.

'Walk! Where do you think you're going? Walk!'

Fear made my mouth dry, but the only thing to drink was rainwater. I lifted my head as I walked and let it run down my cheeks, licking the rain on my lips.

'Vickram mallah, I swear, I'm going to have that girl!'

Behind me, I heard the deep voice of the one named Vickram. 'No,' he said. 'I'm the one who's going to use her first!'

My clothes clung to me; the rain had turned them to thin rags. I was caught in a nightmare, near-naked and exposed, trying to run but unable to advance fast enough as my feet sank in the mud.

My mouth was still dry with fear. I gathered my courage and turned around to face them. 'Please, brother, give me some water.'

'I'm not your brother, I'm your husband!' one of them laughed nastily.

They shoved me forward.

The one I was least afraid of was Vickram, the mallah. Though he said little, when he spoke to his men it was in a calm voice, while the other one, who had shouted that his name was Baboo, bullied his men, yelling and grunting at them.

He smelled like an animal and in the faint dawn light I could just make out his features. He had a large nose, the sharp teeth of a wildcat and only one eye. His other eye was white.

He kept pushing me forward with his thick hands, giggling and telling me how much he was going to enjoy using me.

We had walked the whole night, across the fields and into the ravines. The rain had let up, finally, and the men halted where two paths crossed by a small river. They washed their faces and rinsed their mouths. Lying down between two rocks, I drank with my face in the river. My skin was damp and cold, my temples throbbed, and my feet had been cut by the sharp stones of the hillsides. For hours I had been wanting desperately to go to the toilet.

'Please,' I said, 'I would like to relieve myself.'

'Do you think we're stupid?' asked Baboo. 'Do you think we're going to let you get away?'

'Leave her!' said Vickram.

'Stay there!'

'Go on.'

In the early morning light I saw their black faces, horrid

and ferocious. They didn't look much like policemen, even though they were all wearing uniforms, with cartridge belts across their chests, rucksacks and heavy boots with thick rubber soles so they didn't make a noise as they walked.

I looked around. We were high in the ravines, surrounded by rocks and bushes. Somewhere far below were the plains and the river. Some of the men had rolled out their blankets to lie down, while others slept on the bare ground with their heads on their rucksacks. I tried to relieve myself behind a bush, quivering at the thought that one of them would sneak up on me. I returned and, as I bathed my feet in the river, I saw that most of them had gone to sleep.

I approached Vickram, careful to keep a respectful distance.

'Please, brother, let me go now. I beg you.'

But I had got a bit too close to him for one-eye's liking.

'You! Come over here with Baboo!'

Baboo had become angry when I approached Vickram. He seemed to have his own men, while Vickram had his. They had settled down to rest in two separate groups. And it seemed they couldn't agree on whether to rape me or kill me.

I backed away with my hands still clasped together beseeching Vickram.

'Please, my brother, let me go home . . .'

'Don't be afraid,' he said.

He handed me a sari and some plastic sandals from his rucksack. The ogre was watching him . . . 'Be careful,' he said slyly. 'She'll start getting ideas. You better come here with me, you little hussy!'

He came over to me and grabbed me by the hair to drag me back to where he was sitting.

'Stay here. And stop calling him your brother.'

He pushed me to the ground and sat down beside me.

Vickram said nothing and I was too scared to move now. With my eyes, I tried to implore him to help me.

He motioned to me to wait.

Squatting down there, I lowered my head between my knees and didn't dare to lift it again. Some of the men had opened their rucksacks and began to bite at dry salt biscuits. I had to content myself with water.

Throughout the night, during the insane dash across the fields and into the jungles, I thought I had fallen into the hands of policemen. Now I was certain they were bandits. I had been accused of being a dacoit who lived in the jungle and came out only to pillage and now I had been kidnapped by real dacoits. They didn't have four arms and four ears, as Rukmini and I had thought, but they were monsters nonetheless. They had dark, dirty faces with rough features, thick moustaches and bands of cloth tied across their foreheads, and they spoke in a language I barely understood. Why did they kidnap me? If they had been hired to punish me, why hadn't they done it yet? Why didn't they just rape me and kill me right there? In the village I might have had a chance to escape or defend myself somehow, but out here in the wild there was nothing I could do. I didn't even know where I was.

All I could think was that it was to the one named Vickram, whom the others had said was a mallah like me, that I owed my salvation for the moment. But he paid no more attention to me than he would to a fish washed up on the riverbank. The one-eyed Baboo wasn't a mallah. He was taller than Vickram. He had said he was a gujar. I had never heard of this caste, but he must have been a thakur of some kind.

The men were eating and joking among themselves. Nobody spoke to me. They were talking about rupees. My head was spinning, trying to think of a way to save myself. I wondered if my parents had gone to the police, whether Mayadin, or the Sarpanch, or both of them had been behind it. With my head between my knees and my eyes shut, I began to pray. 'God, if you exist, if you can see me, make them release me. Make the one named Vickram help me.' But deep in me I knew that if God existed, I wouldn't be there with those bandits.

We had hardly been there any time before they packed their rucksacks again and began to put their boots back on. I got dressed too, wrapping the sari Vickram had given me around my damp petticoat, and we set off again.

Baboo made me walk ahead of him. If I stumbled, he cursed me. I braced myself, fearing I would be beaten, but the blows didn't come . . . Instead, I felt his lone eye on my back. I had no idea which direction we were taking. We were walking in single file along narrow paths cut deep in the hills by the rains. Around me the terrain was rocky and empty, with just a few trees; no fields, no animals, no people.

After we had been marching for an hour or so, I saw smoke rising in the sky. It was coming from a rough-looking settlement tucked away in the ravines. Near the wooden huts, the trees had been cut and logs piled up. There was one little hut a short way from the village, half-hidden in the earth. We came up to the hut and a man greeted us. He didn't seem to be afraid of the dacoits. The men asked him for clothing for me and some things for themselves. He disappeared in the direction of the village and came back with a pair of black trousers, a blue T-shirt and several pairs of rubber-soled shoes. Baboo pointed at the shoes and told me to find a pair that fitted me. The man nodded to his hut. I realised he meant for me to change in there. He didn't seem surprised to see me with all those men.

There was an old man sitting on a stool nearby, watching us, and I thought of trying to ask him to get help from the village, but the bandits surrounded the hut while I changed. There must have been more than thirty of them in all.

The trousers were black ones that men wore. I pulled them on under my petticoat. I kept my blouse on under the T-shirt and folded my sari under my arm. Without my sari I had nothing to cover my head, and my hair hung loose. Baboo was waiting outside the hut, reclining on an old khat that shook under his weight. He caught me by my hair and made me sit down beside him.

Vickram was standing a little way off.

'Take your hands off her,' he said. His voice sounded cold and menacing.

Suddenly he was surrounded by five or six of Baboo's men, pointing their rifles at him. Warily, he watched as Baboo, who still had me by the hair, stretched out like a fat bullock on the khat. 'Why are you trying to protect her?' asked one-eye. 'Why her? We've had so many other girls before. What is it about this one? You're on her side, is that it?'

'I told you not to touch her. She belongs to my community.'

'So what? Who cares? You don't even know her. She's not one of your family.'

'If you touch her, I'll shoot you,' said Vickram.

'If you shoot me, I'll shoot you, and then what? We aren't both going to die for this little hussy, are we? She's the one we should shoot!'

The rest of the men looked at one another. They couldn't understand why the two leaders were arguing. 'What are we doing with this bloody girl?' asked one of the men. 'We should've got rid of her long ago, eh Baboo?'

Vickram didn't move.

'Don't get hasty, Baboo. You've done whatever you like up to now, and we've put up with it. This one, you don't touch!'

Was he protecting me just because I was a mallah? It seemed I wasn't the only one who didn't understand. The men were murmuring that they had never seen Vickram like this before; they were asking what was wrong with him. I could only hope it was because he was a mallah, and even though he was a bandit, and I was just a poor peasant, he had taken pity on me. Whatever the reason, it was the first time a man had ever tried to defend me. I couldn't believe it.

Baboo backed down. He pushed me from the khat, like a child tired of playing a game, a game he was used to winning. I could sense a battle brewing between the two men, and I wanted Vickram to win – not so much for his sake, but for mine. My body wouldn't be able to bear any more torture. My hatred of men was so strong I desired only to be a man myself. I hated men, but all I wanted was to be like them, to have their power, and their freedom, to no longer be just flesh for them to toy with.

The afternoon passed slowly. I lay on the ground but I couldn't sleep. As night fell, we left the hut and began moving again. I heard one of the men say we were heading for a village called Raipur. I had never heard of it, and I still had no idea where we were. To us, the jungles had always been places filled with terrible dangers. We were always told never to leave the plains, and never to stray from the paths. All I knew was that I was far from the banks of the Yamuna.

We walked the whole night long again, halting from time to time for a short rest. By morning, we had arrived at the village, stopping a good way outside it just as we had done before. Even from afar, I could see it was a prosperous village. The houses were solid and well-made, with windows and carved wooden doors.

They sent one of the men to find someone named Raja. From the way the men spoke of him he must have been important, perhaps a local prince or a Brahmin, I thought. We waited the whole day, and it was almost evening when Raja finally came. He arrived with two other men on a motorcycle. One man was driving it and Raja and the other man were sitting sideways. The entire gang bowed to this Raja, and some of them approached him to touch his feet. He was well-dressed, like the politicians we sometimes saw visiting our villages. He wore a white shirt and black trousers, and black leather shoes that shined.

He noticed me looking at him. I had been keeping as far from the gang as possible, not saying a word, so as not to annoy one-eye.

'She's just an infant, Baboo,' said one of the men who had come on the motorcycle.

Raja looked around at the gang. 'Don't any of you touch her,' he said.

'That's what I told them,' said Vickram.

But the gang members protested to Raja: 'In that case,' they said, 'we might as well get rid of her. Vickram doesn't want her and she can't run very fast. She just holds us up.'

Did getting rid of me mean killing me, or leaving me there in the jungle? If they abandoned me near a village, I was sure I would be able to find my way. It was a sudden glimmer of hope. I lifted my head to look at the ogre, hoping he would agree.

Baboo shook his head.

It was as if my presence had divided the gang. They seemed to be splitting into two groups, the mallahs on one side, the thakurs on the other. It was the thakurs who were refusing to let me go.

'We went a long way to get her,' said Baboo, 'and we aren't just going to let her go now. If we do that, they'll say she made fools of us.'

Who were 'they'? I wondered. The ones who had hired

the gang to kidnap me? It was not hard to imagine who they might be . . .

Raja tried to reason with Baboo. 'She's just a poor girl. She hasn't done anything to you.'

Like Vickram, Raja seemed to have pity for me. He was well-spoken, and I thought he must have been someone very important. When they addressed him, both Vickram and Baboo used terms of respect, though Baboo was clearly irritated by Raja's comments.

'I have always told you that you act without thinking, Baboo. Why is it you are always after girls like this?' asked Raja. 'It's all you ever think about. I have told you to leave them alone. One day you will get yourself killed because of it.'

'I couldn't give a damn! If it's the last thing I do, I'm going to have that one! I'm not going to let her go.'

'You aren't going to lay a finger on her!' said Vickram.

'Either we get rid of the girl,' said Baboo menacingly, 'or we get rid of Vickram.'

I was watching Vickram, praying to him silently to save me. He came towards me, and shone the light from his torch on his own face this time.

'Take a good look at me,' he said.

It was a handsome face; narrow, with a fine nose. He had a thin moustache and his skin was pale and soft, almost like a girl's skin. Despite the scar over his left eye, there was something in his look that made me trust him.

'I am Vickram, the mallah. Remember my name, and don't forget my face.'

'What has got into you?' bellowed one-eye. 'What are you trying to prove? That you're a mallah? Are you doing it to get at me?'

'I want her to be able to identify me, that's all. Let's stop this, okay?'

Vickram returned to where his men were standing. Raja nodded, signalling that the matter was closed. He went back to his motorcycle and, before he got on, each of the gang members bowed to him and touched his feet in turn. As he rode off in a cloud of smoke and dust, some more men arrived from the village with potatoes and chapatis. The members of the gang forgot their quarrel and settled down to eat. I was still sitting apart from them, and Baboo still had his lone eye on me.

'You!' he roared. 'If you try to run away, I'll shoot you down.'

Among the men who had brought the food from the village was one Vickram greeted as his uncle. He joined the other three gang members who seemed to be Vickram's men. I had caught their names: Madhav, Raghu Nath and Bharat. The name of Vickram's uncle was Bare Lal. He brought a plate of food over and handed it to me. They never seemed to be very far from his side, and now they were all eating except Vickram. He was smoking a cigarette, deep in thought.

'Come on, eat!' said Bharat. 'It'll be all right, Mastana, don't blame yourself.'

I had heard his men calling him Mastana earlier. It was a word full of warmth and admiration, a nickname for someone handsome and carefree, and I was surprised to hear anyone calling a bandit Mastana. Nor had I ever seen anyone smoke so much. He sucked on the cigarette with a serious frown and when he had smoked it down to the filter, he shook another out of his pack and lit it with the first.

'We should never have kidnapped her,' he said after a while. 'We've been tricked.'

Baboo grinned, his mouth full of food. He pointed a finger dripping with ghee at me. 'If that girl is yours,' he said, 'she's mine too!'

He picked up his rifle suddenly and fired. I heard the shot explode near me and dived sideways. But it was only a game. All the men laughed to see me curled in a ball on the grass, quaking with shock. Vickram said nothing.

Once the food had been eaten, we set off again in the dark. This time we descended from the ravines to the Yamuna where a ferryman was waiting with a boat. We floated down the river until we reached a village called Bejamau. It was morning by the time we got there and people were bathing and washing their laundry in the river. Everyone seemed to recognise Vickram. They surrounded him, pleased to see him and full of questions. Then they noticed me.

'You've got another girl!' they said, looking surprised. 'Why have you brought her here?'

'It's not your problem. You don't have to be concerned about her.'

The gang members all climbed out of the boat, leaving me in it, guarded by four men. 'Don't move,' they warned me. 'If you don't do what you're told, we'll kill you, understand? Vickram's not the one in charge here, it's Baboo, and he's dangerous. You better do what he says.'

The others headed off along the riverbank towards some steps that led from the water's edge up the hillside to a temple. After a few minutes, Vickram's uncle, Bare Lal, came back to get me. In front of the temple, sitting cross-legged and immobile on a straw mat, was a sadhu. He was very old and his body was nearly naked and covered in white ashes. He was so thin he seemed to be made only of bones. Long strands of hair fell over his shoulders. His eyes were closed.

Bare Lal ushered me forward. 'His name is Sidh Baba. You can greet him.'

He was a holy man, a guru who seemed to be venerated by Vickram and his men. They each knelt down and touched his feet as he murmured his prayers. Then they withdrew to a respectful distance.

Vickram spoke to the sadhu. 'Forgive us for what we have done,' he said. 'We have kidnapped this girl. Forgive us for this bad deed and give us the strength to protect her.'

Baboo heard this but didn't interrupt. I felt a nudge from one of the men. I advanced and knelt down too, touching the guru's feet. As I did, I began to whimper with relief.

The sadhu opened his eyes. They burned like two round coals in that face white with ashes. He said something I couldn't understand, and one of his devotees translated it.

'What are you doing with all these dacoits at your age?'

I was so stunned, I couldn't answer.

'I'm fed up with this,' said Baboo angrily.

The holy man looked at him and murmured something else that the devotee translated.

'Will you shut up and sit down calmly, please.'

Baboo looked around at all the men and sat down.

Then the devotee leaned towards the holy man to hear what he said next, and whispered something to Vickram.

The men took me away from the temple. I didn't understand what was going on, other than that the argument had flared up again and that the strange, ash-covered man sitting in front of his temple had the power to make Baboo obey him.

Bare Lal told me that the sadhu drank only milk, spoke only through his nose, not through his mouth, and that it was extremely rare that he spoke directly to someone, as he had spoken to me. The temple was small and covered with white mosaic. It was set above the steps by the river, but with the monsoon the water had risen almost to the top of the steps, right up to the doorway. I hadn't been able to see the white temple from the boat. It looked so peaceful and safe under the blue sky that I couldn't stop myself crying.

The holy man had spoken to me! His temple was dedicated to Shiva, the smiling god who lived on the sacred mountain, whose rage had the power to destroy demons. Perhaps Shiva would protect me now!

They brought me back to the river and, with the boat loaded down by the gang, we set off again. Nobody said anything about where we were going. Nobody said, you're going home, Phoolan. Night fell and after a while we got out on the far side of the Yamuna. We had to start walking again, walking through fields, then climbing again, up the rough slopes of the ravines, dodging between sharp limestone rocks and the dry thorny bushes. If I hung on to the branch of a tree even for a second to catch my breath, I heard a voice behind me telling me to keep moving.

I hadn't seen my family for two nights.

19

The bandits had encircled some large, three-storey houses belonging to rich families. They had burst in and quickly made their way up to the roof terraces and they were waving their torches and firing their rifles into the night like devils. From up there, they could survey the whole village. Baboo Gujar was shouting through a megaphone that one of the men had been carrying.

'It is I, Baboo Gujar Singh, and you are nothing but dogs!'

That morning, they had divided the village up into 'sectors'. Vickram and his men had gone to the other part of the village but Baboo had made me go with him, and now I was sitting on a cart, guarded by two of Baboo's men, taking part, terrified, in my first pillage.

Some of Baboo's men were running around the house looking for girls, the rest were barging into rooms and dragging out trunks that they burst open by firing at the locks. They were stuffing handfuls of gold and silver jewellery and bundles of rupees into their pockets, and battering any women who screamed in protest. No one tried to resist them. The men who lived there had all run away to hide when they heard the rifles. I could only see shadows fleeing in the dark and hear the panic-stricken cries.

Suddenly Baboo shouted to the men guarding me, 'Show her what to do.'

They shoved me inside the house, into a room where some men were smashing everything; they were emptying the cupboards and overturning mattresses and slashing them open. Two women crouched in a corner were sobbing hysterically and covering their faces with their saris. Baboo was in a state of high excitation, his lone eye rolling, his teeth bared. He strutted around the room with his rifle in his hand and pointed to a wooden trunk with a heavy iron padlock.

'Open it!'

The women shrieked. One of them took a key from her sari and fumbled with the lock. She opened the trunk.

'Take their jewellery and give them a beating for good measure. Go on! Hit them! Like this . . .'

Grinning like a madman, he kicked the woman over.

'Take a good look at her,' he announced. 'It's Phoolan Devi. A new dacoit is born, and I'm going to marry her!'

'I can't hit these women,' I said. 'they haven't done anything to me.'

I started crying like the women, and Baboo came up and put his arm around me, fondling me.

'What's wrong, my little sweetie?'

The women implored me not to beat them, pulling the gold bangles from their arms and handing them to me. I gave them to Baboo.

'Go on! Hit that one! Ask her where the rest of it is. You're going to learn how to be a dacoit.'

I refused. I didn't know why he wanted to involve me. I didn't want to become a dacoit, I wanted to get away from them, or stay there with those poor women, and die with them if I must.

As Baboo stuffed the gold bracelets in his pocket, he noticed a young girl hiding in a corridor. She must have been about my age – no more than sixteen. He motioned to his men and three of them dragged her trembling in front of him. He lifted her head to see her face and gave a nod to his men. They took her outside. I heard her screaming and pleading with them to stop. They were raping her. I covered my ears, unable to bear her cries. She was begging for mercy; she could do nothing to stop them and I could do nothing to help her because I was a prisoner just as she was. Baboo had picked her up with one hand like a hunk of meat and given her to his men. I, too, had been helpless prey like her. I couldn't bear it any longer. I ran out of the room, but one of the bandits caught me in the yard.

'You don't like it? The little whore thinks she's too good for us!' he shouted. He picked me up and dumped me on the cart outside. I could still hear the girl screaming in the night, the screams of a child . . .

Why had Vickram left me in the hands of these men? He had abandoned me to the whims of a bandit who raped girls as though he was simply relieving himself. He came around from the back of the house proudly zipping his trousers and adjusting his belt, his lone eye rolling with satisfaction. Then he sat on the cart and began to fondle me, telling me he was going to marry this tender little chicken who had tried to run away, as though it was all a joke.

The men had finished their looting and were leaving, firing their rifles in the air as they hurried from the village to meet up with Vickram. He and his men had hijacked a tractor with a cart from two peasants in the fields, and Vickram was driving it. They sat me on the big spare tyre with Madhav, one of Vickram's men, to one side of me and a thakur on the other. My head was spinning.

'Don't worry,' Bare Lal whispered to me, 'we're going to get you out of his clutches.'

He was Vickram's uncle, the one who had given me food.

But Baboo had heard him. 'Hey, you there!' he barked. 'What are you doing whispering in her ear?'

Bare Lal ignored him. He was the only one who spoke to me. At first I had taken him for a thakur because he was tall and wore a moustache. He had the good skin of a rich man and a ferocious expression. But I was relieved that he seemed to have taken charge of me because he was older than the rest of the men and I hoped that meant he would protect me.

We rode on the tractor for hours through the night, stopping at dawn in a small clearing. I guessed we must have been somewhere near the Yamuna, because I heard Vickram say to Baboo that if they let me go with the two peasants, they could show me the road to Auraiya. I knew that was a town on the far side of the Yamuna, upriver from my village.

Some of the others agreed. I heard the men saying they should let me go, I wasn't worth fighting about. I was too much trouble. 'We don't need to carry a caged bird around with us,' said one of them.

My heart started to flutter with hope. If we were near Auraiya, then we must be near the Yamuna. I could see the red walls and straw roofs of a village not far off. I threw myself in front of Baboo with my hands together. I touched his feet begging him to release me.

'All right. She can go wherever she likes.'

I didn't know whether to believe him. I lifted my head to try to look directly in his single, hateful eye, to see if he was mocking me.

'Go on, my little chicken, see if you can get away from me!'

I stood up and hesitantly I took a few steps with my back to him, but I didn't dare run. I thought I was almost free when I heard the crack of a rifle shot.

I froze. The sleeve of my T-shirt was singed. I had been grazed by the bullet! I leapt aside like a goat and stood there, petrified and trembling. I didn't dare to move in case he fired again. I had my eyes fixed on the burnt sleeve just inches from my heart.

'Are you crazy?' Vickram shouted. 'Why did you fire at her?'

They began to argue again and to threaten each other with their rifles. I was still frozen, not daring to move.

'You are mallahs, a worthless pack of dogs. We aren't letting her go just because you say so.'

Two arms hooked under mine and carried me back in front of Baboo.

'Do you still want to run away?'

'No.'

He punched me, slapped me, lifted me up with one hand and threw me to the ground. Then he started trying to pull my trousers off in front of the others.

'I'm fed up with this. I'm going to use her right here! Let's see if you can do anything to stop me . . .'

'Don't touch her,' Vickram said.

I struggled to my feet, hanging on to the branch of a tree as he tore away my T-shirt, exposing me. He yanked the T-shirt again, pulling me to the ground and rolling me over like a sack of grain.

'Let me go, please,' I begged.

Then I heard Vickram's voice near me. He spoke calmly, but his words terrified me. 'Forgive me, Baboo,' he said. 'We shouldn't be getting so worked up about her.'

'That's right,' said Baboo. 'There's enough of her for both of us.' He drew his sword from the sheath at his belt. 'We'll cut her in two. Ha ha!'

Vickram didn't flinch. 'Why don't you do this right, Baboo? She's not married. Marry her first!'

Baboo sniggered. 'I bet ten *lakhs* I do marry her,' he said. He must have thought the idea of marrying me funny in some perverse way.

'If it's a matter of money, I'll give you twenty *lakhs* to let her go.'

'I'll give you forty *lakhs*, but I'm keeping her! I'm not letting a girl of your caste get away, mallah. I'm keeping her. I can do whatever I like with her, and she's only good for one thing . . .'

'Let's go to the temple, and then you can marry her. We'll make a nice wedding for you.'

Baboo laughed. 'All right.' He let me go.

Once again, I had been spared, though I still couldn't understand why. It was bewildering. For a moment, I even forgot my fear.

Vickram seemed to be the cleverer of the two. Baboo was nothing but an ignorant ogre who wanted to prove that he could do whatever he liked with me. Vickram's men were mainly all mallahs, plus a few members of other low castes. There seemed to be about a dozen of them, and just as many thakurs. Vickram's men didn't run around the villages looking for women to rape, like Baboo Gujar's men, but the two gangs had apparently joined forces. They travelled by night, stopping at villages for supplies and lying low during the day to rest. They had everything worked out. There were villages where they were safe, where they could find food, and in these villages they handed out some of their loot. And there were other villages where they plundered the houses of the rich and raped the women.

The next day, as we were passing by a village named Madhapur, the ogre saw a girl by the road and asked her for a drink of water. She looked like the daughter of a Brahmin, she was thin but pretty, perhaps twelve or thirteen years old. She went away and naïvely came back with a pot of water, as I might once have done. We were just passing that village, we hadn't come there to pillage, and the girl was no threat to the men. But that didn't matter. Baboo raped her right there.

Vickram had gone somewhere with his men, leaving Bare Lal there with me. Two thakurs crowded around me so I couldn't see what Baboo was doing. Afterwards, we waited for hours as Baboo's men rampaged through the village in broad daylight. Most of the villagers had fled in panic, but there were still some in hiding. I sat on a khat by the wall of an empty house, flanked by the two thakurs, waiting for Baboo and his men to return, listening to shrieks and moans and occasional rifleshots. The sounds made the thakurs restless. They teased me but didn't dare touch me for fear of Baboo.

When Vickram finally returned, Bare Lal explained what had been going on. 'Baboo raped a girl again and the others ransacked the village looking for more.'

Vickram shook his head. 'He'll pay for it. Sooner or later, someone will do it to his own mother.'

The two guards didn't like to hear this. 'Don't talk about Baboo like that. Do you want us to tell him?'

Vickram paid no heed to them. I had noticed that he spoke only to Baboo, and he seemed to be furious with him this time. He took the megaphone and used it to summon the gang, shouting that the police were on their way. Instantly, the men came running from every direction, some still clutching their trousers.

Vickram grabbed my hand and we headed off into the nearby forest as the rest of the gang followed, scattering through the trees. The men regrouped again on a road by a bridge that crossed the Yamuna. There was a sign pointing to Auraiya, but we took the opposite direction. As we ran, I noticed a frightening painting of Kali, the black goddess, on the garden wall of a temple. Kali, like Durga, has the power to destroy, to slay demons. I fell on my knees in front of her, begging her to save me from these demon dacoits! She wore a necklace of human skulls and her arms waved, brandishing swords and daggers. But the arms I felt picking me up belonged to one of the demons, who was telling me we couldn't stay outside; it wasn't safe on the road.

The entire gang swarmed through the doorway into the grounds and then into the temple. I was paralysed, thinking they were going to marry me to the ogre right there. I couldn't go in. I collapsed against the wall outside, feeling as though I was about to vomit, but I couldn't vomit. There was nothing in my belly but fear.

Baboo wouldn't leave me there. 'I'll kill you, I'll cut off your nose, I'll gouge your eyes out if you try to run away!'

Bharat told me not to be scared.

'Help me, Bharat, help me! I want to die. Let me go and find a well to drown in. There must be a well near here!'

He was short and chubby, with a dark face, and he smiled consolingly when he saw the tears running down my cheeks. 'Don't do that, Baboo will kill me! He will hold me responsible!'

I just shook my head. 'Even if I survive, my life is ruined.'

There was no wedding. It was still daytime and the bandits were too nervous about being near the road. They made their offerings to Kali and we left in a hurry. We scattered in the jungle again, moving without a halt as night fell. It must have been almost dawn by the time the men came together and finally stopped in a clearing to rest.

In the dark, I could hear the noise of a pump not far away, which I knew meant there was a well somewhere . . .

Baboo's men stretched a tarpaulin across some stakes, creating a shelter to protect their chief from the rain. They spread a groundsheet underneath for him to sleep on and gave him his cushion. The rest of the men slept under the trees, on the bare ground, with only their rucksacks for pillows. It was cold and the earth was damp, but Baboo settled down comfortably in his makeshift tent.

He clicked his fingers. 'I don't want to sleep alone. Bring me the girl.'

Vickram was still sitting up, with one of his brown cigarettes in his hand. 'You should get some sleep,' he said to Baboo. 'Tomorrow you're going to marry her. You'll need your strength.'

'Shut up, you! I want her now!'

I heard Vickram's voice in the dark, telling me to do as Baboo said. 'Obey him. Go in there and lie down with him . . .'

I began to sob.

Vickram nodded. Reluctantly, I got up and went into the tent, where I lay down, still sobbing, beside Baboo. He raised himself up on one elbow and inspected me with his hideous eye.

'Aaah!' he growled. 'What a pretty little hussy she is!'

He began to fondle me with his large, disgusting hands. I closed my eyes and prayed to Durga to whisper in my ear when the moment was right to flee.

I heard Vickram outside the tent. 'Are you going to marry her tomorrow?'

'Eh? Yes. Of course I will.'

'That's what you say now, but I bet you won't do it.'

'Shut up and get me a cigarette.'

I heard Vickram walking off and felt the weight of the ogre's body on me. Then I heard Vickram returning, but there was a sudden silence outside the tent.

I opened my eyes and saw Vickram and Bare Lal in the tent. Baboo was on top of me and he hadn't seen them. 'Where's my cigarette?' he growled.

Vickram was carrying his rifle. 'You miserable dog! Get up from her, or it's not a cigarette I will give you but a bullet in the back of the head.'

The ogre scrabbled frantically to get up but his legs were twisted around mine. Vickram fired.

I screamed. I thought I was dead. I heard two more shots, and I felt something warm touch me. It was blood!

'I'm dead,' I screamed, 'I'm dead!'

I tried desperately to crawl from under him. Somebody tried to pull me out. They lifted the ogre's body but he fell forward on his belly with a thud. My legs were still pinned under him, I was unable to get up. I heard the cracks of more rifleshots outside the tent. There were shouts and the sounds of people running, and then silence again.

When I finally managed to get out of the tent, I saw corpses lying everywhere. Four of Baboo Gujar's men were dead, all his lieutenants, and two more had been shot as they tried to flee. I ran as fast as I could in the direction of the well, and when I reached it I plunged my hands in the bucket of water, sobbing with shock as I washed the ogre's blood from my neck. In the distance I could see shadows jerking with glee, doing a mad dance. It was Vickram and his men kicking the ogre's corpse.

Death had brushed close by me, leaving a repulsive smell of blood and burnt flesh in my nostrils. Since I had been with them, I had grown used to the bandits shooting in the air. It was a noise like the fireworks during the Diwali festival. But this time, the noise of the rifleshot right next to my ear had been like thunder, and the smell of gunpowder so strong I thought I was the one who had died. My blouse was drenched in blood and sweat, and I saw a shadow coming towards me, somebody tall, with a moustache.

It was Bare Lal. 'It's over,' he said. 'Come.'

His fierce expression turned to a smile.

'What about the rest of them?' I asked.

'They ran away like rats,' he said triumphantly.

Vickram was sitting next to the ogre's corpse, writing something on a scrap of paper by the light of his torch.

'What is he doing, Phoopha?' I asked Bare Lal. I was still trembling, and addressed him as uncle out of respectful fear.

'He's writing that Baboo was killed in the name of Phoolan Devi. It's the rule.'

He folded the piece of paper and slid it into the dead ogre's shirt pocket, then he laid Baboo's rifle on his lifeless chest and put his sword across it in his hand. Loot from the day before was bulging from Baboo's pockets. Vickram didn't touch it.

The rest of the thakurs had fled, but Vickram's men were all there. They had dived for cover when the shooting started and now they emerged from hiding and began to congratulate Vickram, saying they had all had enough of this dog who raped or bullied everyone. There were around twenty of them. Fifteen were mallahs, there were two Brahmins, and some who belonged to a caste of leatherworkers called chamars. For Vickram's men, Baboo was more than just an embarrassment; he gave them a bad reputation, and bandits, I was beginning to learn, depended on goodwill. They needed people they could rely on for information and villagers willing to supply them with food.

They had been planning the ambush for days, using me to distract the ogre and waiting for their moment. I was the bait for their trap. Because of me, they were able to take him by surprise. It didn't matter to me for a moment that I could have died too . . . Vickram the mallah had succeeded in avenging the insults of Baboo the thakur.

We left the scene of the massacre and headed off into the night at an exhausting pace until we came to a vast lake. Everyone threw themselves down to wash their faces and hands. Fear finally loosened its grip on my stomach. My heart stopped pounding. I knew that these were dangerous men. Vickram had killed Baboo just like that. Bare Lal had killed one man, Bharat had shot another, Raghu Nath and

Madhav had each killed a man, and I still didn't know what they had in store for me, but I didn't care. I washed the ogre's blood from my clothes. The night air was cold but refreshing, like the water of the lake.

I turned to Bare Lal. 'Phoopha,' I said. 'I'm hungry!'

'There will be food when we reach the village. It isn't far.'

The sun was up by the time we got there. The village was bustling and Vickram immediately began handing out rupees, announcing that Baboo was dead.

'Hurrah! Long live Vickram!' the villagers cheered.

They were all mallahs, happy to be rid of the ogre who raped their wives and daughters. It seemed as if the entire village crowded around Vickram wanting to touch him in gratitude. Someone draped a garland around his shoulders as though he was a god. I heard him ask one of his men if I had eaten yet. They pointed at me. I was sitting a little way off eating dal and chapatis.

'Good,' he said.

I hoped he would let me go at last. I asked his uncle.

Bare Lal made a face. 'He has killed in your name, Phoolan. You owe him your life. You must obey him now. Who knows what he will ask of you. You must be patient.'

Vickram still hadn't spoken to me directly. But I sensed he was watching me. Why, I didn't know, nor did I care. He had saved me from humiliation and perhaps death. He was the first man who had ever been able to defend me. My father had only ever cried and begged impotently. Even if I was only the bait for their ambush, Vickram had avenged me! Even if I had to die, I thanked Durga and Kali and all the gods and goddesses for this one satisfaction.

Vickram was the first man to treat me like a human being, not a slave, or a piece of flesh. If he let me go, I resolved to request one more kindness from him. 'Brother,' I decided I

would ask him, 'avenge me of Mayadin. Deliver me from
that demon. Make the people of my village treat me like a
human being too. Tell them Phoolan Devi is not a pariah.
Give me the taste of victory, as I have given it to you . . .'

20

News of Baboo Gujar's death spread rapidly along the Yamuna. In a village called Asta, all the women came out and garlanded Vickram. 'It was a good thing you did,' they said. 'A pity it took so long!' Everybody seemed to like him. They said he was courageous and fair, he had never mistreated a woman and he gave money to the poor . . . But he frightened me nonetheless. I had seen him kill Baboo and his lieutenants in cold blood.

The memory of that brutal slaughter made me shiver. In the villages, death came in fevers from diseases or snakebites, and in childbirth. But I had never witnessed violent death, I had never seen a human body go suddenly limp like that, never smelled the singed flesh of a gunshot wound. And I had witnessed it amid such a torrent of my own fears that it would be carved in my mind for all time. Baboo had been rutting like an animal, groaning and panting. He lived only to rape, all he thought about was rape – until his head exploded. But I had escaped him. He hadn't been able to rape me. I was the last woman he had seen, and the only one he hadn't been able to possess. And what was even more satisfying, I had been the agent of his death.

I exulted in a new and powerful emotion, the satisfaction of dealing out justice. I felt as though I was walking in early morning sunshine, after the mist clears over the river. Once I was free, I decided, I wouldn't go back to my village, so that my family would no longer be persecuted. I would go and help Rukmini with her children.

The bandits had told me to wait in the boat that was tied up on the Yamuna. Vickram was able to hire the services of certain mallah ferrymen without a problem. He didn't take the boat or terrorise them, he just paid the usual fee. The large wooden boat rocked gently on the calm, shimmering water. The sand was grey here, not like the yellow sand near my village, and there were no kachwaris. The river here ran through a narrow valley. The hillsides were dry, covered in scrub and dotted with a few trees. The soft sunlight sparkled on the water. How many days had it been since I was kidnapped by dacoits? I wondered. It might have been five or six days, I couldn't even begin to recall. Time passed differently with them. They lived by night as much as by day, eating in different places, at any time of day, sleeping wherever they could, in clearings in the forest or in the fields, and always moving, never turning back. The bandits had no courtyards to sweep out, no wheat to grind for chapatis, no cows to mind, no planting or harvesting to do. A few days before I had been afraid of them, but now I was almost proud to see all the villagers honouring them.

Two of the men were keeping lookout in the boat with me while the others had gone to the temple. Exhausted from all these emotions, all these thoughts, and with the boat rocking gently on the water, I dozed off.

I woke with a start. Bare Lal had returned with news: 'We have chosen to stay with Mastana. All the men agreed! He is our leader! Now he wants to see you. He asked us what we ought to do with you and we decided he should keep you!'

A shiver of fear ran through me.

Bare Lal and the two men who were guarding me brought me to the doorway of the temple and made me sit down. Vickram was sitting on a step and the rest of the men were all sitting around him. He was younger than most of them, perhaps twenty-five years old, but even his uncle treated him with great respect. He was also the thinnest of all of them. I had never seen him close up in the daylight before. He didn't look very strong. He was pale-skinned, and his long black hair was still wet from bathing. He was wearing a police uniform with his cartridge belt slung across his chest and his rifle, the one that had killed Baboo, strapped to his shoulder. He had a white cotton cloth tied across his brow.

His black eyes narrowed on me. I saw that they were ringed with fatigue. 'Do you like me?'

Nobody had ever asked me such a question. Surprise and embarrassment made me lower my head. I blushed with confusion. I had no idea what to answer.

Around me, the others began laughing, teasing me and making remarks I didn't understand. I giggled, and I began to cry. I couldn't help myself. I was disappointed and excited all at once. I had expected him to say I was free to go, perhaps even to bring me back in triumph, but I was still his prisoner, and I had no idea what he meant by his question.

He came towards me and stroked my hair gently. 'Don't cry,' he said. 'Why are you crying? I'm not going to hurt you.'

His gesture was new to me as well. Nobody other than my mother and father had ever shown me tenderness. No one had ever touched me like that, certainly no man.

'Well, Phoolan, do you like me?'

I tried to smile at him through my tears.

The gang seemed to be encouraging him.

'Keep her, Mastana! Give her lots of love, so she forgets all the rest! Give her lots of love!'

And I thought it must have been something sweet and delicious because they said it would make me forget the bad things that had happened to me.

Often I didn't understand the words they used. I thought they were all better-spoken than me, but in fact my dialect was different from theirs, and in towns like Orai the dialect spoken was different again. The judge, the lawyer and the prison guard had all used words I didn't understand. In my village we spoke Bhundelkhandi, and Vickram spoke a dialect called Chaurasi. Many of the words were different, and I had trouble understanding him. I didn't know the word love in their dialect. I thought it must be something to eat – because it was something you gave, something sweet and delicious from the way they said it. But I understood his gestures . . .

He sat down in front of me and wiped the tears away from my cheeks with his hand. 'I know everything that happened to you. I know what the thakurs did. Do you still hate them?'

'I don't even know who they were.'

'Then forget the past. With us, nothing like that will ever happen again.'

The others were silent now. They must have felt sorry for me.

'Poor girl,' said Bare Lal, 'look how she's crying!'

His pity for me made the tears flood again.

I felt strange – happy, but still frightened. A man had touched me softly, he had stroked my hair and touched my cheeks. A hand had caressed me like my poor father's hand, but a hand with the strength he never had. I felt I could trust him, something I had never felt about a stranger or a man before. Gradually, I stopped sobbing, and my tears dried. If I stayed with him, perhaps I would be happy: no more beatings, no more pain, no more humiliation.

'Tell me how you feel about me? Do you think I'm worthy of you?'

I laughed at his question. The men in my village all wanted the women to respect them, but they never asked them if they deserved it. The women would surely have answered no.

'Don't laugh. Be serious! You must say it in front of everyone. Say it! They want to hear it from your lips . . .'

'Go on,' said one of the men, 'say it! If you don't we'll never get anywhere. Do you like him or not, yes or no?'

Vickram's uncle told me not to be afraid. 'If you don't like him, we'll work something out so you can stay here, but you won't have to live with him. Tell us.'

I took a deep breath. 'Yes, I like him.'

'Louder!'

'YES, I LIKE HIM.'

'Again!'

'No. You're making fun of me!'

They all began to laugh. 'Okay,' Vickram said. 'That's enough.'

He had kidnapped me from my family; there was no one else to protect me but Mastana.

He sent some men to get provisions and the rest of us returned to the boat.

When the men joined us, the others saw they were carrying paper bags full of cakes and sweets. The festivities began. They fired shots in the air and began to sing wedding songs, but Vickram stopped them.

'Wait! First you must all make a vow. You must swear that I am your leader and you will obey me. You will never try to harm me and you will treat this woman as though she was your mother or your sister. Swear it!'

Each of the men leant over the river and took up the sacred water in their cupped hands. 'I swear that Vickram is my leader,' each of them said. And they opened their hands to let the water return to the river. The men repeated the gesture. 'I swear to treat Phoolan as my sister, and anyone who breaks this oath shall die.'

They had brought garlands of red and white flowers for the ceremony, and plenty of food, and we headed off down the river and back into the jungle. Vickram wanted music and all the things that made a real marriage, but I protested.

'I can't marry you. I was already married when I was little.'

'Don't ever say that! You aren't married. Don't ever mention your first marriage. I am your first husband!'

He hung a garland of marigolds around my neck, and then I hung one around his neck. He made the mark of *teeka* on my forehead. The vermilion dot meant I was married. In the shade of a large banyan tree, with only my new family of outlaws as witnesses, Phoolan Devi had married a dacoit! There was no *baraat*, no temple, no music, just shouts of joy in the jungle, and rifleshots that scattered all the parrots from the trees and scared away the jackals.

The sun went down over the river. I had gone through the ceremony without saying much; intimidated by the simple ritual, and I had the funny feeling it was all a dream. Although he was kind to me, Vickram intimidated me most of all the men in the gang, especially after Bare Lal had replied to my question about love with a chuckle.

'Can you eat love? You don't eat love, Phoolan, you make it!' he had exclaimed. 'A man and woman together, you know? That is what giving love means. It has nothing to do with sweets you eat.'

Love was complicated, I decided. When I thought I loved my bullock that was one thing; when Vickram asked me if I liked him, it was something else, and when Uncle Bare Lal laughed and said love was what a man and a woman made together, that was something else entirely! I had only ever known violence, and love made me very afraid . . .

The sun had gone down and it was time to leave the banks of the river, where there were too few trees for cover.

We climbed back in the boat and set off towards Raipur, where we tied up the boat. Vickram told the men to go back into hiding in the forest, except Madhav who was to come with us to get food and supplies. He announced to me that we were going to visit his family: his uncle and his grandfather lived there, he said.

But it was just a pretext. There was neither an uncle nor a grandfather in the village. Vickram had wanted us to be alone. After Madhav left with the food for the men, he took me to a little house near the woods on the edge of the village, a rich person's house built of concrete. The house did belong to a member of his family, but it was a cousin, not his uncle.

He introduced me. 'This is Phoolan, your relative. I have just married her!'

The people in the house greeted me warmly. I could hardly see them in the light from the oil-lamps, but there were three or four men. I lowered my eyes. I had no sari to cover my head.

'It's a good thing, Vickram.'

'She is going to sleep. She's very tired.'

He led me upstairs, where there was one small room, with a wooden bed, a blanket and a stool in the corner. I was nervous about what would happen next. But at least we were in a village, I thought, and there were people downstairs. I was relieved when Vickram went back downstairs to talk with them.

I could hear his deep voice below as I fell asleep, in a slumber so profound I didn't even remember where I was when he woke me. I sat up with a start.

Everything flooded back. 'Has your grandfather come?' I asked.

'No.'

'Where is he? Is he coming?'

'Let's just say I'm the grandfather. We're married now

and we're going to live together. The others won't always be with us, you see.'

I was wide awake again. I was married, I remembered, but what did this marriage mean? Was it some kind of charade, or was I really married? What was his family going to say about me? I couldn't hear a sound downstairs. The others must have left. I was alone with him, and anxious now.

'You ought to take off your uniform.' He handed me a lunghi to change into.

'No . . . I can't in front of you.'

'Okay, I'll go downstairs.'

A lunghi is a man's garment and I couldn't see how to put it on properly. I had to make do with wrapping it around me, and I sat there waiting on the bed in the dark. There were no windows in the room. If it was a real marriage, I would have to obey him, but what if it wasn't? What was I going to do there all alone with this man? I wondered.

He came back and sat on the bed beside me as he took my hand. 'Don't worry, I'm not going to hurt you. Are you afraid?'

'Yes,' I said. I told him I was afraid of all the men in his gang.

'Why? We are married now. They were the ones who suggested it, and they were our witnesses.'

'My parents will beat me for it.'

'We shall go to see your parents and ask them for their blessings. Don't you realise you're married now? Don't you understand? I married you for life, and you're lucky to be married! Baboo did terrible things to other girls and they will never find husbands . . .'

'Why do men misbehave like that?' I asked. 'Why did you kidnap me?'

'What happened is what happened. Forget about the past. Tell me about your in-laws. Who were they? Which village?'

I didn't dare. The memories were buried deep, far away and long ago.

'I will take revenge on all the people who hurt you or mistreated you. Don't be afraid, tell me yourself what happened.'

I told him. I said I was just a child, and he was old and evil. I told him that the name of the village was Maheshpur. I told him what had happened there. I told him everything.

'You swear it's true?

I swore it.

'Right. Forget it now. Forget the past . . . Do you like me?'

'Yes, I like you.'

'Can I lie down beside you?'

'Oh no! The people here will punish me!'

'But I brought you here so they could see you! I wanted them to know you are my wife. Why would they want to punish you?'

I told him about Mayadin, about the Sarpanch's son, the police, the thakurs who came all the time to my village looking for me.

'Is it true you were raped?'

I could only lower my head. I couldn't speak. I wanted to hide my face, vanish from his sight. I began to cry.

'I know . . . Don't say any more. Don't tell anyone else, ever. You have had enough pain. It is good to tell me and you must listen to me now. You must do what I tell you, me and nobody else. If I say something and you listen to me and do it, everything will be fine. And you must never tell anybody about what we do, the places we hide, otherwise I will beat you. But right now just listen to me. I'm not going to force you, I'm not angry, I don't want to hurt you. If you like me, if you want me, one day you will tell me of your own free will. Stay here on the bed, I'll sleep on the floor next to you. Don't be afraid, Phoolan . . .'

'I'm not afraid. You can sleep on the bed, I'm not afraid,' I said. 'Stay here beside me, but not too close.'

We had been talking for hours and my head was heavy and my eyes were burning with fatigue. I had never talked to anyone like that before, for such a long time. I had never talked to anyone at all. It was always orders: come here, do that, shut up. Or insults. Talking was new to me, saying what was on your mind or in your heart, saying the things that choked you, expressing the pain that twisted your heart.

It was sweetly painful to be able to talk without shame or fear to this man I hardly knew, whom my family didn't know, who had kidnapped me from them. He was respected by so many people, and he was so handsome, that I couldn't believe he belonged to my community. And that I belonged to him now.

He kissed me, the first time a man had done that. It was the first time a man had asked if I was afraid, if I was happy.

I didn't know if this moment of calm and security was called love. But many years later, thinking about it, I would ask myself why didn't this man, if he loved me as he said, just let me go? Then I wouldn't have become a bandit like him. I would have had a family, children, cattle in the shed, a fire in the hearth.

Or I would have died, and none of it would have mattered.

21

Did I want to go home? No.

Did I believe in God again? Yes.

Did I have hope for life? Yes.

But to tell a man I loved him . . .

No, I couldn't say it. I couldn't bring myself to believe I belonged to him, that he was going to protect me.

I had told him I was sleepy, but I couldn't sleep. I lay with my eyes wide open, staring in the dark. He had promised he wouldn't hurt me, but he was stronger than me, and he was a man, and a man for me meant rape. Talking with him, I had been able to forget, but whenever he came close to me, I instinctively withdrew. I couldn't help myself. It was going to take more than one night to rebuild my trust. And I was still his prisoner.

As I lay there, I tried to comprehend why this man was being tender with me while all the others had only wanted to humiliate me. I was just a poor simple little peasant, naïve and uneducated, and he knew how to read and write, and survive in the jungle. I knew very well that he was in control of my destiny, even if he had said that if I didn't want to live in the jungle, we could go and live in a town. It was too much to believe, too much to hope for.

The world was still full of menace for me, and I made my way in it as best I could, taking each new step in terror. I was sixteen years old, and I had been a woman only since the last monsoon, but I had already been wed twice, and survived more pain than any of the other women of my family. My mother had never had to suffer at the hands of my father. He was never violent, and she was the one who decided everything for him. Rukmini wasn't afraid of men, Choti laughed about them, and Bhuri was too young to know. I thought of the insults I had been showered with: I was a bad girl, a loose woman, a bitch and a whore. I had been to prison, bringing shame on my family and my village. But I had brought none of it on myself. Putti Lal had abandoned me. I had done nothing except claim what was ours from Mayadin.

I slept finally, so deeply and for so long that the sun was already high when I woke. Vickram had already bathed. He was dressed and sitting on the stool, reading. I had been woken by the sound of voices. Bare Lal and Madhav had arrived. They were in high spirits.

'You're still asleep?' asked Bare Lal. 'Time to get up!'

'Did you sleep well in that bed?' joked Madhav.

They both laughed. And then they noticed my jewellery – a watch and a necklace Vickram had given me the night before. It was a gold necklace. 'I didn't steal it,' he had said to me solemnly. 'I borrowed the money from my father and I had it bought in town for you.' I didn't even know how to tell the time with a watch. As for the necklace, it was the first time I had ever worn gold. The ring I wore in my nose was made of silver, and my bangles were made of plastic.

Bare Lal examined all my finery and laughed even louder.

'Are you the big dacoit who stole all that?'

'Don't speak to her like that!' Vickram told his uncle.

Bare Lal frowned. 'All right. Sorry. We must go now before the police come. We've been here twenty-four hours. It's too long.'

'Not yet,' said Vickram. 'I have to pay a visit first . . .'

*

We went without the rest of the gang, just the four of us in the boat, to a village called Bejamau, a large village with many small, mud-walled houses and a few larger houses made of concrete, just like my village. People of many different castes lived there, though most were jatavs. Vickram took my hand and led me down the main path through the village, past the well where women were gathered with pots on their heads, stopping in front of a small house.

'Amma,' he said with a chuckle as he pushed open the wooden door, 'meet Phoolan, your new daughter!'

There were five women sitting there in the yard in front of me and I didn't know which of them was his mother. I tried to pull my hand out of his – it was impolite to hold hands like that in front of his family – but that just made him laugh, and he took my hand again.

'Buppa this is Phoolan, your new daughter.'

His father examined me in silence. He was still young, much younger than my father. Then a very old woman bowed down in front of Vickram and touched his feet.

'Phoolan, this is my mother-in-law.'

I didn't understand right away. I was still too embarrassed about him holding my hand in front of all these strangers, and uncomfortable about the way I was dressed. I was wearing trousers and a man's shirt in front of all the women in saris; I couldn't even cover my head. Then I realised. His mother-in-law! That meant he was already married . . .

One of the women was bouncing a child on her knee. The woman was young, and very pretty, and the child must have been about two or three years old, a little girl so sweet I had trouble taking my eyes from her. She had the same fine features and pale colouring as Vickram!

'Is that your little sister,' I asked him, 'or your daughter?'

'I don't know. Who knows?'

He was making jokes about it! The little girl's mother

smiled at me. She seemed happy too, and not at all embarrassed, unlike me. Vickram introduced me.

'Rajeshwari, do you know who this is?'

'No.'

'This is Phoolan. She is my wife.'

I was sure the young woman had been kidnapped like me, and that he was making fun of her.

Pretending I urgently needed to relieve myself, I tried to run away as soon as I got outside the house. But Uncle Bare Lal was there talking with some people. He was surprised to see me and caught hold of me.

'Where are you going, Phoolan? What's the matter?'

'Leave me alone. Don't speak to me!'

How many other women had he kidnapped like that? Rajeshwari was older than me, perhaps twenty years old, and prettier, a thin little doll with nice light skin. Did this mean he had a wife in every village? Did he have children everywhere he went? How many of us were there?

His uncle wouldn't let go of me. 'You mustn't go anywhere alone. You shouldn't leave the house.'

'I want to go to the toilet.'

'There is a room in the house. Use the pot.'

'Leave me alone! Who are you to tell me where to go? I can go where I please!'

I was sitting in the boat with my arms folded in displeasure. Madhav was the first to find me. I saw his dark face peering over the side of the boat with surprise. There was childish amusement all over his rough dacoit features. Vickram was behind him, still in high spirits. He seemed to think it was comical too.

'Come, I'll introduce you properly . . .'

'No! You're a wicked man. How many women have you kidnapped and ruined like this? And why are you laughing at me?'

With both hands, he grabbed me around my waist and lifted me out of the boat.

'Let me go! Leave me alone!'

People watched us with astonishment. But Madhav had realised what I was talking about and tried to explain. 'You don't get it. She's his first wife! He was married when he was very young to this girl. You mustn't hate her. You mustn't be angry with him. Come!'

'No. Leave me alone! I'm staying right here.'

Vickram had to go and get his wife to explain it to me. The poor girl had tears in her eyes. 'You are my sister now. Why are you angry with me? I have nothing against you. I'm very lucky. From today, I'm giving you my husband. Stop behaving like this. Think of me! If you don't like me, Vickram will be angry with me.'

I was embarrassed, and the more she pleaded the more embarrassed I became. All the villagers had gathered there, and they were sitting under a banyan tree watching us. My temper only seemed to amuse them. 'She is Vickram's new wife?' they asked. 'Where did he find her?' Yes, it was me, Phoolan, and I felt stupid. Beyond my family and my village, I knew nothing. I lost my temper and got angry about things I didn't understand. Rajeshwari seemed good-natured, and it wasn't unusual for a man to have two wives, especially if he married young the first time and if he could afford to support them. I wasn't exactly happy with the idea, but that's how it was. Vickram had done nothing wrong.

'I wanted everyone to know we were married,' he said. 'I didn't want to keep it a secret from my family.'

I told him I understood, finally. It was hard for me to suddenly find myself in another community, where life was different. Vickram's family were mallahs, but they weren't as poor as my family. Their house was made of bricks and concrete, and they had a large courtyard with plenty of rooms for them and for their cattle. They had enough to eat, and there was plenty more stored in their house. I wasn't used to it. Compared to my family, these mallahs lived like thakurs. Vickram had been to school. There was no Mayadin to beat them or demean them, and no thakurs to make them toil like slaves for nothing. They didn't have to live in dread, they could laugh and joke and discuss things openly. In my house, we were beaten before we could explain, we cried before we could speak, and the only thought we had when we woke in the morning was where we would find enough to eat that day.

After a meal with the whole family, a plentiful meal with piles of chapatis and heapings of dal, we prepared to leave. Vickram's mother-in-law gave me a present, two hundred rupees, and the others each gave me notes of five or twenty rupees. They put their hands together in prayer for our happiness and bowed to touch my feet. The women even stroked my hair in admiration.

Just before we departed, Vickram picked up his little daughter and said, 'Look, it's your new Amma! Say goodbye!'

The little child had the same straight nose, the same warm, large eyes, and the same pale skin. She had beautiful thick black hair. She ran after me and tried to climb up my trousers, calling me her Amma. It would be nice, I thought, to have children one day, like everyone else. I wondered what the little girl's mother really thought of me. I hoped she had at least found me pretty, and worthy of Vickram. But what did the others think? They had asked nothing about my family or my village. Vickram had simply said, 'I'm married to her.' It was as if I had come from nowhere. Though it had been just days since I last saw them, my parents, my sisters and brother, Mayadin's field of hora, the Nadi, the cows, all of that, seemed far away.

After we left there, we returned to the temple, not far away, at a place called Ghatapara, to see the holy man covered in ashes. Vickram prostrated himself before the sadhu, and recounted the circumstances of Baboo Gujar's death.

'You have done a good thing,' said the sadhu through his devotee. 'You should have killed that demon a long time back!'

Then he opened his eyes that burned like coals in that white face and spoke to me.

'You have vanquished the demon, you are the incarnation of Kali the goddess herself!'

The words of the sadhu were a blessing from the gods whom I thought had abandoned me when I was sent to prison. Before, I had searched everywhere for God. I used to go to the temple with Buppa to pray and ask for blessings. But inside that police lock-up I thought all the gods had abandoned me. I had wept at my fate and cursed them for letting me be punished unjustly. It was the others who should have been punished, the ones who always wanted to hurt me, but nothing ever happened to them . . .

I went down to the edge of the river to bathe, to purify myself before I returned to pray in the temple. God had not abandoned me! I wasn't alone in the world. He was looking after me. I prayed for a long time. I thanked God for delivering me from the demon, for giving me the strength to survive, and for sending me someone to defend me.

I was going to walk at his side through the jungle, eat and sleep peacefully at his side, and forget, if I could.

Reunited with the men we left the cover of the jungle to cross a plain where many peasants were camped in tents. A dam was being built not far from there and the people were using the earth churned up by the gigantic machines to make bricks.

'Who are you?' one of the peasants shouted. 'Get lost!'

Madhav grabbed him by the neck. 'We're Vickram's gang! Now, what's the name of that village over there?'

'Maheshpur.'

I remembered that name. 'That's my in-laws' village,' I said. 'It's where he locked me up and beat me!'

But I couldn't remember the house. I had tried so hard to forget. All I could recall was the piles of wood outside for the fire. As we headed towards the village, Vickram asked people if they knew someone named Putti Lal.

It wasn't long before a man replied that he knew him. 'Show us where he lives,' said Vickram, 'and then make yourself scarce!'

It was here that I had been tortured for the first time. The man whose memory still gave me nightmares lived in this village. But when Vickram said I would be able to do whatever I liked with him now, even strangle him with my bare hands if I wished, I began to tremble with fear. Vengeance was something I had craved with my whole being, but when the possibility of tasting it was suddenly handed to me, it was too abrupt. I wasn't prepared. The thought of Vickram's men ransacking his house filled me with glee, but I shrank from the idea of exacting revenge myself.

Vickram seized me by the arm and shook me. 'It's now or never. Tonight you're going to become a real dacoit!' He kicked the door down and barged into the courtyard. 'Where is Putti Lal?' he demanded.

An elderly man emerged from his house and rashly answered, 'It's me. I'm Putti Lal.'

It was him. He looked older than I remembered. He was wearing rumpled pyjamas and slippers, and seemed half-asleep. The men looked at him doubtfully. 'That's the one?' they asked me. They thought he looked more like someone's father or grandfather.

'Did you marry Phoolan Devi?' Vickram asked.

'Yes.'

'Let's see if you really know her. What was she like?'

'Oh, she was very wicked, a real little whore!'

I was standing behind Vickram and I heard what he said. The blood began to throb in my head. The evil dog hadn't realised what was about to happen to him. He was looking at Vickram with a satisfied smile. He must have thought Vickram's men were police.

'So you are the bloody dog! You married an eleven-year-old girl and you dare to say she was a whore? You were thirty-five years old, a widower!'

He stepped aside and shone his torch on my face.

'Here she is, Phoolan Devi! Recognise her?'

Before he could reply, Vickram's men jumped him. They dragged him out in the street and started beating him with their lathis.

'What is Phoolan like?' they kept asking him. 'What is she?'

They beat him mercilessly, as he had beaten me. I heard his bones cracking, and saw him spitting out his broken teeth as he pleaded with them to stop. Meanwhile, I wanted to find the woman, the one who had punished me for nothing and starved me half to death. I was going to deal with her myself! But I couldn't find her anywhere. I did find some things my mother had given Putti Lal, some pots and utensils, and I found the cow my parents had given as part of my dowry. I led the cow out of the house, but Vickram stopped me.

'We can't take the animal with us. It is better just to give this bastard a bloody good hiding, to teach him not to call you a little whore.'

Vickram walked off and cut a thick branch from a neem in the street in front of the house. He handed it to me. 'It's your turn now. Go on.'

The men had tied his hands behind his back, as he had once done to me. The little whore remembered everything he had done now: what he had tried to do with his knife, how he had molested me and raped me, how he had put his serpent in my hand, in my mouth. And how he had struck me when I screamed with fear, how he had crushed me with his fat body when I tried to get away . . .

I did it to him now. For the first time, I beat someone the way they had beaten me. I had the power. All the men were behind me, cheering me on. I beat him harder and harder, driven half mad to be able finally to quench my thirst for vengeance!

The crop made from a neem branch wasn't as vicious as a lathi, but it tore his clothes and seared his skin, leaving long red weals. I flailed at the serpent that had made me so afraid. I whipped it until it died.

'Are you going to do that again?' I shrieked at him.

I crushed his serpent. I stabbed him in the crotch with the stick the way he had tried to stab me and I jumped on his serpent and crushed it!

Vickram threw his head back and laughed at my madness. 'Talk about a beating! Did you see what she just did?'

He groaned, trying to plead for mercy, begging me to forgive him. The men were still cheering me on: 'Kill him! Kill the bastard! Go on!'

He covered his head with his arms and rolled at my feet, to touch them. He croaked, trying to call for help, but he had no voice left. 'Don't come near!' shouted the men. 'Let her finish it. It's Phoolan Devi chastising her bastard dog of a husband!'

None of the villagers showed their faces in any case, apart from a few who must have had something against him as they joined in with the gang's cries of encouragement.

Vickram picked him up by the scruff of the neck. He was

still whimpering for us to have mercy on him, as I had whimpered. Blood was streaming down his face. Two of the men held him there while Vickram waited for him to open his eyes.

'I am the husband of Phoolan Devi! Do you hear me? If you ever say it's you again, I will kill you! Are you the husband of Phoolan Devi?'

'No. No.'

'Did you torture her?'

'Yes. I did.'

'Did you abandon her?'

'Yes, it was me who brought her back.'

'What is she like?'

'She is a goddess, a good woman. I am the guilty one. It was all my fault!'

He was almost naked now, with his pyjamas ripped to shreds and blood all over his crotch. The men released him and he crumpled to the ground, but the rage that had been loosed in me would not subside. I wanted to cut him into pieces, to rip his guts out. Vickram held me back. 'That's enough. If you want to continue I'll give you a gun. Do you want to kill him?'

'No.'

Killing him would have been too good for him! It would have been too kind after what he had done to me. It wasn't enough. It was the serpent in him that I wanted to destroy.

The men brought him to his feet again, and we drove him naked and bloody, with his hands tied behind his back, through the village, beating him all the way to the main road.

One of the villagers had given us a sheet and we tied it over his head and left him for dead by the roadside. It was night, and I was hoping a cart or a lorry would pass in the dark and run him over, crushing him forever.

Vickram left a letter on him: *Warning: this is what happens to old men who marry young girls!*

I learned later that he was found by police the next day in the same spot, still alive. He hadn't even been able to crawl back to his house.

I felt good. I felt relieved. I had never before felt such release. Before, I had accepted everything. I had endured all the beatings, swallowing my rage. That night, for the first time in my life, I had tasted revenge. I had tasted it for myself!

As we left Maheshpur, I swore to myself I would do the same thing to all the bastards like him. I would crush them! Otherwise there was no justice for girls like me. The only thing to do with men like that was to crush their serpents, so that they could never use them again! That would be my justice!

The jungle was going to be my home, my village, and the men I marched with, my family.

After the satisfaction of that night, Vickram said to me, 'Never think about tomorrow, Phoolan. Just say to yourself that today you are alive, and tomorrow you might be dead. It's not an easy life, but don't hope for any other. Do you think you'll be able to make it?'

'Yes,' I answered.

22

We kept to the banks of the Yamuna for the most part, staying near the villages, but sometimes we had to cross forests and jungles. We were running, always running, running, running, for leagues and leagues, and it was usually night-time. My hair got caught in the low branches and the thorny bushes tore my clothes. But Vickram held my hand so I wouldn't fall behind, and when I ran out of breath, he would shout, 'Come on, you can do it!' The pace was relentless. We travelled for miles in the night, crossing fast-flowing tributaries at a leap. Vickram would cross first and shout back, 'Jump, or I'll come back and push you!' He wouldn't let me rest until we reached our destination in the morning.

In some places the river crossed thick forests and in other places it wound through steep, rocky ravines. Climbing the bare hillsides was the hardest thing. There were no footholds and nothing to hold on to with your hands. The sandy earth slid away as you tried to scrabble up, taking you back down with it, and there was nothing you could do except start all over again. But I was proud of myself. After a while, I no longer slipped as we scaled the ravines and I reached the top at the same time as Vickram.

It was always night when we moved around, and sometimes tigers followed us. I could hear them growling in the dark. I lived in the wild, surrounded by the cries of animals

I rarely glimpsed: the squawks of birds, the grunts of wild boars and the rustling of snakes. The jungle was frightening but beautiful and the more time passed, the more I learned. If you were thirsty, all you had to do was stretch out your hand to pluck a delicious wild fig. Sometimes we heard the rifleshots of hunters chasing a deer or a rabbit, and the men would roast a whole animal over a fire and eat it. I had never eaten meat before. I was a vegetarian, like my father. He believed it was wrong to kill an animal just to eat it. We hardly ever had meat in the villages, in any case. Most of the gang's food came from villages: potatoes or chick-peas or dal, and wheat to make chapatis. Shepherds gave us milk and peasants gave us eggs. And we had plenty of mangoes, as many as we could eat. We just took them from the trees.

Informers in the villages told us which houses to plunder and who to punish. Vickram Mallah had a network of spies, people who belonged to his family or his community or villagers he had avenged against a cruel Sarpanch, or a thakur who was persecuting them. Sometimes I cried when I thought about my parents. I wondered if Mayadin and the others were still harassing them. I would have liked to go back home to see my mother and father but Vickram explained to me that if I went back, the thakurs wouldn't leave me alone. They wanted me dead. I would have to wait.

I was becoming a dacoit, despite myself. I wore the uniform of a police inspector with two stars, while Vickram had one with three stars. But there was one thing I needed to learn . . .

In the beginning, the men had thought it funny to pretend to fire their rifles beside me, shouting 'Bang!' as I dozed just to see me leap in the air with fright. Vickram had warned me not to say too much to them. I was to speak only to his uncle, Bare Lal. I had to ask him for food or drink, and never speak directly to Vickram in the presence of the men. The men seemed to like me, but I was unnerved by them. 'Don't ever get too close to them,' Vickram had warned. 'They are dangerous, they have no morals. If you have to speak to them, be firm, and speak with authority. The only person you can count on is yourself.' They obeyed him because he was their leader and in principle they would obey me too but he said he didn't want me to be defenceless. I decided I would learn to use a rifle, so they would stop harassing me with their bang bang.

Vickram gave me his 306, a light rifle, he explained, but a good one. It was nearly as big as me and difficult to lift.

He hung a target on a tree.

'Go on, squeeze the trigger . . .'

The explosion in my ear was so deafening I dropped the rifle.

The men thought this was the funniest thing they had ever seen. But I picked up the rifle and fired again, closing my eyes with each shot at first, but planting my feet squarely and bracing my shoulder for the recoil. When the men started complaining about the waste of bullets, Vickram turned to them. 'I don't care if she uses ten cartons or fifty cartons,' he snapped, 'I want her to learn to aim properly!'

I hated the noise of the shots exploding right in my ears as I pulled the trigger back, but after a few weeks, I could at least hold the rifle up and shoot. It would be two or three months, though, before I could aim the rifle at something and stand a chance of hitting it.

One morning, we were busy laying out our clothes to dry on the banks of the river. The sun had not yet risen over the trees when one of the lookouts whistled. It was the police!

So much the better, I thought to myself, they would arrest us and put us in jail, and I would be released one day because I hadn't done anything bad. But I was hurried into the boat by the men, and the police started shooting as soon as we pushed it out on to the Yamuna. We were trapped by the current, a sitting target – and they knew it. I could see them at the top of the ravine. We had been caught in an ambush and they never intended to capture us alive.

'Take cover!' Vickram shouted, and I crouched down with the rest of the men as he dived into the churning water. His head disappeared under the foam for a moment, and I threw him a lifebelt. All I could see was his arms holding his rifle in the air. Each time his head came up above the water, he fired.

'Shoot, Phoolan,' he shouted. 'Shoot!'

I fired twice, blindly, at the hillside.

The police were trying to kill us. The river was so rough the churning water drenched us and the men could barely make headway against the current. Vickram clung to the lifebelt. We couldn't let ourselves be carried downstream in the direction of Kalpi because more police would surely be waiting there. They kept firing at us as the men rowed desperately against the current. Finally we reached a bend in the river with forests either side. The current wasn't so strong there and the men were able to haul Vickram back in. Out of sight of the police now, we managed to reach the bank. Nobody had been hurt but we had to abandon the boat and run for hours to be certain the police lost our trail.

We hid for three days after that, with nothing to eat or drink. Vickram kept asking me if I was all right, if I could hold out. I told him I could. I didn't want to seem weaker than the men. They played music and sang and danced or played cards as though they weren't bothered by their empty bellies.

I was beginning to understand how hard their lives were.

For most of them it wasn't a life they had chosen. They had been caught up in land disputes or family feuds like my fight with Mayadin and because they couldn't get justice from the police, they had taken it into their own hands. From the police all they would get was a beating while the rich men they accused laughed with satisfaction. It seemed the rich were never satisfied and always wanted more. Even the ones who had become bandits for the money were never happy. They found that once they had money, they couldn't spend it, they couldn't go back to their villages. They had to keep running through the night and hiding by day.

Perhaps it was the hunger, but I no longer wanted to return to my parents, even though I didn't know what sort of life I would have in the wilds with these men. It seemed we were forever on the move from the river to the jungle and back to the river. There was not a single woman there for me to talk to, just men that I had to be wary of despite their vows of loyalty and Vickram's presence. I had to eat alone, and keep a little way from the rest. I was a woman alone, a woman whose food was cooked for her by a man, but a woman nonetheless, with a woman's problems, who had to live among these men in the best way she could. I had to take my baths in a secluded corner, keeping a constant watch for wild animals and for the men.

They were bandits. There were no laws or restrictions to stop them, yet they never tried to lure me aside or molest me. They never said anything dirty to me. They behaved respectfully. In the villages there were all kinds of customs and duties, but the men there behaved at times like dogs. I decided I liked the jungles and the hills. For the first time, I was being treated with respect. I got used to battling with the mosquitoes, and waiting: waiting for nightfall to pack up and move; waiting for the scout to return from the nearest village with food and information about potential lootings.

Two informers had asked Vickram to do something about a

rich man in their village who was not paying what he owed to the people who worked for him. A pillage was decided on and the house was identified. I listened attentively to the orders from our chief: stay in twos, never alone; never let anyone come near you during the action; if you or your partner are in danger, whistle; when you hear a whistle, stop what you're doing and regroup . . .

Late that same evening, Vickram was looking over the wall of a roof terrace, with me at his side. 'The chief must stay high up somewhere to be able to survey the village and control his gang while they loot the houses.' He told me I had to take over his duties. 'Shoot in the air to give the signal! That's how we warn the villagers.'

I did as he said and fired in the air, while he screamed through his megaphone. 'The rich are the real enemies of the poor! You've made life miserable for these poor people, now we are going to make you pay!'

He shouted his name, and mine: 'I am Vickram Mallah, and Phoolan Devi is here with me!' He turned to me and smiled.

The target of a looting always had to know who was punishing him, and the whole village had to hear it too. It was the code of dacoits.

I didn't know if anyone noticed that night that I was a woman. The villagers were much more frightened than me. Despite the shots and the panic, I wasn't scared. People were running in every direction, fleeing their houses, but we weren't in any danger. About fifteen of the men had gone into the village while the remainder spread out in the surrounding fields keeping lookout.

It wasn't enough to plunder the houses of the rich; they had to be given a lesson, Vickram explained. I didn't participate that time. With their lathis, the men took care of the rich man the villagers said had been exploiting them. When they finished, they departed with the gold, silver and rupees from his house, firing shots in the air.

My apprenticeship as a dacoit was in hand.

Sometimes one gang would join forces with another. The first gang we joined up with was led by Baba Ghanshyam, a tall, hefty man with a long beard and long hair that he wound around his head inside a white turban. He looked frightening, but his eyes betrayed his intelligence and he spoke with sympathy to me when I told him I had been kidnapped. He told Vickram I had no business with a gang of dacoits and they ought to let me go. Vickram replied that I had enemies and if I surrendered to the police, he would have to put up bail so I wouldn't have go to prison. They decided to celebrate their union with two lootings in my name to get money for my bail. Just to taunt the police, they decided they were going to carry out the raids in the district of Kalpi.

Everything went off as usual in the first village, but in the second, we found ourselves surrounded by police.

Vickram wanted me to insult them with the megaphone. 'Tell them what you think of them, go on! They were the ones who mistreated you, don't forget . . .'

I was too timid to shout through the megaphone. I was sure they couldn't hear my voice at first, it was so frail. But soon I found it was intoxicating to bawl in the night.

'Dogs! Bloody dogs!' I shouted.

Vickram grabbed the megaphone and his voice boomed like thunder. 'You have ruined the life of Phoolan Devi! It was you who tortured her, and now you're going to pay!'

The police retreated from the rifleshots that seemed to be coming from every corner of the village, and as they did, I fled with the rest of the gang. But on the outskirts of the village I found myself tangled in some fencing wire as I tried to slip through in the dark. My hair was caught in some barbed wire and I couldn't free myself. The others had disappeared ahead.

Suddenly I saw two shadows near me, wearing uniforms. I couldn't tell if they were police or bandits.

I held my breath.

'You,' one of them shouted, 'did you see anyone pass by here?'

They were police.

'No,' I mumbled. Luckily, there was no moon that night to reveal me. They also got their clothes caught in the barbed wire, diverting their attention. But they soon freed themselves and I saw the beams of their torches fading in the distance.

I kept struggling with my hair. My uniform was torn and my hair was still caught in the wire, but I didn't dare to shout for help.

I had been there for what seemed like hours, growing frantic with silent desperation, when at last I heard Vickram's voice.

'Phoolan, where are you? Phoolan!'

'Here!' I said. 'I'm here!'

He cut my hair with a slash of his razor, freeing me.

'Two sipahis! Why didn't you shoot them?' he said when I whispered what had happened.

'I was alone, I couldn't get both of them!'

He and Madhav had left the others to come back for me. He thought the police had caught me and I could see anger in his eyes at the risk they had been forced to take to find me. I thought I saw fear too – not for himself, but for my safety. I felt his hand in mine again as we ran through the fields. The police detail from the station at Kalpi wasn't far away. Behind us in the night we could hear the noise of lorries. They must have called for reinforcements. I was so exhausted I stumbled with every step, and Vickram picked me up and carried me on his shoulders.

We reached the Yamuna and jumped in a boat, but as we crossed, we saw more police waiting on the opposite bank.

'Who's that?' they called out in the dark.

'I'm the DSP from Kanpur,' shouted Vickram.

They believed he was a Deputy Superintendent of Police because they didn't ever imagine a bandit could speak so well. Vickram could even speak English.

'I'm in charge here,' he said.

We headed the boat downstream until we were shrouded in darkness again and climbed ashore. The race began again, but we saw no more police that night. They had lost our trail. By dawn, we were deep in the jungle, singing and dancing like children as we counted the loot.

There was no more looting for a while. My feet hardened from running, and I grew tougher too. The next two operations were kidnappings, both thakurs. The first thakur had been denounced by the father of a girl who had been raped, and the second was a police informant. I didn't even see what they looked like. I didn't want to know. They disgusted me. The men corrected them with their lathis and then we collected the ransoms.

After this, the two gangs split up. Vickram and Baba Ghanshyam divided the state territory into two sectors. His men had been paying me too much attention, Vickram had decided.

For more than three months, I had been running through the jungle with Vickram. I must have been in my eighteenth year by then, but the barber had cut my hair short and a long time had passed since I last wore a sari. I lived like the men, dressed like them and ate what they ate. I slept where they slept, under the stars, or under a plastic sheet with Vickram, my husband. He had taught me many things. Most important of all, I was learning not to fear his approaches. Slowly, I was learning to trust this man.

Madhav, who was Vickram's cousin, knew how to write and count and kept a record of the gang's money. He put the bundles of rupees in envelopes and wrote the amounts in a book. Vickram counted the bundles after him, in front of everyone, and put the envelopes in his sack. When the time came, Vickram gave out the shares. He also distributed the rifles and if a man wanted to leave the gang, he had to return his rifle or buy it.

I watched and listened . . .

Though I wasn't supposed to talk to the gang members, I started to become friends with the ones closest to Vickram: the tall Madhav, who never said much and liked to read books; Bharat, another distant cousin of Vickram, and Raghu Nath. Bharat and Raghu Nath were always singing and dancing together like two little monkeys.

Bharat started to call me his daughter, just to tease me, and although he was short and chubby, he would insist on carrying me across rivers on his shoulders when the waters were high. He had a dark face and a loud, booming laugh. He was always making jokes and even stealing, for him, was a prank. He told me how in his village he used to steal blankets from people as they slept, having first cut a thorn bush to throw over his victim while he got away. He became notorious as a bicycle thief. His technique was to hitch a lift on one and then ask the owner to stop so he could relieve himself. Usually, the owner would feel the need to relieve himself at the same time, and Bharat would run back and jump on the bicycle. He said he had stolen more than a hundred bicycles before the police caught him and gave him a bloody good hiding.

Everybody laughed to hear Bharat tell this, but I noticed

the men wouldn't tell funny stories about their bandit exploits when they were happy. They would tell them when they were sad, when they heard that someone had been captured or killed by the police.

During the day, Vickram used to read. It was a holy book, like the story of Rama that the Brahmin in our village used to read. Vickram kept it in the branches of a tree so that nothing would dirty it. He explained that the book should never touch the ground, because it was pure, and the dirt from people's feet would soil it. One day, he put the book down in his lap and said that I would have to choose an emblem. I picked Durga. Like the goddess, I was driven by my hunger for justice, for revenge over demons. That was what gave me my strength. When the rich did bad things, our duty as dacoits was to make them pay.

My language had changed, and my habits too. I had forgotten how to cook chapatis and fetch water from the well. But I had learned how to clean a rifle and load it with bullets . . . In the jungle, one of the men prepared the food and I was served like the others. Water belonged to everyone, whether it came from the river or a spring, and there were fruits right within your reach.

I was free as a bird, but I was beginning to miss my family. I told Vickram I wanted to see them. I had heard nothing of them since the night I was kidnapped during the monsoon, in the month of Shravan; and the month of Margsheersh, that always followed the rains, the coldest month of winter, had nearly passed. I wanted to go back to my village, but Vickram said I was not to go alone. He didn't want me to be captured or have to surrender to the police. For a time, he had talked about putting money aside for my bail, but he didn't mention that any more. He agreed to take me, but he said there was no question of me staying. I would be arrested, and it was no longer possible for me to plead innocence and say I was the victim of a kidnapping. Phoolan Devi had become a dacoit. I could no longer fetch water from the well and mind the cattle; I was the wife of Vickram Mallah, dacoit, deliverer of justice and vengeance!

When we had split with Baba Ghanshyam's gang, we each decided to operate in different sectors of Uttar Pradesh. Ours had included my village and, one day, we found ourselves not far away. I wanted to go at once but Vickram sent someone ahead to see if it was safe. The scout returned with troubling news. My mother had told him the family had no money, no food, and Buppa was ill. They were broken-hearted with sorrow and shame, she had said. The police had taken all their supplies and harassed them almost daily. But the scout said the village was quiet for the moment; a fair was taking place in a neighbouring village and everyone was there.

Vickram decided we would go in that night: Bare Lal, Madhav and Bharat would come with us, while the others waited in the fields outside the village. Bare Lal never let Vickram enter a village alone.

I led them in the darkness to my house, keeping close to the mud walls as I had done so often before, with Vickram close behind me this time. The village was quiet. I could hear dogs barking in the distance, and the familiar smell of forage and cowdung brought tears to my eyes. The last time Vickram had come here, he had kicked down the door. This time, he followed me into the yard. We waited for my mother to come out.

She nearly ran when she saw his uniform, thinking it was the police again.

'Amma! It's me, Phoolan!'

She was very thin. Deep lines were drawn on her face, and my father's face was expressionless. It was as if he had cried so much he was no longer capable of any other emotion. He held me in his arms, clinging to me. They looked more weary and tormented than ever, and my father was in a dreadful state. He released me and just sat down on the ground like a rag doll, covering his face with his hands and mumbling a prayer.

I gave my mother two hundred rupees. 'Take it, Amma. I don't have more right now.'

'I don't want your money. I want you to come back home. We have nothing to eat. The police beat your father and me and they took all our grain, all we had! Because of you, we have nothing. Nobody will help us!'

My father looked up and whimpered. 'Why did fate take you away, Phoolan? Why did fate do this to us?'

My mother sat down on the khat and began to cry too. I squatted down and put my head on her lap. 'Don't cry, Amma,' I said. 'That's how it is. My life is a struggle, and your lives too, now, because of me. I'm going to teach that Mayadin!'

The noise had woken Bhuri and Shiv Narayan. Bhuri had grown; she must have been about nine years old, but she was thinner than before. 'Phoolan! I thought the bad people took you away!' she said. 'Have you become a bad person too?'

Vickram had been watching us in silence, and my father was looking up at him with his lifeless eyes. 'You have ruined my daughter's life,' he said. 'God will never forgive you!'

'No, old man, we were the ones who saved her. Look at her, she's still alive, isn't she? We killed Baboo Gujar for her, and I married her. I am protecting her. If I leave her here with you, the thakurs will come to kill her. If she gives herself up to the police the jackals will do what they did last time.'

'You have ruined her life, Vickram Mallah!'

'How many men do we have to shoot so she can live in peace here, Buppa, how many? Everybody here mistreats her. But if you really want it, I'll make her give herself up!'

My father said nothing more.

The young man in uniform carrying a rifle on his shoulder looked at my ageing father with compassion. He had taken his daughter, but to return her to her humble, wretched father would be to condemn her to death. There was no more to say. Amma put her hands together in prayer and bowed to us, giving us her blessing.

'Take good care of her, please,' said my father.

Vickram knelt down and touched his feet.

'Buppa, I beg you, forgive me . . .'

It was time to leave. It would have been too dangerous to sleep there, and the men wanted to see the fair before we moved on. There would be musicians and a troupe of dancers, but I was only interested in one thing: Mayadin might be there too . . .

The insults, the beatings and the hunger that was ravaging my family were all his fault. He was a mallah like my father, but he still preferred to side with the rich and let his own uncle die of starvation. He was the one who had ruined my life, not Vickram.

We could hear the music from afar and see the lights. There was a stage with hundreds of people sitting in front, but neither my mother nor my father would be going to the fair. The music and the flowers were not for them. The feast was not for them.

'I want Mayadin,' I said.

The gang arrived firing their rifles in the air as usual. Nobody in the crowd moved; they were all paralysed with fear. We surrounded the stage and I snatched the megaphone. The people sitting on the grass gaped at me in amazement. They couldn't believe it was Phoolan, the daughter of Devidin, in front of them, dressed like a dacoit, with a rifle in her hand.

'The feast is over, you dogs. Where is Mayadin?'

There was a stunned silence. I was sure he was there, hiding somewhere . . .

'Nobody knows? Well, do you know what I'm going to do to all of you?'

It was so quiet, I could hear them urinating from fear on the blankets that had been spread out on the grass. Then they tried to offer me their timid excuses: 'It wasn't us, we never did anything to you, let us go!' They never saw anything, they never did anything, they never lifted a finger to help.

'Get out of my sight, all of you, get away from me!'

He was there. I was right, but I only found out as the last of the villagers left. I should have checked them one by one. He had been lying on the ground behind someone so I wouldn't see him, and he had managed to crawl away on his belly, they told me. He had scurried with all the rest of them in terror of Phoolan Devi, the pariah of Gurha Ka Purwa.

That night, I felt again the power born of rage surging through me, overwhelming me. To see my parents hungry, crying, and cringing in fear just a few hundred yards from there, and then to see all of the villagers laughing and enjoying the show . . . It was like an explosion in my spirit. If I had laid eyes on Mayadin, I would surely have killed him right there. And if there had been any police in the crowd, I would have made them dance too with my bullets! But Vickram gave the order to retreat.

He tried to calm me. 'Listen. We'll send a message to his brother-in-law. What was his name? Mansukh. We'll tell him the police want to see him. After all, he was the one. He didn't rape you but he was the one who encouraged the others. You can't kill someone from your own family, from your own community. You will be damned for all time, your reputation will be ruined. And your parents will only suffer even more. We'll bring him to you. You'll be able to do whatever you like with him!'

I wasn't satisfied, but this Mansukh would have to do in the meantime. Men who thought they could abuse the honour and ruin the life of Phoolan Devi, a poor, defenceless mallah girl, deserved to die! To let them live would be to allow them to ruin the lives of other girls. I thought about it the whole night long, lying awake in our camp in the fields under the cold, starry night. I thought about my mother's haggard face, my father's lifeless eyes, and about Mayadin. He had slithered away like a cowardly snake at the sight of me. I thought about what Vickram had said, how he had tried to explain the difference of caste to me, and about the subtle but unforgiving rules that governed them. A mallah could loot a thakur if he was rich, and punish or kill him if he was a rapist. If the thakur was honourable, then the mallah would respect him. Vengeance could only be exacted on behalf of someone of your own community. A mallah could avenge another mallah, but he couldn't take revenge against someone of his family or his community . . .

It was to these rules, this unwritten code, that I owed my life. But I still couldn't accept it, I couldn't abide by it, because I was a woman. I had no place in this hierarchy of caste. I was lower than all of them, and the demons I had to slay were more devious. Whatever caste they belonged to, they were all men.

The next day, they brought me a substitute for my vengeance.

Mansukh was skinny and short-sighted. I recognised his ugly face, the way he squinted all the time. He was one of my demons. Because he was involved with the police, it had been easy to get him out of hiding. A villager had told him a policeman wanted to see him and he assumed it was safe to come out of his house. He was still wearing his nice clothes from the evening before, a clean dhoti and kurta, like a politician, with a blanket around his shoulders. Fear was not part of his life, until he saw me. He had followed Vickram and his men into the forest thinking they were police, but when he saw me, and my rifle, he threw himself at my feet, his voice quivering with terror as he begged for my forgiveness.

He admitted everything. He was the one who had fabricated the robbery charges against me. He was the one who had said to the police, 'She's a hussy, you can do whatever you like with her!' And now he was weeping and pleading with me to let him go.

'Look at him Vickram,' I said. 'That was how I was in the police lock-up. I cried like him, begging them to let me go. I cried for help and he didn't give a damn!'

'It was not me, Phoolan,' said Mansukh now. 'Mayadin told me to do it. It was the others. I just did what they told me.'

'You threw me into the clutches of those policemen in front of my father. Take her, take the hussy and punish her, you said. I was crying that day, and I'm still crying. Look at me . . .'

Vickram had been watching the man trembling at my feet, listening to his confession. 'Take him to the road,' he said to his men. 'She will do it.'

They dragged him out of the forest back to the road and tied him up. Vickram handed me the rifle. 'Go on, do it here,' he said. 'Kill him.'

All of a sudden I was the one who was frightened again. He was on his knees, bound up and moaning. How I had longed to beat them, to see them quivering in fear.

'I can't do it.'

'Yes you can. You have to. If you don't kill him, I can't do it for you. Remember what he did to you. You were the one he did it to, not me.'

I closed my eyes and fired.

Three of the men fired at the same time as me. When I opened my eyes again, his body was lying on the road. He was dead, immobile. Blood was beginning to seep on his nice white clothes.

I had been delivered from the fear of firing at a man, delivered from the hesitation. I had avenged myself with something more than words or screams or tears. I had the means of justice in my hands, and all I had to do was plant my feet squarely, close my eyes and squeeze the trigger to be rid of a demon. He would never be able to harm anyone else the way he had harmed me. It was simple and terrible.

I went up to his corpse and gave it a kick.

'If you hadn't done it, you wouldn't have died like this.'

Vickram left a note on his corpse. He read it to me first. *'Police dogs this is in store for you. Phoolan Devi.'*

There was no turning back now.

The very next day, the police put a reward on my head. Surrendering was out of the question, they would just shoot me on sight. I had become a criminal, like the others.

But what they called a crime, I called justice.

23

It was not yet dawn when the lookout whistled to warn us of people approaching. We were camped in a field near my village where the hora grew so high it hid us. I could see figures advancing slowly in the faint light and they would soon be close enough to open fire on us. The men quickly pulled on their boots and grabbed their rifles, lying low.

There must have been at least a hundred of them. They were from my village, and I recognised the person leading them.

'Stop!' I shouted. 'It's my mother.'

What was she doing with all those people? We had sent her a message that I would be coming to see her again before we left the area, but that she shouldn't say anything to anyone.

Vickram was nervous. 'Maybe she's brought the police.'

The Pradhan was beside her, walking at the head of the throng of villagers. Apart from my mother, they were all men; all the rich men of the village, and they were walking slowly, like pilgrims, and wearing garlands as though they were on their way to a temple. I could see no uniforms, no rifles.

Vickram waited until they were close enough to hear us. 'What do you want?' he shouted.

'We have come to bring you our greetings,' said the Pradhan. 'We have come with her mother. She is our mother too – and her daughter Phoolan is a goddess. We have come to ask Phoolan to bless our village, to purify our houses with her presence.'

They had brought garlands and carried trays of sweets and rupees as offerings. They bowed humbly, joining their hands in prayer to me. Some of them fell to their knees and touched the ground with their foreheads.

'Namasteh . . . Namasteh . . .'

They were praising me as though I was a goddess!

I looked at all of them, the Pradhan and all those men with their filthy landowner faces, their fat, contented cheeks and their bushy moustaches. They had come to get down on their knees and ask for the benediction of Phoolan Devi!

'Go to hell! All of you!' I bellowed.

And my mother was there with them!

'You,' I exclaimed at her. 'How dare you come here with them. You know what they did to me and now you're on their side! Where were they when I came out of prison? Where were they when you begged them to lend you money for my bail? Where were all of these men when we were forbidden to draw water from the well?'

'You must forgive them, Phoolan. If you have any pity left, you must forgive them.'

They were afraid. They had been stricken with fear since I executed Mansukh. The Sarpanch was right there in the middle of them. I cocked my rifle and took aim at him, but Vickram stopped me.

'Let's hear what he has to say first.'

'You,' I shouted at the Sarpanch. 'Step forward, you bastard, away from the others . . . Now, talk!'

The lies and excuses began again. It wasn't his fault, it wasn't his idea, it wasn't him. I had been subjected to terrible atrocities, but he had had nothing to do with these injustices. It would have suited them all if I had ceased to exist, if Phoolan, the little mallah girl who was tortured, humiliated and driven from her village, had vanished in silence and shame. But here I was, a goddess!

'Who ordered my kidnapping?'

'I wasn't the one who told Vickram to do it! Not me!'

I turned to Vickram. He was white with anger. He fixed the Sarpanch with his stare and stepped up to him. 'Have you forgotten who I am? Look at me, I'm Vickram Mallah, and it was your family that asked me to do it. You didn't want her in your village any more. Are you calling me a liar?'

Vickram struck him with his rifle butt.

'Tie him up,' he commanded.

The villagers fell back mumbling their pathetic pleas while the men trussed the Sarpanch up like a chicken. When they released him, he rolled and twisted on the ground to reach my feet and touch my shoes with his forehead.

'Forgive me,' he whimpered. 'Please, release me, oh goddess! You are truly a goddess! You are the incarnation of Durga!'

'And what are you? Bastard! When I lived in your village like an ordinary person you said I was evil. Now you say I am a goddess!'

I took a lathi from one of the men and thrashed the Sarpanch hard across his back. I struck him just once and left him there, humbled and reduced to nothing, with his face against the damp earth.

Some of the villagers came forward and garlanded our men. One of them approached me with a tray of sweets and rupees.

'I don't want your gifts! I don't want your cash. I will burn them in front of you!'

The crowd of villagers began to cheer. 'Long live Phoolan Devi! Long live Phoolan Devi!'

I had spared their pathetic, lying village chief and now

they were singing my praises! I took the wad of rupees from the tray. There must have been twenty thousand rupees wrapped in a bundle. I set fire to it. I was disgusted. But at the same time, I was excited. It was a delicious feeling to have them at my mercy, like having an empty belly and being able to eat your fill. They all implored me to come to their houses, to share their food and give them my blessing and protection. I decided I would go with them, but it would be at my father's house that I would eat. I would share his food, and his poverty.

When we reached the house my father was mortified with awe and fright to see all the important villagers approaching him, chanting that Devidin's daughter was a goddess. Fear was all he knew, and he feared for my safety as always.

'Be careful, Phoolan,' he said. 'It was you who killed Mansukh, wasn't it? I knew it, I was sure! The police came here and I was sure it was you. You shouldn't have done it, Phoolan. It was evil. You have done an evil thing!'

'It's too late. I did it and it's too late. Would you prefer me to forget too? You remember the lock-up where they shut me in. He was right there in front of you, telling the police to torture me. Have you forgotten? You were crying. "Leave her, Don't hurt her," you kept on begging! That was Mansukh. Well, I didn't forget. I killed him, and today I'm going to shoot Mayadin too!'

My father fell to his knees.

'Pray, Father, pray for your daughter Phoolan!'

Outside I could still hear the villagers cheering. 'Long live Phoolan Devi! She has taken pity on us! Long live Durga! She has spared the Sarpanch!'

'Listen to them, Father, listen . . .' There were hundreds of them around the house. I opened the door to show him. They were on their knees, like him, as though his house had become a temple.

My father's face slowly lit up. It was a look I had never seen on his face before. A glow returned to his lifeless eyes. The strength he never had, I had given to him, by means of the fear I inspired, by my presence and my rifle. He stood up, proud for once in his life to be the father of Phoolan Devi, the goddess honoured by the whole village. For the very first time in his poor mallah's life, the entire village was paying tribute to him. 'They respect you now,' I said. 'They never respected you before.'

I saw that he was proud – so proud, he looked away shyly.

The crowd parted and I saw someone approaching. He was wearing old torn clothes like a poor man, and every few steps he would stop, kneel down and touch the ground with his forehead as though he was coming to a temple to ask forgiveness. It was Mayadin, kneeling and scraping his nose against the ground as though I was a divinity. Instead of his usual finery, he was dressed in rags, and he was carrying a silver platter laden with rupees. There were bundles and bundles of rupees on it. He thought he was going to be able to buy his life!

'Buppa, look! Look who it is! He dares to come to your house! I'm going to kill him right now!'

But Vickram grabbed the barrel of my rifle and Madhav snatched it out of my hands. 'Don't do that! If you kill him we're finished. Our reputation will be ruined.'

'I have to let him live because of your reputation? This is what you are asking me?'

'No,' said Vickram. 'For your father. This man is his nephew, he belongs to his family, to your community. You have to spare him for your father's sake. Look at your father, listen to what he says.'

My father went down on his knees again to beseech me. 'Not him! Not our own family. Phoolan, I beg you . . .'

Mayadin came up to us with his rupees. His face was black with fear and the tray was shaking in his hands. He knelt and put it at my feet, remaining there with his forehead to the ground. He was at my mercy.

'I don't want your filthy rupees.'

I would have liked to swipe his head off with a sword. I wanted to kill him, but it was as if a trick was being played to prevent me doing it, driving me mad with frustration. Madhav wouldn't give me back my rifle, and the jackal Mayadin was trying to pay me his respects.

'Forgive me, Phoolan. Spare me, Phoolan. I will do whatever you ask. I will give your father the land. I will help him. I will give him everything my father should have given him.'

My father was still on his knees, crying and imploring me to spare Mayadin.

'Let him live,' said Vickram. 'He is asking you for pardon. Forgive him, for your father's sake.'

'Get out of here with your filthy rupees!' I said. 'I'll give you your miserable life for nothing, because that's all it's worth, nothing!'

I didn't know what else to say.

The villagers cheered and began to sing again, 'Long live Phoolan Devi!' They were cheering because, against my will, I had been forced to spare one of their hyenas.

Vickram took the money, and Mayadin thanked him profusely for accepting his offering. He put a garland around Vickram's neck and with his finger made a red mark of devotion on Vickram's forehead.

Vickram had accepted the money I refused. The traitor! Right there, I demanded to know why.

Vickram took me aside. 'Listen to what I say, Phoolan. You have to respect your father's wishes and spare his family.' I just glared at Vickram angrily, and he said the same thing again, but he was never going to be able to make me believe it was the right thing to do. If I had given in and spared Mayadin, it was because my father was crying, and I had never been able to stand to see my father cry.

And because of the land, the stolen land that had been the cause of all of it. Mayadin was going to give him the land, it was in his reach, but my father was refusing to accept it.

'I want only five bighas of land, Phoolan. That's more than enough.'

'Why not eighty? That's what he stole. It's all yours. It belonged to your father.'

'It's enough, Phoolan. I don't need more.'

'Buppa, as long as I have a megaphone to shout through at them and a rifle to scare them they will sing my praises, because they can't hurt me any more. They are the ones who fear for their lives now, so they are nice to you and Mayadin offers to give you the land he stole. But what would happen if I no longer had a rifle one day, if they were no longer afraid of me?'

'Five bighas. I ask for nothing more.'

They signed a paper putting five bighas of land in the name of my brother, Shiv Narayan. Afterwards the thief wanted to abase himself in front of me again, to thank me for my mercy, but I couldn't even stand to look at him.

'Don't come near me. If you come anywhere near me again, I'll kill you.'

Vickram pocketed the fifty thousand rupees Mayadin had brought.

I knew I was going to regret having given in to my father. Every time I thought of Mayadin after that, my heart tightened with anger. He had been in my grip, but instead of squeezing until there was no life left in him, I had released him. For him to have escaped with his miserable life meant I had been right all along. There was no justice for me after all.

I left the crowd outside to their jubilation, walking around and around our yard with Bhuri and Shiv Narayan following me.

'Leave me alone!' I shouted at them.

I had been forced to spare Mayadin and watch Vickram accept his rupees. My head was spinning. How could Vickram have behaved like that towards my enemy? Where was his honour? Could I trust him, or was he two-faced, like the rest of them?

'How could you do that to me, Mastana?' I asked him. 'How could you take his money after all he did?'

'You have to understand. I was only protecting your reputation. He never harmed you directly, he wasn't the one who asked me to kidnap you.'

'He accused me of robbery! Wasn't that enough, having me arrested? He came to sign the complaint. If he hadn't lied and denounced me to the police, if he had protected me like a member of my own family, I would never have gone through all that humiliation!'

I was exhausted. I didn't want to hear any more arguments. I couldn't sit down, I couldn't drink, I couldn't calm myself down. All I could do was shout, 'Shut up, all of you, shut up! Don't try to explain anything else to me. I've had enough!' All I could do was walk around and around our yard the way I had walked around that police lock-up. 'If that's how it is,' I yelled, 'I'm leaving!'

It was my father who grabbed me by my hair as though I was still a child. 'Don't be angry Phoolan. Calm down. I'm your father and I know some things you don't. We must forgive. I know you hear me. Promise me to forgive, Phoolan. Ask the gods to help you. The gods know how to forgive. If you are the reincarnation of Durga, you must forgive.' He paused. He was crying again. 'You are still my little girl, and I know you aren't going to kill him. Promise me.'

'Why do you still cry, Buppa?'

'Please, Phoolan, I beg you, don't kill him.'

'Stop crying! All right, all right, I won't kill him.'

They were all standing there, my brother and sister, my mother, my father with his hands outstretched. The crowd of villagers was behind them in the street, watching me. I ran from there as fast as I could.

Vickram and the rest of the gang followed me, heading towards the river. I had tears in my eyes now, but I didn't turn around. I shouted back that I would see them in six months, maybe . . . I meant my family, not my village. And as I ran, I realised what lay ahead of me. I would have to harden my heart. Not all victories could be won with rifleshots. My return as a bandit to my village had taught me much. I had always suspected it, and now I had proven to myself how cowardly and spineless these people were. They had wept as I left but they weren't crying because I was going away. My father was the only one weeping for me. The rest of them were weeping with relief. Durga had spared their village from her fury. It was to my rifle they were saying farewell. They were afraid of power – any kind of power. That was the only thing they truly worshipped. And I had learned about the compromises you had to make with justice: you could kill this one, Phoolan, but you had to spare that one . . . And I had learned not to hope for peace; there was nothing in this world that would give me peace.

We crossed the river before the sun set and headed towards the forest, marching all night.

I walked in silence. Vickram was still trying to explain what he had done, but I refused to speak to him.

'Your parents were so wretched. You had to forgive that fellow for their sake. You'll have your chance later, another day. What does it matter?'

I wouldn't talk to him, I wouldn't answer his questions, I refused even to eat any food. Even his men were angry with him. Like me, they wanted to know why Mayadin's tribute had ended up in his pocket. But he was the leader, and it wasn't a looting, so they had to accept it.

After the hours of marching we arrived at a village deep in the jungle called Simra. I settled down to rest as far away as I could from Vickram. With my bare feet cooling in a stream, I contemplated the forest surrounding me. From now on, this was my home, my life.

As I stared at the trees, something snapped inside me. I didn't know what to do any more. I was tired of thinking.

I watched a little bird with blue wings flutter away from the shore. He didn't have to thank anybody except God for the insects he ate; he could sing and fly higher than the tallest trees, up towards the light; he could fly into houses and peck at grain in the stores, and drink water from the stream if he was thirsty. He didn't have to obey the rules of men. But I still did. Compared to the bird, I was powerless.

We stayed in Simra for eight days. Disappointment nagged at me – and annoyance at having been forced to give in to the will of others, to cede to the blackmail of tears. It had been intoxicating to hear the mob shouting 'Long live Phoolan!' But it was deflating to know they were only cheering because they were cowards. And it was humbling to me to realise that without Vickram, they wouldn't have called me a goddess and prostrated themselves at my feet. Without him, I would have been silenced by them long before.

24

Shri Ram was Vickram's guru, the bandit who had taught him all he knew. They had been in prison together but Vickram had been released while Shri Ram stayed locked up in the jail at Kanpur, awaiting trial for robberies and other crimes. I knew that Vickram admired the older dacoit, but because I hadn't been talking to him because of what happened with Mayadin, it was only through Uncle Bare Lal that I learned that Shri Ram and his brother Lala Ram had been released. Vickram had paid eighty thousand rupees to bail them out; at least that explained why he hadn't spat at Mayadin's money . . .

Vickram left the morning after he heard this news, borrowing a scooter from the village and telling everybody as he rode off that, to celebrate the return of Shri Ram, we would be going that night to make offerings at the temple and to give out sweets and rupees in the villages.

'I want you all to welcome him as your leader,' Vickram said as he left, but I had a feeling Shri Ram's arrival was going to be a bad thing. The men were uneasy too. It was the usual story: mallahs and thakurs could never get along.

Night came and Vickram still hadn't returned. After a half-hearted meal shared with the men, listening to their grumblings, I settled down to try to sleep.

'The Ram brothers are dangerous,' Bare Lal had warned while we ate. 'If they come here, keep yourself to yourself.

They are thakurs, and Shri Ram has the same bad tendencies as Baboo Gujar. Don't go anywhere near him.'

It was early in the morning when the lookout woke us. He had heard a tractor approaching.

'It's only us!' Vickram shouted.

There were about ten or fifteen people riding on the tractor with him, and one of them was Shri Ram.

Vickram came straightaway to get me from where I was sleeping. 'Come and greet him . . . Come, Phoolan. You have to pay him your respects.'

He had a mat placed under a tree and invited Shri Ram to sit down. Then he put a garland around his neck and announced, 'You are our leader now.'

Shri Ram wore a dirty pair of trousers and a T-shirt. He had red hair, and red eyes that ran over me slowly from head to toe.

'So this is Phoolan!'

He looked me up and down again, the way thakurs always looked at mallah women, twiddling his red moustache. I took an instinctive dislike to him. If I really was a goddess, like the people of my village had said, I would have transformed the garland of flowers around his neck into a rope, or a snake, right there and then.

'So this is Phoolan,' he repeated. 'And she sleeps with everybody! She's the gang's girl!'

Vickram became annoyed. 'Don't talk like that about her,' he said. 'We're married. She's my wife . . .' Immediately, Bare Lal moved closer to his nephew, and Bharat and Madhav put their hands on their rifles.

By saying what he said, Shri Ram had insulted them too.

'Phoolan is our sister,' said Bare Lal. Have you no respect?'

Vickram turned and gestured at him to keep calm, but Bare Lal looked around slowly at the rest of the men and then said to Vickram, 'Get rid of him. We don't want him here. He may be your leader, but he isn't ours.'

Shri Ram raised his voice to silence them. 'I don't care whether you like it or not, Vickram has made me the leader,' he barked, and without another glance at the men, he took Vickram aside to confer with him.

The men mumbled discontentedly and I slipped away to the edge of the clearing to sit by a tree. My instincts told me not to trust Shri Ram. Because of what he had said, I decided I would rather die than have to touch his feet.

After a few minutes, Vickram came over to me and whispered in my ear. 'You must excuse him, Phoolan. He knows he made a mistake saying that. He won't say it again, he promised me.'

I could see him playing with his moustache and grinning as he watched us. I didn't know if he had really promised or not; all I could sense was his treachery and lust.

'Don't let him stay here, Vickram. He was undressing me with his eyes!'

'I told you he said he was sorry. I owe him everything, Phoolan. Please, come and sit with us. Don't embarrass me in front of him.'

I came and sat down with them – but away from Shri Ram – as Vickram explained about me. He told him all about the way Baboo Gujar had treated me. Without saying it, he was letting Shri Ram know that if anyone touched me, he would kill them.

Shri Ram nodded his head as he listened. Then he stood up and, in front of everybody, bowed to me with his palms together. 'Please excuse me, I didn't realise.'

He was lying. I could tell, even if Vickram couldn't. I could see the lust in his red eyes . . .

Not long after that, I was sitting quietly away from the men, under a tree, and he came and sat down beside me. The monsoon had returned and it was raining softly. I was watching the drops of rain falling under a banyan tree.

'What are you doing, Bahanji?' he asked.

'Nothing,' I replied. 'You can see very well. I'm sheltering from the rain.'

I didn't like him calling me his Bahanji, his sister-in-law. He looked around him, and I could tell he was making sure the coast was clear. I stood up and got out of his reach as fast as I could.

'Who do you think you are, you little bitch? You little piece of shit! You think you're too good for me? How can people like you – backward caste people – think you're better than us? One day I'm going to teach you to obey me!'

I ran in tears to Vickram as he shouted behind me. 'She is lying! Why do you keep her in the gang? She's a hussy. She keeps on tantalising me. Get rid of her!'

Again Vickram's men pointed their rifles at him and warned him not to speak to me like that. Vickram had to calm them, taking them aside and trying to play down what they all knew in their bones, that Shri Ram was a thakur and he despised them. They didn't want him as their leader. They didn't share Vickram's respect for him. Shri Ram might have taught Vickram about being a bandit and prison might have made them close, but the others had nothing in common. One by one, they began to quit the gang.

The older ones were the first to go. The tension was increasing and they knew from experience it meant trouble. Raghu Nath and Bharat no longer danced and sang together the way they used to. Some of the older men tried to persuade Bare Lal to leave with them, but even though he had spoken out against Shri Ram, he insisted on staying. 'I know I'm getting too old for this,' he told them, 'but I have to look after my nephew.'

There were about a dozen thakurs with us now, men that Shri Ram had recruited himself. They ate apart and spoke only to each other. And his brother Lala Ram had joined him too. Our men said he wasn't as dangerous as his brother, and they barely resembled one another. Lala Ram had dark skin and black hair. He was short and chubby. He was the younger of the two but that didn't stop him criticising his brother, telling him off in front of everyone for behaving badly.

When we were on a raid, Shri Ram would pick on members of our community. He would beat them and make them crawl in front of him, insulting them. 'Say it, mallah,' he would spit, 'say you are nothing but a dog!' If he could have got away with it, I'm sure he would have raped mallah women too, but all the men kept their eyes on him, even his own brother.

At the same time, the mallahs who no longer trusted Vickram because of his devotion to Shri Ram began to rally to me. They guarded me around the clock and they would only take orders from me, not their so-called leader. It infuriated Shri Ram to see this. He kept insulting me behind Vickram's back, calling me a low-caste whore. I warned him to watch his words. 'You insolent shit,' he said. 'How dare you talk back to me! How dare you pretend to be the leader!'

A dangerous situation was developing. The men wouldn't stop squabbling. If a thakur decided something, the mallahs were against it. If Shri Ram's men wanted to do one thing, Vickram's men wanted to do something else. Somehow, though, they managed to carry out plenty of looting, and there was no shortage of money or supplies, but the men were becoming enemies. I kept warning Vickram to beware. I knew Shri Ram was evil. I tried to persuade Vickram to leave him and his gang of thakurs, but he said I was misjudging him. 'Shri Ram is a very just man,' he insisted. I was convinced the red devil wanted to kill us, but Vickram was blinded by his admiration for him, and he couldn't see the trap waiting to close around us.

But he couldn't fail to notice how Shri Ram always picked on mallahs and spared thakurs, and hearing him always calling us pathetic – a caste of peasants whose men were only fit to wash his feet and women were only good for one thing – Vickram began to realise he was making a mistake.

He had heard rumours too, though he didn't want to believe them at first: Shri Ram was only staying with us mallahs while it suited him; he intended to kill us and take our money as soon as he got the chance. And it was clear that Shri Ram didn't like the way Vickram and I had become popular among the lowly castes for helping them against thakurs. He had been infuriated once when, in the middle of a pillage, a mallah from our gang had called him a wild animal because he was manhandling a peasant.

Pretending an informer had told us the police were planning an ambush, Vickram and I began sleeping apart, with our rifles at the ready. The other mallahs mounted a guard, sleeping spread out in different places. That way, it would be harder for Shri Ram's men to take us by surprise.

Looting was almost a respite. We carried out one raid after another, running through the jungle without rest, from one forest to the next.

Sometimes we didn't sleep for days and nights. I was the only woman and there was nobody I could talk to about my problems. Often we camped far from a river, without a drop of water for washing. I walked for days cursing the God who had made me a woman. Somebody heard my curses at least: our men started to nickname me Phool Singh, the masculine version of my name. It was a tribute to my fortitude, but when Phool Singh had an ache in her tummy, she would have given tens of thousands of rupees just to be able to bathe in the Yamuna in the cool of the evening.

The men in our gang treated me like a man and addressed me as a man, but with Shri Ram, it was still the same. He stared at me, his eyes filled with lust, pulling at his moustache, his fat lips murmuring obscenities.

I stared back and made a gesture, pretending to cut off his moustache.

'Look at her! Just look!' he exclaimed. 'Now she is threatening me!'

Finally Vickram proposed that we settle accounts and split into two gangs.

'You have money and men now. You can mount your own operations. We shouldn't be having these problems of caste. You are a thakur so make a gang of thakurs and we will have our gang.'

But Shri Ram had something else in mind. 'Here,' he said, 'take my rifle if you want, and kill me, or I will kill myself, but I want only to stay with you, Vickram. You are like my son. Why did you get me out of prison if you didn't want me with you?'

Then Shri Ram looked over at me. 'She is your problem,' he said. 'You listen too much to her. She's made you lose your head. You have no more respect for me because of her, so go on, kill me if that's what you want!'

He even began to sob and fell on his knees in front of Vickram.

'All right, all right! Forget what I said. Stay . . .'

Shri Ram got up from where he was kneeling and slapped Vickram on the back.

Really, he was congratulating himself.

It was his idea to give the men some distraction by playing a game of kabaddi. He said it would take our mind off things. We were camped in a wide clearing and he marked a line down the centre. Then Shri Ram made a show of choosing the teams at random.

'Vickram and I will be the captains, but the teams won't be drawn by caste. We'll pick them by lots!' He held a stone in one hand and a leaf in the other and nodded at them from side to side with his chin like a big red parrot.

The men were divided into two teams; a man from one team would run to the other side shouting 'Kabbadi!' and try to touch his opponent while the men on the other team tried to grab him. When I was little I used to play the game in the village, but with the men it was much rougher. I had no intention of taking part. There was no question of letting a man touch me, and I had other reasons . . .

The men had put down their rifles to play the game. I watched from a distance, making sure I could survey the whole clearing from my vantage point. When he saw me crouched silently by my rucksack, Shri Ram groaned, 'Vickram, tell her to put down her rifle and join in. She's a good runner!'

But Vickram had ordered me not to move. He had told me to keep my eyes on Shri Ram and keep my rifle in my hands from the moment he put his down.

Life was becoming unbearable. I was constantly on my guard, watching every movement around me.

The game became a tournament, and each time they played, I had to watch the men, afraid that, if Shri Ram didn't turn on us, at any moment the police might surprise us in the middle of the game without our arms.

One evening, about a week later, I was sitting by the river while the men were getting ready for a game when I heard a bullet whistle by my head. It had passed right next to me. All the men had dived for cover when they heard the gunshot; all except Shri Ram, who just stood there with a sly grin.

'Sorry! I was aiming at a bird!'

He had shot at me deliberately. I had seen him take his rifle and pretend to aim in the sky and then lower the barrel. Now it was going to be his turn to dance . . . I lifted my rifle and, waving the barrel left and right, aimed at his head.

He turned and ran with a scream.

'I didn't mean it!' I shouted after him. 'I can't hold the barrel steady!'

I lowered my rifle and the men started laughing. For an instant, our eyes met. In his I could see all the hatred and frustration of a thakur who couldn't crush me or frighten me. I hoped he could see pride and contempt in my eyes. I hoped he got the message that I would have killed him if Vickram hadn't been there.

The men were waiting for a showdown, but Vickram just laughed, trying to defuse the situation. 'You wanted to hit a bird, well Phoolan did too! Why are you running away?'

Vickram signalled at me to calm down. He was afraid of a confrontation between the two gangs that would lead to a massacre. I didn't even know how much longer he thought he was going to be able to put up with it. We were never together any more. We hardly even spoke to one another so as not to provoke Shri Ram's jealousy.

One day, a villager invited us to his daughter's wedding. We often went to the festivities in a village, and if the parents were poor, Vickram and I would give money to help the bride's father pay her dowry. Sometimes I would perform the *kanya-daan* ceremony in place of the bride's mother, giving presents to the groom. It was because the money of the rich went to help the poor that the villagers protected us, and I hadn't forgotten the way my family had struggled and starved to be able to pay our dowries.

As we were leaving for the wedding, Shri Ram suddenly

decided he wanted to join us. He wanted to bring along his brother, Lala, and some of their men. For several days, Lala Ram had been trying to placate his brother, and the tension between us had lessened. We decided to let them come with us. The moon was high and a wind was blowing across the plains when we set off. Most of Vickram's men had gone on ahead to the village, to make sure it was safe, but Uncle Bare Lal was with us – and Shri Ram and his men.

We crossed the fields until we came to the road to the village, where we came by a man waiting with a pile of watermelons. The man recognised me. 'Here, Phool Singh, look!' he said. 'I have nice melons for you!' We had been walking for some time and we were far from our camp. I was thirsty. Lala Ram accepted a piece of watermelon and encouraged me to have one too. 'Eat! They're good!'

Lala Ram was standing beside me and Bare Lal was with the rest of the men who had spread out in the fields, waving their torches around in case it was a trap. I didn't notice that Shri Ram had fallen behind.

Vickram took a slice of melon and began eating it, talking with the man by the pile of melons at the side of the road. Suddenly a shot rang out – and then another – and Vickram collapsed to the ground.

Instantly I fired in the air to warn the others, thinking the police had ambushed us. My head was spinning. In the moonlight I could make out only shadows, but I suddenly saw Lala Ram coming towards me. In a flash, I realised it was Shri Ram who had fired the shots. I pointed my rifle at Lala Ram.

'Back, you bastard, or I'll shoot you!'

I fired over his head to show him I was serious.

There was no sign of Shri Ram. 'I know you shot Vickram!' I shouted into the night so he would hear. 'If you shoot, I'll kill your brother!'

I heard someone running behind me and Shri Ram appeared again. 'What do you mean?' he asked. 'I'm right here. It wasn't me who shot him. It's this fellow who gave you the watermelons. He must be mixed up in it. I was by the trees back there having a pee.'

'Don't move!' I said. I still had my rifle aimed at his brother. The man with his melons was still standing there frozen with fright. If he had been the bait for an ambush, he would have dived for cover when the first shot was fired.

I was alone, surrounded, but I could hear the shouts of our men as they ran back from the direction of the village. Shri Ram's men didn't dare to move an inch. They were waiting for a signal from their boss. I had his brother in my sights and I was calculating my chances of shooting Shri Ram before he shot me . . . I thought Vickram was dead, and I didn't care if I lived or died.

'Phoolan . . . Here . . .'

It was Vickram's voice!

He struggled to his feet with his rifle in his hand. When I heard him, tears of relief streamed down my face, but I didn't take my eyes off the two brothers. They still had their rifles pointed at us.

I drew close to him as we waited for our men to reach us. 'Don't move, or he'll shoot us both,' whispered Vickram. 'I saw him do it. But don't accuse anybody, whatever you do, don't say anything!'

He shouted at the two brothers in his deep voice.

'Nobody move. I'm not dead.'

The moon was bright enough for me to be able to see the bloodstains on his uniform. He had been shot in the back! It could only have been a coward like Shri Ram. He was the only one behind us. The others had been ahead of me but he had fallen back and nobody else would have shot Vickram in the back.

He had been shot with a twelve-bore gun. There was blood bubbling out of his back, his clothes were burnt and there was a stink of sulphur. But Vickram had spoken firmly. He didn't want them to know how badly wounded he was. He asked the melon-grower to give him a cloth. 'Any cloth,' he said. The man took off his shirt and gave it to Vickram. He tied it around his waist, covering the wound, and he whispered to me again, 'Don't worry Phoolan, it's not serious. I can still stand up. Stay calm and wait for the others to get here.'

He had been hit above the waist, I couldn't see exactly where. The blood was flowing heavily, down his trousers and over his shoes, but he ignored it. His expression was fixed.

Our men finally reached us. 'What happened?' said Bare Lal. 'Are you hurt badly? Who shot you?'

'We don't know,' said Shri Ram. 'This peasant here was mixed up in it.'

The men turned to the farmer, who was too terrified to move. Vickram quickly cut in. 'Leave him,' he said. 'He didn't have anything to do with it. Tell him to bring us a cart, quickly.'

Vickram was still on his feet, with his rifle in his hand, and his men around him now. There were ten of us. I counted Shri Ram's gang. There were eleven of them.

Vickram spoke slowly. 'Don't come near us, or I'll shoot. And I don't know which one of you I'll hit . . .'

They didn't move.

'Somebody shot me in the back and I know who it was. I don't want to lay eyes on you again. You're a band of cowards, you aren't worth shit. Get away from here! Go!'

Our men knew instantly that Vickram was trying to avoid a bloodbath, and Shri Ram's men understood too. If any one of us opened fire, we might all end up dead there in the fields. The hatred was so tangible I expected the guns to go off at any second. The silence was so intense I could hear the grass rustling in the wind.

Shri Ram was the first to move. He turned and, with a slow wave of his arm, gestured his men to follow him.

They walked away slowly, stepping back without taking their eyes from us. And then in the dead of the night all we could hear was the sound of them running, fleeing like rats.

Not until there was silence did Vickram slump against a rock at the side of the road. I lifted his head and put my rucksack under it. Bare Lal shone his torch on Vickram's wounds.

'He's lucky,' he said. 'Two bullets, either side of his spine. Any lower and he would have been paralysed.'

Vickram was pale. He was sweating heavily and shivering.

'It's all right. He isn't going to die. It'll be all right,' said Bare Lal.

'It hurts, Phoolan. It's burning me! Put water on it . . .'

I ran to a stream, sobbing as I filled my canteen. If he died, I thought, what would become of me? As I ran back to him I felt my wet cheeks grow cold.

The shirt he had tied around his waist where the bullets had hit him was already soaked red with blood. Two holes had been burned in the lower part of his kurta, just above his hip. The bullets must have gone right through him. I poured the water slowly over his wounds. It was no good. The blood was still flowing from him in spurts.

I heard the men whispering that he wouldn't make it, he was going to die. I prayed to God not to take him from me. 'Damn you,' I cursed. 'Don't give me a man to protect me and then take him away from me! Damn you!'

I cursed all the gods, shaking my head in a rage and frustration as I knelt beside the only man who had given me love.

*

Half an hour later, the melon-grower came back from the village with another man at the reins of a bullock-cart, and we laid Vickram on it. I sat with his head in my lap as we lurched forwards. He must have felt my tears falling on his face. He opened his eyes.

'Don't cry, Phoolan. Don't cry. I'm doing fine. It doesn't hurt any more. The pain has gone.'

'I'm scared! I don't want you to die!'

'Don't be afraid. I love you. You're my wife. I'm not going to leave you.'

The cart brought us to the village, where we changed our clothes quickly before setting off for Orai. The man with the cart said Vickram was bleeding too heavily for us to take the bus, and he offered to take us with his cart. He said we could tell the doctor Vickram had been in an accident and he had found him.

I took off my rifle and my cartridge belt and gave them to one of our men. Then I took a sari from my rucksack and put it on over my uniform. Phoolan Devi had to look like the wife of a villager found injured at the roadside. I took off Vickram's watch and his jewellery to give it to the man with the cart, and I was about to give him my bangles too, when Vickram stopped me.

'Keep them.'

'What for? He's a poor man and he's taking a big risk.'

'You are my wife. I want you to keep the jewellery I gave you.' He tried to smile at me. 'It's a long time since I've seen you in a sari . . .'

He lifted himself up. 'See, I can move. It's going to be all right.'

Reluctantly, our men headed back to the jungle. Vickram could only be seen in a town and there would be too many police around. Bare Lal said he was coming with us. He took off his uniform and put on a dhoti and kurta, and the three of us set off. We had to trust the villager with the cart. He seemed to be cunning, at least. He told us to say Vickram had been hurt when a lorry backed into him, piercing him with two metal rods.

It was still night when we reached Orai. We tried to keep to the shadows, out of the light of the streetlamps, so as not to be noticed. If we were stopped by police, they might recognise Vickram. He was unconscious, and the mattress we had put under him was drenched in blood.

Bare Lal and the cart driver left us under a neem tree and set off to find a doctor, but they soon returned saying that all the doctors they could find either refused or said we had to make out a police report first. It was morning before they found a young doctor who was prepared to come, but only for a hundred rupees. He took one look at Vickram and said, 'He's not going to make it, he's lost too much blood.' Then he looked at us and asked, 'What's his name? Where does he come from?'

The doctor wanted to see the wounds, but Bare Lal stopped him. 'If you agree to operate, all right, otherwise leave him.'

The doctor didn't like this. He took Vickram's pulse. 'If something isn't done quickly, this man is going to die!' He opened his bag. The long needle brought back bad memories. I knew nothing about medicine, and the only injection I had ever had was long ago, in my childhood, when my father had rescued me from Putti Lal.

Bare Lal paid the doctor his hundred rupees and told him to go. The cart driver went looking for another doctor. It was mid-morning by then and people were milling around us, curious to know what had happened. They were jatavs and people who belonged to other lowly castes, and some of them brought warm milk for him, but Vickram couldn't drink it. The injection had brought him around again, but his face was the colour of sand and his lips were blue. Bare Lal and I moved the cart into the shade and waited. Time passed slowly. I cradled his head in my arms helplessly. Soon it was midday, and there was still no sign of the cart driver or a doctor.

I barely heard Vickram whisper, in his voice that used to be so strong. He was saying we should take a taxi to Jhansi to find his brother Rampal. 'He is a teacher in a school . . .'

I had never been that far before. Jhansi was a big city. How many hundreds of schools would there be? I wondered. But Bare Lal said he knew someone there who might be able to tell us where we could find Vickram's brother. It was going to take several hours by road, and it would be late by the time we arrived, but we had no choice. The cart driver returned, saying no one would help us, and Vickram was unconscious again. We put him in the taxi, wrapped in a blanket, and set off.

We were heading southwards on a black tarmac road busy with traffic, leaving the Yamuna far behind us. I had never been so far on a road before, nor had I ever ridden in a car, but I was to upset to care. I asked Bare Lal about the man he knew in Jhansi. 'Can you trust him?' I asked. 'Does he know about Vickram?'

He told me not to worry. 'The man is a Pandit, an important man who owns many wheatfields. Rampal used to work for him and he will be able to tell us where to find him.' I prayed silently he was right. From time to time, Vickram shivered and asked for water, and then he fell silent. The driver of the white taxi noticed, but said nothing.

Jhansi was almost at the border of the next state, Madya Pradesh. A red fort where a Maharajah once lived looked out over the city from a hill. The city was much bigger than Orai; there were tall buildings with many floors and I had never seen so many people before. It was evening when we got there and the stalls and shops were lit up. But all I could think of was Vickram. His breathing had grown so faint I could hardly hear it.

The Pandit was a rich man who lived in a large concrete house. Bare Lal went inside and soon came out again with him.

'Who are you?' the Pandit asked when he saw me standing by the taxi. He was well-dressed, with grey hair.

'It doesn't matter,' I said. 'Where is Rampal?'

'He's not around at this hour. You must come back later. Are you Vickram's wife?'

'Yes.'

He must have mistaken me for Vickram's first wife, and I left it at that. I feared he would have heard of Phoolan Devi. He said we could come in and wait, and I decided to risk telling him.

'Vickram is with me,' I said. 'He's been injured and he needs help.'

The Pandit called his wife out of the house and they looked inside the taxi. There was already a crowd gathering around us, looking at the pale, sweating man in the back wrapped in a blanket. The Pandit shooed them away and made the taxi driver back up to the gate. He took Vickram out of the taxi himself and carried him inside. Bare Lal paid the taxi driver and anxiously watched him drive away. The taxi driver had seen the blood . . .

We entered a large room lined with shelves stacked with provisions. There was a big bed in the middle and the Pandit put Vickram down on it. He looked at his bloody hands, at the blanket drenched in blood, and at Vickram's pallid face. 'What happened?' he asked.

'Please . . . We need help.'

I was worn down with desperation. I didn't know what else to say to him.

'What do you expect me to do for you? He's been shot, hasn't he?'

I told him what had happened. There was no point in trying to pretend. He must have known Vickram was a bandit anyway, because he knew his family.

'It was an ambush. He's going to die. Please, help us! It doesn't matter how much it costs, we'll get you the money, but you have to find someone to help us!'

'Wait here,' he said. 'I will make a telephone call.'

Though I could hear the Pandit talking in the next room, I didn't know who he was talking to. 'I don't know,' he was saying, 'they just told me he was injured in the back by a metal rod . . .' I thought for a moment there must have been someone in the room with him. Then I realised the Pandit really was rich. He had electricity in his house, and a telephone. I had never spoken into a telephone. I knew that they existed but they were as much as a mystery for me as the tangle of wires that hung on the electrical poles outside.

Vickram was stretched out motionless on the bed and Bare Lal and I were waiting beside him. He had stopped bleeding, at least. I feared the blood must have all drained out of him. But I saw his thin lips moving and, listening closely, I heard him asking me to hold his hands.

They were cold. I rubbed them slowly to warm them. In the electric light his face looked white, as though he were already dead.

The Pandit had trouble persuading the doctor to come. He ended up spinning him a tale about a fight between three brothers, saying the third brother had tried to separate the first two and a gun had gone off. The doctor told him he would have to report it to the police, whatever the story, and he wanted two hundred and fifty thousand rupees. The Pandit asked us if we agreed. Bare Lal went to speak on the telephone. The doctor finally settled for a hundred thousand rupees in cash and another thirty thousand after the operation. I promised the Pandit I would find the money.

Vickram's brother arrived soon afterwards. I didn't know Rampal. He was shorter and heavier than his brother, with wide shoulders and thin hips and a high, almost feminine voice. He burst into tears when he saw Vickram and greeted me politely as the eldest of his sisters-in-law. But he was of no use to us. He fell at his brother's bedside and wouldn't stop sobbing that he was going to die.

I told him to pull himself together. The dealing on the telephone had already left me at my wits' end. We were going to have to take Vickram from the house to a mill in the countryside that belonged to the Pandit. The doctor was going to operate on him there. We couldn't stay in the city. The taxi driver who had brought us had seen the blood, and might have already told the police.

It was midnight when we called another taxi. We wrapped Vickram in another blanket, with Bare Lal propping him up on one side and Rampal on the other. He looked ill or perhaps drunk, and the taxi driver didn't ask any questions. Bare Lal was tall and with his moustache, he looked like a thakur. His fierce expression silenced the taxi driver. The Pandit didn't come with us. He said goodbye to us from his doorstep as though we were leaving after a family visit, and I climbed in the front seat of the taxi with the end of my sari over my head.

An hour later we arrived at a large grain mill. Three men were waiting for us inside the gate. As soon as the taxi left, they went to work.

They carried Vickram to an empty room, gesturing us to wait outside. I could hear Vickram speaking softly. 'Water, Phoolan. A drink, Phoolan . . .'

One of the doctors came out and asked who Phoolan was.

'It's her, she's his wife,' said Rampal, without thinking. I hoped they wouldn't make the connection with Phoolan Devi and Vickram the Mallah. Our names were known and there was a price on our heads. I followed the doctor with my sari over my head into the room. They had cut away his uniform with scissors and laid him naked on his belly on a table. One of the doctors was washing the blood from his wounds with a sponge. Vickram wasn't calling for me now. I could only see his profile. He looked pale still but calm, as though he was only sleeping.

I stayed there for a few minutes watching what they were doing. They took metal instruments out of their bags and set them in rows on little white trays. 'You'll have to leave now,' said one of the doctors. 'We're waiting for the anaesthetic to take effect, and then we'll operate.'

I didn't want to leave. I didn't trust them. I didn't trust anybody. They had begun to open the skin on his back with a long thin silver knife. The edges of the wound were hanging open either side. The two doctors made a sign for the third one to make me leave.

As we waited in the hall, I asked Uncle Bare Lal, 'What is anaesthetic?'

'It puts you to sleep so you don't feel the operation. Don't worry.'

Rampal was sobbing beside him, wringing his hands. I squatted down on the floor beside them in the empty hallway. Through the window I could see the dark night and the cold moon, the same moon as the night before, when Shri Ram had shot him.

'Bare Lal, we're going to get the bloody red bastard.'

'Vickram will get him.'

Despite everything, I wasn't tired. I could see the field again, and I heard the booming sound of both barrels of the shotgun going off almost at once and I saw Vickram crumple again. In that moment, I had believed he was dead. If the red devil had aimed better, he could have triggered a massacre. We might all have been killed if Vickram hadn't been so cool-headed.

Vickram was intelligent and loyal. It was his loyalty that had enabled those traitors to get him. He had taught me so much – that the rivers flowed from far away in the mountains, where the gods lived; that our country was so large I would never see the end. He knew how to read newspapers and books, he was well-spoken, he was fair and honest, and he had told me that he loved me. I loved him too, like a brother, a father, a leader. He was part of me, part of my soul and part of my being. He couldn't die, because if he died, I would die.

'Don't cry, Phoolan, it's going to be all right.'

'I know, Bare Lal.'

Durga was going to save him.

It was nearly noon the next day when I heard him calling.

'Phoolan, come, where are you?'

I dashed into the room.

'I feel better. Much better!'

He smiled at me, and I couldn't contain myself. I laughed with relief at the sound of his voice.

25

I was squatting in the corner of the room with my sari over
my head, listening carefully to what the doctor was saying.
He had removed some stitches from the wound and now he
was changing the bandages. He had nearly finished his work.

Vickram had flinched while he took out the stitches, but
he hadn't cried out once. 'What are you made of?' the doctor
had asked. 'I heard that two dacoits are in the area,' he added
casually. 'Vickram Mallah and Phoolan Devi. And one of
them, Vickram, has been shot.'

'I hope you don't think we're dacoits,' said Vickram.

'No, no, but I've been told they're hiding somewhere. The
whole town is full of police, and they're checking all the
hospitals and clinics.'

For all we knew, the doctor might already have
denounced us, but Vickram kept calm.

'Another week in bed and you'll be fixed up,' said the
doctor, touching Vickram's back. 'There's still a fragment
here that was impossible to get at. You'll have to be careful
from now on. You said you are a lorry driver . . .'

'That's right.'

'Well, you take it easy now.'

He had doubted us from the start. That was why he
wanted so much money. Vickram couldn't yet walk properly, but it was clearly time to leave.

The doctor said he would be back the next day as usual to

check up on Vickram. He had been there every day since the operation, but he was always alone. I hadn't seen the other two doctors again. At the door of the mill, he turned to say goodbye to me and I could sense him trying to catch a glimpse of my face under my sari.

'Namasteh,' he said.

'Namasteh, sahib.'

I went back inside.

'Did he ask you anything, Phoolan?'

'No, but he keeps looking at Bare Lal and me.'

'You'll have to leave me here. If the police come, it doesn't matter about me, but I don't want you getting killed.'

I knew I wouldn't be able to eat or sleep if we left him there, I would be too desperate with worry. 'I can't leave you here alone,' I said.

'We don't have any other choice. I can't walk and I don't want all three of us getting caught. I want you to go away from here with Bare Lal right now.'

But I had always been stubborn, ever since I was a child. I had an idea. Lorries had been coming and going every day from another part of the mill, and I went to talk to some of the drivers. I told them my husband was ill and asked if they would take him and his brother to Kanpur. One of the drivers was going there, and we agreed on a price.

The doctor had warned Vickram to lie still. When he tried to walk, he said it felt as if his body had been cut in half. He gritted his teeth and Rampal supported him.

Less than an hour after the doctor left, Vickram and Rampal were in the lorry and on their way. They weren't going to Kanpur. Rampal was going to halt the lorry en route and get off with Vickram to head for a little village where they would be able to hide in the house of a shopkeeper they knew. Bare Lal and I were going to take the train back to Orai and walk from there to Gauhani, the village where

Vickram's family lived. We were going to get money he had left with his relatives and join him later. We needed the money to stay in hiding. In my village, the amount the doctor had pocketed for the operation would have bought a house and cattle and fed a family for a year and a half. I didn't know how to count, but I could judge the value of a bundle of rupees, and we didn't have many bundles left. We needed more money urgently, and there was no question of staging a raid to get it for the time being.

We reached Gauhani as night fell and found it was under police watch. A tent had been pitched next to the village well and the police were sitting there waiting outside it. I don't know who they were expecting, but when the sipahi on duty saw a little woman with her head covered by a sari shuffling along timidly by the mud walls, accompanied by a well-dressed thakur, he didn't think there was anything unusual about it.

Vickram's uncle didn't believe me. 'He is dead. The police say so. Who are you to come asking for his money?' he asked. Even if he did believe me, he said he had no money. 'And if you don't leave here right away I'll call the police!'

Vickram had told me he had left fifty thousand rupees with his uncle, but it was as if he preferred not to believe Vickram was still alive. We left his house and, right under the nose of the policeman leaning on his rifle half-asleep, we went to Vickram's father's house, a few streets away. But Vickram's father didn't believe us either. 'It's a lie! The police told us he was dead. They showed us photographs.' I asked him who he believed – me or the police. He had recognised me from the time Vickram had brought me there after our marriage. He began to cry as I told him what had happened to his son, but he said Vickram had left all the money with his uncle, and he had nothing, just a big family to feed.

There were three older sisters who were already married; Vickram was the fourth child and Rampal the fifth, and there were two more boys and three daughters after that. He said he could only give us twenty thousand rupees. There was no point in arguing with him. The day was wearing on. We took the twenty thousand and left to see one of Vickram's aunts in a neighbouring village.

She collapsed in tears when she heard that her nephew had been shot, but was still alive. For her too, Vickram was surely dead, and she snivelled that she had no money either. I was beginning to lose my patience.

'Vickram left five hundred thousand rupees with you! He said so! That's why he sent us here. All we want is fifty thousand for the time being.'

She repeated that she had nothing. I wondered how many more people I would have to beg for Vickram's money.

'Wait until he comes back. Just wait!'

The aunt started taking off her bangles and earrings. 'Here . . . Sell them, and my necklace. It's all I have!'

I refused but Bare Lal told me to take them. 'We need cash.'

He was right. I realised we were powerless without our uniforms, and without the men. Frustration put me on edge, and I was starting to get nervous. We had been in the area too long, trying to get help from a family that only seemed to care about Vickram as long as he was alive, with his pockets full of rupees. We were taking too much of a chance staying so long in Vickram's village. I had another plan. I told Bare Lal we could go to my village. My parents had nothing, but Mayadin had plenty . . .

We left on foot, the thakur and the little woman in her sari, and nobody tried to stop us. We headed towards the Yamuna and from there we continued by boat. We came ashore at the village called Gorha, a few miles before mine, and there, we told someone to go and warn the Sarpanch that Phoolan Devi was back.

Bare Lal was uneasy and I knew that we were running a big risk. They might go straight to the police. The goddess with her rifle and her uniform was a little woman in a sari now, and her gang was a long way away in the jungle. I was afraid, but I knew that fear could be my weapon too. And I was right. They were too scared to tip off the police. The delegation from my village, led by the Sarpanch, came to meet us in the fields as instructed. I let them think the gang was covering me, waiting in the trees with their rifles, and I told them that far from being dead, as they all hoped, Vickram was recovering. He had sent us to collect contributions to his get-well fund. He wanted ten thousand rupees from each of them.

To see Mayadin, the hypocrite, throw himself at my feet again and pray for Vickram's recovery made my stomach turn. He even dared to ask if he could come and pay his respects to Vickram too. I told him he had done me enough harm, and I reminded them that Vickram was protecting their village . . . In other words, if they didn't pay, thakurs might come to pillage them and there would be nothing Vickram or I would do about it.

The money was there the same afternoon.

'Oh what a good idea!' laughed Bare Lal when he saw it. 'You managed to get all that money without firing a single shot! They came here and gave it to us with smiles!'

When they heard that Vickram was injured, the people of Gorha offered us money too. 'We give it willingly, we don't want it back,' their Sarpanch said. Without us asking the poor people of Gorha brought us contributions of a hundred rupees or two hundred rupees each. Vickram was a saviour for them, one woman said. 'Thakurs used to come here and break people's legs and rape the girls.' They said they were happy to pay their respects to Vickram.

I didn't know how to count the money but Bare Lal said we had what we needed now. Our next priority was to find the men. We knew they would be hiding somewhere near a village named Asta, and we had to walk back to the bridge at Kalpi and then take the bus to Orai to reach it. When we got to the village, nobody seemed to have heard anything about any dacoits. There was no sign of them until we noticed a man in a field carrying a heavy sack. I went over to him and asked him if he knew anything about Vickram's gang. He shook his head, so I told him who I was.

'You aren't Phoolan!' he scoffed. 'She wears a uniform and rides a horse. She doesn't walk like a peasant, wearing a sari.'

'Look at me, you fool! Take a good look at me.'

'Oh, Bahanji! Excuse me, Phoolan. I didn't recognise you. These supplies are for Vickram's men. Raghu Nath ordered me to bring them.'

Little Raghu Nath!

'Go and tell them I'm here!'

I couldn't wait to join the men, to get rid of my sari and carry my rifle again. Then we would be able to go back and get Vickram.

The men all thought he was dead too. The newspapers had reported that the police had cremated him in the hills, and they were protecting his family against Shri Ram and Lala Ram. They had made his parents sign an official paper confirming he was dead. Raghu Nath showed me the news-paper and read it to me. The police said they had cremated him because they couldn't show his family the corpse.

Raghu Nath brought me my uniform. 'Please put it back on, Phool Singh. You are the leader now. We all agree that you should take over.'

I told them Vickram wasn't dead. 'The police are lying! Who do you believe, me or this newspaper?'

I explained that it had cost a lot of money for the operation and he was recovering, but he was still their leader. 'As
soon as he can walk again,' I promised them, 'he'll be back.'

But it wasn't yet the moment to put my uniform back on.
Bare Lal and I had to return to get Vickram alone. The men
wanted to come too, but I told them it was too dangerous to
travel in a gang and promised we would return within two
weeks or less. The only thing I took with me was my rifle.
Bare Lal said we would be too conspicuous carrying arms,
but I didn't want to travel around with all that money and no
means of defending ourselves.

'You're not afraid of dacoits, are you?' joked Raghu Nath.

We left the camp half an hour later and began to retrace
our route back to the main road to Kanpur and the village
where Vickram was hiding with his brother Rampal. As we
drew near the road, we stopped at some mallah villages looking for places to hide our rifles. In one of them we learned
that another of Vickram's brothers, Sukpal, had been
arrested by the police. They had beaten him for information,
and the police were boasting that I was about to be captured along with a dacoit who was accompanying me. There
was a ten thousand rupee reward on my head and five thousand on Bare Lal's head. It was far less money than we were
carrying, but it would be enough to feed an informer for a
long while. We would have to be careful. And we were
warned that it was going to be impossible to reach the road.
The police were everywhere.

Bikku and I kept to the fields, with our heads low. The
warnings were well-founded. There must have been five or
six deputy superintendents and whole lorryloads of men in
uniform.

It was too late to turn around, we couldn't get back to
warn the gang, and Bare Lal feared that one of the men had
already been captured and told them of our plans, otherwise

how else would they have known I was with another dacoit? To be safe, we decided to split up. We hid our rifles in a deep pit used for storing the mustard harvest. Bare Lal was going to hide in the wilds, while I set off to try to contact the Pradhan of a village nearby called Kothi-Shala. He was a man we could trust, and he might have more information.

It was still dark, just before dawn, when I located his house and knocked gently on the wooden door.

'Who is it?'

'Phoolan . . .'

He let me in nervously.

'Have the police been here?'

'Yes. They're looking everywhere. They know you're in the area. They even know you are wearing a blue sari. You can't stay here. They're all over the village during the day.'

He gave me a lunghi, and I removed my sari and wrapped the long white cloth around me. Then, with a pot of water on my shoulders, I left calmly along the village path.

'Where are you going?'

Two policemen were blocking my way.

'To the fields, to relieve myself.'

It was an advantage being eighteen years old but looking only fifteen. In a petticoat and lunghi I resembled any other village girl on her way to wash. They didn't give me a second glance. Phoolan Devi had a reputation as a dangerous dacoit. Just like the villager in the fields, the police too imagined her to be twice as tall as me, armed to the teeth and galloping across the fields on a white horse.

Outside the village was an orchard of mango trees. I climbed a large tree and hid myself among the thick leaves. It was a hot day and soon I was parched with thirst, but it was too risky to go near a well. I quenched my thirst with a juicy mango. The sweet fruit gave me sustenance but I didn't know which way to turn next. Behind me was a village full of police, and in front of me it was the same. I scrambled higher up the branches, hoping nobody would be able to see me in the dense foliage, as I waited there in the tree until nightfall.

Once it was dark enough, I climbed down and made my way back to the Pradhan's house, knocking lightly on his door again.

He was even more nervous this time.

'The police are still here!' he whispered in the dark.

Apparently, I had been seen left and right all day long. All the villagers were hoping for the reward. But the other news was not good. One of our men had been arrested. His name was Ramkesh. They had captured him on the bridge at Kalpi and he was the one who had told them Vickram was with his brother. That was why they had arrested Sukpal and beaten him. They had got the wrong brother.

'You can't stay here,' said the Pradhan. 'They might come back at any minute. They're saying that Vickram is dead and you're alone and they will have no trouble cornering you. They're looking everywhere, but they only have a vague idea what you look like.'

'I have to find Bare Lal. He's hiding in the jungle. We planned to meet tonight near the mustard ditch to get our rifles.'

The Pradhan agreed to go and look for him. He gave me some food before he left, and as I ate, I tried to think of what I would do if Bare Lal had been arrested too. He was carrying the money, and if they found him, they would probably shoot him down.

Almost an hour went by before the Pradhan returned out of breath. The police had stopped him and questioned him. They had warned him they didn't like to see him walking around the village at night. But he had located Bare Lal. He had the rifles and he was outside keeping watch. The

Pradhan gave me some clothes that I could run in – a pair of men's trousers, a red T-shirt and some shoes – and we left, crawling in the dark on our hands and knees in the ditches beside the mud walls until we reached the open fields. We decided we would try to reach a village called Bhabroli before dawn. It was too dangerous to move around in daylight. One of Vickram's sisters lived there and she might be able to hide us, at least for a while.

Fatigue was starting to weigh on me. My legs were getting heavier as we ran. I had spent most of the day in the branches of a tree and it was so long since I had slept that I could hardly even remember what it felt like. I thought we would never make it to Bhabroli before the sun came up, but Bare Lal knew the route and made me keep up. He said we could get there by daybreak if we were lucky.

The village was quiet. As we approached the first few houses, I glanced down a path to make sure there were no police and suddenly a figure sprang up behind me.

'Oh my goodness! A woman! She walked on me. She walked on my body!'

It was an old man who had been sleeping on a mat on the ground outside his little house. I had tripped over him. I was wearing trousers and shoes and carrying a rifle; it was still dark, but the old man was shouting that a woman had walked over him. I halted, but we heard someone coming from the house and Bare Lal pulled me away. He kept running but I couldn't keep up. I began to laugh. I was laughing crazily and I couldn't stop. I was laughing and running and crying at the same time.

'How did he know I was a woman, Bare Lal?'

'I don't know, your weight maybe. You were too light.'

'But I just tripped over him!'

I don't think I had ever laughed so much in my life. I was still tittering like a madwoman when we found Vickram's

sister's house. We were being hunted, we were in mortal
danger, my nerves were stretched to the limit and I was
exhausted, but I was laughing . . . I couldn't even stop when
Vickram's sister melted in tears as she opened the door.

'He is dead. My brother is dead!' she grieved.

We had to tell her the whole story before she would settle down, but I could tell that she loved her brother and we
were safe with her for the time being – that is, the time it
would take to find a place to hide the rifles before we set off
again. But it was hard find a good cache for a rifle. If you left
them in a pile of rubbish or just buried them in the ground,
they would rust, and afterwards they might jam. We were
still looking for somewhere when daylight came, and by
then it was too late to leave the house. We had no choice but
to risk spending the day there.

Vickram's brother-in-law volunteered to go to Orai and
get a newspaper. They wanted to know what had happened
to young Sukpal, and we wanted to learn what the police
were up to. He came back three hours later and read us the
newspaper.

Bharat and Madhav had been killed; the two men closest
to Vickram. They had been ambushed on the road to Delhi.

I felt a tremor in me, a terrible sadness. Bharat had
become very fond of me, and used to call me his daughter.
But I felt worse when I thought of Vickram. They were the
men he trusted the most. Madhav was Vickram's cousin, the
son of his father's sister. He was a big, heavy man with a
pock-marked face. He never said very much, but was always
busy reading or writing. He was educated and used to keep
the accounts for the gang.

Vickram had once told me how it was because of Madhav
he had become a bandit. Madhav had fallen in love with a
girl named Kusuma. She belonged to a different caste and
her parents were scandalised when she told them about

Madhav. They had already arranged her marriage. But she wouldn't give up Madhav. In the end, the two of them eloped. The girl's family accused Madhav of kidnapping her and they took their revenge by having one of Madhav's uncles kidnapped. The uncle was never seen again and Madhav asked Vickram to help him take revenge. They were less than sixteen years old and, going from vengeance to vengeance, they became dacoits.

This woman had always been unlucky for Madhav. For a while, before I joined the gang, he had brought her with him to the jungle. But she became pregnant, and it was impossible for her to stay with them. Vickram told me once how he had been forced to make Madhav take her to live elsewhere. That was how she ended up in Delhi. In the city, she was able to live anonymously. But the police must have known somehow. Madhav had been killed with Bharat as they were trying to reach her. He was a kind man who had gone to school until he was fourteen and could have continued his studies if he hadn't met her. And I couldn't help thinking he would still be alive if he hadn't fallen in love with her.

With Madhav and Bharat gone, Vickram was alone. The newspaper story also said a reward of five thousand rupees per head had been paid to an informer. We would have to be careful. Our lives could be bought cheaply.

We waited until night fell before we departed. I was wearing one of Vickram's sister's saris and Bare Lal was dressed in some old clothes he had got from Vickram's brother-in-law. We reached Orai on foot and took the bus in the direction of Kalpi, getting off after a while to take a dirt road to the village where Vickram was hiding in the shopkeeper's house. Rampal was still there with him.

My manic laughter had deserted me. We had the money, and the rifles were hidden in another mustard ditch near his sister's village, but I was also bringing bitter news for Vickram.

Before I could open my mouth, however, he took me in his arms and danced me around with relief. 'I was afraid you were dead. It's been three days.'

I was relieved too, and I didn't know how to begin to tell him that two of his best friends were dead, one of his brothers was in prison, and his men had disbanded.

I showed him the newspaper . . .

He began to cry as he read it. It made me ache to see him cry, this man I loved. To try and bring him out of it, I told him how angry I had been with his family.

'I don't want to know about them,' he said. 'It's their fault. There were always quarrels in my village with thakurs. My father and my uncles had been disputing with them since before I was born. And Madhav's family too . . .'

It sounded like my own life.

'Kusuma's family told her Madhav wasn't suitable for her; he didn't belong to their caste.' Vickram shook his head slowly. 'If we all had the same rights, Phoolan, Madhav and I would never have become dacoits.'

I knew I needed him near me at each instant of my life, and I couldn't think what I would do if he had died, like Bharat and Madhav. He was still weak, but he seemed to be in better condition. He had got back a bit of colour in his cheeks: he didn't look so yellow any more. The piece of gunshot was still lodged in his back, but the risk of infection seemed to have passed. He could walk a little now, though it was painful for him, and I noticed that he couldn't straighten himself fully. Though he tried not to show it, it must have hurt him greatly. He soon had to lie down again.

With his head on my lap, he spoke to me softly. 'You can heal me. With your soft warm hands you can make me better.'

I chuckled. The doctor had forbidden me to touch his wounds before, because of the risk of infection.

Slowly and gently I massaged him.

'Your hands, Phoolan . . . I love the touch of your hands. Whenever you touch me the pain disappears. It's true. You *are* a goddess. It's thanks to you I'm still alive. Stay with me . . .'

He said things to me that he had never said before. He begged me for forgiveness. 'I have ruined your life,' he said.

I told him it wasn't true, he had saved it.

We waited in the shopkeeper's house for many days, until Vickram had recovered some strength and the police had given up their search.

I knew that two boys from my village were studying law in a big city, Lucknow. I thought we would be safer out of the district and the crowded cities seemed like good places to hide. I managed to make contact with them and we went there by taxi, crossing the bridge at Kalpi with our heads low, still looking out for sipahis.

I managed to find the boys and they introduced us to a lawyer. I was hoping we could make a deal with the police, and Vickram seemed to go along with the idea. The lawyer suggested that while he tried to negotiate with them, we could go to Nepal. We would be safe there and he said he knew a doctor who might be able to perform another operation.

We set off northwards for the Himalayas.

We went in the lawyer's car to the mountains: myself, my invalid husband, Uncle Bare Lal and the lawyer. I had become accustomed to travelling by then. I had seen the cities and the railways, and the teeming crowds, always going here and there with their suitcases and their ration tins full of food. I was used to the flat horizons of our country that Vickram said was so big it never ended, and I knew the empty, barren ravines. But when we crossed the border into Nepal and the road began to wind its way up the mountains, I felt a sensation of calm and wonder.

In the stories the Brahmin used to read to us in the village, the mountains were where the gods lived. I understood why they chose to live there, surrounded by the clear white peaks. The air was light and fresh. In the lush green valleys, with the sun shining, there was a feeling of peace and beauty. And best of all, we were able to walk around freely for once, without worrying about being identified.

It was the first time in my life that I had no fear of anyone, no fear of thakurs, nor of the police. It was the first time we had really been together, Vickram and I, just an ordinary wife with her husband. I told him how much I needed him. I wasn't afraid any more. I no longer withdrew from his touch. I welcomed his embrace. I trusted him. Vickram must have felt it too. He turned to me one evening as we walked through the streets and said, 'I owe you my life, Phoolan.'

Vickram went alone to see the doctor. He told me afterwards that the doctor had looked inside his body with a machine. He had said it would be impossible to operate on him. The piece of gunshot was lodged in his spine and would always cause him pain. There was nothing they could do. It was too dangerous to try to remove it, and he would always have to be careful: a fall or an awkward movement might leave him paralysed.

Vickram didn't seem to care. 'Right,' he said. 'Let's go. I have things to do.'

I was scared to go back to the jungle. We were happy in the mountains. 'Just a little while longer,' I pleaded, 'stay and rest a little longer.'

Bare Lal agreed. 'We have enough money for the

moment,' he argued. 'We should stay here. We can do as we please here.'

I kept trying to find excuses to stay, to prolong the chance to sleep the whole night untroubled by nightmares, the happiness of being able to live like everyone else. The lawyer said he was looking into the possibility of us surrendering. He said he would see what he could do. We would have to pay, of course, and I was reminded of my father's case against Mayadin . . . I wasn't very hopeful.

While we were there, I begged Vickram to take me to the cinema. It was the first time I had ever been. I had no idea what it was, though I had seen the posters in the towns.

When I came out of the vast dark hall, I couldn't remember the story, just the people dashing about and singing. I had thought at first they were alive in front of me and, when a woman fired a revolver at a man, she really had killed him. But then their faces grew so large, I wondered how it was possible.

Bare Lal told me that a machine had captured their beings to make living images of them. I wanted to go back in the cinema at once, but Vickram had other thoughts.

'I want my revenge . . .' he said.

26

Bare Lal agreed with me. It was too dangerous to return to the badlands along the Yamuna. 'You've got enough money,' he said. 'You can stay in the city and give up your old life. What are you going to do in the jungle, chase after Shri Ram and Lala Ram to kill them?' The old uncle shook his head in vexation. 'All that is finished now.'

Vickram was twenty-four years old and I was nearly eighteen. We could have changed our identities, Vickram could have found a job, and we could have led a normal life. Vickram was resourceful. I was sure he would have been able to survive in the city, and he could have taught me how to as well.

'If you really want to go back to the jungle,' I decided, 'leave me here. I don't want that kind of life any more.'

'No,' said Vickram. 'You have to come with me. Now that Madhav and Bharat are dead, I need you. Don't I mean anything to you?'

A wife had to be faithful to her husband until she died. I had been wedded to a monster when I was still a child, and now I was married to a bandit. But though I wore the jewellery Vickram had given me, it wasn't a proper marriage. My mother and my sisters hadn't been there to bathe me in oils. I wasn't a wife who kept the fire going in the kitchen, preparing the chapatis; I was Phoolan Devi the dacoit, wife of Vickram Mallah the dacoit. I didn't want to have to keep on running through the night, fleeing all the time from the police, or other dacoits, but I wouldn't have been able to live in the city without him. I wasn't clever enough, and I didn't know how things worked there. You had to be able to read and write in the city, otherwise people could deceive you. I only knew how to read faces and how to understand what people said. I could tell the difference between an honest face and an untrustworthy one, between a promise that would be kept and one that would be broken, but that wasn't enough. A woman couldn't live alone in the city. She would be easy prey. Without a husband, she would be singled out, and without a family she would be considered a prostitute. With no one to defend her, any man could take her.

It was the month of Shravan again, the monsoon season. That meant it had been a whole year since I was kidnapped. To be born a woman, I knew, was to be born powerless, to be unable to exist alone. I would have to return to the jungle . . .

Before we did, we went to make an offering in the temple at Ghatapara, the one by the Yamuna where the old ash-covered sadhu lived, near the village of Vickram's first wife. Dacoits always gave a third of their loot to the gods. It made no difference whether there were temples or mosques on the territory where we operated, we had to give the gods their due. Vickram always obeyed the rituals.

He prayed inside the temple while I prayed outside, at the top of the steps from the river, keeping one eye on the pilgrims who had come to drink and anoint themselves from the well. We were in an area where we might be recognised again.

Afterwards, we set off, walking for hours with our feet soaking in the monsoon torrents. I had almost forgotten what it was like in the open, but there was no turning back now. We were heading for Gauhani, Vickram's village.

Vickram was determined to settle his scores. He had changed, he had become bitter and hateful, especially towards thakurs. He kept saying that he wouldn't have become a dacoit if his father hadn't made him embark on an endless war against thakurs. His father had ruined his life, he said. His father was a quarrelsome man, he explained, always rowing with thakurs in his village. After Vickram had helped Madhav to avenge his uncle's disappearance, some thakurs had come to their house and assaulted Vickram's sisters. He and his cousins Madhav and Bharat had gone after them with a gun. There was a shooting and three people were killed. For the boys, there was no turning back.

When we reached his village, Vickram went straight to his father's house. 'Don't call me your son any more!' he told him. His uncle turned up and Vickram lost his temper, threatening to kill him because he had been living off his money. 'Why should I let you live?' he asked. 'You practically accused Phoolan of wanting the money for herself!' I reminded him of what he had said to me when I wanted to kill Mayadin: you cannot kill a member of your own family. Vickram snorted in annoyance. 'You're never going to let me forget that, are you?' he said, shaking his head. He threw his uncle out into the street, and we departed quickly. Vickram was depressed. He said his family only cared about him because of the money.

We found Raghu Nath hiding in a safe house in a nearby village. I had always liked Raghu Nath. He was short and skinny but quick and clever as a monkey. He had managed to avoid the police and he had been lying low, waiting for us to return. In the meantime, he had formed a new gang with five men. Uncle Bare Lal was still with us and we had a new recruit named Misra, a hefty young man who had been sent by Vickram's brother Sukpal to replace Madhav as Vickram's bodyguard. That meant we had nine men. Once we retrieved our rifles, Vickram's gang was back in business.

As soon as we were reunited, we pulled off two raids on neighbouring villages. Vickram wanted to let everybody know he was still alive. He had been disgusted when he learned the police had killed a poor shepherd in the hills to stage Vickram's death. They had dressed the shepherd's corpse in a uniform like the one Vickram wore and put a rifle across his chest. Then they took a photograph to make everyone believe it was Vickram before they cremated his body. Vickram's family had even performed all the proper rites on the thirteenth day after his death. We found out it was the deputy superintendent of police who had worked out this scenario to discredit Vickram so the villagers wouldn't help anyone associated with him and nobody else could use his name.

To prove he was still alive, Vickram had a rubber stamp made so he could sign his name to our lootings in blue ink. In big letters it said: PHOOLAN AND VICKRAM ARE BACK FROM HEAVEN.

'I don't want them to think you're doing this all alone,' he laughed.

He stamped it all over the doors of the houses of the rich like a curse.

After the two operations, we retreated to the ravines north of the Yamuna this time, and Vickram wrote the police a letter telling them where we were hiding and inviting them to come and get us! It wasn't long before they showed up.

'Here I am!' Vickram yelled through his megaphone. 'It's me, Vickram Mallah. You didn't really think I was dead, did you? Look at me, sipahis! I'm alive, and my days as a dacoit aren't over yet!'

We were spread out on high ground. Our men were lying flat ready to shoot, but Vickram was standing on the ledge. He seemed to be enjoying exposing himself to danger. He dared them to come forward and try to take him, and when they retreated, guessing it was a trap, he insulted them. 'Don't just run away. Cowards, come back and fight!'

He began to chase after them, leaping between the rocks and bushes like a lynx and firing at them as he ran. Shots from the police whistled by his ears but he didn't seem to care, he didn't take cover. He was even able to corner some of the sipahis. 'Hands up!' he shouted. 'Say it! Long live Vickram Mallah! Say it!' He had them in his sights. They dropped their guns and he fired at their feet to make them dance.

I was above him on the ledge, firing to give him cover and watching as the police retreated. He was a good leader. He could shoot better than the police, he could predict how they would react, and he knew the land by heart. He knew they wouldn't risk coming into the ravines after us. And despite his injury, he was able to leap faster than a gazelle, always one step ahead of their sights. It was as though he was taunting destiny, daring death to come for him again.

The police returned to their lorries and jeeps. We could have killed many of them, but we didn't. We didn't want to kill for no reason. Avenging yourself against an enemy was one thing, defending yourself during a looting something else, but even in an ambush, Vickram behaved honourably. He had achieved what he wanted: the police had seen with their own eyes that he was still alive. Vickram and Phoolan were back.

He discussed everything with me now. We worked out our plans together and then we consulted the men. It was the bandit life as before, but I had time to visit my parents. The rest of the men hid in the next village while Vickram came with me. My mother was happy to see me again but asked why the two of us didn't just surrender, before we were killed. Vickram promised her that that was what he intended to do, once he had finished what he had came back to finish with the help of his Durga! Father begged me not to kill anyone. 'Killing a human being is the worst thing of all. You will be damned for eternity,' he warned. I promised him I wouldn't do it. As for surrendering, it was something all dacoits talked about doing one day or another. It meant negotiating terms with the police, having money for bail, and then, perhaps, finally being able to leave the jungle for good. But I didn't really believe it would ever happen.

I looked at my village of mud and straw and I wasn't sure if what I felt was regret or relief. The huts, the cattle, the fields and the well, the wretched toilings of my community, none of it mattered to me now. I had the freedom of the jungle. I realised I could breathe more easily in the barren ravines than in this desert of poverty.

Before we left my village, a woman came to me and flung herself at my feet.

It was Kusuma, the woman Madhav had been trying to reach in Delhi when he was killed. She had managed to make her way to my village, and she had been waiting for me to come. She begged me to take her with me. She said she wanted to become a bandit too and stay with us. She was crying and shaking her bangles under my nose, offering them to me in exchange for protection.

'They wanted to put me in jail as an accomplice! I have no money, I'm scared, and with Madhav gone there's nobody to help me. Please!'

She threw herself at my feet again and she wouldn't stop crying.

I took pity on her, but when I rejoined Vickram and the others, he wasn't at all happy to see her. At first I thought it was simply that he didn't want a woman with us in the jungle. He took me aside and explained that she had caused trouble the last time she was with them by making eyes at the men. But I still felt sorry for her. She had nobody to protect her, and I knew how that felt. I persuaded Vickram to give her a chance.

The problems started right away. She flirted with all the men, including Vickram. She was a real woman, pretty but vain, and always either in tears pleading for pity or else trying to seduce someone. It was as though she couldn't help herself.

Bare Lal was the first to complain. 'She follows me around all the time and contorts herself in front of me. An old man like me! Do something, Vickram. Send her away or I myself will thrash the shameless little hussy!'

I took her aside and tried to warn her not to do such things. I told her she should leave the old man in peace. But from the look in her eyes I could tell she didn't care.

'It's because he's Vickram's uncle, is that it? That's why you're making eyes at him, because Vickram's the leader?'

She tossed her head.

'From now on,' I said, 'you stay with me. You don't go near the men!'

But I might as well have been asking a leopard to change her spots. She was the very incarnation of Sita, the goddess of pleasure. But she knew how to make herself useful too. She cooked and fetched water from the river. Even as she cooked the chapatis on the iron griddle, though, she couldn't stop herself talking to the men and making little gestures to them.

It was Raghu Nath next, little Raghu Nath who was clever as a monkey but not wise enough. She slipped away with him to let him make love to her.

Her shamelessness disgusted me.

'You're always running after the men. First one and then the other. Do you see me going around speaking to all the gang members like that? What kind of woman are you?'

'Oh, Bahanji,' she said, leaning her head to one side and calling me her big sister to try to win my sympathy, 'you are different. I can't live without a man. That's how I am.'

She said she didn't want to belong to Raghu Nath anyway, because he was just a little fish. 'I want to be with Vickram.'

I blushed with embarrassment and gave her a furious slap. And then I went to see Vickram to ask him what she had been saying to him.

He just shrugged. 'She is crazy! She wanted me to take her as my wife instead of you.'

'You must have encouraged her. Why didn't you tell me?'

'No. She said stupid, evil things. She said she was prettier than you and that she loved me more than you. So I asked her what she would do with you, and she said, "We can get rid of her." I kicked her out. I don't want her, Phoolan, you know that. She belongs to everyone.'

'Why didn't you tell me about this?'

'I didn't want to upset you. All we have to do is leave her on the main road. She can find her way back to Delhi.'

His faith in me, his frankness, and the sincerity between us made me trust him. I never doubted for a moment that he really loved me, and the security of knowing that made me take pity on her again.

'We're the only family she has,' I said. 'We can't just leave her on the road. You don't know what the police will do to her. Wait until her case is heard. Then she can go back.'

Vickram accepted. 'Whatever you say, Phool Singh!'

It was night, everyone was asleep, and the thing I had been dreading for a long time finally happened.

The lookout saw them arriving and in an instant we were on our feet with our rifles. It was a delegation from the village. There were about a dozen of them, men we knew and thought we could trust. They were unarmed and they said they wanted to speak to Vickram about his quarrel with Shri Ram.

I felt the ground shake under my feet. This time, it's the end, I thought. We had constructed a makeshift hut under a neem out of wood and branches and we invited one of the villagers, a rich landowner, to come forward and tell us what he had to say.

'We have come to try to end this trouble between you and Shri Ram. He swears he didn't try to kill you, but there are others who say they would like to. There are bad men loitering around here. You must negotiate with him, Mastana, for everybody's sake.'

Vickram clenched his fists. 'I'll shoot him as soon as I lay eyes on him!'

I had the feeling a trap was being laid for us, but I couldn't see it yet. These men knew that Vickram had once looked up to Shri Ram and they were counting on his loyalty. But my female heart was not so trusting . . .

'Shri Ram missed him the first time,' I said to the emissary, 'and now he wants a second try. That's why he sent you here, isn't it?'

'You shouldn't listen to this woman, Vickram. She shouldn't have any say in these matters. It's up to you to sort this out. He says he didn't shoot you. He is a thakur and he was the leader of your gang. You should hear what he has to say before you accuse him.'

Vickram thought for a moment, and then he said, 'All right, bring him here.'

The villagers left and I pleaded with Vickram to ignore them. 'Don't get mixed up with him again. We don't need him.'

'We can hear what he has to say. What's the difference?'

Shri Ram had been his guru, the one who taught Vickram everything, even betrayal. And Vickram knew it. He had wanted to kill him before but now he was willing to meet with him. I couldn't understand it. He was a thakur, the villager had said, he was once Vickram's leader, but I was nothing. If I couldn't convince him, I decided I'd leave him to it. He was the master of his destiny. But if Vickram didn't kill Shri Ram then I would!

I feared that if Shri Ram managed to win over Vickram and persuade him he hadn't tried to kill him, he was bound to come after me next. He hated me, I was just a little mallah whore to him, and for all I knew perhaps I was the one he really wanted to kill.

It was still night when the villagers came back with Shri Ram and his gang. The men were edgy. They were all against the return of this thakur. Like me, they didn't want any reconciliation. I tried to keep as far away as possible from their discussion, squatting in the grass with my rifle in my hands at the ready. From there, I could see him congratulate Vickram on his recovery and sit down to talk with him. Only Lala Ram came over to where I was sitting and bowed to me, returning to join their men. I sat watching them for what seemed like an eternity. It was almost dawn and a soft light was spreading over the fields. From time to time, Vickram would stand up and walk around before sitting down again. He must have been having difficulty containing his anger.

Shri Ram's men had sat down to one side of the neem, and our men were grouped the other side. Not one word was exchanged between them. In the silence, I could hear what Shri Ram was saying. 'Get it out of your head that I fired at you. It was the peasant. He wanted you to think it was me. I prayed you were still alive, and here you are, my brother, safe and sound!'

And then he spoke loudly for me to hear. 'Call her. She looks as if she is still annoyed with me!'

I didn't move. I had a suspicion that Vickram was only pretending to believe him, but I didn't know what he was planning. If he was pretending, I would have to pretend too. But I still didn't go anywhere near them.

As the sun came up, the villager who had served as a go-between departed and both gangs raised camp to go into the jungle for cover. There were eight of them and nine of us, not counting Kusuma.

I had forgotten her. But as soon as we pulled the stakes up to pack the tents, she rushed towards Shri Ram, throwing herself at his feet. She had decided that he, the thakur, was the real leader, and she was going to do her seduction dance for him. He was ugly and terrifying, but Kusuma was the kind of woman who only went after men with power. She followed him with her looks and graces like a little lost cat. Because Shri Ram the thakur wanted to reclaim his place as leader, Vickram the mallah didn't interest her a second longer.

As we walked across the fields and up into the hills, I tried to warn Vickram about what she was up to, but he didn't care. 'She's a lowly woman. Let her do what she wants,' he said. Shri Ram didn't mind either, not even when his more sensible brother Lala warned him about her. He just shrugged his shoulders. 'If she wishes to run after me,' he said, 'let her do so.' He strutted in front of her with his men in their safari suits. We mallahs only had our sipahi uniforms bought from police in need of rupees. He wanted to know how Vickram had managed to get his wounds seen to, where he had gone and who had taken care of him, but Vickram avoided replying. He said his wounds had healed on their own, just like that.

Shri Ram kept going on and on about what he called the incident, trying to say he wasn't responsible and trying to find out who had helped us.

'Nobody. I found a good hiding place and waited,' was all Vickram said.

That night, the two gangs slept apart, all except Kusuma, who shamelessly lay down beside Shri Ram.

But Vickram and I didn't sleep. We were awake the whole night arguing about him. Vickram told me not to provoke Shri Ram, to keep calm for a few days. 'He still owes me a lot of money for his bail. Let's settle our account with him and get rich, and after that we'll go our separate ways.'

Two more days passed and Shri Ram and his men were still there, and he was still trying to provoke me.

'Well, Phool Singh, have you forgiven me? I'm your brother and you are my sister,' he would say. 'Why don't you come here beside me, Bahanji?'

I had no intention of going anywhere near him. I didn't believe him for a second, neither his eyes nor his words. I could see on his face that he was lying.

It was raining and we had been walking half the night through the jungle. We were nearing Vickram's sector, not far from Bejamau, his first wife's village. The ground was soggy, making it heavy going. When at last we halted to make camp it was difficult to hammer the stakes for the tents down in the soft earth. I was exhausted but I couldn't sleep, and I lay listening to the rain. But finally the rain stopped and in the morning the sun came up and everybody got up to relieve themselves and wash before raising the camp again.

I bumped straight into Kusuma, standing right in front of the men in her black bra and panties. I was so shocked by her that for once I spoke to Shri Ram directly. 'What are you doing there both of you? Tell her to cover herself!'

'Not all women are like you, Phool Singh! She likes me, and she doesn't mind showing it!'

A woman in our community would never have dared to

behave in that way. How could she impose the spectacle of her lewdness on us like that? I told Vickram he had to do something about it. He was angry too. He grabbed the woman by the hair and broke off a branch from a tree.

'I told you not to cause trouble,' he said. 'Is a beating the only thing you will understand?'

'I can do whatever I like,' she shrieked.

Her insolent reply seemed to enrage him even more. He threw her to the ground and started to thrash her. The men looked on, some contemptuously and others with a grin. Nobody said a word. She screamed and yelled for help but her red-haired saviour didn't budge. Nearly naked, with her bosom in the air and her flabby hips shaking, she revolted me. She was bright red from Vickram's beating and still tearfully proclaiming her love for Shri Ram. But he had got what he wanted from her and he wasn't going to lift a finger for a wretched low-caste woman like her, a nayan. Let the mallah see to her!

I was probably more ashamed than she was at that moment. She didn't seem to realise that a thakur would always look down on lower castes. Especially if he had just slept with one of their women.

I couldn't bear to see her shamed any further. 'Leave her, Vickram!' I shouted. 'Let her go.'

I turned to her. 'You behave like a prostitute, Kusuma. You chose Raghu Nath, you tried Vickram but he didn't want you and now you are with Shri Ram. Choose once and for all. Don't keep sleeping with everyone. If you like Shri Ram say so, stay with him and marry him!'

'Marry him yourself and I'll marry Vickram!'

Before I even knew it I had given her a fierce slap across her face. She spun around and fell to the ground. 'Don't ever say that again!' I warned her.

Vickram was right; all she would ever understand was

beatings. If I had known then what a demon this woman was, I would have crushed her like a rat as she lay there on the ground.

I could sense danger approaching there in the bright morning light, a shadow circling around us like a vulture. I knew by then that death has a smell, and I could smell it coming . . .

Vickram must have sensed something too. He decided that morning the two gangs should separate. We would make our way by different routes to the temple of Shiva where we always made our offerings, he decided. Shri Ram went along with this. He didn't seem to mind Vickram giving orders. There was something wrong.

In the afternoon, we reached the little white temple by the river at Ghatapara, where the holy man Sidh Baba sat. Vickram had decided to ask for his money from Shri Ram and to make the split permanent. He showed him the account book that Madhav used to keep for Shri Ram to verify.

'Very well,' said Shri Ram. 'You just give me two days.'

The sun was setting when Vickram came to sit at my side by the Yamuna. Swollen by the monsoon, the water had risen all the way up the steps of the temple, as it had the first time I was brought there. The water was rushing past in a muddy brown torrent and it was drizzling lightly. The wind blew a fine, refreshing mist in our faces.

My feet were dangling in the water and with a neem branch I was brushing off the insects trying to bite my calves.

Vickram stroked my head, smiling. 'You are playing like a child. Can I play too?'

'Here, play.'

We were two uniformed children with our guns over our shoulders. He swatted the water with the branch and then turned to me suddenly.

'Phoolan,' he said gravely, 'I've ruined your life. I have done something bad.'

I didn't say anything this time.

'And if I die, what will become of you?'

I wasn't expecting such a question.

'Nothing's going to happen to you. If we split up from them everything will be all right.'

'I have a strange feeling today,' he said.

'If that's so let's leave today, right now.'

I saw tears forming in his eyes. He looked so young, and so scared all of a sudden.

'Nothing will happen, Mastana,' I said hurriedly. 'You escaped death once already. Nothing will happen.'

I wanted to show him my firmness and courage but seeing him cry made my heart tighten. Over his shoulder, at the top of the steps behind us, near the doorway of the little temple, I could see Shri Ram and Lala Ram. I could see his red mane, like a devil's. He must have been itching to know what we were talking about, sitting there by the water like children.

Vickram plunged his hands in the river and brought the water up to his face to wash away his tears. Drops of water fell from his thin moustache and I saw that his lips were trembling. I would never forget how he looked that evening, as the sun set, red as blood.

'Let's go. In a couple of days it'll all be over, and I can see my family,' Vickram said. 'I want to see my father again, to tell him I didn't mean what I said the last time.'

We boarded the two boats, and slid gently along the river in the rain towards the mouth of a tributary near Bejamau, Vickram's first wife's village. The men were tired. We hadn't slept properly for several nights. Bare Lal tied our boat under a clump of neems, and we settled down to sleep. Shri Ram was soon snoring in his boat with his arm around Kusuma, lying on her belly beside him. Lala Ram and the other thakurs fell sound asleep too. But I was thinking about Vickram and his tears. He had sensed danger too. He must have felt it deep inside him to cry like that. I had to try to do something. I got up quietly and woke Misra, Vickram's bodyguard.

'Listen,' I whispered. 'Vickram cried a lot today. Let's kill those two. You kill one and I'll kill the other.'

'No. You have to tell Vickram first. We can't do it alone.'

'They're snoring. We could throw their rifles in the river without them even knowing.'

'No. If you want to do it now, wake him and tell him.'

I woke him softly.

'We can't settle things like that,' he said.

'I want to kill them now.'

'Phoolan, they're asleep. I'm not going to kill somebody while they're asleep. And it's for me to do, not you.' He smiled at my disappointment. 'Don't dirty your hands. It's up to me to kill this demon.'

It was too late anyway and someone grumbled that we were disturbing them. The demon had woken up. We heard the hoarse voice of Shri Ram from the bottom of his boat: 'These bloody mallahs never stop chattering day or night.'

I should have killed him that night. I should have done it alone, without any help. I could have slithered like a snake into their boat and thrown all their rifles into the Yamuna, and then fired point blank at Shri Ram. His men would have fled. And Vickram wouldn't have died the next day.

But who was I to defy destiny?

27

Bejamau was hidden in a ravine a few hundred yards from the shores of the Yamuna, reached by a dirt path that wound up the hillside. Vickram asked his uncle Bare Lal to accompany us to visit his family there. He hadn't seen his first wife or his children since he was injured. He invited Lala Ram to come with us too, so Shri Ram wouldn't suspect we were plotting something if we went alone.

I had spent the morning in a tense silence, with my nerves buzzing. Shri Ram had announced that he was going to marry Kusuma. Good for them, I thought, even if his brother didn't agree. Lala Ram protested that a thakur couldn't marry a nayan, a sub-caste of shudras, like mallahs and jatavs, whose role was to serve others. She was impure, he complained. But Shri Ram didn't seem to care. 'You can say what you like,' he retorted, 'I'm keeping her.' He said he would make her their servant and she could serve them all, she could massage them, wash their feet and pick the fleas from all their heads. He told his men to wait by the river and brought her with him to the village.

Uncle Bare Lal walked in front with the others, and I followed behind up the steep path, calculating our chances: Vickram and me, plus eight men, against Shri Ram and Lala Ram, plus seven thakurs . . . Raghu Nath had left our gang two days earlier, when Vickram had beaten Kusuma and brought up the matter of money with Shri Ram. He shared my apprehension. Raghu Nath was cunning, and he feared the two men were going to affront each other.

I hated that day even before it had begun . . .

The afternoon passed slowly. Vickram was preoccupied with his baby boy, who had a fever. Though I didn't know it at the time, his wife had been pregnant when Vickram first brought me there and it was the first time he had seen the new baby. He was in the jungle when he heard that he had a son, and the news had saddened him. Seeing the baby put him in a strange mood. I was uneasy too. The baby was ill and, as soon as he sat on my lap, he vomited. I feared they would think I had put a curse on the child because Vickram had married me, but the baby's mother was happy to see me. 'Sister, don't forget me,' she said as we left.

I gave her money for the baby without Vickram knowing.

The baby didn't resemble Vickram. He looked more like his mother. Vickram's daughter was there too. She still looked like him, though she had grown taller and put on weight. I woke her from her nap and it made me happy to see she remembered me.

As we returned to the boats, Lala Ram continued to complain about his brother's marriage. And Kusuma kept trying to provoke me.

'I'm getting married tomorrow, Bahanji,' she chirped. 'What do you think of that?'

I told her I was delighted for her.

Even Vickram congratulated Shri Ram. 'We'll have a nice feast!' he said.

But I wanted to know what Shri Ram was planning. I hadn't slept properly for two nights. I was fraught with the premonition of danger. While Vickram had been with his son, I had seen Shri Ram with the account book in his hand.

'This mallah dog thinks he can tell me what to do,' I heard him mutter to his brother. 'He dares to ask me for money!'

I knew things would not go as Vickram planned . . .

I was relieved when, at last, night came. I was glad the day had ended. A bed had been prepared for Vickram under a tarpaulin hung across some branches to keep the rain off. He lay down on it, exhausted. With my pillow under my arms, I asked Bare Lal where I should sleep. Vickram reached over and touched my hand.

'Come to me,' he said tenderly.

'No, you're tired.'

'Yes, come here close to me.'

Since his injury, I usually let him sleep alone. The doctors had said he needed to get his strength back. Though he never complained about it, I could see that the gunshot lodged in his back was still giving him pain. In any case, in the jungle, we were mindful of the others and we slept apart for safety's sake too. But I hadn't been able to lie close to him for so long, I wasn't used to it. I told him it was dangerous, and I felt shy, but he insisted.

I lay down beside him. He took my rifle and put it next to his, at arm's reach.

I heard Bare Lal whisper in the dark. 'Phoolan, we've found a bed for you.'

'It's all right,' Vickram said. 'She's here with me.'

We were so weary, so exhausted. The rain fell gently on the canvas and the wind rustled the trees, and I must have been too tired to heed the ominous quiet. Why did I let myself doze off, why that night after so many wakeful nights spent on the alert, a night when I knew something was dreadfully wrong? The reassurance of having him near me removed all my anxiety, and I fell with him into a deep sleep.

It was to be our last night together, the only night we ever ignored our rule of safety in the jungle and slept together like husband and wife.

I didn't know where I was when I heard the shots. There

was a deafening explosion, then more explosions. My ears were whistling from the noise of gunfire and my head was spinning as though I had been drugged. Vickram was still beside me, but his voice was faint, far away in a fog. 'Phoolan. It's him. The bastard has shot me . . .'

I groped for our guns in the dark but they weren't there. Vickram raised himself up, reaching for his rifle, and Shri Ram fired another bullet into him.

'Give me my rifle and I'll show you how brave you are, you bastard!'

Shri Ram kicked him in the chest.

'Phoolan,' he said. 'I'm dying!'

'No, no,' I said. 'It's nothing. I can't see anything . . .'

I couldn't believe what I was hearing. I still thought I was dreaming. Vickram was still sitting up and talking, as though nothing was wrong. The shadowy figure in front of us, I saw now, was Shri Ram. He had fired two or three times at Vickram, but I wasn't hit.

'Filthy dog!' he spat. 'You thought you were the leader of this gang, you thought you could tell them what to do!'

I couldn't understand what he was saying. I couldn't get up. I was dizzy, and there was a nauseating smell in my nostrils that I recognised. It was the chloroform we used for kidnappings. I could feel it all over my face, in my mouth and my eyes. I didn't know where I was but I could hear Shri Ram somewhere cursing us. Then I saw him smash the side of Vickram's head with the end of his rifle barrel.

'Stop,' I moaned. 'Don't kill him. Kill me instead!'

He hit me with the rifle butt and I fell to the ground.

Where were the others? I thought. I crawled back up on the khat and saw Vickram lying on the ground.

'I'm dying, Phoolan, I'm dying . . .' he stammered.

Shri Ram grabbed me by the hair, someone took me by my feet and someone else held my arms. I could hear myself wailing alone in an immense forest that echoed with the sound of my voice.

'Kill me! Kill me!'

I couldn't see Vickram. I didn't know if he was still alive or not. But I was still alive, somewhere in the dark.

Then I saw the bodies of four of our men on the ground. Uncle Bare Lal was dead. There was a rag that must have been soaked in chloroform next to his face and a pool of blood under him. The other four were tied up, but I couldn't see who was alive and who was dead.

The rain on my face woke me a little from the heavy, nauseous sleep. I guessed they had drugged the men and taken their rifles. That was what they had been planning for two days; that was why they had slept so soundly the night before. But I was still alive – and I realised with terror they weren't going to kill me right away . . .

Kusuma fell on me, tearing at my jewellery. She pulled at my bangles and the gold necklace I wore, all the presents Vickram had given me. The thieving hyena pulled everything she could from me, laughing. She took my watch, and a ring I wore bearing the head of Durga. Then she tore my clothes from me, leaving me naked for the men to tie my feet and hands.

They threw me into some thorn bushes, kicking me back with their feet on my chest to force me into the bush. They knew what they were doing. I could feel each thorn of the babool bush piercing my flesh like a knife. Then they carried me to the river and dumped me in the boat.

I heard them untying the rope and the boat set off. In the clear night I began to comprehend the horror that awaited me: they were going to torture me . . . Lying bound in the bottom of the boat I looked up and saw the red-haired demon. He was grinning. 'Well?' he sneered. 'What are you going to do now?'

'Why didn't you kill me too?'

'Oh, you can still be a great deal of use!'

I was still conscious. I could hear the sound of the oars and the water splashing against the hull. I could see the sky and the stars and feel the rain falling on me – and I prayed. I tried to persuade myself that Vickram wasn't dead, that he was going to protect me. Then I felt the boat hit the shore again and they put a blindfold over my eyes.

I was in a village. I didn't know which one. I heard Shri Ram wake the villagers with a shout.

'She killed Vickram the Mallah! The little whore, she killed him! But we caught her! Come and see!'

I heard people there as I was thrown to the ground. Then it started . . . Shri Ram was the first, then the others, thakurs, anyone who was around.

I heard Shri Ram encouraging them, telling them to use me, to take advantage of me while they had me tied up like that.

They passed me from man to man.

'Say it!' shouted Shri Ram. 'Tell them what happened to Vickram. Admit it, bloody bitch! Admit you killed him.'

For the first hour, I still had the strength to beg. I implored Kusuma to help me. I couldn't see her but I could hear her voice, as dry as a crow's. 'Call your husband to save you now!' she cackled. 'You were so proud, you thought you were so clever, now you're getting what you deserved!'

I didn't know what village we were in. I didn't know how many hours it had been, how many days and nights. Four or five times at least we went from one village to another, and each time I was paraded naked in front of the villagers. Each time, Shri Ram called me a mallah whore. He said I was the one who had killed Vickram and, hurling me to the ground, told the villagers to use me as they pleased.

I heard the voices of men, but I could feel nothing. My

being no longer existed. I thought I had died, like Vickram.

'Kill her,' I heard Lala Ram saying to his brother, 'but don't trail her around like this from village to village.'

I even begged them to kill me as well.

They fell on me like wolves. They dragged me and picked me up and I fell and they dragged me up by my hair again. I saw things I would never be able to forget. I saw crowds of faces and I was naked in front of them. Demons came without end from the fires of Naraka to rape me. I prayed to the gods and goddesses to help me, to let me live, to let me run through the damp fields, climb the ravines, to let me have my revenge and slay the red-haired demon. Then the darkness returned, and another man was grunting over my body, an old man, a spirit sweating with the stench of death.

And then it ended.

I was on a khat. I could feel the sun behind my eyelids – and then I felt the heat all over my body, burning my wounds. I was outside a village somewhere, still naked, but without a blindfold now.

I could hear men shouting. 'No, no, she's dead, I'm not touching her!'

'She will die soon if you don't give her some water.'

It was a woman's voice.

She gave me a sip of water. With blinking eyes I followed the end of the rope that still bound me, until I saw a hand gripping it firmly like the leash of a dog.

My body was covered in blood and bruises. I didn't know how many days and nights it had lasted.

'I beg you, sister, cover me. Please cover me. I am a woman like you.'

But the woman disappeared and Shri Ram was standing in her place.

'You piece of shit! Mallah bitch! You thought you could

bully us around and give us orders. You understand now who you belong to? You remember now why you were born?'

The woman covered me with a blanket. I curled up under it and closed my eyes in pain and horror.

He lifted me up and threw me off the khat. He started beating me again with a lathi and the blanket fell away. Then he lifted me up by my hair to look in my face.

'Now you are down to your level – nothing but dirt.'

I could hear them arguing. One of them wanted to kill me right away. 'Otherwise she will die and then you won't be able to shoot her.'

Someone else said they should hand me over to the police alive, then they could claim the reward. If I was beaten much more, the police wouldn't be able to show my corpse to the newspapers because people might think they had done it.

Shri Ram said if he had his way, he would bring all the thakurs in the world to use me.

Someone said there was nobody else there who wanted to rape me.

I tried to wriggle back under the blanket lying on the ground. But one of them picked me up by the shoulders and another by the feet and, letting the blanket fall so I was naked again, they carried me back to the river and dumped me back in the boat.

The four men from our gang were still there tied up. I only began to cry when I saw them. Their wrists had been broken, their lips were blue and their faces were covered in blood.

'What about Vickram. Is he dead?'

'Shhh. Don't talk . . . Yes.'

I heard them talking about supplies and the boat set off in the direction of Simra, the village where the thakurs had come to us pretending to ask for a reconciliation.

There, they made us get out. They made us lie down in a row, tied up on the bank under the neems. Lala Ram and one of the other men said they were going to get the police. The police would be able to pretend to ambush us and kill us. They had planned it all right from the start, and the villagers who had come to us to propose the truce between Vickram and Shri Ram had been in on it too. I heard Shri Ram asking them for his money. They had collected funds to pay Shri Ram to get rid of us, because we belonged to a backward caste and we defied the rule of thakurs. We were a lowly tribe and now we had been shown our place, they said. By killing Vickram, they had reminded us who gave the orders. They wanted to pretend I had done it to show I was disloyal – a whore! – and on top of it all they hoped to collect a reward and let the police share in the glory.

My body was dead, but my mind was working again. I heard it all. But I also heard the villagers say it was undignified to let a woman be seen like that in the village. They were poor villagers, not thakurs, and they wanted the thakurs to dress me. They didn't know what Shri Ram was planning. They didn't understand why he wanted to inform the police. Shri Ram insulted them but they wouldn't let him leave us there. They decided to go and ask the Brahmin what to do.

One of the men from the village came back with a pair of trousers and a bush shirt.

'Get up and wash yourself,' he said.

The villager who had brought the clothes forced me to put boots on my swollen feet, but I was still tied up and I couldn't dress on my own. He untied my hands. 'Let her dress herself,' he said, 'while I fetch my father.' Painfully I pulled on the trousers and tried to wrap myself in the shirt. Crouching by the shore, I plunged my hands in the water and brought them to my face. Shri Ram was still arguing when the villager returned with an elderly man wearing a long white kurta.

I recognised him! He was a Brahmin. He knew me! He would save me!

'Shri Ram Thakur,' said the old Brahmin, 'it is a good thing you have done to kill this Vickram! He was a cursed dacoit! And you should do away with this demon in the same manner!'

It was his son who had brought clothes for me but now the Brahmin wanted them to kill me! Shri Ram was satisfied to have found a powerful ally. Was there nobody to help me?

'Bring them to my house,' said the Brahmin. 'We shall give thanks there for the death of Vickram.'

I could barely stand up, but they forced me to walk ahead of them. My feet slipped and my legs buckled; I saw the trees spinning around me, but the old man prodded me forwards.

'Walk, you bloody bitch. Move!'

His voice was vicious and pitiless.

The village was a short way from the river but the path seemed so long I thought I was going to die before we reached it. Two guards were holding me up in silence. Kali was a member of Shri Ram's gang, but he belonged to a low caste, like the other guard. Shri Ram said a thakur would become impure if he touched me, so they had been ordered to do it. I stumbled forward, dazed by the sun. I could tell by my shadow that it must have been the middle of the day, and the village seemed to be deserted. It was as if nobody wanted to see the spectacle of my humiliation this time. A few old men watched me pass on my way to the Brahmin's house. It was a large house with concrete floors, but the old Brahmin had me taken to a hut made of mud and straw at the side. Shri Ram's two men were left to guard me. While one waited outside, the other, Kali, came in with me.

He sat down on the ground and looked at me. 'It's not right what they did. It's disgusting.'

'Help me, Kali! Kill them! Kill Shri Ram! I'll do whatever you want, for the rest of my life, but kill him for me!'

'There are too many of them.'

'Then give me your rifle and let me go. You have to help me. You aren't a thakur like them. Have pity on me.'

'I can't help you. They would kill me too.'

I could hear Shri Ram and Kusuma laughing in the house. They must have been celebrating their marriage – and Vickram's death. I didn't even know why I was still alive. They killed the men but raped and tortured the women to remind us of their power over us. With the memory of what they did to me, the pain returned, the way it always did. I could feel a thorn from the babool bush lodged so deeply in me that my back had swollen. Every movement hurt. I felt as though my whole body was broken. I didn't have an ounce of strength left, not even the willpower to chase away the images from my mind: naked and humiliated in front of thousands of people. I would never be able to forget them all looking at me . . .

As the sun was setting, the Brahmin appeared at the door of the hut with Shri Ram. They're going to kill me now, I thought.

'Have her brought to me first,' said the Brahmin.

'All right. You go right ahead and enjoy yourself.'

The old man that I thought I could respect, who I had addressed as Buppa the last time I had seen him, was going to rape me too.

The two guards brought me out. They shoved me into the house with my hands tied again and we went through one room into a large courtyard at the rear. The two guards were still with me but the Brahmin dismissed them.

'Stay in the house you two! I don't need you.'

The courtyard was large, and the red earth was hot from the afternoon sun.

The Brahmin pointed at the barrel of water in the corner. 'Drink.'

I fell sobbing at his feet. 'Buppa, please, don't do it. Don't assault me. Not you too.'

'I would never do that. Now, calm yourself, child. Drink and get your strength back. But if they kill me after this, don't let them get away with it. Do to them what they did to you, Phoolan Devi. Durga will give you the force you need to avenge yourself!'

It took me a moment to gather my wits. The old Brahmin had tears in his eyes. He was going to help me, he was going to save me!

The Brahmin brought me a cup of water and an old twelve-bore shotgun. He had three shells in his hand. The gun was country-made and I hoped he didn't expect me to try to shoot Shri Ram with it.

'Drink, and take this. You will need it.'

I hardly had the strength to swallow.

'Do you want to eat something?'

'No. Nothing, only water.'

Slowly my chest untightened and I began to breathe again. It took a few minutes more for my legs to stop shaking. By then, the guards were knocking at the door to the courtyard, and I could hear Shri Ram shouting from outside.

'Hey, Brahmin, would you like me to send in some reinforcements! Ha ha!'

The old man still had tears in his eyes, but he bellowed back. 'Let me finish what I am doing by myself!'

The Brahmin indicated the mud wall of the courtyard. Normally I would have been able to climb over it easily, but I didn't have the strength to haul myself up. He showed me an opening at the base of the wall, and began clawing at it with his hands to widen it. He helped me to get through it, pushing my shoulders as I squeezed through feet first. There were fields on other side of the wall. He passed the shotgun through the hole, and then slid through after me, helping me to walk. Behind his house was a field of maize and we stumbled through it to a neem tree in the middle. 'You can hide here. I must go back to the house.'

'Stay with me. They'll kill you, Buppa.'

'Oh, I don't think so! I am very old and they have at least some respect for me. I will send the two guards here. I will say you managed to slip away with them. They have no place with those thakurs, and they will do as I say.'

'He has no respect for anyone, Buppa. He will kill you and your family too.'

'My family has already left the village. I sent them away earlier. Do not fear for me. God is protecting me.'

I watched him return to the village, his white turban disappearing over the top of the maize. A thakur would pay homage to a Brahmin as long as it suited him, but this old man didn't belong to Shri Ram's caste and I was sure he was going to have to pay with his life for freeing me. He was old and thin, with grey hair, but he had more courage than any of them.

I lay there sprawled under the tree, hidden in the tall grass, clutching the shotgun to my chest. I didn't have the force to move even an inch further, not even to save my life. I closed my eyes and felt myself drifting away into sleep . . .

No! I mustn't sleep!

The last time I fell asleep, they killed Vickram. If I fell asleep again, I knew it would be my turn to die.

I heard shouts from the Brahmin's house and I saw two figures running in my direction. It was Kali and the other guard. Had the Brahmin managed to persuade them to join me, or were they trying to recapture me? I lifted my aching body and started to stumble through the field.

'Hey, where are you, Phoolan? Wait for us!'

It didn't matter. I couldn't run. I waved my arm and let myself fall to the ground.

'Get up, quick!'

They picked me up and dragged me through the field. We couldn't run very fast but night was falling and the darkness would give us cover. After a moment, we came to a river bordered by steep hillsides covered in thick bushes. Behind us, we heard shots and people yelling and screaming. We clambered up to the crest of the hill. From there, we could see the village in the distance. It was almost night but I knew well enough what the red demon and his thakurs were doing, they were beating and torturing and killing.

Kali and the other guard were lying a few yards away. 'Auntie,' whispered one of them, 'they will kill them all and then they'll come after us!'

We could see flames and smoke climbing in the night sky. It looked as if Shri Ram was putting the village to the torch. I learned later that he had not only killed the rest of Vickram's men, but, after his men had tied up and beaten the Brahmin, he had doused him with petrol and burned him alive.

From the ledge we watched the flames rising and the sinister clouds of smoke, and then night had fallen like a black curtain.

We lay there hidden in the bushes, still as mice.

By a miracle, I had escaped the bloodlust of Shri Ram, and I vowed that if I survived, Vickram's vengeance would also be mine.

28

None of us had been able to sleep, and I hadn't eaten for more than two days. On the morning of the third day, from the ledge we saw an army of police surrounding the village.

Hunger was one thing, but thirst was harder to bear. We were literally dying of thirst. The parched hilltop had turned out to be a trap, with open fields all around, impossible to cross until we were sure it was safe. We had no choice but to lie low and keep watch with the vultures circling over us; holding our breath to hear the slightest movement – a rat scurrying through the bushes, or a hyena howling in the night. In the silence, I could hear my heart pounding in my chest. I could feel it beating in great suffocating blows. I needed desperately to drink.

I was so thirsty I wanted someone to tell me why I shouldn't just go back down to the burned village and give myself up to the police. They would shoot me down, but what difference would it make? Without water, I would soon be dead. What was the point in hiding? Even if we managed to get away from there, we would still have to hide from the police on one hand and Shri Ram and his gang of thakurs on the other.

He had wanted people to believe I was Vickram's killer. He had trailed me through the villages naked, like a madwoman, a demon, and now we were trapped. I was still alive, but only just, and for how long? The faint hope that Vickram wasn't dead, only wounded and hiding somewhere in the jungle, was receding with each passing hour. The thakur dog had judged well which one of us to shoot first. I couldn't take it any more. I decided to climb down from that ridge, cross the fields, and die for a drink of water.

I lifted myself up and as I did, I heard a faint rustling noise in the bushes at my feet. A large snake with black and yellow scales slowly uncoiled his body and raised his head in front of me . . .

I froze.

As slowly as I could, I brought myself to a crouching position, ready to spring. He watched me with his golden eyes set in that black face as though he was going to say something to me. I was watching him too, and all of a sudden, without being able to help myself, I began to cry. I cried big, sad, lonely helpless tears, the tears of a frightened child.

'Who are you? You want to bite me? Did God send you to bite me?'

He listened without moving. The two boys retreated in fear.

'He's going to bite you Auntie! Kill him!'

'Who are you? If God sent you to kill me, go on. If he sent you to protect me, then help me . . .'

He extended his neck, moving his fine head from side to side. Ever since I was a child, I had been followed by snakes – but I wasn't in the habit of speaking to them like that. My mother used to send me to stay at my grandmother's house during the monsoon, when the village sometimes flooded and filled with snakes. Every year, one or two villagers died after being bitten by them, and my mother was afraid for me. Some snakes frightened me and others didn't. But I had never spoken to them before. I didn't recognise this type, so I didn't know if he was dangerous or not, but he was large and strong and, though his bite was probably poisonous, it almost seemed as if he had come just to talk to me.

So I talked. I told him all about my sufferings; about Shri Ram and the nightmare I had just been through. And he moved his head from side to side, studying me as he listened.

The two boys were petrified.

'Maybe it's someone you know,' Kali whispered. 'Someone from your gang. Look how he is listening to you.'

He puffed his neck, his eyes fixed on mine, and made a hissing sound. He *was* listening to me, I was sure. One minute my throat was dry, the next minute my thirst had vanished.

All of a sudden, he turned and slithered towards a rock. He pulled himself up on top of it, looking away in the distance, and then he turned back to me. Twice more he made the same gesture with his head, looking away in the same direction and then turning back to me.

'I should go that way?' I asked him.

He moved his head from side to side and hissed again. Then he turned his head and pointed with it. Kali understood too.

'He's telling you to follow him, Auntie. He is showing you the way!'

'Is it true? You will show me?' I bowed to him with my hands together in relief and prayer. 'Whoever you are,' I said, 'don't abandon me now. Watch over me and give me the strength to survive.'

Majestically, the snake slithered away.

All three of us followed him around a rock on the other side of the hill, away from the village. We crossed the bushy slopes in the heavy sun until we came to some trees. After fifteen minutes of crossing that rough terrain in the afternoon heat I noticed a stream of water. It was coming from a small spring in the rocks! We were saved!

I drank for a long time, cupping my hands and letting the water flow into my mouth. Then I brought the water up to my face and let it flow from my hands over my head. I bathed my wounds. The soft, fresh water, flowing over my swollen body gave me hope; my strength returned, and with it my will to survive.

I closed my eyes and prayed to the snake: Whoever you are, stay by me, be my golden eyes, show me the way and I will obey you.

When I opened my eyes, he was gone.

Kali and the other boy, whose name was Charan, were walking ahead of me in an immense wheatfield.

At the slightest sound we ducked down, making ourselves invisible like the snake in the grass. Thirst was burning in our throats again, and we spoke little. I had decided to head back past Simra to the Yamuna, and then to follow the river, to reach the house of one of my maternal aunts near a village called Delkhan.

Maybe the snake really was guiding us because we reached her village without anyone seeing us. We advanced carefully towards the outskirts. The mallahs lived in a clump of houses at the top of the village, near the hillside. The heart of the village was lower down, near the river. We waited until nightfall to pass through it to reach my aunt's house.

I told Kali and Charan to hide in the ditch while I looked inside. My aunt was in the yard, cooking chapatis at the fire. She was alone, so I signalled the boys to follow me with a whistle. My aunt was astonished to see me there with two men in uniform. She hugged me and asked what had happened to me. I told her nothing. We were in a region controlled by thakurs and Shri Ram surely had informers everywhere. Silence was the best protection. Besides, I was too bruised and weary to repeat all I had said to the snake on the ledge.

Suddenly, I heard voices behind me. I couldn't work out where they were coming from at first, but as I turned I saw some figures. They were villagers and they had recognised me. 'Catch hold of her,' one of them shouted, 'we'll hand her over to the police.' Without even thinking, I dived behind the cattle in the yard and yelled out a warning.

'Bastards! Dogs! I'm going to kill you!'

I unshouldered the shotgun and fired in the air, a single shot. The villagers panicked and fled from the yard and I ran around behind the house followed by Kali and Charan intending to retrace my steps out of the village. But someone blocked my route. It was one of my cousins, Ram Sevak.

'Not that way, it's the way they came. There's more of them and they're looking for you.'

That left only the ravines, the cover of the jungle and the night. But the jungle there was too dense and hilly. It was hard to make headway without heavy boots and knives. A little way from the village, we circled back down to the river, and decided to risk taking the main road. The road traversed another small village and people watched us passing, murmuring to one another. It was the middle of the night but the villagers still weren't asleep.

'It's Phoolan Devi. It is her. We must tell her!'

They said they had heard that I had been killed along with Vickram. They followed us all the way to the temple at the edge of the village, eager to hear the details, to know why I was alone and who the two boys with me were. I just had time to answer them before I saw a gang of men coming down the road, wearing uniforms and carrying rifles.

At first sight, I took them for dacoits. 'Who are you?' I shouted.

'You,' came the reply. 'Identify yourself!'

'It's me, Phoolan,' I said, thinking it was Baba Ghanshyam's gang. Some of them dived into a ditch and began firing while the others took cover. I shouted to Kali to run for cover too, realising I had made a dangerous mistake. They were police. I fired too, just once, to cover my retreat. That left me with only one shell.

Fleeing in the night, I lost my two companions. One of the boys had been heading for the jungle and the other vanished in the fields. I had left the road too and I soon found myself back on hilly ground, climbing and falling in the gulleys and climbing higher again, the way Vickram had taught me, desperate to reach the ridge as rifleshots cracked in the night beneath me. Finally, I came to a ravine with a torrent below. A tree hung over the raging water. I climbed out on a branch overhanging the river, the longest one I could see, and I jumped.

I twisted my foot as I landed on the opposite side and I could still hear shooting behind me. But I scrambled onwards. I had to reach the summit of the ravine. I climbed again to the top of a small tree. It wasn't very solid, but I had no choice. I climbed all the way out to the end of a branch. It creaked dangerously under my weight. I didn't dare to move.

I couldn't move. My legs were giving way under me. I was out of breath and my heart was beating so hard I thought it was going to burst. I didn't know which way to go. Habit had driven me up the ravine, but maybe they had the whole valley encircled. I wasn't even sure if it was the police. It could have been thakurs, Or Shri Ram and his men, still after me.

About an hour after that, from my perch, I saw the lights

of vehicles arriving below in the village. I heard shouted commands echo across the hillsides. I was almost relieved. It was police reinforcements arriving and they were going to conduct a house-to-house search.

Slowly, I climbed down from the tree, testing each branch before I put my weight on it. If one of them broke it was a fall of several yards to the ground. When I got down at last I sat on the ground, lying flat to catch my breath again. I was covered in cuts and grazes and I could still hear shooting in the distance. They must have been searching for me in the fields, shooting at shadows, or at the two boys, Kali and Charan. But I was out of their range for the time being. I knew they wouldn't come up there in the dark for fear of an ambush and I now realised they must have thought I had a gang with me. When I had shouted out my name they wouldn't have imagined for a moment I was alone. It would have been madness on my part to give myself away like that. And when I had called to Kali to take cover the police had all dived in the ditches too. They must have thought Phoolan Devi's gang was right in front of them!

My second shell had given me a second chance, but if they found me now, the third one would be for me. I decided I would kill myself rather than give them the pleasure.

At the bottom of the hill I could see the police. There were dozens of them searching in the fields and the others were gathering the villagers together, getting ready to search their houses and barns. I could see the lanterns and hear them nervously barking orders. They were frightened, thinking they were looking for a gang of dacoits.

There was no more gang. Vickram was dead and I was alone. Physically, I was in tatters. I was eighteen years old and I bore the scars of tortures inflicted on me by men who were not men but beasts and dogs. My wrists had been broken in a police lock-up and they had never healed properly. I could hardly hold my shotgun steady enough to aim. I had to hold it with both hands, and I had only one shell left . . . But for the sipahis, I had become Phoolan Devi the Untouchable, the Queen of Dacoits!

That night, I vowed silently to the snake who was now my ally that I would be a woman no longer. Whatever I did from then on, I would do as a man would do. Evil had left its mark on me. I had survived the evil of men, and I had nothing more to lose. I was stronger than ever.

29

On the far side of the hill was a river, swollen to a raging torrent by the monsoon rains. I wasn't strong enough to swim across so I followed the river for a while, walking along the banks with my feet sinking in the mud, and then I continued barefoot through the jungle. Large owls white as spirits in the moonlight watched me from the branches. I walked and walked, my mind empty. My only thought was that I had to make headway.

By dawn I had crossed into another valley and I was heading towards Kalpi. Outside a village, I climbed a neem and stayed there for hours, half-asleep but still watchful. I was cleaning the shotgun, poking it with a twig to clean the chamber. As I was trying to load it, my last cartridge jumped out of my fingers and fell to the ground at the foot of the tree.

It was the only one I had. I was about to climb down to retrieve it when a dozen policemen came down the path and halted in the shade of the tree directly below me. Their boots were clogged with mud and they took them off and started shaking them against the trunk of the tree.

I could hear every word they said. They were talking about me. 'I've had enough. She must be far away from here by now.'

'Who knows where she's hiding?'

Remaining still as a snake in the branches, I kept my eyes on the cartridge that was lying at their feet.

But they didn't know how to see. Their eyes were like buttons, sewn up tight. They didn't lift their heads once. I even climbed from where I was sitting up to a higher branch and they didn't hear me. They didn't know how to listen either.

Survival wasn't something you learned. Everyone must fulfil their destiny and I had begun to believe that it was my destiny to survive. To survive to avenge myself was what drove me on. I would never forget what the red devil had made me suffer. Killing him would be too kind! I was going to cut him into pieces, one piece today and another the next day, so he would be able to watch me throwing him, slowly, slowly, limb by limb, to the dogs. Even after death, in my future lives, I wouldn't forget. My hunger for vengeance was so strong it woke me in the night. I used to try to sleep by thinking of Vickram's face, hearing again the sweet words he said to me before the end, but I couldn't. Images of my humiliation kept coming back, I could no longer see his face, and I would scream in horror. My body was one enormous wound, I was already dead, and I couldn't halt as I walked and walked, trying to make headway, trying to get home.

A shepherd's wife found me and nursed me in her hut. My hands were broken and she mixed a pomade of mud to soothe them. While I waited for them to heal, I managed to send a message to the brother of one of our dead men.

Some mallahs from my community came in a boat to get me. I saw my mother again.

She beat her chest like a martyr when she saw me, crying yet again for forgiveness for having brought me into the world, for the fresh horrors I had been made to suffer. They already knew about everything, all that I had been through.

It had made the rounds of all the villages. She cared for me, bathing me and covering me with compresses, and at last, after two more days, I was able to sleep.

For the first time in my life, the people of my village were on my side, even the Sarpanch. His son Suresh presented me with a rifle – as if to make amends. I knew it was only because they were more afraid of the thakurs now than they were of me, but I accepted it.

With the rifle, I left for the jungle again. My first objective was to start my own gang. I contacted a dacoit named Balwan, a shepherd from the gadariya caste, and he let me join his gang for a few days, long enough to kidnap two rich merchants of the vaishya caste and rake in fifty thousand rupees in ransom for each of them. My share was twenty-five thousand rupees.

Balwan had about a dozen men. He offered to let me join him, saying we could run the gang together, but I didn't want to get into a situation like that again. I didn't need anyone's protection this time and I wasn't going to take orders from anybody. I was going to be the leader, I was the one who was going to be obeyed from now on. I knew that having two factions in one gang could lead to caste rivalries and infighting. And I knew too that Balwan was a hot-head, who wouldn't hesitate to kill his own men if he suspected them of informing. He had liquidated some jatavs in his gang that he suspected of having killed his brother, and I didn't want to see dacoits turning their rifles on each other again.

Since I didn't want to join him, Balwan proposed to lend me money for arms and supplies. But I didn't want to owe anything to anyone either. I knew that to be able to assert your will, independence was essential.

Talking with him for hours, I reached a conclusion. 'It's simple Balwan,' I explained. 'I don't consider myself a woman any longer. I don't want anybody's protection, nor their help. I want to control everything myself. If I take a gun from you, I'll pay you for it.'

I was wary of Balwan. He was the sort who only became a bandit for the money. He had started out as a petty thief, stealing sheep and goats. He was too excitable and I felt he couldn't be trusted. For him, everything came down to money, and I wanted men with other motivations.

'If there are men here who want to follow me,' I told him, 'let them say so, but I will decide if I will take them or not.'

The first to come forward was Lakhan, a tall fellow in his thirties with a thick beard and long hair tied back in a knot, who was to become a friend and brother to me. Until he quit his old life to join the gang, he had worked in a bank. He was clever, and he seemed to be honest, so I decided to make him my accountant.

While I was with Balwan, his old boss, the fearsome leader of an infamous muslim gang, contacted us. Baba Mustakim had a good reputation among dacoits. He was renowned for his honour, so I accepted a meeting. I was surprised to see he didn't look at all like a bandit. He was well-dressed and courteous. He said he had heard about what had happened and he too wanted to help me. I bought an automatic rifle from him, a costly weapon. I gave him the twenty-five thousand rupees I had and he said I could give him the rest later.

I talked through the night with Baba Mustakim. Muslims were usually poor and had as much to fear from thakurs as my community. Baba Mustakim was determined to join me and it wasn't until the early hours of the morning that he finally acknowledged my reasons for refusing his help.

'If you don't want my aid, then take ten men from my gang,' he said. 'Choose them yourself.'

I wanted men who got along with each other, but most of

all I wanted men driven like me by a hunger for vengeance. A man who was only looking for rapes and rupees was a bad dacoit, but a man with a grudge against my enemies would make a good dacoit. That was what I thought. It was a conclusion I was going to regret.

I took them aside one by one and asked them the essential question: 'Do you want me as your leader?' If the reply was affirmative, I asked a second question.

'Am I a man or a woman for you?'

I was in a hurry. I was anxious to find the red demon, and that was how my gang came into being. There was Man Singh, who was to become my lieutenant, my brother. The others were Baladin, Ramdas, Jhallar, Laltu, Jageshwar, Muniram and Kharag, who was nicknamed Vishnu because he was always doing crazy things like making tea by boiling rupee coins. I already had my tall accountant, Lakhan. They were all from castes of shepherds or leatherworkers, castes compatible with my own.

Man Singh was tall and bearded with long, wavy hair that tumbled to his shoulders. His appearance frightened me at first. Deep lines ran across his heavy brow; he had a penetrating gaze, and the nose of an eagle, but Baba Mustakim told me he was one of the oldest members of his gang and that he would be a great help to me. He explained that Man Singh had become a dacoit for the same reason as me. His two uncles had refused to share land they inherited with their sister, Man Singh's mother. They denounced Man Singh to the police because he used to supply Baba Mustakim, who was his childhood friend from a nearby village. When the police came for Man Singh, they killed his brother. Man Singh escaped to join the dacoits.

Baba Mustakim called the rest of his men together and ordered them to stand.

'Swear before Allah never to look upon Phoolan Devi as a

woman. Swear to think of her as your own brother. I myself will kill any one of you who breaks this vow. She is my brother, and she is yours also. Allah be praised!'

'Long live Phool Singh!'

He tied a red cloth around my head, the symbol of vengeance.

Before he and his men left for their camp in the hills nearby, Baba Mustakim gave me a present, a stamp like the one Vickram had made to let everyone know he was still alive. This one was in my name. It said:

PHOOLAN DEVI QUEEN OF BANDITS.

Two days later, I used it for the first time to stamp my name on doors the way Vickram had done during a looting. Balwan and Baba Mustakim insisted on joining us with their men as we staged our first operation, a daylight raid in the middle of a bustling town. Not just any town either, but Kalpi, where, as a terrified girl, perhaps three years before, I had been held in a police lock-up.

It was summer again and the sun was beating down, filling the streets with a suffocating heat. The attack began with the torpor at its peak, at three o'clock in the afternoon. Our objective was to kidnap a couple of well-to-do merchants from the silversmithing bazaar. The windows of their shops shattered under our rifle butts and the owners ran from us, leaving all their precious necklaces and bangles. Encouraged by Baba and me, the poor people dived on this treasure. 'Take it! Help yourselves!' shouted Baba Mustakim, laughing. Staging a raid with me seemed to give him much enjoyment, and it was a pleasure for me to see the thin hands of the poor overflowing with the shining trinkets, but we had our hostages and very soon it was time to leave.

We had planned to cross the railway tracks to reach the

safety of the bush, but the police were waiting for us, dug in behind sandbags beside the railway line. They had held their fire hoping to get us all and, because I was ahead of the others, leading the way, I found myself caught in a sudden hail of rifle fire.

'Run, Phoolan, run!' shouted Baba.

The bullets whistled past as I dived down for cover; the air was hot with the smell of gunpowder. The police were one side of the railway line and our men had dropped back on the other side, returning fire. I was caught in the middle.

Stones from under the railway sleepers flew in the air around me. The police were using grenades too. As I crawled on my belly back to the men, I thought we would never make it out of there alive, but somehow, keeping low behind the mound of stones under the tracks, we managed to reach the rail bridge at the Yamuna. There, we broke up into small groups and lost the police.

By nightfall, our two hostages were still alive – but only just. As well as being terrified, they were exhausted and dehydrated from running without a pause in the blistering heat for so long. The men had arranged to meet up at Baba Mustakim's village, Giloli. We arrived at ten and the others were all there by midnight. As soon as we were all together, the police descended on us again, their rifles blazing. This time we had to flee without the two hostages. They would have died in our hands.

We contented ourselves with releasing them with a threat: 'If you don't send us money, you know what will happen. We'll be back. You will pay, say it!'

'We will pay! We will pay!' they bleated.

The clash at the railway line had lasted for hours, but nobody had been killed and I came out of it without a scratch. It had been exhilarating to pull off a raid in the middle of a town! I had proven that I could lead a gang as well as any man; I had led my men into battle and come out unscathed. I was sure that someone was protecting me, a spirit that hungered for vengeance like mine.

Sometimes, after I had settled on a plan, a little girl came to me in my head and whispered, 'Don't go that way, Phoolan, the police are waiting.'

The little girl was Durga, the goddess, protecting me. The men believed it too. My conviction gave them courage.

'It was thanks to you we got out of there alive,' they all said.

Baba Mustakim said I brought good luck. Balwan agreed.

I relented, accepting their company and the help of their gangs.

We were to be allied for six months.

During that time we carried out a raid on the day of Diwali, the festival of light. On that day, everyone sweeps and tidies their house in honour of the goddess Lakshmi, the wife of Vishnu, who couldn't abide poverty and dirt. In the village we used to give the walls a fresh coat of cow dung. We painted signs on the ground and the walls and in the evening, we lit the lanterns and put candles and oil-lamps everywhere. In the towns, the streets were hung with garlands of coloured light bulbs.

There was a village that we had been surveying for a while, where a rich landowner lived, someone who owned a great deal of property. Every time a peasant was in debt or put his land in hock, this greedy vulture took advantage. He never extended his credit terms, he would never accept a delay in repayments and, for want of a few hundred rupees, he stripped poor families of all they had. In the name of the poor and in honour of the goddess Lakshmi, we decided this man was going to pay . . .

We had heard he had a great deal of money hidden in his

house, and we began simply by threatening him. On the morning of Diwali, a messenger brought him a letter from us. 'Give back to the poor the land you have taken.'

He sent a reply right away. 'I have already received all manner of threats from dacoits!'

The following day, we paid him a little visit.

He lived in a large villa set in beautiful gardens surrounded by fortified walls. We'd heard that he had four or five armed men but his servants and guards fled at the sight of our gang, which must have been nearly fifty strong that day, swelled by all the dispossessed farmers who joined us. He was old and it wasn't very difficult to overcome him.

I slapped him across his face.

'Well, old man. You think you're a Maharajah, but you own nothing. You exploit these poor people! You persecute them and then you take their land and everything they have. What is your excuse?'

'No, no, Bahanji, I haven't done any harm. I haven't hurt anyone. It's my right!'

'Don't call me your sister! Where is the loot?'

He was so afraid that without any resistance he showed us where he kept it all. All we had to do was dig in his beautiful garden, and there it was. I had never seen so much gold and silver, so much jewellery. It was as if he knew the loans could never be paid back. He had simply buried in clay pots everything he had received in pawn against loans. There was a pot full of gold and one full of silver, and another one full of the deeds to property that people had pawned too.

'You're going to give back what you stole to each and every one of them!'

Standing on the roof terrace of his villa, I summoned all the villagers through our loudhailer, all those who had pawned their wives' jewellery, their fields, and even their houses. I told them to come and get their property back!

They came running to get their deeds and, crazy with delight and disbelief, went off to tell those who lived further away.

'Are you still a landowner, old man?'

'No, no. I swear it.'

We took as much cash as we could for ourselves – a fortune, nearly two million rupees, said my accountant Lakhan – but we had to leave the rest of the riches, all the unclaimed jewellery. It was too heavy to carry.

On another occasion, in a town, we redistributed part of a hoard we had taken from the cloth merchants in the bazaar. We must have given away a hundred thousand rupees that day. People mobbed us, screaming for everyone to come.

'Phoolan Devi and Baba Mustakim are giving out money!'

But I craved a different satisfaction . . .

And then, worsening my frustration, I missed Shri Ram and Lala Ram by minutes. An informer had told us which village they were hiding in and our men surrounded it. We knew which house they were in but by the time we got there, it was empty. We grabbed some villagers and I began to beat them with my bare fists. 'Where are they?' I shrieked. 'Where have they gone?' One of the villagers said they had left disguised as women, and I remembered having seen two women just fifteen minutes earlier. I had even remarked to Baba that they were walking oddly, and I suddenly realised why they had been carrying wood in the direction of the forest. I had been right, they weren't who they pretended to be, but Baba Mustakim had warned me not to interfere with women, saying it would ruin our reputation.

I was beside myself with frustration. I insulted the villagers for hiding the red dog. I stripped them and beat them. I fired at the ground to make them dance and I paraded them naked through the village hearing them sing my praises.

'Long live Phoolan Devi! Long live Phoolan!'

I shouted through my megaphone: 'Come out Shri Ram. Wherever you are. Come out if you have the balls!'

I gave vent to my anger that afternoon on the men that had shielded them. They were the same ones who had left me naked and defenceless; they had watched me being tortured without lifting a finger. I was boiling with rage. I needed to make them suffer what I had been made to suffer. I beat them between their legs with my rifle butt. I wanted to destroy the serpent that represented their power over me . . .

I crushed, burned and impaled!

And then I laughed to see them leap like castrated horses and fall at my feet and cry like women, begging and pleading for mercy, as I had.

People of my caste heard all about it. If a mother wanted to protect her daughter, or a father his wife or his sister, they knew all they had to do was say to the rapist that Phoolan Devi would punish them.

And I did.

I helped the poor people by giving them money and I punished the wicked with the same tortures they inflicted on others, because I knew the police never listened to the complaints of the poor. I knew there were hundreds of girls who had been forced to undergo dangerous abortions to avoid disgrace, or else throw themselves in the river or drown themselves at the bottom of a well because they were treated like prostitutes, and they were afraid. They were all afraid.

When we were on a raid, if I saw a servant girl in the house of a thakur, I would ask what her duties were.

'Oh, she is just a servant,' the thakurs would always say.

But if I took the girl aside and asked her, the reply was

usually different . . . 'They drink all night and the men torture me, the father and the son and the uncles, they do
whatever they like with me . . .'

I heard it often enough.

That's why, whenever I heard it, I crushed the serpent
they used to torture women. I dismembered them. It was my
vengeance, and the vengeance of all women.

In the villages of my region where there was no justice
other than the lathi, where the mallahs were the slaves of the
thakurs, I dealt out justice. 'Who stole from you? Who beat
you? Who took your food? Who said you couldn't use the
well? Who stole your cattle? Who raped your daughter, or
your sister, or your wife?' The guilty one was brought before
my court. He was forced to suffer what he had made others
suffer. He was stripped and given a good hiding with our
lathis in front of all the villagers. Then I would make them
dance, I would make them sing a playback song with my
words:

> *What are we going to do with him?*
> *Make him dance, make him dance!*
> *What are we going to do with him?*
> *Kill him or make him dance?'*

Sometimes they would sing and dance naked in front of
the villagers.

'Phoolan Devi is good and kind!' they would say.

'Long live Phoolan Devi!' said the villagers.

Sometimes they didn't dance . . .

There was one old man, a filthy old hog, who raped all
the girls in the villages of his district. We took him to the
jungle with us and kept him for eight days. 'Tell me, tell me
everything,' I said. 'I just want to be sure, and then I will let
you go.'

He told me everything, all the names, all the girls and the women he had tortured and humiliated. He even admitted that he had used young boys, and then anything that was female: sheep, dogs and goats. He had violated his own daughter and his daughter-in-law.

This thakur was a pervert and a sadist. Nothing could satisfy his greedy lust. The men of my gang were sickened.

His serpent first, then his hands, then his feet . . .

I cut them off.

I did it before the image of Durga, to give her peace.

On the last day, one of the men finished him with a bullet.

30

'*How beautiful your hair looks . . .*'
It was Vickram's voice, deep and reassuring.

I heard it often, and with it, the memories returned . . .

Sitting by a river, I remembered a time when I was bathing in the evening not long after he had killed Baboo Gujar. I was still scared. The smell of death hung about me and I couldn't seem to wash it away. We had been marching for days through the jungle, climbing the hills and crossing the rivers to reach that place by the river near Asta. We were deep in the forests, at a place where five rivers met. The monsoon had transformed the region into a vast lake. There was water everywhere, as far as the eye could see.

My hair was so long and matted with sweat and dirt that water alone couldn't untangle it. Vickram had handed me a bottle of oil.

'Use this.'

I had never seen oil in a bottle before, and it smelled so nice that I thought it must have been very expensive. 'Take as much as you like and pass it on.'

As I passed the precious bottle to Uncle Bare Lal it slipped from his wet hands and fell, smashing on the pebbles. I cried out and cupped my hands to try to save the oil before it ran away. Then I poured what I had retrieved on to a piece of the broken glass. I would have so liked to show it to my mother and my sisters.

'Leave it,' Uncle Bare Lal said. 'It's nothing. There's plenty more where that one came from.'

I believed that something as beautiful as that must be unique in the world. The world for me then was not very large: a few villages, the river, a forest, and some small farming towns, Kalpi and Orai. Where would you be able to find another bottle like that? I wondered. The oil was softer than the softest soap.

Vickram had given me a comb to use but I was embarrassed to bathe in front of him, afraid that he would come near me in the water. Sensing my shyness, he had gone a little way along the shore to bathe. I fought for a long while with the comb and the knots in my hair, and I was sitting on the bank when he came to sit beside me. The warm, late-afternoon sun was drying my hair and the humidity made it wavy.

'How beautiful your hair looks,' he had said.

In the sharp, cloudless sky, the sun was setting slowly, an enormous ball of orange fire. It made me sad to see it going down in the lake.

'What are you thinking?'

'The sun is going to die in the water,' I said.

'What makes you think that?'

'There's no more land, this is as far as the world goes, so the sun will drown.'

It was the first time I had seen the sun set over such a vast stretch of water, so vast you couldn't see the opposite shore. But they couldn't understand that my world then had a limit, that it ended where I could no longer see it. They both laughed, and Uncle Bare Lal said, 'So you think this is the end of the world? What's under us then, another world growing?'

I had tried hard to grasp what these men were saying. I had only ever seen the plains and the river. Ever since I was a child, I had watched the sun die on the far side of the

Yamuna and a new sun born in the morning. For me, the world was very small, but I was so afraid of them that I wished I had kept my sadness and anguish to myself.

It was stupid of me to think the sun was going to die in the water. It was so handsome, so deep and red over the shining water, that it couldn't just die like that.

We had returned to the same place a month or so later, after we were married, and everything was different. The waters had receded, the mist was lighter, and I wasn't so scared. Vickram took the time to explain things to me.

'You see, it isn't the end of the world. The sun doesn't die. Each morning it gets up again for you. And this evening it won't fall in the water. It goes to bed in one part of the country and gets up in another.'

I didn't know what a country was. I had never heard that word.

'A country is like India, for example. That is our country. It is very big and the world is even bigger. There are many many countries.'

Running through the jungles with Vickram, crossing the plains and the rivers, I had begun to glimpse how large my country was, and I thought I would never know where it ended.

'India goes all the way to the sea,' Vickram had said.

I had never seen the sea. There were many countries in the world. China was the other side of the mountains and America was the other side of the sea. But how could it be that America didn't just float away? I wondered if it was attached with a rope.

'The world is round, Phoolan. The countries of the world and the seas are all on a gigantic ball!'

The world was so large that the sun never died. It just kept going around and around.

I was trying to learn, but there was so much to know.

The first time I saw Vickram handing money out to the poor in the villages, I asked myself why he was doing it. I would have liked to know why he didn't give it to me instead. With just one of those banknotes I could have gone back to my village. But he gave them all away and soon there was not a single one left for me.

Then, one day, he gave me a banknote. He told me it was worth a hundred rupees! I didn't know what a hundred rupees was. For me, five or ten rupees was a lot of money. I didn't know how to count, but Vickram taught me how as we gave out money together in the villages.

'Give five hundred to him and a hundred to him,' he would say.

I learned to recognise hundred rupee notes. I listened to everything he said and I did as I was told. I hadn't chosen him but he was a mallah and he respected me. Before it was my father and all he had tried to teach me was to submit to the will of the rich and the thakurs. 'Look at the other girls,' my father would say, 'they don't say anything, they don't answer back their betters.' According to my father, you had to take off your shoes – if you had any – and walk barefoot past a thakur, otherwise they could beat you for your insolence. According to him, you had to drink water from the river and not from the well if the Sarpanch forbade it.

But according to Vickram, we could keep our shoes on in front of anyone and we could drink water from the well like everyone else. We all had the same dignity before God.

I forgot that Vickram was dead and I was still alive. I heard his voice and I saw him again sitting under a tree in the jungle as I sat watching and listening and learning from him. I used to like to hear him read the newspaper aloud. I had learned everything from him. I was his silent, attentive pupil and, gradually, I began to form my own ideas about the rich and the poor, about money and men.

I used to like to see him with the men. He was a good leader, kind and fair. The only thing I never understood about him was his loyalty to the red demon, his obstinate trust, all the way to the end – to his death. The evening before, when Vickram had cried by the riverbank and his heart was heavy with dark foreboding, we could have fled. That same night, when I wanted to kill Shri Ram, he had prevented me.

'You can't kill a sleeping man . . .'

And yet that was to be the trick destiny played on him.

The last thing he taught me, as he died at my side, was never, never to trust anybody again.

But there was worse to come.

Durga may have been protecting me, but I hadn't received the blessing of Sarasvati, the goddess of wisdom.

31

An informer had told us that Shri Ram and his gang were hiding out in a village named Behmai.

The region was one of high, barren hills carved with deep ravines, with few trees for cover. Behmai was tucked away in one of the ravines, far above the banks of the Yamuna. The men agreed to go after the two brothers as soon as we heard they were there. Three boats carried us as close as possible by river and we set off on foot up the sandy hillsides to reach the village.

We discussed our tactics as we marched through the night: Baba Mustakim, Balwan, Man Singh and myself. We knew that Shri Ram's gang was large and well-armed. They were all thakurs and they could get everything they needed from the villages in the region, be it food, guns or women. We would be on their territory, but Baba Mustakim's men were excited and I was too. Soon we came to a shepherd village called Ingwi comprised of straw-covered, mud-walled huts. We made camp nearby while it was still dark. I couldn't sleep, knowing my vengeance was at hand.

In the morning, Man Singh went to Ingwi to find out if anyone had seen Shri Ram. 'This was the place they brought you,' he said when he returned. The villagers had told him how to reach Behmai. They said Shri Ram was there. And there was more. 'That was where he humiliated you,' he said.

It was midday when we halted again at the top of a ravine to eat. The month of Magh had passed and Phalgun had begun. In a few weeks, it would be spring. The sky was clear, a pale, soft blue above the sandy orange hillside, and the sun was high. Out of the silence a voice came screeching through a powerful loudhailer.

It was the amplified voice of Shri Ram echoing in the ravines. He owned a loudhailer powered by a heavy battery, I knew. He was probably bellowing at us from the roof of one of the houses in Behmai and he was insulting Baba Mustakim.

'You think you can get me, Mustakim? Me, Shri Ram the thakur, you and your muslim pigs!'

He insulted Balwan too. 'And you Balwan, a shepherd, a caste of shit! We have already given you one lesson and now you want another.'

He had been tipped off. We had lost our chance of taking him by surprise.

The men had their boots back on and their arms at the ready in a few minutes. We spread out, advancing in the direction of Shri Ram's voice. The ground was hard and dry and there were no trees for cover but we still couldn't see the village until we had wound our way further up the ravine. All the time we could hear Shri Ram taunting us.

We decided to split into three groups. Baba Mustakim was to lead his men around one side of the village and I would take my men around the other. The third group, led by Balwan and Ram Avtar, was to take the main path into the village. Shri Ram would have no choice but to retreat. Then we would have him in our trap. We were counting on Balwan's group to drive him out and into our crossfire.

As I came around my side, I could hear Balwan yelling from the village and rifle-fire cracking like thunder. His men were terrorising the villagers. I was following a dry creek across some bushy terrain for cover, wondering what was going on in the village. Shri Ram had insulted them so much, pouring abuse on Balwan's shepherd caste and on muslims, that they were insane with resentment by the time they entered the village. The men were still firing and the villagers were screaming. They must have been rampaging like madmen in search of Shri Ram and his gang. Suddenly, ahead of me, I saw some men fleeing from the rear of the village and I realised it was Shri Ram and his gang.

As I fired in his direction, I heard Baba Mustakim calling to Balwan and his men to join us. I shouted the same thing. 'Over here! They're getting away!'

But Balwan and his men must have been too preoccupied with their looting. In the heat of the moment, I hadn't noticed that two of my men, Man Singh and Baladin, had gone to join them.

Baba Mustakim and I met up beyond the village with our men and together we chased Shri Ram and his gang. I had seen about five or six men escaping from houses at the rear of the village and now they had a head start on us. We were too far behind to see who they were but I was sure Shri Ram was somewhere in front of me, hidden in a crag or lying flat behind a bush. I could see figures flitting from rock to rock, setting off clouds of dust and firing in our direction before vanishing again. They had fled before Balwan and his men and it was impossible to approach them now. The cowards didn't dare to face us.

We exchanged fire for a while, driving them further up the ravine, but at about a thousand yards from the village they stopped shooting back. They must have retreated and run. They knew the terrain and we didn't. If we advanced now, we might find ourselves in a trap. We decided to return to the village in case they tried to double back and trap us from behind. Baba Mustakim was furious and I was beside myself with anger. We had missed Shri Ram by a whisker of his red moustache.

As we headed back along the path towards the village, I heard women wailing and the shouting and whooping of Balwan and his men as they fired shots in the air.

'Long Live Phoolan Devi! Victory to Phoolan!' they were shouting.

More than twenty men were killed that day, twenty thakurs.

Madness had taken hold. Women were running in every direction, screaming and begging for mercy above the noise of gunfire.

Balwan wanted to torch the village.

'Imbecile!' Baba Mustakim yelled at them. 'It's out of the question. There are families here. You are crazy!'

Instead, Baba Mustakim gave the order to retreat.

'It is a disaster for us,' he said. 'The newspapers will be full of it! All the police in India will be chasing us! If we stay together now we haven't got a hope. We must split up.'

Balwan left the gang and we never heard from him again. Baba Mustakim took three or four of his men, including Ram Avtar, and I took seven men including Man Singh.

The chase Baba Mustakim predicted began. It was going to last a long time.

Over the next few days, the radio didn't stop talking about Behmai, the little village in the arid heartlands of Uttar Pradesh, and Phoolan Devi, the dacoit who had gone there to slake her thirst on the blood of thakurs.

The Queen of Bandits came with her entire gang to kill us, villagers said, because Shri Ram had killed Vickram and raped her. Shri Ram was a thakur and the men they killed were thakurs too. Phoolan was the one who did it, the villagers said. They had seen her, and denounced her to the army of police officers that arrived in the devastated village, now inhabited only by goats, children and widows.

In all the newspapers Man Singh was able to find they called me a bloodthirsty madwoman, the Bandit Queen of Chambal, the badlands where the Chambal river meets the Yamuna. There was such an uproar the Chief Minister resigned from his post because of me. The story swelled like the neck of a snake. I was described as a monster. Some witnesses said I was two yards tall, some said I was ugly as an ape, others said I was beautiful as a goddess, and one day there was even a photo of me in a magazine. But it wasn't me. Nobody had ever taken my photo. Only the villagers of my district knew what I looked like. The newspapers called what happened a massacre of thakurs by low-caste dacoits. I was called the Bandit Queen, a poor mallah girl who, ever since her lover was killed by thakurs, had wielded the fearsome sword of Kali, the patron saint of thuggees.

Then we heard on the radio that the new Chief Minister in Kanpur had called for reinforcements. The entire state was on alert. The army had been called in and they had orders to shoot us on sight. The worst of it was that Shri Ram, my only real enemy, was still alive, while I was being tracked through the jungle like a blood-crazed tigress accused of devouring little lambs.

But nothing was going to stop me finding him.

If I heard that someone had been sheltering him – and usually it was someone who had some kind of connection with the police – I would deal with them. I didn't kill wantonly, I punished.

All the time, the only one I wanted to find and punish, to cut into pieces and throw to the dogs, was Shri Ram. I wanted to see the dogs devour him, tearing at his flesh and gnawing at his bones. My only craze was for his blood.

I was told about a certain Pradhan, a corrupt man with a reputation for dealings with the police, who had hidden Shri Ram in his village for a time. Like Shri Ram, this Pradhan was always on the lookout for a helpless girl to satisfy his lusts.

We arrived at his house in the night, pretending to be sipahis. I was wearing my uniform, and carrying my rifle, with a white turban over my red headband. Man Singh and the others were dressed in their uniforms too. The Pradhan let us in without imagining for a moment that it was Phoolan Devi in his house. He gave us money, thinking I was a young police officer and that Man Singh was my superior. It was his custom to grease the palms of the police, and he offered us whisky too. In the jungle, nobody ever drank alcohol. We asked for water and got him talking.

After a while, I told him my chief would like to loosen up a little. 'You don't have a woman around here, do you? We heard you always had one.'

'Oh yes, I have many, many! I have to have one every day. You just have to take one from the village, there is no shortage of the little things. I have had them all at one time or another!'

'How much do you pay them?'

'Pay? What do you want me to pay those bitches for? A good kicking is enough for low-caste bitches like that.'

The men listened without saying anything as he proudly told us of his exploits. Then he decided he would get two women for us.

'Only two,' I joked. 'What are we going to do with two. We need one for each of us.'

He laughed nervously and called his servant, sending him

to the village with instructions to fetch the daughter of so-and-so and the wife of someone else. He gave a list of names.

While we were waiting, I mentioned Shri Ram. 'Why did you let him stay here?'

'Oh, Shri Ram is a very good man for getting girls. He finds them in every village, everywhere he goes. He knows exactly how to get them.'

'What sort of women?'

'Mallahs, jatavs, whatever you like.'

'The thing is, my chief would like you to let him have your wife for the night . . .'

'Oh no, he cannot have her. She is a Kshastriya! We are all Kshastriyas here, and we don't do such things. Tell him to be patient and we will find him a very pretty girl, very pretty.'

Two young girls arrived, poor girls with dark skin, dressed in rags. They must have been fifteen or sixteen, perhaps even younger. The Pradhan started telling them what they would have to do for us, dribbling with lust as he spoke. I could only think of myself at that age, hiding in fear from men like him, hiding in trees and cowsheds and whimpering with humiliation.

'Hey, Pradhan, I heard there was a very pretty girl in the next village . . .'

'Yes, the daughter of a Brahmin. She is very beautiful.'

'We're going there later. We have heard that Phoolan Devi and her gang are around here and maybe she knows where they're hiding!'

'Let me come with you! She is much more beautiful than the girls around here. They are all dark-skinned and horrible. My sons prefer girls with light skin, too, and the Brahmin's daughter is so light-skinned and pretty!'

'We can't take you along. If our superiors found out we might lose our jobs.'

'That's really too bad. Well, anyway, we still have these two. You go ahead . . . I will help myself to another drink.'

He was intoxicated but we had drunk only water. He was reeling as he took his shirt off and ordered one of the girls to lie down. She obeyed without a word of protest. She shut her eyes and waited, terrorised and downtrodden by the knowledge that her caste didn't have the right to refuse this pig, a member of the so-called martial caste of Kshastriyas.

I pulled off my turban, and shook my hair so it fell to my shoulders, putting the barrel of my rifle right under his nose.

'You filthy bloody dog! Do you know who I am?'

'No. What is happening here?'

'You wanted a woman?'

I smashed him between the legs with my rifle butt and he fell on all fours moaning with his behind in the air. I beat his arms and legs. The two girls huddled in the corner, trembling like lambs. I gave them both a slap.

'You come when you're called, is that it? He whistles and you lie down . . .'

'He would beat us. He wouldn't let us have any food.'

'Then get away from here, don't stay here in this bloody village. Go and live somewhere else.'

He looked ridiculous, naked, on all fours, pleading with us to excuse him. We tied a rope around his neck like a pig and dragged him through the village calling everybody out, all the girls and women he had raped.

'When he assaulted you, did you ever see him naked like this? Take a good look,' I shouted. 'Make him turn around and dance for you!'

His wife came out and begged me to be merciful to him. She said she had children to feed and she would be helpless without him to provide for her. Were they all cowards, every last one of them? Was I the only one who rebelled?

'Today he begs me to pardon him but tomorrow when I'm

gone it'll be the same as before.' It was pitiful. 'Don't worry, I'm not going to kill him. He will live, but he will never be the same as before.'

I called to one of my men.

'Cut this thing off!'

'Eh? Why don't we just kill him?'

'Cut it, or I'll do it myself!'

'If you are able to do it, Bahanji, then I am able also!'

He took out the long razor he used for shaving and sliced off the Pradhan's serpent.

But my men decided it wasn't enough. They said we ought to cut off his nose as well. He was an informer, mixed up with the police, and police spies had their noses cut off! That way, in future, everybody would be able to see whose side he was on.

I gave his wife enough rupees to take him to the hospital, with his serpent tied around his neck.

Some weeks later, I saw him again in his village. I asked what had happened and, still quaking with fear, he told me he had to pee through a plastic tube.

'Have you come to kill me this time?' he asked pathetically.

'Why should I bother? You can't harm anyone now. Who are you going to hurt with that plastic tube? Who are you going to denounce with a hole instead of a nose?'

That was how I punished some of them. The first time, it had been in an outpouring of rage, not long after Vickram's death. Then I said to myself it was justice pure and simple for them. Without their organs they wouldn't be able to persecute women any more.

But I never killed without reason.

32

It said in the newspaper that the Chief Minister had offered a reward of a hundred thousand rupees for information leading to my capture and five thousand for Man Singh. He had vowed that in six months he would have me, alive or dead, and that Phoolan Devi would cease to terrorise the region. I saw metal birds in the sky spitting fire. There were helicopters over the treetops and lorries and jeeps on the roads. In the ravines, whole army divisions were deployed.

Don't trust anybody, that was what Vickram had said, not even your own men. Especially not your own men. The reward of a hundred thousand rupees might have tempted Man Singh or Baladin, or even Lakhan, my loyal jatav accountant. My only true friend, the only person I could really trust, was my Sten automatic rifle. It was an ally worth a hundred and eighty thousand rupees – more than my own head – though I paid only fifty thousand for it to a shepherd in the Chambal valley.

He was alone in the hills with his flock when we came across him. We had gone into hiding in the badlands, the deep, desolate ravines between the Chambal river and the Yamuna. I asked the shepherd for a drink of water, and because he was staring in fascination at my rifle, I asked him if he had ever seen one before.

'Yes. I have one in my house.'

'Really, and where did you get it?'

'When I was taking the flock through the forest I found it on the ground.'

'Well, don't tell anybody. I'd like to see it.'

I expected him to come back with an old army rifle of some kind, but he returned with his wife, his father and some other shepherds and they put a sheaf of millet down at my feet. The rifle was hidden inside. It was a first-class weapon, a three-speed Sten automatic. I tried it out while the shepherds watched me in awe, as though I was some kind of god to be able to load, aim and fire a rifle.

'You stole it from the police?'

'No, Lalloo, no! I really did find it in the hills.'

He had called me a young man, thinking I was a boy because I was wearing a cap and I could handle the gun.

'How much do you want?'

'I don't want money. What am I going to do with money here? If you want it, take it. I don't know how to use it. We hid it but we are afraid a thakur will come and beat us and take it.'

I gave him fifty thousand rupees, an enormous sum of money for a shepherd.

His father had never seen so much money in his whole life. 'You are rich, my son!' he said. 'With this we will be able to buy land.'

'Do you know Phoolan Devi?' I asked.

'Yes I have heard of her.'

'Do you know what she looks like?'

'She is very big and strong. Sometimes she comes to steal my goats.'

'What? She steals your goats – and doesn't pay you?'

'No, she never pays.'

'Then it is not Phoolan who is stealing your goats.' I took off my hat and shook my hair out. 'Look at me. I am Phoolan Devi. Do I look like her?'

He gaped at me with his eyes wide.

'The woman in the valley is very big and there is one man with her who has a gun and another with a lathi, and they are always stealing my animals.'

'This woman is tricking you! Next time you see her, tell her she is lying and that you have seen the real Phoolan Devi.'

'She won't believe me! And they have a rifle! And the man will beat us with his lathi.'

We waited there for two days. Man Singh and the others were impatient. They thought the man was lying and, even if it was true, they thought it wasn't worth getting mixed up with, but I suspected it wouldn't be long before I saw my double. The shepherd said she came once a week to steal his animals. On the afternoon of the second day, a woman and two men arrived.

We watched them from behind the trees. The young shepherd came to me and told us they were the ones. 'They threatened us, they said we couldn't let our animals graze here if we didn't give them one.' As they walked away, we caught up with them. The woman was wearing a ragged old uniform. She was much bigger than me, but she had a red band around her head.

'So you are Phoolan, and this is your gang. There are just three of you?'

'Yes, that's right, I'm Phoolan Devi!'

'All right then. I am a police officer. We're looking for Phoolan Devi and I'm going to beat you and lock you up in prison.'

She was so frightened she peed in her trousers.

'No, no! It's not true. It's not me, I swear. We're from the village down there. This is my husband and my brother-in-law.'

I gave each of them a slap, and the woman swore that she

wouldn't do it again, she wouldn't steal any more goats from the poor. She admitted she had been doing it for six months. The first time, it had worked so well that she couldn't help coming back to do it again. She said they had sold the goats in the market so I told her she would have to give the money to the shepherds.

'I don't have it. We are poor too. We don't have any land or animals. It was only to be able to eat, I swear!'

At first I had been annoyed, but now I felt sorry for her in her old trousers and T-shirt, with her funny turban on her head. And the other two looked as pitiful as she did.

'Take this.' I gave them five hundred rupees each. 'Buy a bigha of land and don't ever come back to feed your family by stealing their goats.'

The shepherds became indignant. They wanted me to kill the three of them. This woman had been stealing animals from them and they had no hope of ever getting any compensation.

To shut them up, I gave them each a bundle of rupees too.

It satisfied me to give money to the poor. I liked to have that power. The first time Vickram gave me a hundred-rupee note, nothing would have pleased me more than to be able to run home and give it to my mother, but I was still a prisoner in the jungle then. I could imagine their happiness when they went home to their houses with their bundles of rupees that represented not wealth for them but survival. It wasn't riches they clutched in their hands, it was relief, the relief of being able to fill their bellies, to buy grain for the winter and wood for the fire. I would have liked to have endless bundles of rupees to be able to give to all those who had nothing, as once I had nothing.

Most of all, I liked to be able to give money to women. I very rarely gave it to men. They could work in the fields, go from village to village, find money somehow, but not the women. Nobody helped the women, not even their husbands. They didn't give the women a rupee. Without money, women were forced to suffer hunger and humiliation, and even sell their bodies like sacks of flour, while the men spent their money drinking and gambling.

The shepherds watched me giving out the money as though I was Lakshmi, the goddess of plenitude, herself. But I knew by then that what I had given them was hardly more than nothing.

In all our lootings, I saw real riches just once.

After I had separated from Baba Mustakim at Bchmai, I found myself with only seven men. My lieutenant Man Singh and Lakhan, my accountant, were still with me. We had been getting restless hiding out in the Chambal. Eventually, a gang led by Ram Avtar, one of Mustakim's men, joined us, bringing our strength up to twenty-five in all, most of them muslims.

We decided to raid the palace overlooking the Yamuna at Jagamanpur, an isolated town at the foot of the hills on the edge of the Jalaun plain. The palace was an immense building with hundreds of people bustling outside who fled in panic when we arrived. I climbed the marble staircase in the courtyard up to a terrace, and then up another staircase to the rooftop.

'My name is Phoolan Devi,' I shouted through my loudhailer. 'I am here to loot this palace. Where are you, Rajah? Show yourself!'

The palace emptied, the servants running everywhere. The women were fleeing, tangled in their saris and terrified by the shots we fired in the air. I had heard that the wife of the Maharajah would be a fancy prize. She was said to be covered in gold. I descended from the roof, hoping to catch her.

'Don't be scared,' I reassured the women. 'We're only here to steal!'

It didn't calm them. Far from it. They flew in every direction like parrots in their bright-coloured saris. Men dressed in brocades and silks were fleeing too, and I grabbed one of them and stuck my rifle in his belly.

'Are you the rajah?'

'No, no! It's him, that one, running away there.'

I wouldn't have taken him for a rajah. He looked like any man from a village with the end of his dhoti trailing behind him. He hadn't had time to knot it properly and he was trying to gather it up as he ran half-naked from our assault.

'Hey, why are you in such a hurry,' I shouted at him through my megaphone. 'Dress yourself first. We came here to see you. We heard that you had never let a dacoit into your house, you shoot them all down.'

I laughed. I had never seen a man running so fast. His dhoti was flapping like a white sail in the wind.

The host left us to explore at our leisure his deserted palace. We were free to marvel at the marble hallways, the silver mirrors, the swords and the rifles hanging on the walls. I pulled down a silver sabre. The handle was studded with pearls and precious stones. Even the sheath was made of silver. It looked very old and there was something engraved on it. I showed my trophy to one of the men and he said it was the names of the father and grandfather of the Maharajah.

I brandished it like a warrior.

'Look at me,' I shouted to the others, 'I'm Durga!'

I ran out on the balcony and waved it at the sipahis who were firing at us from the town.

'Hold your fire! Get your swords, cowards, and fight Durga!'

The bedrooms were even more beautiful. I found some of

the men standing awestruck by an enormous bed with dark red coverings and long red curtains. It was covered in velvet: a pool of soft velvet with velvet pillows floating on it. I threw myself on it, rolling on the ruby-coloured velvet, while the men searched for money and jewellery, but there wasn't any. Everything was on the walls: gold and silver, velvet and silk. There were carpets on the floor and furniture studded with precious stones. We ransacked all the drawers. Everything in the palace was made of precious things, but there wasn't a single rupee. There were all kinds of flowers in great tall vases that scented the air like a forest in springtime. But no rupees.

All this luxury, all this beauty, the perfume and the flowers, began to irritate me. This rajah dog slept on a bed covered in velvet while I slept on hard earth.

One by one, I smashed the magnificent vases, pouring curses on the boastful rajah. My family's house was hardly bigger than his bed! Two of the villages of my community could fit in his courtyard!

Outside I could still hear rifle fire. The local police were shooting at us from afar. So vast was the palace and the gardens full of flowers that surrounded it that they were firing without being able to see us. There weren't enough of them to launch an attack and reinforcements would take a while to arrive.

One of the men had dressed as a rajah, in a silk brocade jacket, and he was admiring himself in a mirror of polished silver. There were so many beautiful objects, but they were too heavy to transport and they would be hard to sell. There was an enormous hookah, as tall as me, made of silver, that I wanted to take, but the men laughed at me.

'Can you see us running through the jungle with that?'

After an hour we had found little to make it worth our effort but the men still wouldn't leave. They were trying out all the beds and sitting at the tables and dancing on the carpets, playing at being princes, bowing to each other and laughing like children. I had to grab them and shake them to get them to leave.

I had wanted to prove to the rajah that we could come into his beautiful palace if we liked, and I had done it. But we were going to leave with our pockets empty.

Half an hour later, we were in the middle of the little town, at the market. There, among the people selling cucumbers and melons from their kachwaris, like my mother used to, I felt like Maharani.

The people threw themselves to the ground to touch my feet. 'Long live Phoolan Devi!' they cheered. 'Give us money!'

I gave away so many rupees that I had to borrow more from the men. I gave away a ring that Baba Mustakim had given me, everything I had. I kept the sword from the rajah's palace for a while after that but it was too heavy to wear and I ended up giving it away to a shepherd.

It hadn't been a pillage that day, we just wanted to prove we were stronger than the rajah who ruled the town. I had laughed to see him running away holding up his dhoti. I was satisfied. Me, a low-caste girl, laughing at the ridiculous rajah!

I didn't laugh very often, and I knew the men had started to find me bitter, always angry and aggressive. At times they were even afraid to speak to me. There were moments when I hated them all, and times when I loved them like brothers. I had confided in no one since the death of Vickram. Inside, I was still empty.

One evening, in the jungle near Etawah, as I was resting in the twilight under a tree, I dozed off and woke abruptly with the sickening feeling that one of the men was trying to molest me. But there was nobody near me. I looked around and saw a snake. He was black, with a wide neck. I called the guard quickly. His long body was already coiled around me. I could feel his muscles rippling against me; cold waves of strength gripped my body.

'Hurry, there's a snake on me. Make him go away!'

The guard was a muslim, one of the members of Baba Mustakim's gang. 'Don't move,' he said.

All the men knew I was followed by a snake. They all gathered around me.

'Don't kill him,' I said. 'I forbid you to kill him.'

He went of his own accord, disturbed probably by the sound of the men. He released me slowly and slithered off, turning his head around once to look at me before disappearing in the forest.

The snake was my friend. I believed he was the spirit of a dead person coming to see me. Whenever he returned after a few days, or a few weeks, I said to him, 'Oh, there you are, back again.'

Or else it was the little girl . . .

I often heard the voice of a little girl in my head saying, 'Don't drink that water, don't go that way, don't stay any longer in this village . . .'

33

When I heard on the radio that Baba Mustakim was dead, my first reaction was to wonder who had denounced him. Then I began to doubt that it was true. I had lost count of how many months I had been running through the jungle with my men, from one valley to the next. The monsoon had come again and we decided to make for Guloli, the village where Baba Mustakim's family lived. The more I thought about it the more I was sure he wasn't dead. The police could easily have made up the story to panic us, as they had done with Vickram the first time he was shot.

Baba used to leave half of his money with a Pandit in Suroli and he had bought lorries in the Pandit's name, Suttan. His financial base was there, near his family, in the heart of a muslim community. Suroli was a hindu village and Guloli, adjacent to it, was a muslim village. The Pandit was the only hindu in Baba Mustakim's circle. I never liked him much. There was something in his look that troubled me. He had grown rich with the help of Baba Mustakim and in the back of my mind I knew that, if he really was dead, the Pandit could no longer be trusted.

It was the middle of the night when we reached the twin villages. We located his house, a nice house, built of concrete, with two storeys. Pandit Suttan welcomed us warmly and tearfully confirmed that, alas, the news was true, Baba Mustakim was dead. 'He was on his way to see his sister at

Dastampur. He was unarmed when they got him. Someone had given him away. Three other men died with him and they weren't even bandits. The police said it was a shoot-out, but they weren't even armed. What a sorrowful thing!'

The death of Baba Mustakim was like losing a father for us, but for the Pandit it meant losing his biggest source of income. He asked for our protection, saying we were the only ones who could help him now. I didn't reply. We had been isolated these last months, and we needed money. It had been impossible to stage the kind of raid that would improve our finances, just a few minor lootings to be able to survive and get more ammunition. The raid on the palace at Jagamanpur had been fruitless. And for the moment, it seemed to be impossible to find Shri Ram, to satisfy my thirst. He had vanished into thin air.

Meanwhile, we were hearing every day on the radio that so-and-so had surrendered and someone else had been shot down, denounced and then assassinated by the police . . . It was as if there was no one left in the jungle apart from Phoolan Devi's gang.

The Pandit offered us food and asked where we were going to hide. I told him we were going to Mustakim's cousin's house in Guloli. 'I am going to see his family with Man Singh and Baladin. I will leave three men here and we will return tomorrow. Though I was mistrustful of him, I didn't want him to doubt us. Leaving the men with him was a mark of confidence.

It was five o'clock in the morning, time to go to ground. It had been months since we dared to move around by day. We intended to spend the day with Munna, a young cousin of Mustakim whom I knew well. I had been there several times before. When we reached his house, we talked for a while, Munna, his grandfather and I, about Baba, remembering the times we had spent together . . .

At about eleven o'clock in the morning, I heard a series of explosions in the distance.

'What's going on, Munna?'

'Oh, fireworks probably.'

'Go and take a look.'

He came back in a panic. The police had invaded the village. The shots we heard had come from the other hamlet, Suroli. With a shawl over my head so that my uniform wouldn't be noticed, I climbed up on to the terrace of his house. The police were everywhere: in the narrow streets, in the courtyards of the houses and on the terraces. I had never seen so many police in one village. With my binoculars under my shawl, I tried to make out what was going on beyond the village.

It was going to be impossible to get out. There were lorryloads of sipahis everywhere. We were under siege. Somebody had informed on us, the Pandit probably. I was sure his tears had been false and his deceitful look had been showing his true feelings. No one else there would have even thought of denouncing us. Nearly everyone in Guloli was muslim and Mustakim was a hero for them.

I came down quickly from the terrace. The three of us were caught in the trap: Man Singh, Baladin and me. Over a loudspeaker, the police announced that the area was surrounded and they were going to evacuate the villagers. 'Phoolan Devi's gang is hiding in your village! Each villager must show some means of identification to the police. Please co-operate.' They were going to empty the village and then come in after us! If we tried to pretend we were villagers without papers, we would be caught. I could already hear a helicopter growling over our heads and there was another one approaching.

As the villagers left their houses in trepidation, Man Singh and Baladin tried to find a way out of the village, but the streets were filled with uniformed men.

'Three men have already been killed,' said the voice through the loudspeaker. 'Three bandits from Phoolan Devi's gang.'

They must have been the three men we left at the Pandit's house: Laltu, Ram Shankar and Subaran. There were just the three of us, plus Jageshwar and Kallu, left now – five in all – and I didn't know where the other two were. We had three automatic rifles: I had my Sten, Man Singh had his 306 and Baladin had a 303. Our only consolation was that we had plenty of ammunition.

By midday the village had been evacuated. An hour later, the battle began.

There was only one thing to do: keep moving from house to house, through the streets and courtyards, over the roofs and walls, shooting when they shot at us. Even if we were only going in circles, we had to keep on the move. They were dropping grenades from the helicopters, demolishing the houses behind us as we moved. Soon the village was transformed into a battlefield. They were trying to bomb any point from which a shot was fired, and in their panic they bombed their own men as well as us.

We threaded our way along the alleys, diving through doorways and hiding in courtyards. It was impossible to face them man-to-man. They were going around in groups of a dozen and they were armed with machine guns.

By nightfall, we had found a hiding place in one of the deserted houses.

'Five of Phoolan Devi's men have been killed!' they announced over the loudspeaker. They must have got Jageshwar and Kallu too. They were keeping score. There were only three of us left.

Suddenly, the whole village lit up as bright as day again. They had brought powerful lights to illuminate the streets. I could see shadows flickering along the walls as they went from house to house, communicating with walkie-talkies. They had some kind of password to recognise each other. If only we knew what it was! There were so many of them that, with our uniforms, we might have been able to lose ourselves in their midst. I tried to listen but it was no use, I couldn't understand their language. We had no choice but to keep moving from one house to the next. When they checked one house and moved on, Man Singh, Baladin and I would steal in behind them. Whenever they surrounded a house, we slipped over the wall into the next one.

At one moment, we dropped down the other side of a wall and found the house already occupied by a dozen policemen. We had landed in the courtyard. They were sitting just inside a doorway, smoking in the dark.

Man Singh clasped his rifle and looked at me.

I shook my head. There were too many of them. I motioned my two companions to sit down in the corner of the yard and pretend to be dozing. I did the same.

'Because of that bloody woman you can't even have a smoke in peace,' we heard one of the policemen say.

'Nobody knows what's happening. We'll end up killing each other at this rate. Some men have already been hit.'

They got up to leave the house and we followed behind as though we were part of their squad. As they went into the next house to search, we slipped back into the courtyard.

They were in every house, behind every wall. There was no way out. The essential thing was to stay together in case it came to a showdown. Slipping from one house to the next and being shot at all afternoon had left us exhausted. They had been so close to us at times that I was sure they had seen us, but they kept shooting at shadows, giving themselves away.

We spent the night without sleep, without even speaking

to each other, hidden away in the ruins of a house they had bombarded during the day.

When day broke, the rat run began again.

'Phoolan Devi is wearing a uniform and a turban,' they said over the loudspeaker. 'The others are in police uniforms.'

We had to change our clothes. We looked around for a terrace where someone had left clothes to dry, made our way up and snatched them. Behind us the police dropped grenades from the helicopter, destroying the terrace. We stumbled under the rocky debris that fell around us.

We had managed to get lunghis for Man Singh and Baladin and a sari for me. We slipped into another house and changed, hiding our uniforms hurriedly. I just had time to adjust my sari and hide my cartridge belt and my rifle under it when the door to the yard opened with a crash and I saw a squad of sipahis outside in the street. I was in the courtyard but, luckily, Man Singh and Baladin were inside one of the rooms.

'What are you doing there?' one of the sipahis yelled at me. 'You were told to evacuate. You'll get yourself killed!'

He must have taken me for a young muslim woman. I answered in a tearful high-pitched wail. 'I was scared, I didn't know which way to run.'

'You were lucky with all that shooting.'

One of the other policemen nodded. 'That bloody Phoolan must be doing the same thing right now. She must be hiding somewhere.'

They forgot about me and moved on. I had been lucky, because they didn't know what I looked like. And they had other business too. I noticed they were carrying jerrycans full of petrol. They weren't just searching the houses, they were looting them too, like bandits. And they were going to burn the village down afterwards to cover their activities. I could already smell burning. The grenades had started small fires everywhere.

'Phoolan, give yourself up!' said the voice from the loud-speaker. 'Come, Bahanji. We won't punish you. We won't kill you.'

Man Singh and Baladin wanted to surrender. They thought we were going to die in that village. For me it was out of the question. 'That's how they got Mustakim and the others. They told them they wouldn't be harmed and then they shot them down. If you go near the police, Man Singh, I will shoot you down myself!'

My throat was itching with thirst but there was no water to be found anywhere. The police had smashed all the pots of water they found in the houses.

Twenty-four hours had passed already, it was mid-morning on the second day, and the battle began again.

They fired, and we fired back, slipping over a wall or down an alley, and they fired again. The hours passed and they were still there in force, searching the houses they had already searched, shooting through doors, dropping grenades from the helicopters. Night was falling and somehow we had to get out of there, but there was no way out. In the fields beyond, the villagers were waiting for the battle to finish.

Gradually the shooting ceased and there was silence. It was almost dark. Over the loudspeaker, they gave the order to cease firing. They must have been killing each other in their frantic search to find and kill us. We couldn't breathe because of the smoke from the fires, and we still hadn't found anything to drink. It was going to be our second night hidden inside a house, without hope.

The roof of the house had collapsed, destroyed by a grenade. There would soon be nothing left of the village. They said over the loudspeaker that they were going to burn all the houses. If they did that, we were finished.

I was going insane. 'I've had enough!' I said to Man Singh. 'I'm going to shoot myself!'

'Remember what you said: if we have to die let's take some of them with us at least.'

Forgetting we were cornered like rats, I fell asleep from exhaustion. I was sound asleep, and in my sleep I heard a little girl's voice . . . *Take off your shoes and go around behind the mosque. There's a house there, in ruins. Hide in there!*

I woke with a start. The house where we were hiding was near a mosque. I had seen it during the day, but the street that led to it was filled with heaps of rubble from the explosions. We would have to crawl over the debris of the bombarded houses to reach it.

I woke the others.

'Baladin, Man Singh, let's go! Leave your boots here.'

'What's happened to you? The police are everywhere. Listen, you can hear them talking on the terraces.'

'We're moving,' I said. 'We're going to hide over there behind the mosque.'

We had barely stood up to leave the room when we had to drop on our bellies to the ground in the yard.

'Hey, you over there! Do you want to get yourself killed?'

We could see shadows and torchbeams on the walls. And more voices.

'Don't shoot. You heard the order.'

They had mistaken us for police and they were waiting for us to shout the password. We didn't move. The silence lasted for several minutes.

'It was just dogs,' one of them said at last. 'There's nobody in there!'

They laughed with relief and we saw the torchbeams moving away.

We crawled over the rubble, silent as snakes. The beams of their torches played on the walls around us, but the police wouldn't enter the ruined houses in the dark. They were afraid to injure themselves or be cornered by us. It was almost as if they were scared to come face-to-face with us. They must have had orders to remain in groups. Slowly, so as not to make a sound, we inched our way on our bellies towards the mosque.

We had to make our way around to the back. There really was a house there, a little house, no more than a hut, and it was in ruins. The roof had collapsed, but we lifted away some of the rocks from the doorway and crawled inside. Man Singh buried himself under a pile of fallen rocks. I hid under another pile and Baladin covered himself with straw from the roof.

We tried to close the gaps around us with rocks, so as not to be seen. It was as though we were closing our own tombs over us. If I was going to die, I thought, it might as well be there as anywhere else. I was too exhausted to care.

We said nothing and we didn't move until morning.

At one moment in the night I heard police walking by us. 'She got away. The people here must have helped her.'

The villagers had helped us in the beginning. When we were running from house to house trying to find a place to hide nobody had given us away. They were still evacuating the village and I had given the villagers all the money I had left, nearly fifty thousand rupees. I had thought then my last hour had come, and the women wept for me saying, 'Allah be with you!' The muslims were poor, as poor as mallahs. In a hindu community, where everyone feared and respected thakurs, I might not have been protected.

The next morning, the voice from the loudspeaker confirmed what the police had said. 'You may return to your houses. Phoolan Devi is no longer in the area.'

We heard footsteps and the sounds of people wailing and moaning at the devastation, but it was midday before I dared to poke my nose out from under the rocks. Thirst was the hardest torture to bear. I had no more saliva left to swallow, and the smell of the helicopters had given me a headache. Suddenly I heard a funny noise. I lifted my head and shook the dust and sand from my hair. A woman yelped in front of me. She had just squatted down and lifted her petticoat to pee when she saw me. She must have thought at first that I was a demon, but she had enough wits about her to realise who we were.

'You are the bandits! You must get away from here. They have killed many people in the village already and they destroyed all the homes. Please, go away from here right away. You have brought a curse on us!'

We made our way to the edge of the village. The police lorries were still there but the police appeared to have given up the search. The helicopters had gone. Keeping low, we made our way through the fields to the Yamuna. We fell on the water like thirsty dogs, without noticing that three army boats were moored a little further up, two on the far side and one on our side. Lifting my head from the water I saw squads of police on the road, but they were paying no attention to us. We were dressed in ordinary clothes, ragged and dusty. We were just peasants. They weren't looking for Phoolan and her gang any more. I had officially escaped the police trap. There must have been a thousand men trying to catch me. The Prime Minister, Indira Gandhi herself, said she wanted the dacoits responsible for the massacre at Behmai to be brought to justice. Well, Laltu, Subaran, Jageshwar, Kallu and Ram Shankar were all dead.

I drank, dunking my head under the water, as I tried to decide what to do next. I wanted to return to the Pandit's house, to find out if he had denounced us and cut off his nose if it was him. And if it wasn't him, then he was the only one who could help us. We had no money and the police were still looking for us everywhere in the district. We left, walking normally with our rifles under clothes. They had spent two days and nights trying to corner us, but it was as though Durga had blindfolded them all!

We followed a canal that led back to the two villages. The canal was dry and there were tree-lined mounds either side. Walking in the empty canal bed, we were out of sight. We had almost reached the Pandit's house when we encountered a man relieving himself in the canal. 'Don't go any further, Pandit Suttan's house is full of sipahis.'

So it had been him after all! The man told us the Pradhan had been seen leaving the village on a motorcycle to fetch the police from Kalpi. But we couldn't go there now. He would be able to keep his nose for the time being. We climbed out of the canal and crossed the fields, heading back into the jungle.

I learned later that it was one of my men who had given us the chance to escape. Wounded in the leg by a grenade and captured by the police, Kallu told them he had helped me to reach the jungle before he died. A policeman was even suspected of taking a bribe to ferry me out of there in a helicopter.

We stopped at the next village, Tunna, to offer our thanks to the gods. I had no money left but Man Singh and Baladin still had some. When they saw us arriving at the temple, the villagers fled in terror. The Brahmin had his eyes closed in prayer and I lifted my rifle into the air to show we meant no harm.

'Don't be afraid. We're only here to make an offering, to thank the gods for letting us live!'

Man Singh handed me a thousand rupees and I gave the roll of notes to the Brahmin, asking him what he had been praying for.

'I was giving thanks for your death. Yours and Man Singh's!'

'Eh?'

'They all say you are dead. They took your body to your village to show it to your parents.'

'You dare to celebrate my death! After all the help I have given you jatavs!'

'It's because of Man Singh. He killed seven men here in Tunna.'

It was true. Three months before the massacre at Behmai, Man Singh had come here on a mission of vengeance. The Brahmin hadn't recognised him beside me covered in dust.

But I wasn't angry. Alive or dead, I realised we had become legends for them. They saw only our rifles, and it was the same for the police. The radio and the newspapers wouldn't stop talking about me.

If only they had talked about me before, I thought, when I was being mistreated and I was the one crying out for justice. But the bad things done by the poor were all anyone ever talked about, not the bad things done to them.

34

'If any of you ever betrays me,' I always warned the men, 'I will kill you!'

Being the gang leader meant having to be suspicious of everything and everyone. I could never let two men go together to a village for example. Two men together might plot something, while one alone wouldn't be able to cause much trouble.

But nobody ever threatened my authority, not because they were afraid, but because they trusted me. And I respected their confidence in me, I took care of my men. I made sure they were fed and protected and if the police were after us, I was always the last to run. I waited until they had reached safety, exactly as Vickram used to.

But now I had no gang any more.

There were only three of us left after the battle at Guloli. The police wanted me dead or alive, but I wasn't afraid of the police. I was afraid of treason. There was a big reward on my head, enough to tempt the most loyal of men.

And then Baladin disappeared. He went to a village near the jungle saying he was going to get some food and he never returned.

Food became an everyday problem. There were too few of us to go into the villages. Sometimes the only way to get something to eat was to capture someone who had some food and take it from them. Without Baladin, and with the two of us reduced to stealing food, Man Singh began to lose heart. He was fed up with being on the run, he said, having to hide in the ravines and not being able to walk along a road or bathe in a river without seeing sipahis. He said we ought to go to his village, Barahai, in the district of Almanipur, where his brother would be able to hide us for a while. We trekked across the ravines for several days but when we got there, Man Singh's brother just tried to talk him into surrendering. 'You have to give yourself up,' he insisted. 'We don't want any more bandits around here!' For the whole night Man Singh was harassed by his family's pleas. Finally, he decided to stay, and I left for the jungle alone. I decided I would go on, gang or no gang.

I had no contact with anyone. I couldn't eat or drink or sleep at regular hours. I had to move through the night, the way we had always done, and sleep during the day, but I was on my own now. There were times when I bought food from someone in a field and walked the whole night to be able to sit down and eat in security. For companionship, I had the monkeys, the bears and the wild cats. The jungle was never quiet, except when danger approached. The birds were always singing and their cries told me things. They told me when a wild animal was near, or a man. I didn't know the names of the birds, but I learned to recognise them by their calls and their colours. I knew which one pecked at the bark of trees and which one caught fish from the river with his long beak. The presence of animals comforted me. I never doubted they were on my side. Hearing a monkey laugh made me feel I wasn't entirely alone. The bears made strange growls at night that were almost reassuring. And the peacocks kept me company, talking to me all day long.

I ate wild fruits and berries and snacked on salted peas. I bathed in the clear rivers and slept in the clearings, because you couldn't sleep under a tree at night; you couldn't breathe wondering what was going to fall on you. During the day, the shade of a neem or a banyan tree was welcome but at night it was better to be in a clearing in the forest.

For nearly three months, I spoke to nobody except the animals. I sat and reflected in solitude.

The monsoon had long passed and the fields of barley and millet were high. Water was becoming scarce but it was possible at times to approach a well during the day and in the wilds, when I saw shepherds, I would ask if they knew of a spring. The problem was to be sure it wasn't poisoned. There were rumours that the police left poison around for me, as though I was a wolf that preyed on chickens. I used to watch the little fishes in the water before I drank. If any of them were floating belly up I wouldn't drink, but if they darted through the water in silver shoals, I knew it was safe.

Whenever I was seen, I had to move on. I couldn't trust anyone. I was always moving, climbing to the top of a tree to see if there were any sipahis around, and moving on. The slopes of the ravines, muddy and slippery during the monsoon, became dry and hard in the hot season. I had to claw my way over them in the heat, always moving.

Once, I found myself close to my village. I hadn't even been aware of heading there and I wasn't sure whether I should go in. I needn't have worried. I was so thin that the first person I met didn't even recognise me. I turned away . . .

At last, I don't know how, two of the members of my old gang, Muniram and Kharag, managed to find me. Muniram belonged to a caste of potters. I used to call him uncle because he was much older than me. Kharag we used to call Vishnu, the crazy man. He had a very odd way of making tea by boiling rupee coins. Who could like tea made with rupees? I had certainly never drunk it, but I was pleased to see him brewing it in front of me again. They told me they had heard that Man Singh hadn't given himself up after all and we decided to see if we could find him.

In Man Singh's village, the only person we could find from his family was only an old uncle living in a half-ruined house. One of Man Singh's brothers had been shot in a battle with the police and the rest of the family had fled from the village and gone to live in Orai. The old uncle told us that Man Singh had been too scared in the end to give himself up. He had been afraid he would be killed by the local police before anyone contacted their superiors. The uncle said his nephew was hiding out in the house of one of his aunts, three hours walk away. Man Singh's uncle came with us through the forest and when we arrived at the aunt's village, he went in alone. We waited under a tree beside a canal in the dark.

At midnight, we heard footsteps.

'Give me the food and get away from here!'

I recognised Man Singh's voice, but I waited until I could see him right in front of me, to be sure he was alone, before I called out. I trusted nothing and nobody, not even the oldest member of my gang. There was no way of knowing if he really had been too afraid to give himself up, or if he had made a deal with the police.

But all he had with him was his rifle. We hurried away at once. We had heard that Balwan had been ambushed and killed in that area. In the hot season, that plain became a desert and it was too easy to be seen. The jungle was not far away and we were safer there. We found a clearing and slept until midday, and then the four of us held a council.

Man Singh said he didn't trust his family any more. His uncle had told him he should kill us, and that way, he could give himself up.

'Go on then,' I said. 'Kill us.'

'Phoolan, I have been in your gang since the beginning.'

His face turned sad, and I noticed he had become much thinner. His brow was lined and his long hair that fell in curls to his shoulders was tangled and dirty. He looked at me wearily and shook his head.

'How did you survive all alone?'

'I managed . . .'

I tried to keep my misgivings to myself. I didn't think Man Singh deserved my suspicion but it had become second nature to me since Vickram's death.

We decided we would try to find the others. Muslim, one of Baba Mustakim's cousins, was on the run somewhere in the region of Etawah, with five men from Mustakim's old gang. The police had been pressuring his family to make him surrender too. Everybody was talking about surrendering, but I wasn't going to.

We found Muslim almost by accident. We had looted a village near Etawah. It wasn't much of a hoard, but it was our first operation in a long while. At least six months had passed since we last raided a village and, even though there were only five of us, I wanted the police to know I was still alive. As usual, all sorts of rumours were circulating. The latest one was that I had committed suicide. Someone who wanted revenge on a man who had stolen his land had told us who to loot, and we got some silver and gold, and some rupees out of it. Afterwards, we were bathing near a spring in the forest and we saw someone heading our way carrying a sack. He turned away suddenly when he saw us. Man Singh ran after him and caught him. The man said he was carrying supplies for Muslim.

'Go and tell him that Phoolan Devi and Man Singh are looking for him.'

Muslim too thought I had lost weight during my months alone in the jungle. I told him he looked skinny himself.

Everyone was looking thin. We had only fruits to eat most of the time, and we dreamed of chapatis, dal, rice and ghee.

Muslim told us about what had happened at Dastampur. There had been another massacre there and the newspapers said Muslim and I had been behind it. We had done it, supposedly, to avenge the death of Baba Mustakim. The truth was that Muslim wasn't even in the region and I was on the run alone after escaping from the grenades at Guloli. Muslim said it was his community at Guloli who had taken it on themselves to avenge his brother. 'They arrived at Dastampur pretending they were sipahis and saying they had come to reward whoever had informed on Baba Mustakim. That's how they found out who it was. They shot them down right there in the village, a dozen of them. I had nothing to do with it, even though Baba Mustakim was my brother, but the police say I was in on it and you too.'

After Behmai and now Dastampur, the state of Uttar Pradesh had become too dangerous for us. We decided to cross the border into Madhya Pradesh.

There, we were at least able to pull off some raids to get the cash we needed for supplies. We started with a kidnapping, then we held up some buses and robbed some rich merchants. Soon, the government of Madhya Pradesh was warning us to surrender too.

The other news from the transistor was more painful. My mother and father had been arrested and imprisoned. It was to try to make me surrender, Man Singh reckoned. Later I learned that at first they had been told I was dead and they would have to identify the corpse. My grandmother had tried to commit suicide when she heard. She threw herself in the river but was fished out in time by the boatmen.

Meanwhile, Shri Ram had disappeared. Nobody had heard even a vague rumour about where he was hiding, or even if he was still alive. I tried not to think about him.

Whenever thoughts of revenge returned to me, they brought back with them all the horrors. To be humiliated like that was the worst thing a woman could be made to endure and the hatred of men was still so strong in me that sometimes I would become enraged for nothing. I would turn on my men for no reason.

'Get away from me!' I would snap. 'Leave your guns and go. I don't want to see you ever again.'

I knew they respected me – they trusted me more than I trusted them – but I couldn't help it, the hatred and rejection I felt was too strong. Luckily they knew me well. 'Wait until she calms down,' they would say to each other.

They would bring me water to drink or some *pan* to chew. I would walk back and forth, incapable of sitting down in those moments. Chewing the spicy betel nut would do nothing to placate me. I was filled with a wrath that came from deep inside, from long ago. It was always there, simmering away. I forgot they were my men.

They would get down on their knees in front of me, trying to make jokes to lighten my mood.

'Like this, Bahanji, you won't have to jump up to slap us!'

But nothing would make me laugh in those moments, except to have Shri Ram there to feed to the dogs. It was as if I had swallowed something poisonous, and I couldn't vomit it out . . . Until the day I received a message from his brother, Lala Ram.

Your enemy is dead.

The two of them had quarrelled over a woman, and Lala Ram had finally killed his own brother. So he had died because of a woman, I reflected. That was my only consolation. But at least the red devil had gone from this world. I would have liked to have been able to kill him with my own hands, but it was a relief. As I thought about it, I realised that I truly didn't care if I died after that, because he was dead, my enemy was dead.

But I still had other enemies.

From that moment on, my old hatred for Mayadin resurfaced to plague my thoughts. Let him live, Vickram had said, because he belongs to your family. But I wanted to settle my scores now.

It was hard to get anywhere near my village. The police were camped to one side of a small forest and we made our camp the other side, out of their sight. When night fell, I hurried into my village. I spent half an hour going from house to house looking for him, but all I found were some of the panches. And then the police attacked. Someone must have told them I was there. When the shooting started, my first instinct was to run home to my house. I was almost at the door before I realised I would be endangering my own family. I retreated from the village to rejoin the men, chased by the police. They tried to cut us off as we headed for the forest, so we turned towards the river. They tried to head us off before we reached the river too. They were right behind us as we reached the bank. There was nothing else to do but dive under the water and swim until we could vanish in the dark.

I was annoyed, but also relieved. I knew I wasn't going to die now, not until I had punished Mayadin. I didn't want him to be able to snigger about me and say, 'That bitch thought she could give me a lesson, and now she's dead.' Oh no! He would be the last one, I vowed to myself! He still had his lesson coming . . .

In the meantime, I contented myself with the thought that I had been able to give other lessons. I had taken money from the rich and given it to the poor; I had helped girls to marry by paying their dowries; I had punished rapists and land-grabbers and informers. I was the one who could hold her head up with honour, not him. I was the one who stood and fought, while he hid in terror.

Man Singh kept saying we ought to make a deal and give ourselves up, but I had no intention of doing that – just the opposite. I taunted the police, sending them messages saying that I was going to ruin their lives and haunt their dreams, and like Durga the goddess I would leave terror and destruction wherever I passed.

It was true. Whenever I entered a village people fled in every direction and the streets rapidly emptied. I didn't even have to lift my rifle. If I grabbed someone, they would fall on their knees pleading with me to spare them, saying they were poor people, chamars or jatavs or what have you, never thakurs. But I knew how to recognise a thakur. They were always well-dressed and well-fed. Their faces weren't lined with sadness and fatigue. A poor person didn't need to say he was poor.

The newspapers wrote that I had cut the nose off this one or that one, in this village or that. It was as if by cutting a nose off someone I scored a point and if I didn't do it I lost a point. But many of those operations weren't even our work; they were carried out by other gangs using our name. I was never so cowardly as to pretend I was someone else. I had always shown my face to the people, telling them not to forget my name, Phoolan Devi, and I expected others to act with honour too. If an informant asked us to punish someone in a village, and we found the police waiting for us when we got there, the informant would be beaten until he told us who put him up to it, and the instigator would have his nose cut off. But if the raid went off without a hitch, the informant was given his share.

I couldn't trust anything or anyone.

Muslim had said he wanted to retrieve some money he had stashed in a village near the road to Bhind, the first big town over the border. The money was with someone he swore he could trust, someone who had never tried to trick him or cheat him, he said, but I had a bad feeling about it. The man was a thakur. I had nothing against him personally, but I had learned by then that money was all too often the root of betrayal.

We camped near the village and Muslim went in alone. He sent someone out with food, someone I hadn't seen in a long time. Raghu Nath had been one of Vickram's men at the start. He was as clever as a monkey and he had a keen nose for his own survival. He had been wise enough to leave us two days before Shri Ram killed Vickram. He had joined me again for a while but he went into hiding after the killings at Behmai.

He came with a bowl of lentils and a khat for me to rest on.

'Lie down, Bahanji,' he said, 'have some dal, relax.'

It was good to see him again, but I was sick that day, and in a bad temper. I couldn't eat the dal. I asked him why he hadn't brought eggs for me from the village instead.

Muslim returned and stared making fun of me.

'You didn't eat the dal I sent you! What's wrong? Don't you like me?'

'No, it's not that. I came to help you get your money, otherwise I wouldn't be here.'

Raghu Nath kept trying to make me stretch out on the khat he had brought, but I suddenly had to relieve myself. I left my rifle and picked up a pot of water and followed a little stream until I was out of view of the camp.

Two sipahis nearly stumbled over me. Luckily, I had left my rifle and I was wearing trousers and a shirt.

'Get away from here, you stupid boy! We're looking for Phoolan Devi's gang. Get away before we shoot you!'

I ran as fast as I could, circling back to warn the others. I had the pot in one hand and I was holding up my trousers with the other. I had a terrible stomach ache and an even more terrible fear of being without my rifle. The lookout saw me running and I just had time to say the police were there when the shooting started.

They fired at the khat – where Raghu Nath had tried to make me sit down and eat the lentils he knew I liked. But Raghu Nath had disappeared now. Muslim was firing back at the police, advancing towards them with seven of his men.

I grabbed my rifle and fired, giving them some cover. Man Singh looked at me worriedly and we called at them to pull back. There were too many police for us to attack. We fired as long as we could to hold them off, but we had to retreat.

As we did, I looked back and saw one of the policemen who had stumbled on me in the bushes. He recognised me.

'I am Phoolan Devi!' I yelled.

We were a few miles away when we saw the reinforcements arriving. There were lorries full of police. We would have all been dead if we had tried to shoot it out with them. I hoped Muslim and the men had got away.

There on the khat I had left behind my shoes and all the money I had with me. I had left behind part of my naivety too. It was Raghu Nath who had denounced us. He had told them where we were. He had brought the dal for me to distract me.

A few months later, we heard that Muslim hadn't been killed in the shoot-out and he was hiding in a village near Bhind, over the border in Madya Pradesh. An informer from the village told us Muslim had made contact with someone in the state police. He was going to surrender.

Everybody wanted to surrender, it seemed. The men wanted to join Muslim and turn themselves in too, even Man Singh.

'Let's find Muslim,' he argued, 'and hear what the terms are at least.'

'Because of him, we nearly got killed. He escaped without trying to contact us and now I hear he is in touch with the police!'

Trust nothing and nobody . . .

'Muslim cannot be a traitor,' said Man Singh. 'A member of Baba Mustakim's family wouldn't betray us.'

Three months passed before we met again in the jungle, not far from the banks of the river Sind, near the point where it joins the Chambal. We hadn't seen Muslim since Diwali and it was the month of Phagun by then.

He was nervous. He spoke quietly, as though he was afraid of something. I was angry with him and told him off for leaving us.

'You're a traitor! The last time, you abandoned us, remember, now what are you plotting? You want to sell us to the police, don't you?'

'No, no. Phoolan. I'm not a traitor. This man, this officer, he came to see me himself, and he said, "Give yourself up, but do what you can to convince Phoolan" . . .'

'If you want to surrender, go ahead – if you think you'll be happy in prison. Not me.'

'But Phoolan, without you, I can't. They don't want to negotiate with us without you. They said Phoolan first, and then they will accept all the rest of us in Madhya Pradesh. Listen to me Phoolan. In Uttar Pradesh they will kill you on sight. We can't even put a foot there any more.'

He fell silent for a moment.

'How many of us are left?' he asked.

*

Aatma-Samarpan.

Surrender. Just hearing the word made me furious. It was a word I had heard dacoits using around me since the start, and now I was hearing it on the radio and seeing it written in the newspapers. My own men were even saying it.

I didn't know anything about the political campaign that was building around me at that moment in the cities. Even if I had known, and been able to understand, I wouldn't have reacted any differently to what Muslim said that day. I didn't know how to live anywhere else but the jungle.

I refused instinctively.

Others had capitulated, but they were all men. With me, Phoolan Devi, a woman, it would be different. What was I going to do, deliver myself to more humiliation once again? They had killed Neera, the wife of Baba Mustakim, and carried her naked body on a bullock-cart through the villages. She was merely the wife of a dacoit, she meant nothing to them. I knew only too well what they would want to do to me, to prove that they were the ones with the power.

Aatma-Samarpan?

Never.

35

Ihadn't seen Baba Ghanshyam for nearly three years and when I did, all the memories came flooding back to me: Vickram, Uncle Bare Lal, Bharat and the others . . . I had been so afraid of them that night during the monsoon when they kidnapped me from my family.

Baba Ghanshyam was so dark-skinned he looked like a buffalo with his big bulging black eyes. He seemed much older to me than he had before. He must have been about forty-five years old by then. I still hadn't learned to count, I still judged the value of a bundle of rupees by its thickness and people's ages by the lines on their faces. He came unarmed and it was strange to see his chubby hands, clasped together as he bowed to greet me, without a rifle in them. He still had the same shock of long hair wound in a white turban around his head. He wept when he saw me, but I wasn't so moved. He had brought his brother Gharam with him.

'You were supposed to come alone.'

'Still the same Phoolan, the same aggressive little girl. You didn't even know how to blow your nose, you were too scared to even speak to us. All you said if any of us came near you was, "Bastard, you're going to die, you've ruined my life, bastard!"'

And he laughed.

'Have you come to talk about surrendering, like Muslim and the others? They keep telling me if I give myself up they will do it too. What is all this talk about surrendering? What is it to do with me if you all want to surrender?'

'Phool Singh, listen to me. If you give yourself up with us, we will get honourable terms.'

'Tell my men what you want to eat,' I said, changing the subject. 'I'll have it brought from Tehengur.'

Now that we had spoken alone, the two gangs could assemble for food.

The Sarpanch of Tehengur brought the food himself on a large tray covered with a cloth. He tasted it first. It was a necessary precaution. I loved to eat bowls of sweetened milk curd and the police could easily put poison in it without me being able to tell from the taste. I had to be careful of *pan* too. The spicy ground betel nut would disguise the poison. All foods, sweet or salty, that could disguise the taste of poison had to be eaten first by those who brought them. That was the rule.

Once that was done, everybody began to eat and talk, and Baba Ghanshyam and I got down to serious discussions. My view was that even if the police pursued us relentlessly, with help from the army too, we weren't just a gang of frightened cats.

'Let them come! We have enough arms and ammunition to fight them,' I said. 'I'm not afraid of dying!'

Baba Ghanshyam looked at me with frustration, mumbling to his brother.

'What? Stop looking at me like that!' I said to him.

But I had heard perfectly well. He was asking how a stubborn child like me could lead a gang with our reputation. They couldn't believe it. They still remembered when I was their captive, terrorised and defenceless. Now they had to deal with me as a gang leader of the same rank as them, if not higher. Most of Ghanshyam's men wore ragged old uniforms. It was cold and some of them didn't even have pullovers. My men – Man Singh, Jay Bir Singh, Muslim and the rest – were well-dressed and well-fed. We didn't look like a gang of beggars. I took good care of my men.

'Your men don't have any woollens, Ghanshyam,' I told him. 'You're not looking after them. How many are there? Eighteen? How much do you pay them?'

Ghanshyam started getting vexed. 'Don't ask me these things, Bahanji! You can have them if you like. Maybe they would like that.'

'In the meantime, I can give you some pullovers. We have plenty.'

'Don't do that. Don't get too friendly with them. Are you trying to turn them against me?'

'Don't get angry. I'm only trying to help you. I've got groundsheets and blankets, pullovers and watches. Your men look like they could use them.'

Ghanshyam accepted.

I almost felt sorry for him. He had a woman in his gang. She told me her name was Munni and she had four children. Earlier, I had given her two thousand rupees. 'Why do you keep her in your gang,' I asked Ghanshyam, 'to cook and do the laundry? It's dangerous. You'll see. One day she'll do something more than the housework for your men!'

By then, the sun had started to set. It was time to go our separate ways.

'*Namasteh . . .*'

'What do you mean? No, wait. Stay here. We haven't decided yet. If you give yourself up we will surrender with you. Let's talk it over properly.'

'Listen Baba Ghanshyam. You have been talking to a policeman and I don't know what he's told you but if you want to surrender, that's your business.'

'Look, just go and see Paras Ram and he will explain. You know that you can trust him.'

Paras Ram was a farmer, the Sarpanch of the village of
Bhadoriya. He was a thakur, a retired army officer, and while
I rarely had good relations with a village headman, especially not a rich one and a thakur at that, he had always
been honest in his dealings with me. I knew I could call on
him in the night for information without fearing a trap. I
agreed to see him. I told Ghanshyam I would let him know
what happened.

It was nearly midnight when we arrived there and Paras
Ram suggested we camp in an abandoned fort in the hills
nearby while he had food prepared for us. He brought it
himself, a tray of fried samosas stuffed with peas and potatoes. I sat down on a blanket in front of him and we spoke
while my men got ready to sleep.

Paras Ram always spoke to me like a father. He was wise
and kind to me. 'Surrendering would be a good answer for
you, Phoolan. You are young, and your family suffers greatly
from this situation,' he said.

'Who would I surrender to? I don't trust the police.'

'I would like you to agree to meet a man I know. He is a
relation of mine, an officer in the army up in Kashmir.'

'He really is your relative?'

'Yes. You can trust me. Would you meet him?'

'When?'

'Tomorrow morning.'

I paused.

'All right.'

The next morning, the weather was bad.

Dawn broke in heavy fog and it was impossible to see
more than a few yards. Nobody had lived in the old citadel
where we were camped for decades, perhaps even centuries,
and there was an eerie quiet around us. The fortified walls
had crumbled but it was well hidden in the ravines. I had

twenty-six men with me by then and I made them take up positions all around, lying flat among the rocks. There could have been an entire army division out there for all I knew.

Towards ten o'clock, the lookout signalled that Paras Ram was approaching, with someone walking behind him. We couldn't see much in the fog. The other man was a vague silhouette. I let them draw closer until I could better make him out. He wore a woollen cap and he had a blanket wrapped around his shoulders against the cold. I could see his breath in the damp mist.

I invited them both to sit down on the groundsheet, without taking my eyes from the face of the new arrival. He was well-fed, about forty to fifty years old, and he had a shrewd look.

'Where are you from?'

He replied with a smile. 'Kashmir.'

'Get up, please.'

Paras Ram interjected. 'Phoolan, we came here in good faith. You don't have to be suspicious.'

I searched the visitor. He had a revolver in one pocket, a cassette recorder in another, and also a camera. I put them all down beside me.

'Now you can sit down. Don't try to trick me. I know who you are.'

'Good. I'm a journalist from Delhi. I write in the newspapers,' he said, indicating the tape recorder and camera.

'First you come from Kashmir and now you come from Delhi. You are lying. I know where you are from. Would you like me to tell you?'

'Yes. Go ahead.'

'You are from the police. You have come from the station at Bhind.'

'How do you know?'

'Your face. Your face tells me so.'

Paras Ram started to get nervous. But the visitor was still smiling. 'All right, I am not a journalist. But I could be your father, and you could be my daughter, and I mean you no harm. You were right. I am a police officer. My name is Rajandra Chaturvedi.'

'What is your community?'

'Brahmin.'

'Would you like something to eat?'

'No thank you.'

He must have been afraid I would try to poison him. I could see that he was nervous about the revolver. He was a government employee and I was a dacoit. If I didn't give him back his firearm, he would be in trouble with his superiors. But he kept smiling and even made jokes.

'Since you have my revolver, there is nothing left for me to do but to become a dacoit too and stay with you!'

'If you wish. I would be pleased to have you. One more man in the gang.'

I emptied his weapon, taking the charger out and putting it in my pocket before giving the revolver back to him.

'Take it. That's what's bothering you, isn't it?'

He was relieved, and smiled again. 'They say you are a terrifying dacoit but you seem to be an honest girl.'

'Then eat now, if you want to prove to me I don't frighten you.'

'You don't want to kill me? You swear that you wouldn't try to harm me?'

'I swear it on your revolver. Durga swears it. If my enemy comes to speak to me like this, I wouldn't hurt him even if he was the most abominable of men. Share this food with me without fear.'

He declined to eat nonetheless.

As I ate, he asked, 'Can I have my camera back?'

'What are you going to do with it?'

'Can I take a photo, just one photo, as a souvenir?'

'No.'

I had never seen a camera this close before and I didn't know how it worked. I didn't know how the photos came out of it, but the word photograph was like an alarm bell to me. The men had always warned me never to let anyone take a picture of my face. It would be put in the newspapers and on posters in the railway stations and after that, everybody would be able to recognise me.

I gave the camera to Paras Ram, not the police officer.

'You still don't trust me, even though I am unarmed. I have information that there are other gangs in the sector, not far from here. Any of them might kill me, but I have come to see you, Phoolan, and if I am shot, you will be blamed for it.'

'Nobody is going to kill you. Now, what do you want?'

'I have a proposition for you. If you want to give yourself up to the authorities in Madhya Pradesh, it might be possible.'

'My family is in Uttar Pradesh. What would become of them? Who would protect them?'

'All that I want is to be able to discuss this without danger, either for me or for you. You can trust me. I'm sure we can come to an arrangement.'

It was evening when he left, under the protection of my men. He had to walk a long way in the misty cold night to reach his car on the road, far down below the ravines.

A few days later, I was shown the newspaper with my photo on the front page, eating with that man, and another photo of the entire gang. Man Singh read what was written beneath.

'Phoolan Devi is a good woman. I will do everything I can to persuade her to surrender.'

He had betrayed me!

I didn't know how they got the photos out of that box, but if I had known he had taken them it, I would have smashed the camera to pieces. He had only come to see me, he said, and now he was saying in the newspaper that he had met me and that I was going to surrender. Why was he doing that? I had decided nothing.

Nobody had ever seen my face in a photograph. He had put me in great danger.

Right away, we raised camp to return to Uttar Pradesh. For nearly two weeks we travelled northwards without halting in a great arc, almost to the border with Rajastan, to avoid being seen. This Rajendra Chaturvedi might like to think I was going to give myself up on his territory, Madhya Pradesh, but that would be for me to decide and me alone.

Muslim wanted to surrender. Ghanshyam and Man Singh wanted to surrender. They were all waiting for me. I didn't know why they all needed me to surrender if that's what they wanted. And I was even more wary now. Meeting police officers was risky. It was dangerous enough when they had guns and reinforcements, but talking with them was worse. Now I had to be very careful. The police in Uttar Pradesh had wanted my head since the massacre at Behmai. I was the leader of the gang that carried it out and they were going to kill me for it.

A few weeks later, we were camped with Muslim and his men near a village called Ambapur, in Uttar Pradesh, when it started again. This time, it was a whole group of them that wanted to see me. The lookout had stopped them and he ran up the hill to warn us.

'There are about a dozen of them. I saw a jeep down below on the road. One of them came up here alone. He isn't carrying a rifle.'

'Who is he?'

'He says his name is Mir Sahib, and he comes from Amraudha. There is a woman with them.'

'Tell them to wait.'

'Nobody had heard of this man, neither in my gang nor in Muslim's gang. The lookout went back to interrogate them and returned in a panic.

'He says he's brought your mother to see you, Bahanji. She is in the jeep with your brother Shiv Narayan.'

I hadn't seen my mother for at least two years but my first reaction was anger. I wanted to know who these people were and what she was doing with them. I told the lookout to let them through and watched her climbing up the hill through my binoculars.

She walked slowly behind the men, helped by my brother. She was thin and her back was bent.

'Phoolan, my child!'

Instead of rushing into her arms I bawled at her. 'What are you doing here? Who are these people and what are you doing with them? How did you know where to find me?'

'I don't know anything. This man Mir Sahib brought us here. He wanted to speak with you. Phoolan, listen to me. They put us in prison for a long time, your father and me. They said you were dead, and then you weren't dead. I didn't know what to believe!'

'You don't know anything! You don't even know who brought you here! You could get me killed! Oh, wait, they paid you for this. You need money, that's it.'

'Phoolan, I beg you. Listen to them. They say you can surrender wherever you want, in Etawah or Kanpur, and they won't harm you.'

Shiv Narayan came and hugged me. My little brother had grown. The last time I had seen him, he was still a little boy, but now he was a young man. He had lively, intelligent eyes and he had grown so tall that he could easily reach my ears to whisper. 'Don't listen to them, Phoolan. We don't even know who they are nor where they come from. Amma let herself be talked into coming with them, but you must be careful.'

My mother was imploring me with her eyes, and with her hands, holding them towards me with her palms open. 'Listen to them, Phoolan, just hear what they have to say,' she pleaded.

The men with her were certain to be police officers. I guessed that they had beaten her or threatened to put her back in prison. She told me the police had been persecuting my family for months. They were being watched around the clock. They had nothing more to eat and my father had no work. If I refused, it was going to cause them more trouble. I agreed to listen to this Mir Sahib, for their sake. I told the men to bring him forward.

'Who are you?'

'I am a journalist. These men too are journalists. We would like to speak to you and take your photograph.'

'No photographs. I don't want my photo in the newspapers. So speak.'

'We have been to see the Chief Minister of Uttar Pradesh. He promised your mother that if Phoolan Devi gave herself up, he would give her a hundred bighas of land, he would arrange jobs for all your family, and they could have gun permits. He promised you would be released after eight years in prison. Whatever the sentence was, he said you would be released after eight years.'

Shiv Narayan took me aside.

'Don't do it, don't go back there. They'll kill you if you do, like they killed the other dacoit, Chavi Ram. He raised his arms and said he was surrendering and they shot him down. Everybody knows in the village.'

I told my little brother not to worry, I hadn't decided anything.

'If you must give yourself up, don't do it in Uttar Pradesh. Everybody says the police there just want you dead. The men in the village talk about it all the time. You have to believe me! I don't want them to kill you, Phoolan!'

I looked at my little brother in admiration. He was intelligent and well-spoken. He had learned to read and write. He wasn't a savage like me.

And he loved me.

'Do you want me to surrender?' I asked him.

'If you think it's the right thing to do, but not with them. I don't want you to die.'

'I will give it some thought. Meanwhile you stay away from these people. If they come saying they are police or journalists refuse to see them, and don't believe anything they tell you.'

I gave three thousand rupees to my weeping mother and the same amount to my brother. Then I turned to the gang of journalists. They were just like the police to me: they showed photos and wrote their stories without knowing the truth.

'You want me to surrender in Uttar Pradesh?'

'That's right. The police have promised you eight years.'

'So what happens if I surrender in Madhya Pradesh?'

'Why would you want to do that? That is not your home. It is here that you must surrender. Uttar Pradesh is your state.'

'I'll think about it.'

I said I would think about it for the sake of my mother, so that they would stop persecuting my family. I might have been a savage, and ignorant of how their cameras worked, but menace and coercion were things I could sense instinctively. I knew how to sniff out their traps, read their faces, and interpret their words. My instincts had helped me to survive in the jungle. I had been through so many close calls with death that I knew at once what lay behind their enticements. They had brought my family to try to soften me and they pretended to be concerned for them. But I knew that if I refused, they would switch tactics and put my mother and father back in prison to pressure me.

And I knew that my little brother was right. They wanted me to come to Uttar Pradesh to give myself up so they could shoot me like they shot the others. I saw myself standing up from behind a bush with my hands in the air and a moment later, there would be a storm of bullets.

I made my decision.

If I was going to have to quit the jungle so that my family could live in peace, I might as well not get killed if I could help it. We raised camp and returned across the Chambal river to Madhya Pradesh, to the region near Bhind.

Two weeks after seeing my mother, I sent word to Paras Ram that I wanted to talk to Chaturvedi again. Man Singh didn't agree. He was against the police officer from Madhya Pradesh. He wanted to give himself up in Uttar Pradesh. He told me he had already made an attempt to negotiate through his brothers. Had he been offered money if I gave myself up with him? I wondered.

Paras Ram arranged for the meeting to take place near his village, on land that belonged to him. From there, we were to bring the two of them with us back to the ravines. We got there first, and before Chaturvedi arrived, I asked the men with me to give me all their rifles and ammunition. I didn't want anybody to be armed.

Man Singh was furious. 'Have you gone completely crazy?'

'If you don't like it, you can leave. Or would you like to shoot him? You're the only one who would stand to gain anything from that.'

'God! Why are you always accusing me?'

'Because I know what you are thinking. You keep saying

your brother wants me to surrender with you. How much money have they offered your brother for me? How much?'

Man Singh didn't answer.

Don't trust anything or anybody . . .

Rajendra Chaturvedi watched us without saying a word. How could I know if I could trust him? He had already lied to me about the camera, but he was an official from the government of Madhya Pradesh, a high-ranking police officer, not a sipahi without any stripes from the constabulary at Kalpi. I had to take a chance.

We marched for two hours, the men ahead and Chaturvedi behind with me. I was nervous. If one of the men shot him, it would be disastrous for me. I would be accused of having laid a trap for him after he had put his trust in me. He had left his motorcycle with the two policemen from Paras Ram's village. My honour was at stake, and my only chance of survival. If he died, the police of Madhya Pradesh would be crying for my blood too.

We returned to the ruins of the abandoned fort, where it would be easy to survey the ravines. Chaturvedi wasn't used to walking like us and he was out of breath but he remained calm and smiling.

'My government is prepared to accept your surrender,' he said. 'I have been sent by the Chief Minister, Arjun Singh, who is under the instructions of the Prime Minister, Indira Gandhi, herself.'

I had heard of her and I admired Mrs Gandhi. She was a woman, like me, after all, in a world of men. I knew nothing about her life, but I knew she must have had to overcome many enemies, like me. I told Chaturvedi that I would have liked to meet Indira Gandhi.

'That would not be possible,' said Chaturvedi, 'but if you want to meet the Chief Minister for the state, I can arrange it.'

I didn't really know what a Chief Minister was. I assumed he would be a very old government official.

'No, he is a politician. He is the head of the whole state, all the towns and villages, and if you surrender to him, he will respect you. He is under instructions from the Prime Minister to guarantee your safety.'

'And my family?'

'You can bring them here.'

'How many years of prison? I want eight years.'

'Why eight years?'

'Eight years I said.'

'All right, if that's what you want, eight years it will be.'

'I will think about it.'

I thought about it for a long time, more than a month. I had told him I wanted eight years because the journalists from Uttar Pradesh had said eight years. If they had said five, I would have said five. The rules of negotiating a surrender were yet another thing I knew nothing about.

I trusted Chaturvedi one minute, then the next I backed away from him like a frightened cat. He seemed to know a great deal about what was going on while I knew nothing. But my greatest worry was my family. I wanted real guarantees for their safety. Thakurs would never cease to threaten and bully them, I knew. I wanted them to be moved to Madhya Pradesh, and I wanted them to have land and work, the things they had been denied ever since I was born. But I didn't know what guarantee I could have other than words and I knew I couldn't trust words.

Then something happened to prove me right.

Muslim had been wanting to surrender for a while and we had separated because he wanted to give himself up as a gang leader to be able to get better terms. He had a dozen men with him and I had fourteen. But when the surrender was due to take place, he was caught in a police crossfire. Three of his men were killed and he was injured.

I retreated into the badlands of Chambal, convinced that Chaturvedi had broken his word and he was the one responsible.

He trailed us from village to village, and for a while he must have thought we had returned to Uttar Pradesh, but he persevered and managed to keep in contact with us. I wasn't impressed. I thought he was only doing it because it was his job. Finally I agreed to meet him a third time. I wanted to know what had happened to Muslim. An informant had told us he was still alive and under guard in hospital.

I was extremely angry that day. Man Singh tried to calm me and so did Chaturvedi. All these men kept saying I was impatient and aggressive. Chaturvedi was surprised I didn't know what had happened to Muslim. It had been in all the newspapers, he said. He shrugged it off as a misunderstanding between police departments. There was a senior officer in Uttar Pradesh who didn't agree with what Chaturvedi was doing. He wanted to kill all dacoits, while Chaturvedi was under orders to capture us alive. The government of Uttar Pradesh had been annoyed by the intervention of an officer from another state in their affairs.

It all seemed to be easy enough for them to understand, it was all just politics, but I had only my instincts to rely on for the truth. My struggle for survival had taught me to be wary. I didn't know anything about politics, governments or states. All I knew was what I felt in my bones.

I agreed to meet him again.

This time, Chaturvedi came with his wife. She was pretty, with kind, gentle eyes. She had brought clothes and presents for me, food that she prepared specially for me. It had been so long since someone had showed me affection like that, so long, that I didn't know what to say. Chaturvedi also said he was going to bring my family to Madhya Pradesh. He went to meet my mother and brought my whole family back in a lorry, with their cattle.

Finally, another man came, Rama Shankar Singh, an envoy of the Chief Minister. He asked me to record a message for the Chief Minister of Madhya Pradesh on his cassette machine. I recited my list of demands:

- Not to be hung.
- To be tried in Madhya Pradesh not anywhere else.
- To be sentenced to eight years in prison.
- To be imprisoned with my men.
- The families must be given gun permits for their safety.
- They must be given land and work to be able to live.
- All my demands were to be written on official stationery.

And then, in another message, I demanded that they accept the surrender of Muslim and his gang under the same terms – even if he was already in hospital, injured by the police – and the surrender of Baba Ghanshyam.

The wait lasted fifty days, as they said it would.

It was still cold and spring wouldn't come. I was nervous and irritable, anxious about how it was going to turn out. I had made my decision, but every time I heard the birds singing and looked up at the trees I asked myself if I would ever be able to survive in prison.

I was in Paras Ram's house when Rajendra Chaturvedi and Rama Shankar Singh arrived with the letter. It was an official letter. At the top it was marked, *Government of India*. Everything I had asked for was written out beneath, and below that were some signatures. Paras Ram read it out for me and the men.

'Now you must sign,' said Chaturvedi.

I didn't know how to sign my name with a pen. I asked Munim, the gang's accountant, to sign Phoolan Devi for me. Then I turned to the other men. 'Now you are free to choose. You can come with me, or you can leave.'

Man Singh ran out of the room and leapt from the terrace of the house into the road and away into the jungle. The others chose to stay with me.

'You must set a date now,' said Chaturvedi. 'When will it be?'

'In six days.'

They looked at the calendar on the wall.

'*Barah farvari unnes sau tirasi.*'

The twelfth of February, 1983.

36

Six days and five nights.

I saw the sun rise and watched it set again on six days of frenetic liberty, and with the darkness at the close of each day came five nights of anguish.

I was beginning to realise what surrender really meant. I was going to have to hand over my rifle and cartridge belt. I would be taken to the prison at Gwalior empty-handed and defenceless. At least I knew what prison was like. I had been fifteen years old when I was imprisoned before, quivering with terror, but the future was no more clear to me now than it was then. I tried to convince myself that everything would work out well, that they would keep their promise and that I wouldn't be hanged, but uncertainty still gnawed at my insides.

As long as I was still free, I could go to the villages and talk to people. The police followed close behind me. Chaturvedi had said it would be better if I stayed where I was, lying on a khat and waiting for the moment when I would have to go to prison. He was worried that I might commit one last raid. He said if I did, he would have a lot of explaining to do. But it wasn't a raid I needed to calm my nerves; I wanted to see villagers, women and children, poor people like me. I wanted to be Phoolan Devi, the dacoit, for a little while longer, and ask them, 'What's wrong? Who beat you? Who raped you? Is the Sarpanch of this village a fair man? Can I trust this rich man who wants to pay tribute to me? Are you afraid to speak? Take my money and speak . . .'

I needed them. It was their survival too that I had been fighting for. Being a bandit meant taking from the rich and giving to the poor, punishing the rapist and chastising the cruel landowner to make them understand that women and the poor had their dignity too. I needed to see the relief on their faces when I took bundles of rupees rolled tightly with elastic bands out of my pocket and weighed their value in my hands: five thousand, ten thousand, twenty thousand! I wanted to be able to put the bundles in *their* outstretched hands and punish the ones who tried to deprive them of their right to exist. In prison, I would no longer be able to do it; I wasn't even sure if I would reach the prison, let alone survive there.

Chaturvedi told me to stay calm, not to go from village to village, but I couldn't stop myself. They wanted to see me; everybody, from the shepherds to the rich, wanted to see me. They wanted me to bless their villages, purifying their houses with my presence. The rich wanted me to accept their offerings and the poor wanted me to hear their prayers.

For six days, I went from village to village, sleeping in this house or that and trying to forget the lorry that followed me full of police, trying to forget what awaited me.

If Vickram was still alive we would have been able to surrender together. Before he died, he had said to me, 'Once we get the money we're owed from Shri Ram, we'll give ourselves up hand-in-hand, Phool Singh!' We could have lived quietly after that. We would have had to pay a fine and spend a few months in prison. Instead, Vickram died and I became a spirit searching for vengeance, with nothing left to lose, because I too had died with him.

*

It was over. The last night had come.

The police had put up a whole village of tents around a large wooden building in the wilds that belonged to the Department of Irrigation. They had rigged up floodlights and the building was surrounded. I was ushered inside through a crowd of people. They were journalists who swarmed around Chaturvedi as we entered, looking at me intently. Towards midnight, a police lorry drove up with Ghanshyam and his men. Man Singh was with them. He had changed his mind. He was going to join us.

The journalists all wanted to talk to me and take my photo. I refused to let them take my picture, but I said I would answer their questions and they were allowed inside.

'Now that the police have you,' one of them asked, 'do you think they will let you just surrender?' He must have known something. He meant the police were going to kill us.

They started to discuss this, squawking agitatedly around me like peacocks in the jungle. Fear ignited in me; something in my head exploded. 'Get ready,' I whispered to Man Singh. 'Load your rifle. They're going to shoot us. We won't get out of here alive!'

I refused to answer any more of their questions. I didn't care about these journalists, I didn't even understand what they were saying much less what they wanted from me. I spoke Bundelkhandi and I didn't know the language they spoke.

I started throwing whatever I could lay my hands on at them. 'Leave me alone, get out of here!' I screamed at them.

Chaturvedi's wife thought I was cracking. 'Phoolan, what's wrong?' she asked.

'They said the police are going to kill me. Is it true?'

She tried to calm me as I looked around desperately for a way out of there. But there were half a dozen sipahis outside the room where the journalists had been let in; they had been guarding me closely, sticking to my shadow and driving me even more crazy.

'I'm going to kill myself if this goes on.'

But how could I do that? I didn't even have my rifle any more. They had asked me to show them my rifle and then they asked if they could try it and they hadn't given it back to me. I didn't have a revolver either. Unarmed, the fear swelled in me. They had disarmed me to be able to kill me, I was sure.

They had brought my family and put them in one room and I was in another with the pressmen. All the men were together in a large room. There were no khats to sleep on and the food they brought us to eat I couldn't swallow. Panicking, I rushed out to the room where my family were waiting.

'Amma, go away from here. They're going to kill me!'

My mother covered her face with her hands, sobbing.

'Man Singh, they're going to kill us!' I repeated.

'Don't be afraid, Phoolan. We are here. If they kill you, we will kill them.'

The journalists had followed me, buzzing around me like flies with their cameras and tape recorders. I pulled their hair and pushed them out of the room, shouting like a madwoman.

'Why do you want my photo? If you want my photo, wait until I'm dead.'

I hadn't eaten, I didn't drink a single glass of water, and I didn't sleep the whole night. In the morning, a doctor came to examine me. The men panicked, thinking I had been poisoned.

'What is wrong with Phoolan?' Man Singh asked the doctor.

'Nothing. It's the tension. Her nerves can't take it, you know. That's why she is ill.'

At six o'clock in the morning they made us go outside to wait. There were people and vehicles everywhere. The journalists were still crowding around us. Every time I saw someone taking a photograph I wanted to shoot them – but I had no rifle. The men still had their rifles but the only weapons I had at hand were pebbles and sticks. I threw them at the journalists.

The men climbed aboard a bus and I got in a car with Chaturvedi. 'Give me back my rifle,' I demanded.

'No, Phoolan,' he said. 'Calm yourself. Don't get angry with the journalists, they'll write bad things about you.'

The engine started and we drove off. The windows were darkened and I couldn't see anything outside.

'Where are we going? Where are you taking me?'

'To the temple first.'

Outside the temple, the police had to fire in the air to disperse the large crowd that gathered around us. It was like a festival. I asked the guards to give me a rifle. If one of them had done it, I would have killed myself right there, and they knew it. If I killed myself on the way to surrendering, Chaturvedi and all the police and the army would have been responsible. They must have been afraid that instead of just shooting myself, I might even have fired into the crowd. I was furious with Chaturvedi. He was carrying my Sten on his shoulder and I dived at him, pulling at his clothes, to try and wrench it away from him.

At that moment, a journalist took a photo and a police officer lunged at him, grabbing his camera and pulling out the film as though he was tearing out its guts. Chaturvedi pushed me aside and made me sit on the ground like a child outside the temple.

'That's enough! Calm yourself now.'

Half an hour later we arrived in Bhind and the car slowed down by the gates of a large building. It was a school that had been emptied of pupils and filled with police. Our car was surrounded by officers of the Home Guard. They carried no rifles; their only weapons were their long iron-ringed lathis. I had asked for them to be there, for my safety, and I was relieved not to be able to see any rifles around me now. We were ushered along by the guards, who surrounded the car so tightly I could barely see what was happening. The car halted but we couldn't even open the doors because of the wall of people around us.

Slowly, the car inched forward towards some steps and the guards pushed the crowds back. We got out and we were led across the courtyard and through the doors of the school into a large empty hall. The rest of the men were already in there. Chaturvedi told us to prepare ourselves. 'The Chief Minister will soon be arriving. There are toilets and washrooms here and we have provided clothes. When you are presented to the Minister, all you have to do is give him your weapons and pay him your respects.'

That was it?

Hand over my arms and bow to him with my hands together. That was a surrender? I had imagined there would be a Brahmin to say a mantra, and food to eat, or that I would be asked to say something. Beyond the hall was a recreation ground and Ghanshyam's men were already dressed and waiting there. They looked washed and contented, as though they were expecting to be given prizes.

I changed in the washrooms. The uniform I had been wearing, the shirt and the boots that smelled of the jungle, of sweat and freedom, and of the anguish of the last few days, fell in a little heap on the cement floor. I combed my hair, tightened the red cloth around my forehead and splashed my face with cold water. My hands trembled. It had been far too long since I had last been able to sleep.

When I emerged, they gave me back my rifle and my cartridge belt. The rifle had been unloaded but the belt was still full. I could have reloaded in a second.

Outside, I heard a great fuss going on. From the window, I could see a stage. A man was standing on it, speaking to the crowd through a microphone. I couldn't understand a word of what he was saying, but I saw two police officers suddenly start hitting him!

Man Singh laughed. 'He was announcing the names of all the dacoits who are going to surrender today, but when he got to your name, the idiot got mixed up. He said the Chief Minister of the state government is going to give himself up to Phoolan Devi! That's why they beat him.'

I ran to the door. 'Don't hit him!' I shouted, 'It's the truth!'

I relaxed and laughed with Man Singh. The incompetent speaker was shoved from the podium after being given a correction in front of thousands of people who watched it all without a murmur. For a few moments, I forgot the seriousness of the situation. Then Chaturvedi came in to announce the arrival of the CM.

I recoiled, refusing to go out. Who was this CM? 'I want to surrender to the Chief Minister, not the CM!'

Chaturvedi explained patiently that it was the same person. C and M were the initials of his title.

The CM was on the stage, waiting. I had to go first. Police officers surrounded me and asked me politely if they could inspect my rifle, to verify it wasn't loaded. They handed it back to me and I slung it back on my shoulder, then they marched me out and we climbed the steps up to the stage.

It was high up. A sea of faces stretched away below me. I had never seen so many important-looking people in one place. The midday sun was hot, the sky blue, but this mass of people, thousands of people, nearly all men wearing dhotis and kurtas or uniforms as though it was some sort of political rally, made no more noise than a stream rustling in the ravines.

On one side of the stage were three large portraits. One was of Vinoda Bhave, a famous man who had launched the programme of surrender for dacoits. Next to him was Mahatma Gandhi, and next to him, the goddess Durga. On the other side of the stage there were rows of officials.

'Phoolan Devi will now lay down her arms,' a man announced in the microphone. 'The government has taken into account her decision to surrender of her own free will. We have accepted her conditions, er . . . No. She has accepted our conditions.'

It was the same man who had made the mistake earlier. I couldn't help myself. I smiled.

The journalists took hundreds of photos at once and a police officer nudged me forward. 'Give your rifle to the CM now.'

I walked across the stage towards a man in a soldier's uniform with a chubby face and a bald head. He was speaking into the microphone.

I stopped when I reached him. 'It's you? You're the one?' I asked him.

He didn't seem to understand me, so I unshouldered my rifle and gave it to him, and then I took off my cartridge belt and hung it across his forearm. An officer standing near him signalled at me to lift up my hands as I had been told, to pay my respects.

I joined my hands together and lifted them to my forehead in prayer, paying my respects to the CM and then to the crowd. I could still hear them murmuring.

The officer gave me a garland and I placed it around the neck of the Chief Minister. As I did, the officer grabbed my arm. 'You mustn't do that. Hand it to him in his hands.'

'Why?'

The Chief Minister smiled at me. 'Let her do it.'

Then I took another garland and placed it around the portrait of Durga.

In my soul, it was to her I surrendered.

After that it was the turn of Man Singh, and then Ghanshyam, and then all the rest: each time, the same gestures, the same garlands and the same murmurings from the spectators. They all spoke at once, thousands of them. If I had been allowed to speak into the microphone, I would have insulted them for their disrespect.

Why did I have to pay my respects to them like that? Who were they that I should respect them? I was used to people paying their respects to me.

And then the chaos broke out. Standing on the roof of the car, followed by a convoy of police jeeps and trucks, I was taken on a tour of Bhind. Very soon, we were caught in a traffic jam and could hardly move. The guards had to push back the crowds shoving to get a look at me. What was the point of it all, I wondered, why were they displaying me like a monkey to all these people, without even letting me speak? The noise of the cars, buses and motorcycles and the pointless shouting of the crowds was exhausting me.

Finally I was brought to a little house in the forest outside the town, where another gang of journalists was waiting. There was going to be a press conference, I was told, but I didn't know what that was. The guards explained that I would have to answer their questions.

But they all spoke at the same time:

'What are you feeling right now?'

'How does it feel not to have a rifle any more?'

'Why did you trust the police in Madhya Pradesh?'

I had only one urge right then: to flee from there.

Without a rifle in my hands, I felt uneasy . . .

As for the police of Madhya Pradesh, I could only say one thing: they had made me promises.

But I couldn't answer them all. There were too many of them shouting and their questions were making my head spin. So I asked them a question.

'What do you think?'

'I'm personally very happy you have laid down your arms,' said one of them.

'Good. If you're happy, I'm happy. Now, leave me alone!'

I was a wild animal, sick, nervous and aggressive. That's what they said later. They had stared at me in amazement.

'She doesn't look like a bandit . . .'

'She isn't as pretty as they say . . .'

'Your crimes won't go unpunished,' I heard someone say, 'they will hang you!'

I felt as though I was being put on trial. They had placed a table and chair there and they all wanted me to sit on the chair behind the table but I was uncomfortable. I wasn't used to it. Sitting on a chair made me feel ill. I bit my nails until they bled and I was so nervous that I bit one nail off completely.

One of the journalists had a bulky machine on his shoulders aimed at me like a rifle. Munna, from my gang, leaned over to warn me. 'It's an electrical machine that will send electricity to kill you!'

I believed him. Neither of us knew that it was only a television camera and I was being filmed.

'Get out of here! Leave me in peace,' I said to the man aiming his machine at me.

I stopped answering their questions. But they wouldn't stop asking them. It went on for an hour. Afterwards the journalists wrote that I was a wildcat, that I was impolite and all I knew was how to insult people. They said I was stupid and ugly, not any kind of Bandit Queen at all. If I had had my rifle they would have found out what kind of queen I was! If I had understood their language and known what press conferences and a television cameras were, I would have tried to tell them what was going on in my head, but I wasn't even sure that was what they wanted to know.

They had brought me food, but I couldn't eat it sitting there on a chair at the table. I wanted to sit on the ground, as I had always done.

Once that ordeal was over, the police made us get in jeeps to take us to Gwalior. To reach the jail, we passed through the bazaar and there the people looked at me differently. They were poor people who lived in the city. The bazaar was thronging with them and our jeep could barely get through. As we slowed down, they recognised me. Even though the police wouldn't let them near me, I could see respect and admiration in their eyes.

'Long live Phoolan Devi!' they started shouting.

It was the first time that day I had the feeling I was meeting human beings, but the police kept them back. They didn't want them to be able to touch me.

There were three vehicles in our convoy. I was sitting in a jeep with the Police Superintendent of Gwalior, Ghanshyam was in the car behind, and there was a third car following. At one moment, the jeep halted and a police officer jumped out of the third car and came up to us.

'Somebody wants to have a word with you. Follow me.'

I got down from the jeep and found myself seconds later face-to-face with the muzzle of a Sten. I didn't understand what was happening. Suddenly there were police all around me – with their guns trained on the officer with the Sten. I was hustled away back into the jeep and we sped away. The whole thing had lasted less than a minute. A voice came crackling over the police radio saying that Phoolan Devi had just escaped an assassination attempt. The officer had been an impostor pretending to be the superintendent of the Etawah district. He had been travelling in the third vehicle and the Madhya Pradesh police had caught up with him just in time.

The Police Superintendent of Gwalior was extremely vexed. 'Why did you get down from the vehicle?' he asked me. 'You must be careful, Phoolan. We are trying to protect you but they nearly got you and ruined everything.'

We drove at high speed towards the jail now. I thought of nothing else but prison. The trees by the roadside seemed to be receding from me, like the jungle, and my liberty.

A long time before, in the jungle, it had been raining very hard one day, and all I had been able to see before my eyes was water. Water from the sky had flooded the jungle and the Yamuna had burst its banks.

I had been watching a holy man swimming in the river. He had two palm leaves in his hands to help him make headway against the current as he crossed the river. We knew him well but we never dared to visit his temple because he always cursed us dacoits. We had camped on a hill and I was watching him struggling in the water, trying not to be seen, so he wouldn't insult me.

It took him a very long time, but he had finally arrived at the shore near where we were camped. It was the first time he had ever approached us. I went up to him to touch his feet.

'Why do you never come to my temple?' he had asked.

'Baba, you are always insulting dacoits. I'm afraid you will curse me.'

'I'm glad I am having a closer look at you. Come to my temple now.'

We went there and I prayed and made offerings of money

to the statues of the gods. Suddenly the holy man had looked in my eyes and said, 'My girl, you will be in prison in six months' time.'

'Don't say that,' I cried. 'I'd rather die than go to jail.'

I had sworn that day never to speak to a police officer, never to let myself be persuaded to surrender.

As the jeep hurtled on, I realised I had forgotten the holy man's prediction.

I had forgotten my destiny.

37

Heavy iron gates swallowed the jeep and we were made to get out in the courtyard. There were high walls of red brick all around us, so high I couldn't see anything. It was like being inside a fort. A tall iron door swung open in front of us and, after we were led through, closed again behind us.

'Hand me your knife,' said a prison guard to me.

I had refused to hand over my knife at the ceremony in front of the CM and I wasn't going to hand it over now that I was there in prison.

'What if I go outside for a walk? If somebody attacked me I would only have my knife to defend myself. I'm keeping it under my belt,' I said. I didn't understand yet that I wouldn't be going for any walks outside. I had been told I would have freedom of movement in the prison. I thought that meant I would be able to go out to the market to buy food, stop to talk to people in the street, and return to sleep.

There must have been at least twenty guards around me, keeping a careful distance. I was cornered, and suddenly overwhelmed with doubt and desperation. I regretted having signed the paper from the Government of India. If they hadn't dragged my family in front of me to blackmail me, I wouldn't have been there. But the guards didn't move and it took a while to settle the matter of my knife. Some of the guards went to talk to the prison director and offered me a chair while we waited. I didn't want to sit on a chair either.

I squatted down on my heels, the way I always sat. The guards shook their heads in exasperation.

Finally the prison director came and persuaded me to hand over my knife. He told me that nobody had any weapons in there; it was against the rules, and he said with a chuckle that I wasn't going to need it to go outside. He promised he would keep it in a safe for me. I resigned myself. I was too tired to argue.

'I know what you want,' I snapped. 'You want to kill me!'

They said they meant me no harm. They were only going to take me to the women's section.

This time I lost my patience. I squatted down, refusing to budge. They had promised me special quarters. It was a condition of my surrender that I could be with my men. I stood up again and strutted back to the iron door, screaming that I wasn't going to stay there. This time the guards were nervous. They called on their radios for orders.

They ended up taking me to another part of the prison. Another thick metal door closed behind me, and I found myself in a hall with Malkan Singh, a bandit who had surrendered before us, and his men. They took me through there to another hall. Baba Ghanshyam and his gang were in there. Beyond that was another hall, for me.

The hall had many windows, all with bars, looking out on the yard. As soon as I was alone, dacoits came to the bars with garlands.

'Long live Phoolan Devi! Long live Phoolan Devi!' they chanted. I saw my accountant Lakhan; there was Muniram, Kharag and Jhallar, and there were others from Baba Ghanshyam's gang too.

It wasn't how I had imagined prison would be. I felt uneasy in the large room meant for two or three hundred inmates, who I realised had been herded out into the yard to make room for me. There was an iron-framed bed with a mattress and a sheet. I had a stomach ache and I was tired, but I couldn't lie down. I walked around and around the hall, listening to the sound of my footsteps slapping on the concrete floor in the vast emptiness. Finally they brought the prison doctor who gave me a pill that he said would stop the pain. But when he asked where the pain was, I couldn't tell him. It was everywhere.

I fell asleep at last staring at the high, plaster-covered ceiling and the concrete walls.

Three times that first night, I woke with a fright shouting orders to my men. 'Let's go! We're moving.'

The two women guards who were waiting outside the bars woke too. 'Where do you think you are going?' they asked.

I thought we were still in the jungle, we had slept too long and we had to move camp. The irritated looks on the faces of the guards and the concrete walls brought me back to reality. By four o'clock in the morning, I was wide awake again, as I always was in the jungle.

I examined the new jungle I found myself in. Outside the hall, in the recreation yard, were three large trees. One of them was a banyan. On a mound of earth in the middle there was a little temple dedicated to Shiva. The yard was an immense terrain of bare red earth and surrounding it were buildings like the one I was in where the dacoits slept in groups. At one end there was a canteen. I was taken out for exercise, and in the pale morning light I made a tour of my new world.

There was a water tap in one corner where some prisoners were washing their faces. But I walked all the way up to the tall iron gate that we had entered through.

'Open the gate. I want to go out.'

'Please, Bahanji, don't ask me to do that,' said the guard.

'Why not?'

'I'll lose my job.'

'What are you talking about? I can come and go as I please!'

Some of the dacoits came up to me and said I would have to take my walk in the yard, like the rest of them.

'But there's a field of grass out there. I only want to go for a walk there to relieve myself.'

'It's not allowed. You'll have to do as we do now.'

So I had been tricked.

I asked where the latrines were, and they pointed to the building everybody used.

The smell was appalling. I found myself slipping barefoot in shit and I flew out of there before I fainted, cursing the gods. I was cursing so loud the guards made two prisoners clean out the latrine. But all they did was shovel some of the shit in a bucket and throw it in the ditch outside, filling the yard with the disgusting smell.

Next, I decided to try to bathe. They had put up a bamboo enclosure for me with a straw roof, to shield me from the eyes of the men, and there was a pot of water in there. It was an improvement.

But the food brought all my revulsion back. The chapatis were black, and tasted as though the flour had been milled with sand. The dal was black too. There was no ghee, only foul-smelling vegetable oil. The tea they served looked like the water of the Yamuna when it was swollen with mud. I never drank tea anyway, only water. Nobody drank tea in the jungle.

That first morning in prison, I contented myself with eating nothing.

During this time, a crowd had gathered at the exterior gates. There were people climbing the bars and shouting my name and imploring the guards to bring me to them. I stormed up to the gates.

'What do you want with me you bloody dogs?' I shouted. 'Go home to your mothers!'

The prison director arrived, and he was surprised by my anger. 'These people only want to see you, Phoolan. It's normal. I too wondered what you were like when you were in the jungle. They don't mean you any harm. You're not in the jungle any more, nobody is going to put a rifle under your nose.'

He let a group of them come into the prison . . .

It went on like that for several days. They would sit on a bench under the tree and call for me. If I refused to come out, they would come into the hall where I slept.

The journalists were the worst. They always wanted to take ridiculous photographs of me. Because I wouldn't sit on chairs, they said it would be interesting to photograph me squatting on the floor. Interesting! I didn't know how else to sit. I couldn't squat on a chair. If I scratched my head, they took a photo; if I insulted them, they took a photo. I would charge at them and tear their cameras away from them. I hated being photographed. Every time I heard the click of a camera, I turned into a tigress.

On the third day, a man came saying his name was Ashok Roy. He said he had made a film called *Kahani Phoolan Ki* and that he had been waiting to see if I was killed or put in prison to finish his film. He began to show me photos. I lunged at him and grabbed him by the collar of his shirt.

'How dare you? What is all this film business? What is it you want?'

His collar tore away in my hands as I shook him. He ran away in alarm, taking his photos.

I wanted to know how he dared to take these pictures of my life without my permission. I had been to the cinema once in Nepal, but I still didn't know what a film was. Before the man came, some of the prisoners had told me that it was a bad thing, and that I would have very big problems with a film. It was bound to be full of lies, they explained, but people would believe all of them.

'A film is a great catastrophe,' one of the jailbirds had said. 'It will fall like a cyclone on your head.'

For several hours, I wondered to myself what a film could actually be, to be able to fall on your head. Was it something you hung on the wall like a painting of the gods? A film of my life might be something they would show at my trial . . . I had heard that you could shoot a film, and I wondered if it was something you put in a cannon to shoot somebody with, the way you could shoot a gun! I would have liked to ask the man, but he ran off like a startled rabbit. I was relieved he had departed so quickly, but I was warned that it was only the beginning: 'Don't think you're out of trouble yet. Whatever happens, you won't be able to do anything about it. The film is made and all he wanted was to get a glimpse of you. And now that he has, he won't spare you.'

Why did they all want to stare at me? I thought I knew the answer: because I was a bad woman. Why did they want me to sit on a chair? Why did they want to make me eat their terrible food? Why did they come to see what I looked like? Because I was a bad woman. I was like a wildcat in a cage. I wouldn't give an inch. I wouldn't take off my uniform when they told me I couldn't wear it. I snapped at the guards, mistaking the English words they used for insults. They just thought I was funny, though, and it took me a few days to understand why. I was a source of profit for them. People came in their hundreds to see me, and I could be as bad-tempered and notorious as I liked. The prison staff made them pay to see me.

They charged ten rupees per person. The prison director didn't care. He even proposed giving me a share, but I refused. I told him I wasn't there just to entertain people. That didn't stop them. They would charge up to fifty rupees at times. They even had group rates; people came in tens and twenties and more. I would shut myself in a corner of the hall and the guards would come and plead with me to show myself. It was a ridiculous circus that made me so angry I would come out finally, just to insult them. They didn't care; they just laughed.

That was why when, after a week had gone by and the guards came and said I had some more visitors, I ignored them. I hissed that I didn't want any more visitors.

'No. Not the public this time. Your family.'

The government of Madhya Pradesh had lodged my family in a hostel for pilgrims near Gwalior. The whole family had come and I watched them being escorted across the yard: my mother, my father, my sisters and my brother. I showed them into my vast empty cell, as enraged as ever. My father hadn't changed either. He was still as weary and resigned as before.

'Why have you come, Buppa?' I asked. 'It's because of all of you I'm in here! But I'm not going to put up with it. I'm going to kill myself.'

When I was a child, my father always refused to listen to me when told him I wasn't a girl at all. He said I would get into trouble with my tongue. He used to say a girl should be quiet and obedient, not wilful like me. The other girls in my village didn't behave the way I did. They weren't allowed to giggle in public, or walk around alone, or answer back when someone made disgusting suggestions to them. I had rebelled – and my father had never been able to accept it. He had always shied away from confrontations; he had never been able to defend himself. He was a pious, simple man, ready to die as he had been born: in slavery.

The first time in my life that I had doubted my father was when I came out of prison, when I was fifteen, and he had bowed in front of Mayadin. I had been tortured half to death because of that bastard, but my father was fawning in front of him and paying him his respects. That was when I realised there was nobody to protect me, when the police in the lock-up at Kalpi had called me a whore and he had hidden his face . . .

And when, finally, I had Mayadin at the end of my rifle, my father had asked for just five bighas of land . . . His humility terrified me.

That day in the jail at Gwalior – in that sinister, corrupt prison where I was being exhibited like a species of rat – I spat curses on him. But he didn't flinch from my abuse. He put his hand on my brow gently to calm me, as he used to do when I was a little girl.

'Don't be afraid, my child. Look for peace and you will find it. Your life here in prison is easier than the life you led in the jungle. You will get used to it. You mustn't fight with others. Be good and kind. You will find peace.'

'Who are you to preach to me? I'm not staying here. It stinks! Look around you, it's diseased and filthy. Look at this food. I have to make deals to get it from outside, otherwise I would have to eat rot! You always wanted me to submit and now you want me to submit here too!'

My only happiness that day was to be able to see my sisters Rukmini and Choti and Bhuri, and my brother whom I adored. I was resentful towards my father and I couldn't help showing it, but I bitterly regretted it afterwards.

It was the last time I ever saw him. He died before I was able to ask his forgiveness for my anger.

After eight days, I understood what prison was. I knew I wasn't going to leave.

They built a little house for me. The roof wasn't even finished when I moved in. There were two rooms, one with a toilet and washbasin and another smaller one for me to sleep in. My house was enclosed by a high wall with an iron gate. Between the wall and my doorway there was some grass and behind, between the back of the house and the wall, a garden. I began growing peppers, tomatoes, aubergines and potatoes. A ex-dacoit named Karan became my cook.

'Good,' the prison director said. 'You're not a wild animal; make an effort to act like a human being. Greet people properly, with respect, and devote some time to prayer.'

I realised I was going to have plenty of time there at Gwalior. The jungle was behind me, far away. The freedom and excitement of being a dacoit, going from village to village making the law, was behind me. I had to learn to get by in prison. I had no money, unlike other gang leaders. I hadn't become a dacoit for the money. The thing I had liked best was being able to give it away. But to have food brought in from outside the prison you had to have money. I vomited up the horrors they served us. I had only nine thousand rupees with me when I arrived in the jail. Other bandits had pockets stuffed with money. One day, when some journalists learned I had to pay to get reasonable food, they gave me money and offered to bring me fruits. I thought they meant *phoot*, a Hindi name for a wild fruit that I couldn't digest. I refused. When I told the guard, she realised my mistake and roared with laughter.

Another journalist asked me if I had any plans for marriage, if I wanted one day to have a home, a husband and become a mistress. I flew into a rage. I took mistress to be an insult. But he explained that he meant a mistress of the house. He wanted to know if I was going to get married.

I said I had no plans.

The prison director told me Man Singh had said he was

my husband, but when I asked Man Singh, he denied saying
it. He always did have a cowardly streak. He said he had
been talking about his rifle! I had heard, however, that he
had been boasting about many things since we surrendered.
I think he was jealous of me. To put a stop to all this, I
declared in front of everybody that no man was my husband, and that no man ever would be. To my amazement,
though, I wasn't short of offers. A number of men came to
the prison to propose to me. A young man from a Jain family in Delhi came. He was twenty years old and I gently
dismissed him. Then a Punjabi came with an offer of marriage and then a Sikh. The Sikh was burly, with an enormous
turban, and only one leg. He said he was very rich, he owned
a transportation company with many lorries, and he would
deposit a hundred thousand rupees for me in prison. He
already had a wife and children but he still wanted to marry
me.

'I want to prove to the world there are men tough enough
to cope with a woman who has turned out badly. I want the
satisfaction of helping a woman like you in her hour of
need!'

There was even a Frenchman who said he owned facto-
ries. He was rich, he said, and he wanted to move to India
and marry me. He asked how much he would have to pay to
free me. For two hours, the interpreter kept asking me if I
wanted to marry this Frenchman.

I didn't think it so funny that they let people come into
the prison just to stare at me, to take my picture, question
me and now propose marriage to me.

Marriage was forbidden for me. Ever since Putti Lal had
repudiated me and the people of my village had shunned me
as though I was carrying some kind of disease, marriage had
been out of the question for me. Deep in my memory I bore
the scars of the day nobody in my community would help

me haul the dead buffalo out of our house; the day I was forbidden to take water from the well; the day, after I was released from prison in Orai, they called me a whore and asked me how many men I had been with . . . Vickram had helped me to forget those things for a time, but Vickram was gone.

Men were still demons for me. They would always be demons. Whenever a journalist asked me about the tortures inflicted on me by Shri Ram, I couldn't answer. I would send them away. I alone knew what I had suffered. I alone knew what it felt like to be alive but dead. At an age when young women wait patiently for their husbands, squatting by the fire and cooking chapatis, I was a stone in the jungle, a stone without feeling or regrets. I was no longer a woman. A stone couldn't marry a man when it was a man who had made the stone.

38

I was supposed to be released from the prison at Gwalior in 1991. They had promised me when I surrendered that I would be tried, but no trial ever took place. Instead, I received something I hadn't bargained for in my list of demands. I learned how to survive in their world.

Gwalior was the worst place. It was a world of deals and compromises where money was the only thing of value. I learned that anything could be bought or sold. The big-time dacoits battled with each other for the title of kingpin. They exploited the smaller ones and stole from them. They made a jungle out of the prison.

They would steal anything from anybody. They used to boast about how, before they were captured, they stole sheep from shepherds, or how they stole buffaloes or horses or camels that they took over the state line to sell in Uttar Pradesh and all the way to the mountains in Himalchal Pradesh. In the prison at Gwalior, there was a gang leader called Dasyu Sarmrat, the so-called King of Dacoits. He dared to boast to me of trafficking in women! He kidnapped them to sell them to gujars who couldn't find brides. He said he would sell a woman for ten thousand rupees, sometimes fifteen thousand. They all wanted to be princes or kings of dacoits; they all had money in prison, but they never gave a thought to the poor people they terrorised and exploited or the women they tortured.

For a time, there was a prison director at Gwalior who was as corrupt and heartless as them. He let the madwomen mix with the common prisoners and die like dogs, their skinny bodies eaten by rats. I couldn't rest after seeing their half-eaten corpses. All the time I was there I continued to rebel and fight. I protested every day against the filth, the laziness and the corruption. I went on hunger strike twice, trying to obtain some decency for us, and I nearly died the second time. But nobody cared.

In the early days, I had Chief Minister Arjun Singh to look after me. He had encouraged me to learn to read, to greet people with respect, and to speak politely. My mother was able to ask him for things my family needed. But he had only stayed in his post for eleven months after my surrender before he was named Governor of the Punjab. The other dacoits laughed when they heard.

'Call your CM to come and help you now!' they taunted me. Not long after, I found myself even more alone.

The day the Prime Minister, Indira Gandhi, was assassinated, I wept with grief. Though I had never met her, she had done a lot for me and my family and I knew that from then on, there would be no one to uphold the agreement her government had made with me. I would be on my own. The other dacoits laughed and said I wasn't going to get any special treatment any more.

'It's over, Phoolan. Indira's holiday camp is closed!' they said. Not only the mother of India, but my 'mother' too was dead.

After that, I met some political prisoners who promised to fight for me when they were released, but I didn't understand how they could 'fight' for me. I didn't understand what they meant when they talked about my fight being political. The only world I knew outside the prison was the villages and the jungle.

I found out more when I got a television.

The daughter of an industrialist gave me one as a present. It was the first time I had ever seen a television. When the guards switched it on I was astonished. I couldn't understand how such a big picture could pass through such a small cable. It was like the day I spoke through telephone for the first time. I knew what telephones were, and I had seen them being used, but I had never spoken with one. I was handed the receiver and I didn't know what to do with it. I held it at arm's length and dropped it in fright. Each time it rang I picked it up and dropped it again. Finally I heard a noise coming from it and I held it to my ear to hear better.

'Hello, Phoolan?'

It was the prison director calling me at the hospital. I was so impressed to hear his voice through it that I hung up again as though it was God himself on the other end of the line.

I had been sent to the hospital because I was sick. The torture, the jungle, the hunger strikes had left me weak and they had decided they were going to operate on me for a tumour in the prison at Gwalior.

They transferred me to the prison hospital but, just before the operation, a visitor came with food for me. I didn't know who this visitor was. He looked like a guard or a police officer and he insisted on me eating the food he had brought to keep my strength up. But earlier that day, I had been told by the nurses I shouldn't eat before the anaesthetic. I had already been operated on for a cyst since I had been in prison and I wasn't the same ignorant jungle animal I had been at the start. I ran out of the room shouting for help and refused to let myself be tied to the bed. The operation on my tumour could wait, I decided.

The next day, a story appeared in a newspaper saying that Phoolan Devi had gone insane and that I had run away from the hospital after striking a woman doctor. A journalist came to see me soon after and advised me to do everything I could to get out of that prison because my life was in danger. Someone had offered five hundred thousand rupees for my death.

Years went by and I still hadn't been sent for trial. It was as though they had forgotten all about me. All the other dacoits who had surrendered with me were freed after five or six years but it was as if they wanted me out of the way. Even in jail, it seemed, a woman had to wait in silence. The Supreme Court eventually gave me nothing more than a dispensation to be treated in the prison hospital at Delhi.

The night I left the prison, the madwomen of Gwalior were all crying, and the children too. I offered prayers to Durga for my safety in front of the little shrine I had built out of some bricks. They brought me from the women's quarters at midnight and I had to wait three more hours in front of the heavy front gate before they made me climb into an armoured van, surrounded by police. When we arrived at the railway station, I counted them as we waited on the platform, surrounded by people. There were eighteen police officers; four women, the rest men.

It had been a long time since I wore a uniform and carried a rifle, and I had learned by then how to sit on a chair with my feet on the floor instead of curled up under me, the way I used to sit on a khat. In the train I was just a woman in a red sari. Nobody recognised me, but they must have wondered why I was being escorted by police, and why I was crying.

I was choking and sobbing because, before I left, the prisoners at Gwalior had said that Tihar was one prison that nobody got out of; they said I was going to be locked in there and raped and tortured. Even if they were exaggerating, I knew I was going to have to undergo an operation and the train was carrying me away from Gwalior and my family, my mother and my sisters. I didn't know how many months or years it might be before I saw them again. I hadn't seen my mother in a long time and the last time, she had been so sad and distant, as though she was never going to finish mourning for my father.

Suddenly I heard a beggar singing.

'*Durga maiya karengi beda paar . . .*'

He was singing that the goddess Durga would help me cross the river.

My heart lightened. I gave him fifty rupees to continue singing, and he came back three more times to sing for me before the train reached Delhi.

The prison at Tihar was a different world.

I was put in cell number ten. I had a room to myself, with a shelf made of concrete for a bed with a mattress on it. The guards were young women and they helped me build myself a new shrine with a little wooden stool they gave me. I set some little figures of the gods on it and surrounded them with incense and flowers.

As I was praying the next morning, I heard someone calling me from outside the door.

'Phoolan, what are you doing?' There was a knock, and then a woman entered. 'Oh, you're praying. Carry on, excuse me,' she said.

When I had finished I turned to the woman. She was wearing a white kurta and long grey jacket. She had short brown hair like a boy and her face was lively and honest.

'*Namasteh*,' I said. My manners had greatly improved. 'May I know your name?'

'I'm the director of this prison. Perhaps you've heard of me. My name is Kiran Bedi.'

I had heard of her, I had even seen her on the television,

but I hadn't recognised her. Kiran Bedi was the Inspector General of Prisons, a woman respected by the guards and the police. She was knowledgeable and powerful. There was a time when I wouldn't have believed such a woman existed. I was to find out for myself that she had authority, but used it fairly, and she was ruthless when it came to dealing with corruption.

'I'm happy to see you praying, Phoolan,' she said. 'It's a good thing. You are going to have a pleasant time here and, don't worry, you'll soon be released. It's against the law in India for you to be imprisoned for so long without a trial. I'm going to see to it that an appeal is submitted on your behalf.'

It was more than I had ever hoped to hear! A smiling, pleasant woman talking about my freedom, giving instructions for me to be fed properly, and orders for me to be left in peace, orders for them to take good care of me.

When they took me to the Indian Institute of Medical Science, the hospital was well-guarded, with police in the corridors. In Gwalior I had been treated like an animal. Before my first operation there I had the feeling I was going to be cut up and examined like a mouse and then thrown in the dustbin. In this hospital it was clean and they asked me where it was hurting me when they examined me.

They put a thin tube in my mouth and threaded it down my throat. It was a miniature camera, they said, for looking in my stomach. On the TV I saw a large dark stain, like a bruise.

The doctors were respectful and considerate. Before the operation, they explained what they were going to do in simple language. In Gwalior all they had said was that I had poison in my body, as though I had been bitten by a snake. When they had said I was going to be given rhesus blood I had panicked. I thought they meant the blood of a rhesus monkey. I begged them not to turn me into a monkey!

Nobody in Gwalior had made any effort to understand my dialect, or to communicate with me. I was uncultured and stupid as far as they were concerned and I was going to stay that way.

In Delhi, they operated on my stomach ulcer. It was a pain I had had for a long time and it wouldn't go away. After the operation, I had trouble believing it had really happened. It had all gone so calmly and smoothly. I kept touching the bandage to convince myself.

Once the scars healed, as they had promised, the ulcer ceased to gnaw at me. Back in my cell, my rage and worry slowly dissipated. The real poison, that of mistrust and fear, gradually left my system.

One day I heard on the radio that the Government of Uttar Pradesh had dropped the charges against me.

I was so happy, and so dumbfounded, that I punched myself in the head to be sure I was awake. I checked the radio to see if it really was working. The girls in the next cells jumped for joy and banged on the bars with their metal plates. I thought I would go crazy with happiness. The director of the prison at Gwalior always used to say I would end up insane. When he had transferred me to the women's quarters, I was locked up with the madwomen for a while. I remembered what he had said and almost believed he had been right. It couldn't be true, I thought. I *had* gone mad, I was hearing things!

But I wasn't crazy. It was repeated on the news several times that day.

The following morning, Mrs Kiran Bedi came to see me to tell me officially. 'But it could be six months before you are finally released,' she warned. 'There are a lot of formalities. We might have to wait a while.'

'It's fine with me,' I said. 'Let the Supreme Court take

their time. I don't even mind staying here another year!'

When I had gone there, I had no hope of ever leaving. I thought I was going to be sent back to Gwalior and I would end my days in prison, forgotten. I had even asked them why they were bothering to nurse me. Time didn't frighten me in the least.

Over the next few months, I received letters and telegrams from all over India, from people I didn't know, congratulating me.

In February 1994, eleven years after I surrendered, the gates of the Tihar jail in Delhi opened. I was freed on parole, but assigned to my residence, and given police protection. My liberty was provisional, they said, and I would have to wait for the Supreme Court to reach a final decision.

I was no longer the same person.

I was no longer the frightened child who believed the world ended where the fields ended and the sun drowned each night in the river. I was no longer the wild creature who fought with the ferocity of the goddess Durga to survive in the jungle. There was no more vengeance in my heart.

In my village, they say that when the demon Kans strikes with lightning at the birth of a baby girl and kills her, she will rise up in the sky to become the lightning in her turn. The demon struck me with lightning, and I became the lightning for others.

Epilogue

So many people had spoken for me without me ever having been able to speak for myself. So many people had taken my photo and distorted it for their purposes. So many people disdained the little village girl, who was tortured and humiliated, but still not crushed.

So many times I reached out my hands and nobody helped me. They called me a pest and a criminal. I never considered myself to be someone good, but I wasn't a criminal either. All I did was make men suffer what they made me suffer.

I had seen all kinds of bandits. Assassins had tried to take my life, journalists had tried to get my story, movie directors had tried to capture me on film. They all thought they could speak about me as though I didn't exist, as though I still didn't have any right to respect. The bandits had tried to torture my body, but the others tried to torture my spirit.

Now, for the first time, a woman from my community has been able to tell the truth about her life, and testify in public to the injustice we all had to suffer. It was my hope that my testimonial would give help to others: other women, my sisters who have been humiliated, and my brothers who are being exploited.

I wanted to prove that we all have our honour, whatever our origins, our caste, the colour of our skin or our sex.

I wanted respect.

I wanted them to say, 'Phoolan Devi is a human being,' because then they would say it about others.

A new battle began the day I left the prison, but it was going to be different. I still hardly knew how to read or write, but I knew better how to see, hear and understand the people and things of this world. I had survived in the villages and jungles and I prayed to God I would be able to survive in the city, to help those who still suffer the way I suffered.

In my next life, perhaps destiny will not be so cruel.

Let Durga hear her prayer.

> *Sing of my deeds*
> *Tell of my combats*
> *How I fought the treacherous demons*
> *Forgive my failings*
> *And bestow on me peace*